COLUMBIA STUDIES IN
CONTEMPORARY AMERICAN HISTORY

Alan Brinkley, General Editor

See page 385 for a complete list of titles in this series

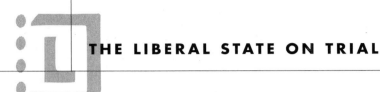

THE LIBERAL STATE ON TRIAL

THE COLD WAR AND AMERICAN POLITICS IN THE TRUMAN YEARS

Jonathan Bell

COLUMBIA UNIVERSITY PRESS
NEW YORK

Columbia University Press
Publishers Since 1893
New York, Chichester, West Sussex

Library of Congress Cataloging-in-Publication Data

Bell, Jonathan
The liberal state on trial : the Cold War and American politics in the Truman years / Jonathan Bell
p. cm — (Columbia studies in contemporary American history)
Includes bibliographical references and index.
ISBN 0–231–13356–1 (cloth : alk. paper)
ISBN 0–231–13357–X (pbk : alk. paper)
1. United States—Politics and government—1945–1953.
2. United States—Foreign relations—1945–1953.
3. United States—Social policy. 4. Liberalism—United States—History—20th century. 5. State, The. 6. Cold War. I. Title. II. Series.

E813.B44 2004
973.918—dc22 2004048405

Columbia University Press books are printed on permanent and durable acid-free paper
Printed in the United States of America

c 10 9 8 7 6 5 4 3 2 1
p 10 9 8 7 6 5 4 3 2 1

Portions of chapters 1 and 6 originally appeared in slightly different form as "Conceptualising Southern Liberalism: Ideology and the Pepper-Smathers 1950 Primary in Florida" *Journal of American Studies* 37, no. 1 (April 2003): 17–45, and part of chapter 4 as "The Changing Dynamics of American Liberalism: Paul Douglas and the Elections of 1948," *Journal of the Illinois State Historical Society*, 96, no. 4 (Winter 2003-4): 368–393.

References to Internet Web Sites (URLs) were accurate at the time of writing. Neither the author nor Columbia University Press is responsible for Web sites that may have expired or changed since the book was prepared

To my parents

CONTENTS

ACKNOWLEDGMENTS

A WORK OF THIS SIZE AND GEOGRAPHICAL SCOPE WILL inevitably run up many personal and professional debts. First mention must go to the archivists and staff of the numerous libraries and archives both in Britain and across the United States who helped me make sense of the tons of material that shaped this work. The archival staff in the Manuscripts Division of the Library of Congress in Washington, D.C. got to know me particularly well, and they were always utterly efficient. Don Ritchie, Associate Historian at the Senate Historical Office in Washington, was a fountain of knowledge on past members of Congress, and also provided transcripts for a number of illuminating oral interviews. Susan Naulty, Archivist at the Nixon Library and Birthplace in California, was an excellent guide through the Nixon papers. Eric Moody at the Nevada Historical Society in Reno introduced me to a recently rebuilt and reorganized archive there. Tim Mahony and the staff at the archive in the McKeldin Library at the University of Maryland provided my initial introduction to archival work in the United States. At Stonehill College in Massachusetts Louise Kenneally and her husband Jim provided much friendly assistance at the Joseph Martin center. John Nemmers at the Claude Pepper Library in Tallahassee acted as guide both to the voluminous Pepper archive and to the social delights of northern Florida. My thanks also go to the staff at the Maryland Historical Society in Baltimore, the Massachusetts Historical Society in Boston, the Kennedy Library, the Bancroft Library at the University of California, Berkeley (in particular David Kessler), the Houghton Library at Harvard, the Schlesinger Library at Radcliffe College, Cambridge, Massachusetts, the Chicago Historical Society, the Regenstein Library at the University of Chicago, the

Library of the University of Florida, and Joshua Lupkin at the Lehman archive at Columbia University. In Britain, I received help in the microfilm room at the Cambridge University Library, at the Churchill College Archives Centre, Cambridge, and at the British Library in London.

I was also privileged to work with such a distinguished group of academic guides. My doctoral supervisor, John Thompson, was the key to the completion of this manuscript, both through his relentless enthusiasm for my work and his flawless proof reading eye. Tony Badger and Jim Patterson also helped enormously in their comments and enthusiasm. Keith Olson at the University of Maryland was not only an academic guide but also my pilot through the bureaucratic maze of U.S. immigration procedures. Donald and Betty Pope of Carson City, Nevada, improved my argument through frequent comment and criticism. I also benefited from informal chats with Robert J. Allison of Suffolk University, Boston, Richard Abrams of Berkeley, Wayne Cole, and Meg Jacobs. Stuart Kidd read a chapter of the manuscript and offered constructive comments. Melvyn Leffler and Gareth Davies offered piercing criticism and insight in questions following a research paper I gave at the Oxford University American research seminar in late 2002, questions that greatly improved the argument at key points. My two readers from Columbia University Press, Colin Gordon and Nelson Lichtenstein, were instrumental in turning a dissertation into a book with their extensive and extremely insightful criticism. My thanks go to all.

I relied on the friendship of a number of people who provided me with accommodation, friendly advice, and support throughout the writing of this book. I want to thank my friends Andrew Kaye and David Eldridge, who completed PhD dissertations alongside me and helped me keep body and soul together while we lived in the United States. Julia Young and Ray Swartz have proved to be wonderful friends whenever I am in San Francisco. Chuck and Alice Barr in Reno, Alejandra Bronfman in Gainesville, and William and Margaret Marflitt in Laguna, California, also provided a bed for the night and friendship at key junctures.

Thanks also to my friends at Columbia University Press, especially to Anne Routon, who has provided ceaseless help, advice, and friendship over the past three years.

My research was made possible by a generous grant from the Arts and Humanities Research Board, as well as the time afforded by an AHRB research leave award. The British Academy awarded me a small travel grant that greatly assisted my archival work in the United States. The University of Reading allowed me both travel money and research time with which to complete this book, and has also furnished me with some wonderful friends, who helped me retain my sanity while completing the final stages of the project.

INTRODUCTION
IDEOLOGIES OF THE STATE IN EARLY COLD WAR AMERICA

HOW WOULD THE ABSENCE OF A PERCEIVED TOTALITARIAN threat in America in the Truman years have affected the development of American politics? Although my purpose here is not to attempt to construct counterfactual history, we do need to understand how the peculiar dynamics of Cold War ideology in the United States in the late 1940s shaped the direction of political thought and action in those years. The question of what happened to the reform thrust of the New Deal has hardly been ignored in the historiography on post–World War II politics, but the fate of American liberalism is usually seen as springing from events and trends in place before 1945.[1] The present study will seek to show that a powerful forum for social democratic ideas existed in the United States at the end of the war, and that the emergence of the Cold War determined the fate of postwar American liberalism and conservatism to an extent underestimated in existing scholarship. While many commentators have noted the rise of anti-statism in American politics after World War Two, few have fully engaged with the state of left-wing thought at the end of the war or recognized the disjuncture between New Deal liberalism and a more ambitious social democratic impulse that gained strength on the American left during the war.

In 1945 many congressional Democrats and their supporters in pressure groups such as the Union for Democratic Action were promoting an agenda in some respects very similar to that of the Labour government in Great Britain, which was seen as something of a model for the American left. A UDA memorandum in November 1946 noted American liberals' "keen and sympathetic interest [in] this brave attempt to establish democratic socialism in war-weary and war-ravished

[sic] England."[2] Yet any transatlantic social democratic consensus rested on shaky ground. American liberals in the late 1940s embraced not only quasi-Keynesian growth politics in their desire to validate progressive ideas in an age of prosperity; they also embraced anti-leftism in a manner which shifted the boundaries of liberal political discourse away from social democratic values and toward a politics that promoted individual freedom at home and abroad, anticipating the civil rights liberalism of the 1960s.

Part of the impact of the Cold War on American politics was to reorient the language of American liberalism away from ideas of achieving greater equality of opportunity through federal intervention in the economy and toward a politics of civil rights. In part this was a result of a powerful revival of anti-statist sentiment in American politics to which liberals had to respond. In part, however, the growth of Cold War liberalism was a consequence of a political logic that sought to distance American political discourse from anything perceived as totalitarian. This study aims to show that what Alan Brinkley has termed "the end of reform" was a result not only of political pressures from the right and from private enterprise, nor simply because the liberal movement had embraced market economics and the corporate welfare state, but also because the Cold War helped to reorient the terms of liberal political thought to preclude popular front alliances across the left of the political spectrum that had formed the mainstay of northern Democratic political power since the late 1930s.[3]

Helen Gahagan Douglas was one liberal Democratic congresswoman who stated in 1946 that she was "jealous for my belief . . . that in our democracy the Government is the servant of the people, and that . . . it will protect the people—all of us, Protestant, Catholic, Jew, or gentile; black, white, or yellow."[4] She was one example, as were many others who built their political careers in the 1940s in organs like the UDA and who would find their political homes in the Democratic Party, of a politician whose political worldview seemed in the mid-1940s to have moved beyond the New Deal. Although Democratic candidates in the 1946 midterm elections stressed the socioeconomic achievements of the New Deal in their campaigns, they also hoped for a more ambitious future for American liberals because of the wartime experiences of the popular front. Liberal activists talked openly about expanding the welfare state, establishing a permanent program of public works (essentially a state sector of the economy), and creating a federally run health insurance system. The wartime alliance between the United States and the Soviet Union, together with the advent of a new period of political upheaval in Great Britain in the wake of the Beveridge report, had encouraged UDA liberal activists and, at times, the administration to experiment with left-wing ideas without fear that they could be associated with totalitarianism in the minds of a majority of the American public, as evidenced by Roosevelt's economic bill of rights speech as late as 1944.

With the intensification of Cold War animosities by the end of the decade liberals like Douglas saw their commitment to social democracy held up as a liability not only by anti-statist Republicans but also by their colleagues in the Democratic Party. The late 1940s provide an appropriate focus for a study of why the United States did not follow the same path as other democratic industrial countries in developing an extensive welfare state. Just as in other industrialized nations, the United States stood at a crossroads that would determine to a large extent its political direction in the postwar era. Politicians like Douglas discovered that their country had chosen a different route to that of other nations, one that helped to disguise the brief flowering of a social democratic impulse in American liberalism at the end of World War Two that the current historiography has not fully unearthed.[5]

We know, from previous scholarship, that New Deal liberalism faced growing opposition from Southerners and fiscal conservatives in the GOP and the business community. The sectional organization of the American party system also forces us to place the developing network of liberal activists inside and outside the Democratic Party into a larger context of regional variations, loose party structures, powerful financial interests, and political rivalries.[6] Even in the wake of the major reorganization of Congress in 1946, conservative southerners dominated most important congressional committees, and the South loomed large in determining the contours of American politics. The present study does not aim to overturn this picture of the American political scene after World War Two, but rather to demonstrate that our understanding of the dynamics of American reform politics in the Truman years is enriched by a deeper awareness of the role of the Cold War in shifting the priorities of American liberals and conservatives. Major battles over the future of the New Deal state, such as the debates over the future of the Office of Price Administration, Taft-Hartley, or federal health insurance, need to be placed in the broader political context of electoral campaign politics to show how local candidates—liberal and conservative alike—navigated the terrain of the early Cold War and saw their political worldviews changed by the experience. By 1952, Cold War anti-statism had overwhelmed the social democratic promise of the early postwar years in the United States, just as it had also trumped the fiscally conservative isolationism of the Republican Party.

The end of America's relationship with the Soviet Union after the war helped to redefine the political language of liberalism to render it less amenable to social democratic ideas. In addition, the Cold War played a role in the revitalization and reconfiguration of long-standing anti-statist sentiment in the Republican Party. Right-wing antipathy toward New Deal liberalism took at least two distinct forms, one of which took priority over the other as anti-Soviet feeling increased. In the early twentieth century opponents of statist measures denied the effectiveness of governmental action to achieve goals such as the equalization of economic and social opportunity. Many followers of free market thought argued that governmental action in fields such as economic and welfare policy tended to aggravate social inequality, harm business confidence, and was in general less effective than nongovernmental forms of economic and social management. But there had always been another, more abstract, kind of anti-statism in the United States that gained added potency from the Cold War. John Foster Dulles argued in 1949 that politicians "should consider not merely whether the professed end is good, but what the process of getting there will do *to* people's character. . . . [We] too, have come to believe, with Stalin, that material things are primary and spiritual things secondary."[7] Dulles's words suggest that images that drew strength from the anti-communist thrust of U.S. foreign policy invigorated an abstract ideology of anti-statism that attracted many political groups previously amenable to a limited extension of government. Cold War anti-statism also pushed many on the right previously wary of the possible consequences of an assertive foreign policy into reluctant support of the new policy of militant anti-communist internationalism. Those who had been suspicious of the state all along could use a growing popular fear of the state derived in part from Cold War images of otherness abroad to reinforce their critique of domestic reform proposals.[8]

The dominant trend of the existing historiography on the fate of liberal reform after the New Deal has been to integrate the effects of the Cold War into an already well-established pattern of anti-statist resurgence. The midterm elections of 1938 had witnessed the fragmentation of the New Deal coalition in Congress, and the revitalization of the Republican Party, a development that was to continue during the war years. Conservatives also benefited from the institutional structures of the American political system, which made the promotion of a coherent liberal alternative to private sector capitalism difficult. It is pointed out that anti-communism as a tool of right-wing interests was hardly new to the postwar era, since it had resurfaced as a brake on liberal reform with the formation of the House Un-American Activities Committee in 1938. Essentially it is often argued that the New Deal as an effort to reshape the landscape of American politics received a near insurmountable setback after 1938, and that any appraisal of the Truman years needs to be seen in this context.[9]

Historians have tended to regard the main achievement of American liberals after World War Two as being their ability to adapt their policies to the new challenges of an era of prosperity after the war. New Deal liberalism in the 1930s had been a series of policy responses to the exigencies and crises of the depression. By 1945, however, the opportunities presented by the wartime mobilization of the economy had largely solved the immediate problems of the depression years, while revitalizing the power of big business in American politics, and creating new problems of how best to ensure the fair distribution of the nation's economic resources. The 1940s saw the resurgence of a Republican and southern Democratic coalition in Congress, together with the demise of New Deal and wartime planning agencies that had constituted a social democratic response to the demands of recession and war but that seemed politically unsustainable in the charged atmosphere of the postwar period. To a number of historians, the establishment in the late 1940s of a network of political operators in the Truman administration dedicated to the promotion of Keynesian, private-sector solutions to questions of continued economic growth represented a carefully planned, indeed politically necessary, attempt to keep the flame of left-of-center reform alive in a hostile political climate. Through such organs as the Council of Economic Advisers, they argue, economists like Leon Keyserling promoted policies of demand management through manipulation of taxes, interest rates, and military spending, which kept the economy on an even keel while relinquishing major decisionmaking to the private sector. The logic of this argument springs from the assumption that the realities of American politics after World War Two proscribed a more social democratic, state-centered development of the New Deal, and the only real discord within this historiographical school revolves around whether the evolution of the "politics of growth" should be seen as a vindication of the might of the private sector economy or as a politically viable way of sustaining liberal ideals in an era of business dominance.[10]

Critics of the direction of mainstream postwar American liberalism have usually focused on the fate of the American labor movement. After the passage of the Wagner Act in 1935 American labor unions had grown considerably in size and political clout, and during World War Two had exercised significant leverage over the political process, through both the role of labor representatives on wartime planning bodies and the evolution of powerful political machines such as the CIO's Political Action Committee. Organized labor emerged from the war committed to securing its new place in America's political order, and prepared to exercise its considerable muscle in the form of massive industrial action to gain an increased share of the economic pie in a period of high inflation and in the face of resurgent business influence in politics. The development of Democratic Party links with the business community after the war, it is argued, combined with the anti-communist hysteria of the Cold War to emaciate labor's political power by the early 1950s, thereby impoverishing liberal politics in the postwar era. Union leader Walter Reuther's vision of a corporate state in 1945 in which labor and management joined with the state in collective economic decisionmaking was gradually replaced by union-management collusion to gain piecemeal improvements in working conditions and wages in exchange for labor's political quiescence.[11]

The present study does not pretend to be a comprehensive survey of the events of the late 1940s; it seeks only to show that the Cold War played a crucial part in the domestic struggle over the extent of federal involvement in American society. Although a significant literature exists pointing to administrative and institutional factors as explanations for the limited progress of social democratic policies in the United States, such studies would benefit from a specific temporal and contextual framework which demonstrates that American state building is contingent upon ideological factors.[12] Much of our understanding of an anti-left turn in American politics still rests on the assertion in 1970 by Richard Freeland that the Truman administration was forced to out-McCarthy McCarthy in its adoption of the federal loyalty program and its tacit acceptance of other anti-subversive legislation.[13] The present study integrates this approach into the broad argument, but is not really concerned with McCarthyism, choosing instead to highlight particular underresearched local battles and developments that demonstrate the logic of Cold War liberalism and its inevitable decline as a force for genuine socioeconomic change. I use specific case studies of political campaigns and debates over policy to illuminate this link between the rhetoric of the Cold War and the failure of the United States to develop the welfare state beyond the partial reconstruction of the New Deal.

In many ways the anti-statist attacks on Truman's Fair Deal simply continued the trend that had emerged in the 1930s, but gained new significance from the existence of a more ambitious form of American liberalism that had established itself on the American political scene by 1945. This is not to argue that there was some alternative to the foreign policy pursued after the Second World War, nor to argue that one could not be liberal and anti-communist. What I do argue in these pages is that anti-communist liberalism was inevitably constrained by its own anti-left rhetoric, exemplified both by a purge of the left and by the growing political importance of anti-statism. Anti-communism was not confined to foreign policy, but was deployed to make a direct attack on the validity of state action in the domestic sphere, and to undermine even those liberal projects that were undertaken in this period.[14]

1. THE DYNAMICS OF POSTWAR POLITICS BEFORE THE COLD WAR

THE SOCIAL AND ECONOMIC PICTURE OF AMERICA IN 1946 was not as straightforward as is often suggested. This chapter aims to demonstrate that the process of American state building had come to a crossroads at the end of World War Two, and that both powerful social democratic political pressures and significant anti-statist interests were vying for political hegemony.

The social context of the mid-term elections of 1946 suggests that the anti-government mandate in America was less emphatic than is often assumed. It is true that one can read the results of the Congressional races of the war years or the roll calls in Congress on progressive legislation after 1941 as showing that the return of material prosperity with the World War dampened down demands for an extension of the New Deal.[1] It is also possible to take at face value the statements of those at the time who wished to read an anti-statist message into the social and electoral upheavals of the immediate postwar period. House Republican leader Joseph Martin asserted in a February 1946 speech that the "deadly poison of bureaucratic waste, irresponsible spending, deficit financing and deceitful political expediency is pulsing in every vein and artery of the nation's economy." Congressman Christian Herter argued in October that the elections would be decided on the basis that people "are tired of too much government. They are tired of vacillating and bungling government."[2] In addition, even before the Republican triumph in the 1946 midterm elections Congress had grown increasingly unwilling to countenance further expansion of the New Deal state, watering down the Employment Act of 1946 and killing off the Office of Price Administration (OPA) entirely.

On the other hand, although the war had in many ways rehabilitated the political might of the private business community and other conservative forces opposed to the development of left-wing politics in the United States, it had also thrown into relief new problems of industrial economy and social policy that strengthened the hand of liberal political actors and pressure groups. An examination of battles within and outside Congress over full employment, OPA, and the International Labor Organization, as well as the rise of a new generation of liberal and anti-statist politicians, shows that what Alan Brinkley has called the "end of reform" was not preordained in 1946. Although it is certainly the case that the 1946 election results and the subsequent right turn in American politics did herald a shift of political power away from the original sponsors of the full employment bill and other social welfare measures, the elections did not mark the end of attempts to inject left of center ideology into Democratic politics. Crucially, it was by no means clear that American policymakers were hell-bent on severing relations with the Soviet Union, or in shifting the emphasis of liberal politics away from an international dialogue of reform.[3] However, whenever communism became an issue in the context of the 1946 elections and thereafter, the social democratic impulse gaining strength in many parts of the industrialized world faced in the United States challenges not only from the Republican Party and organized business, but also from liberal activists, who began to reassess the place of left-wing ideas in a Cold War climate.

The Background to Changing Perceptions of the State: An Overview

At the end of World War Two this broadly social democratic current in American politics still held considerable sway in Democratic Party circles. Progressive interest groups such as the Union for Democratic Action (UDA) led a spirited fight to implement the Full Employment Act in 1945–46 and to defend the OPA from being dismantled by congressional conservatives. In many ways the war had demonstrated what the state could do to stabilize the American economy, and had also thrown up new challenges concerning postwar reconversion that demanded new solutions from government. If during the Depression the Roosevelt administration had often used tried and tested methods of economic stimulation, in 1945 the Truman administration and its supporters formed part of an international social democratic experiment, taking place from the United Kingdom to New Zealand. While the Labour government in Britain was much more entrenched in power than liberals in the variegated political structure in Washington, the development of a political program for the left in both countries was proceeding along similar lines.[4] "It is time for a standard to be raised that goes beyond the slogans and programs of the Roosevelt period," argued Joseph Lash to the New York chapter of the UDA in September 1946. The Depression years had, he argued, vindicated those advocating "the development of democratic techniques for achieving collectivist objectives," including "full employment, economic efficiency, and a structure of economic democracy. . . . Wartime developments have not invalidated this thesis."[5] The imaginations of liberal political activists inside and outside Congress were captured by such questions as how to provide jobs for thousands of returning servicemen; how to control inflationary pressures and regulate demand in the reconversion period; and how to prevent the collapse of the wartime boom after the cessation of hostilities. . "My contacts with workers over recent months indicate to me that they will not remain quiescent under another depression, and I hesitate to think by what means they would rent their anger at such a reconversion," argued Washington UDA direction Paul Sifton in February 1945. "They feel that they have a right to job security, to the opportunity to work and earn a decent living."[6] The passage in 1944 of the GI Bill of Rights had convinced UDA members and their allies in Congress that the initiative still lay with them in the developing battle over who would dominate American politics.

The diffuse structure of the American federal system and the persistence of a conservative southern bloc within the Democratic Party helped to obscure the emergence of a leftist impulse in postwar American politics. New Deal initiatives had in many ways come about in spite of the often intractable opposition of the party's southern wing, a fact that the failed attempt on the part of the Roosevelt administration to purge several southern conservatives from Congress in the 1938 primaries had thrown into sharp relief.[7] The lack of coherent, organized party machines in southern and western states had allowed some left-of-center figures, best exemplified by Senator Claude Pepper of Florida and Governor Jim Folsom of Alabama, to gain control of the levers of political power. There was, however, no established party apparatus to facilitate the development of a united social democratic bloc within the Democratic Party, and no ideologically driven political machine outside a handful of northeastern states through which to shape a liberal-labor political order.[8]

There had, however, been a significant increase in the number of liberals in the Democratic Party as a whole as a result of the New Deal and the war, and the extent of their commitment to the expansion of social democratic reform would decide the future of American politics just as much as the vitality of southern conservatives in the party. Just as important as the continued existence of an anti-statist strain in American politics to a discussion of the fate of the reform impulse in these years is the development of a social democratic network of activists inside and outside Congress whose ideological frame of reference was not simply, or even primarily, the New Deal, but also a politics of equality of opportunity and social welfare that transcended national boundaries. For example, the union of Democratic, Liberal, and American Labor Party forces in New York at the end of the war, or the dominance of the CIO-PAC (political action committee) in the Ohio Democratic Party, or the growing self-confidence of leftist activists who would come to form the California Democratic Council and rejuvenate the party in the Golden State in the 1950s formed part of a mosaic of social democratic expression in postwar America. The mosaic may have been fractured and bereft of the sort of national coherence that helped identify the ideological focus of the British Labour Party or the Swedish Social Democrats. Still, Roosevelt's Economic Bill of Rights in his 1944 State of the Union address symbolized a new start for American liberals in a political landscape dramatically altered by war. When Senator Pepper and Senator Harley Kilgore of West Virginia assembled a liberal Democratic caucus to discuss a postwar left-of-center program in 1945, they could count on more than half the party's Senate contingent, and about 120 congressmen, without counting the tractable contingent of liberal Republicans and southerners.[9] More important perhaps were liberals outside Congress in groups like the UDA or the CIO-PAC, who could potentially use their growing political confidence to push the political balance further to the left in future elections.

The way in which the war had forced the state to engage in widespread economic and social planning created momentum for further left-of-center initiatives, mirroring developments in other nations. The Full Employment bill mobilized a coalition of administration officials in bureaus like the Office of War Mobilization and Reconversion, labor leaders, congressmen, and UDA activists. High levels of employment had been achieved in wartime "through the creation of an unlimited market by the government," argued Fred Vinson, director of the OWMR in a letter to Senator Robert Wagner of New York. Vinson found ready allies in Congress in the form of Wagner, Senator James Murray of Montana, congressmen Wright Patman of Texas and George Outland of California, who began pushing the bill on Capitol Hill. The bill would commit the United States government to "the responsibility to do everything possible to attain full employment in this country," if necessary through public works and capital projects, and not simply through fiscal policy.[10] In his statement to the Senate Banking and Currency Committee on the bill in June 1945, George Outland argued that Americans had a right to gainful employment that had to be enshrined in government policy, a right already embedded in the constitutions of a number of other countries, including Brazil, the USSR, and Argentina. "The prevention of unemployment is everybody's business and consequently the business of government. The responsibility for maintaining employment is too large for business alone or for any one economic group to assume."[11] The full employment bill formed part of a wider program that shifted the focus of American liberalism away from contingent responses to emergencies of depression and war and toward long-range social democratic planning that had emerged hesitantly during the "Second New Deal" of 1935. At a meeting of leading progressive thinkers in Washington in October 1946 to map out the future of the UDA "as a Fabian society type of organization," UDA leader James Loeb "felt the central problem of our times was what were the overall controls needed to guarantee full employment. . . . He thought the problem of the 'mixed economy' was the central one." So central was this question in 1946 that there was a consensus that "foreign policy should be considered subsequent to the investigation of a progressive position on economic policy."[12]

Many saw the state as a valuable tool for re-establishing equilibrium between social groups in America if it could be run more efficiently. Indeed, recent scholarship has demonstrated the continued power of big government in the immediate aftermath of the war.[13] The wartime success of the OPA in maintaining stable prices and supply convinced the Truman administration and its allies that similar state management of the economy would be necessary in the period of postwar reconversion. "It will require some months yet," warned OPA administrator Paul Porter in March 1946, "to build up well-balanced industries of parts and materials in all our factories. . . . It must be clear to all but the most uninformed or the most narrowly self-interested that the decisions of Congress this year will determine our economic future for a generation or longer." In January Franklin Roosevelt Jr. formed a committee of 1,000 to defend price and rent control to preempt a business backlash against government controls that was gathering force with the end of world war.[14] The fight over the full employment bill, which had been all but gutted in the House in December 1945 to the extent that all actual machinery to promote government intervention in the economy had been weakened or eliminated, suggested to liberals that the fight to promote the type of Fabian reform drive evolving in countries like the United Kingdom would not be easily won. Nevertheless, the reform impulse was very much alive and well in American politics in 1946, to a degree that would be unthinkable four years later.

Battles over American membership in the International Labor Organization (ILO), and the development of a social democratic vision on the left through projects like full employment and an American Beveridge plan, brought representatives of the labor movement into the reform coalition. The UDA was vocal in its support for the UAW-led strike at General Motors in late 1945, and this fact caused UAW leader Walter Reuther to note that his union "intends to work with all progressives for an economy of abundance and security." Reuther argued that the GM strike not only represented concern over wage rates, but also prices and the attainment of "mass purchasing power for full employment" as "a serious and permanent concern." At a dinner earlier in the year supporting Henry Wallace's nomination to be Roosevelt's new Secretary of Commerce, Reuther had urged that the administration create "a single, overall agency, with full authority to plan, organize and direct the conversion of our war economy to peace production so as to achieve full and continuous employment." Alongside this corporate statist vision of an alliance between bureaucrats, labor leaders, and business representatives went plans "for a far-flung public works program . . . not as an emergency glorified WPA project, but as a permanent part of a healthy, expanding national economy." This program, together with a comprehensive cradle to grave welfare state, formed a comprehensive blueprint for an American social democracy. Emil Rieve of the Textile Workers Union argued that union members needed to support the retention in government of progressives like Henry Wallace, who had promised sixty million jobs at the end of the war, "for there can be no lasting peace unless there are jobs for everyone—60,000,000 jobs for the 60,000,000 Americans who need them."[15]

The coalition of Democracy and labor had been cemented in 1943–44 with the founding of the CIO-PAC to act as an electoral campaign group for liberal electoral candidates, as well as the participation of key Roosevelt administration figures Arthur Altmeyer, Wilbur Cohen, and Isidore Falk of the Social Security Administration and Federal Security Administration in the declaration of postwar principles of the ILO. At the planning meeting in Ottawa in late 1943 these figures had approved a comprehensive plan for social security, including free health care, public works, and a cradle to grave social safety net which the CIO incorporated into its wish list for a postwar order. This comprehensive welfare state would "appropriately be financed out of general revenue," and the program was adopted at the 1944 General Conference of the ILO in Philadelphia.[16] In addition, the 1943 report of the National Resources Planning Board set out officially the post–New Deal agenda of Democratic liberalism as an economic "Bill of Rights" that postulated a similar socioeconomic program to that of the Beveridge Plan in Great Britain.[17] A tripartite alliance of federal bureaucrats and politicians, organized labor, and liberal pressure groups like the UDA seemed to herald at least the potential of a reinvigorated American social democratic impulse, albeit tempered by the realities of a prosperous society eager to shrug off the shackles of wartime austerity.

This liberal political dialogue over the future of reform after the New Deal gained an international dimension when the UDA looked to London for material with which to promote a reformist agenda at home. In May 1946 James Loeb organized a luncheon for UDA activists in Washington "on the general subject of American Progressives and the British Labor Government." The invitation, sent to prominent liberal activists like Congressman Jerry Voorhis of California and theologian Reinhold Niebuhr, stated that "American progressives must seek to understand the problems confronting this British government and the steps it has taken to meet them." Voorhis was urged to speak at the meeting, and to address "some of the steps that the British Government has taken internally to meet the needs of postwar Britain, including the health program, the beginnings of nationalization, etc." Former OPA head Leon Henderson informed a Town Hall meeting that he had "just returned from England and France. . . . They know that they must both make certain choices to insure employment, that they must not risk the fabric of future freedom to vague laws or to Adam Smith or automaticity."[18]

The UDA set up an office in London to send reports to members back in the United States. The July 1946 issue of the "UDA London Letter" commented on the first year of the Labour government in glowing terms: "This English experiment—to secure basic social change by democratic, rather than totalitarian, means—is unprecedented in world history." A month later the focus was on nationalization of industries, the logic behind which was explained in terms of a desire "to mold the policies of employment and investment so that everyone willing to work may have a job." The National Health Service was described as attempting to provide universal access "to the best medical treatment that science and the nation can provide."[19] American liberal activists formed part of an international discourse on social democratic avenues for meeting the challenges of an uncertain peacetime economy.[20]

This transnational conversation about social democracy revealed, however, significant cracks in the commitment of American liberals to a politics of the left that would only intensify in the emerging Cold War. For one thing, a comparison of the American and British political climates revealed just how limited the social democratic vision was in the United States. In addition, the emergence of deep divisions within American liberalism over the question of relations with the Soviet Union increasingly defined the context of the international conversation among those on the left. A UDA memo written shortly after the 1946 midterm elections argued that the rationale behind the economic integration of Germany into a European economic federation was the threat of "Russian domination of Europe." The author of the memorandum noted "differences in political outlook between the US and the principal countries of Europe," but stated that "our differences with governments which, broadly speaking, are social democratic, are differences in degree of public ownership and central planning. They are not comparable to the fundamental cleavage between totalitarian and democratic systems."[21]

The memorandum demonstrated not only the awareness on the part of liberal activists of the need to adapt the language of reform to the demands of the American political scene, but also the increasing desire by UDA liberals to shift American liberalism away from associations with any sort of popular front on the left in order to emphasize this "fundamental cleavage" between freedom and totalitarianism. British Labour politician Jennie Lee would note in April 1947 that American liberals had changed since the concerted drive to confirm Henry Wallace as Secretary of Commerce and to pass the Full Employment Act in 1945. The depth of the divisions that had given rise to the formation of the rival liberal organizations in the form of the Progressive Citizens of America and Americans for Democratic Action, divisions that manifested themselves far less severely in Europe, demonstrated to Lee that progressive groups "in Britain and America are dangerously out of touch with one another."[22]

As the 1946 midterm elections approached, however, the principal obstacle to the emergence of a social democratic politics in America remained the growing strength of the business community and its anti-statist allies. James Loeb had to admit in May 1946 that the aftermath of the fight for the full employment bill had left many liberals "heartsick. More than that we are rather angry." Despite spending some 90 percent of the UDA's 1945 budget of $90,000 lobbying for the bill, not only had the end result proved less than comprehensive, but also President Truman had not even appointed anyone to the new Council of Economic Advisers. "Those of us who continue to support President Truman," warned Loeb in a letter to Truman's secretary, "despite the attacks on him from both the right and the left, necessarily are weakened by delays of this sort."[23]

The death of Roosevelt and the revival of a conservative coalition of southern Democrats, Republicans and business organizations like the Chamber of Commerce had left liberal Democrats uncertain and rudderless.

While the UDA had a budget in 1945 of $90,000, the National Association of Manufacturers spent more than $3 million in its drive to destroy OPA in the first six months of 1946, half of it on newspaper advertising and the rest on supplying speakers to civic organizations, sending flyers to community leaders, and mobilizing support in Congress. Business leaders like the vice president of Westinghouse Electric noted that the climate of popular opinion had swung far enough since the New Deal to preclude a return "to the tested principles and practices of free private enterprise."[24] Nevertheless, the war had revitalized the U.S. economy to a degree that pushed demands for higher productivity and less regulation to the top of the political agenda. Musing on Great Britain's "considerable progress this year under its socialist government" and its program of nationalization of the commanding heights of the British economy in July 1946, Senator Pepper also expressed frustration at the fact that social democratic politics "is the direction of things everywhere but here."[25]

As the country struggled to readjust to a peacetime economy, it became more difficult to perceive anything but political stalemate. The United States was being convulsed by numerous strikes in its major industries at the same time as massive postwar demand for consumable goods was fueling inflation and creating shortages of meat and durable goods. The state had been responsible for empowering the labor unions in the mid-1930s and its Office of Price Administration had the power to regulate prices and demand. Yet by 1946 the OPA was under threat and conservatives in Congress were drawing up revisions to the National Labor Relations Act in the form of the Case bill to recast the balance of industrial power in favor of management. The carefully controlled broker state of the war years was beginning to break down, leaving the compass of political opinion in flux. On the one hand, the sponsors of the full employment bill in the Senate managed to engender a fair degree of consensus over the need, in Senator Wayne Morse's words, to "make political democracy and the private enterprise economy work cooperatively in this country." After watering down the provisions of the bill relating to public spending, Republicans like Robert Taft claimed that there "is now nothing in the bill to which any Member of the Congress should take exception. . . . It is a bill which provides in effect that the Government shall take thought and shall provide the machinery for eliminating economic depression."[26] The first Senate version passed by 71 votes to 10, the ten opponents being six right-wing Republicans, three southern Democrats, and maverick Rhode Island Senator Peter Gerry. The final conference bill in February 1946 passed without a vote.[27] On the other hand, however, the limited scope of the final Act together with the clear signs that congressional conservatives were mobilizing their resources against organized labor demonstrated the fragility of the New Deal coalition's hold on power in Washington. The war had undoubtedly enlarged significantly the state capacity of the American government, but it was not yet clear which political interests would be best placed to harness the power of the state. The most notable example of this problem lay in the field of federal labor policy, an issue that will be discussed later in this chapter.

The Republican campaign slogan "Had Enough?" seemed designed to appeal to an electorate unhappy with the response of government to the economic problems that had been ushered in with the end of hostilities abroad. The enormous mail bags to Congressmen condemning Chester Bowles as administrator of the Office of Price Administration and attacking the militancy of unions are testimony to much popular feeling.[28] A circular for the GOP campaign committee on labor policy claimed the existence of a link between the fact that the price of a pound of chicken had risen from 39 cents in 1940 to 50 cents in 1945 and the concomitant near doubling of strike cases, from some 2,600 to almost 5,000.[29] In one survey, of those polled who said they had an interest in the 1946 elections (half of those surveyed), 49 percent said it made a significant difference which party won the elections, and a further 31 percent said it made some difference, with only 11 percent saying it made no difference at all.[30] An August 1946 poll found that a large percentage of respondents, 46 percent, thought inflation the most important issue facing the nation, and that for the first time since the New Deal a majority thought the Republicans best placed to tackle the crisis.[31]

Before the Cold War: The International Context of Postwar Liberalism

Perhaps the most striking thing about liberalism in 1946 was that it did not tend to frame itself in terms of American foreign relations, and in cases where other countries did enter into debate, it was more often than not in a positive way intended to reinforce America's leftward direction. For staunch New Dealer Claude Pepper, domestic liberalism went hand in hand with a positive view of social democratic and statist experiments overseas. This was not particularly unusual in the pre–Cold War period. It was no accident that the temporary hiatus between periods of anti-statist political dominance in the late 1930s and late 1940s came during the United States' alliance with the Soviet Union. The absence of the Soviet menace from political debate made it much easier to engage directly with liberal ideas, a notion expressed not only by radical writers in the 1930s but also by members of the Roosevelt administration up to 1945. Joseph Davies as Roosevelt's ambassador to Moscow in the late 1930s was convinced that American liberalism had emerged from the same mainspring as all left-wing movements, but that the United States, in contrast to the USSR, was "holding on to those freedoms which we cherished and at the same time we were trying to bring about greater distribution of wealth and greater equality of opportunity . . . for the underprivileged."

In a 1944 book devoted to the propagation of wartime propaganda Under-Secretary of State Sumner Welles argued that under Stalin the USSR had advanced from "impractical and unproductive Communism toward state socialism."[32] The twin emergencies of the Depression and war had allowed the administration to experiment with left-wing thought without fear that they could be associated with totalitarianism in the minds of a majority of the American public, as evidenced by Roosevelt's Economic Bill of Rights speech as late as 1944.

Claude Pepper sprang from this radical tradition in post-1917 American political thought, which aimed to define more sharply the contours of a domestic reform agenda with reference to the experience of other countries. On a visit to Stalin in Moscow in September 1945, a visit that would help destroy his political career five years later, Pepper enquired about Soviet domestic policy as well as the international situation, and handed Stalin a copy of Henry Wallace's left-wing manifesto, *Sixty Million Jobs*, explaining to him that it "represented what might be called the Roosevelt point of view about our future economic policy at home, that it was the best statement which could be found of the policy of the liberal element in our country."[33] On his return to the United States Pepper claimed that the USSR was "still an immature democracy, but they are reaching out for the things that we enjoy: freedom of press, civil liberties, freedom of the individual. . . . As they get a higher standard of living, they will demand more civil rights." In a speech at Madison Square Garden in July 1945, Pepper argued that it was "Russia which suggested that full employment for all nations should be one of the objectives of the United Nations."[34]

Clearly Pepper had an unrealistic understanding of the nature of Stalin's rule, but looked with some appreciation at the strides made in terms of economic modernization under the Soviet Union's statist socioeconomic program. Keen to push the boundaries of American liberalism toward a more daring state-centered approach than had been achieved under President Roosevelt, and aware that the great enemy of democracy during World War II had been the totalitarian right, not the left, Pepper was one of many popular front liberals after the war who combined domestic and foreign policy into an ideological whole.[35] As Congresswoman Helen Gahagan Douglas of California put it, when "Lenin with the philosophy of Marx and Engel [sic] arrived in Petrograd in the midst of a revolt against the czars and the war, there was small wonder that the Russian people followed him who promised bread and freedom. . . . It is our job . . . to see that . . . through democratic processes the welfare and security of the people which are what make a society solvent increase day by day."[36]

Moderate Florida Democrats such as George Smathers, candidate for the Fourth congressional district, and 1946 Senate candidate Spessard Holland drew no positive comparisons with any country outside the United States. More importantly, however, they did not make attacks on the left through the use of anti-totalitarian imagery to anything like the extent that would become normal a few years later. There might be serious disagreements between, say, Pepper and Smathers about the desirable scope of postwar liberalism, but these rival interpretations sat uneasily side by side, vying for supremacy in the context of the struggles by organized labor and other groups such as the Southern Conference for Human Welfare for a greater commitment by liberals to social pluralism.[37] References in the Smathers and Holland campaigns to foreign relations tended to take the form of vague generalities about the new United Nations Organization. Formulations such as "America as the most powerful nation on earth must exercise its influence on the world and assume its rightful leadership in the formulation and maintenance of world peace" summed up the level of specificity of Smathers' campaign against incumbent Democrat Pat Cannon.[38] The Soviet Union was rarely mentioned in the Smathers primary campaign; rather, he exhorted all countries to "get together to give up a certain amount of their sovereignty." When one of Smathers' campaign workers attended a Cannon speech in Miami in April 1946, he made the note that Cannon had mentioned the USSR, and that the speech had been "slanted to inspire fear," implying that to do so was out of step with the mainstream of the Democratic Party, who still made encouraging, if slightly unconvinced, noises about U.S.-Soviet cooperation.[39] Holland's announcement of his principles for his Senate campaign stated that "I favor and will work for peace and understanding with Russia. Their government and economy are different from ours. We wish them progress in raising the living standards of their peoples." He urged "frankness and realism" in American dealings with the USSR, and, although expressing hostility to any form of "regimentation and collectivism" for the United States, he endorsed and trumpeted the achievements of the New Deal in the fields of social security, banking insurance, and made reference to "enlarged programs" in the future.[40] Holland, like Smathers, made no claims to support Pepper's broader definition of New Deal liberalism, refusing to endorse federal health insurance and musing that some form of anti-labor amendment to the National Labor Relations Act might be necessary to equalize the balance between labor and management.[41] There was, however, no equation of the New Deal state in toto as being a road to totalitarianism, and there was no overriding impression in the campaign literature that statism was the principal issue for Democrats of the 1946 elections, beyond the immediate issue of what to do about labor unrest and the end of price controls.

It was still unclear what foreign policy the United States would pursue in the wake of the war. For one thing, foreign policy was seen as much less important than the manifold domestic issues besetting the nation.[42] More significantly, anti-communism was not yet the principal driving force behind America's view of foreign affairs. Many commentators still believed it was essential to come to terms with the Soviet Union. The message from Stalin in September 1946 playing down the danger of conflict and asserting the need for friendship between East and West was warily welcomed in American political circles. Congresswoman Edith Nourse Rogers (R-Massachusetts) stated that "these statements defining the hope of Russia constitute the most encouraging force for peace since the end of hostilities of World War II." Congressman Emmanuel Celler (D-New York), a supporter of the anti-Soviet strategy in later years, argued in a radio speech in May 1946 that "world power is split between the two great giants—Russia and the United States—opposed in ideology. . . . I think there is enough wisdom in the United States and in Russia to devise a modus operandi whereby these two gigantic political entities may live in peace. We must remember—there must be only one world—but if two should develop, each will destroy the other and there will be no world!"[43] Republican candidate for Congress in New York Jacob Javits argued in a campaign broadcast that the United States should not rule out continuing to send aid to the Soviet Union.[44]

Public opinion polls continued to find the American public confused about the world beyond its borders. While 62 percent of those surveyed in one poll said they were less friendly toward the USSR than in 1945, 54 percent in a similar poll supported the strengthening of the United Nations so it could control all the world's armed forces.[45] It was therefore not simply radicals and fringe figures who opposed the application of anti-Soviet hysteria to American foreign policy. Harold Ickes, moved by the large amount of correspondence he received supporting the continuation of Roosevelt's policy of accommodation of the Soviet Union, replied to one concerned writer in California: "I certainly do not want to see us get into war with Russia nor do I believe that Russia wants to fight us."[46] Although in later months anti-Soviet sentiment intensified, Ickes remained convinced that any surrender to anti-Soviet hysteria would endanger domestic liberalism. He responded angrily to one correspondent after Wallace's dismissal in September disputing the writer's claim that if one eliminated Communism one would "eliminate the Democratic Party."[47] Clearly statements like that published by the UDA in October 1945 that "Russian policy is based upon mistrust of the west, rather than upon purely expansionist impulses" were becoming less common as the relationship between the two nations cooled. Nevertheless, anti-Sovietism had not yet crystallized as the dominant preoccupation of Americans in 1946.[48]

On questions of domestic and foreign policy, then, there still existed in 1946 significant possibilities for vibrant political debates between economic anti-statism as a guiding political ideology and progressive liberalism. The problem was that the growth of anti-communism as a significant factor in domestic politics would provide new opportunities for the reorientation of both anti-statism and liberalism, away from economic issues and toward more theoretical constructs which would appeal to basic American fears of state power. This trend was not yet readily apparent, but it was emerging to dampen the prospects for a general coming to terms with the state by all political groups. The remaining sections of this chapter deal with these ideological developments in more detail, using specific case analyses to illustrate the general trends described above.

The Democratic Party and Democratic Liberalism

In 1946 state-centered ideas of social justice and reform still very much influenced the northern wing of the Democratic Party in the wake of the depression and war. Any commitment to anti-totalitarian ideals in foreign policy was set alongside a general attachment to the ideas crystallized during the New Deal years. Congressional candidates such as John F. Kennedy of Massachusetts and Helen Gahagan Douglas of California, who late in the decade would be seen very differently in the context of the Cold War, were still in 1946 talking the same language. Both represented constituencies dependent on New Deal ideas if they were to have any chance of social and economic advance. Kennedy's seat, the 11th district of Massachusetts, consisted of the union-dominated cities of Cambridge and Somerville with large populations of ex-servicemen and high proportions of manual workers. Douglas's seat, California's 14th district, included downtown Los Angeles, heavily populated by blacks and Hispanics, as well as swathes of southern Los Angeles, containing the poorest neighborhoods.[49] The philosophy of the Democratic Party, argued Kennedy, made it the better vehicle for America in the years ahead: "It stands for full employment and high production.

It stands for an extension of social security, to give full protection to the unemployed and aged. It stands for a minimum wage. . . . for the enactment of progressive legislation that will be of aid to the people, that will preserve our system of private enterprise and strengthen the fabric of our society."[50] There was not a mention of communism or foreign policy in the whole speech. In his platform for the election, Kennedy started by discussing the aftermath of war, but then linked postwar reconstruction to liberal statist legislation at home, particularly housing construction and continued price control. He confined thoughts on foreign policy mainly to the United Nations.[51] New Deal spirit imbued Massachusetts Democrats in 1946; Michael Bevilacqua, candidate for Boston City Council in ward 3, included in Kennedy's constituency, campaigned on the theme "Ward 3 Needs a New Deal," based on leftist conceptions of the state.[52]

Helen Douglas's campaign in California also stressed domestic economic welfare and the continuance of liberal ideology. A successful Broadway theater career and a life in the media spotlight as wife of movie actor Melvyn Douglas had attracted instant attention from California Democratic bosses when the couple decided to get involved in liberal politics in the late 1930s. The Democratic Party in the Golden State was still reeling from internecine divisions that had characterized Upton Sinclair's gubernatorial campaign of 1934 and Sheridan Downey's Senate primary victory over Senator William Gibbs McAdoo in 1938. Helen Douglas, a newcomer to active politics at the start of the war, was by the early 1940s chair of the women's division of the California State Democratic Central Committee, and an active fundraiser in Hollywood. In 1944, shortly before being selected as party candidate for Congress in the 14th congressional district, she orchestrated a fundraising drive that capitalized on the power of the Roosevelt image by constructing quilts with "autographed signatures of men and women who have been prominently connected with the Roosevelt administration" that would sell for $1 a piece.[53] She and her husband formed part of a left-wing political network in California struggling to free the party from the control of a conservative group of party bosses. Her election, along with that of Ellis Patterson in the Santa Monica-based 16th district, symbolized the growing power in California of a new generation of activists searching for social democratic solutions to America's socioeconomic problems at the end of the war.

In March 1946 she had made a long speech in the House setting out what she called her "Democratic Credo." Already the target of anti-statists who saw her as communist-influenced, Douglas retorted that she was "sick to death of the vicious and deliberate way the word Communist has been forged into a weapon . . . of hearing the very program which was initiated by

Franklin Roosevelt . . . called Communistic by those who seek to defeat the majority will of the American people." In Douglas's opinion, Communism was no threat to a strong democracy in which there was economic and social equality of opportunity. Statist measures were vital to the defeat of communism.[54] The speech would cause her many problems in later years, but in 1946 it still represented the optimism of liberal America just a year after Roosevelt's death. She reported with glee the opposition to her of the "oil interests, real estate, home loan" companies, and fought hard to convince her constituents that liberalism was still the way forward for America at mid-century.[55] In this she was of one voice with most Democrats outside the south. The party in California as a whole was divided, but ripe for development as a vehicle for social democratic policies, as the growth of the California Democratic Council in the 1950s would demonstrate. Ellis Patterson in the 16th district had stood to the left of Will Rogers in his attempt to win the Senate nomination, and Rogers presented himself as a New Deal loyalist during the campaign against William F. Knowland.[56] There was also Jerry Voorhis in the 12th district. Outside California there were certainly radicals such as Hugh De Lacy in Seattle and John Blatnik, standing successfully in a Republican seat in Minnesota, but even moderates such as Kennedy and John Carroll (D-Colorado) stressed domestic themes and the value of the state in their campaigns in visibly pluralist constituencies.

As the Douglas campaign indicated, however, by 1946 anti-communism was an issue beginning to destabilize and weaken the liberal consensus on the state. Douglas herself regularly had to disassociate her liberalism from the far left because her political opponents within both parties were beginning to use popular anti-communism against her in Los Angeles. Just a week before polling day, Douglas told her friend Harold Ickes about the latest tricks being used against her. "They've put out an anonymous flyer," she said, "asking me how I happened to go to Moscow, what Stalin said to me, what I told Stalin, etc. . . . This morning I signed an affidavit swearing that I had never been to Moscow, had never been to Russia, and had never seen Uncle Joe." The 14th was normally fertile territory for the left, but in 1946 Douglas was struggling. That she needed to ask for a public endorsement from Ickes, asking him to "stress the fight I've put up for a decent integrated program of public power," suggests how worried Douglas had become.[57] A Democratic Party report made after the election suggested that the "Douglas group in 1946 put on a terrific get out the vote campaign. . . . If the Douglas campaign had not been as vigorous as it was, we would have lost the district at that time." As it was Douglas' margin had been only 8,756 votes out of around 100,000 cast, and this in a district the Republicans should never have had a hope in if the New Deal coalition remained intact.[58] Republicans took note of the result. Analyzing the result in three areas of the district around downtown Los Angeles, each with high populations of either Hispanics or blacks, a GOP report noted that although both Douglas and Rogers had taken these areas, the margins were not as comfortable as one would expect. In downtown itself, Knowland had finished only 100 votes behind Rogers, and Douglas's opponent had run 400 votes behind her.[59] The reasons for the renaissance of Republicanism included the national issues of shortages, strikes, and problems of postwar reconversion, as well as the significant drop in voter turnout, but in Douglas's case both Republicans and her enemies in her own party saw a potent electoral link between her liberalism and images of communism.

Helen Douglas's campaign in 1946 also cast light on a further development changing the dynamics of American liberalism in the wake of World War Two. Her district was the home of the *Los Angeles Sentinel*, an African American daily serving the largest African American community west of Chicago. In an editorial stance that was to change markedly in succeeding years, the *Sentinel* noted Douglas's "brilliant record on the question of atomic energy; her support of OPA, housing, social security and kindred legislation conceived for the common good," as well as her recognition of the ways in which the war had pushed the issue of civil rights for racial minorities onto the political agenda. The paper believed that "Mrs Douglas would be a far more convinced and effective fighter for social security, for adequate price controls, for a far-sighted foreign policy, for safeguarding the rights of labor" than her Republican opponent. The *Sentinel* published in October an opinion piece by Roy Wilkins of the NAACP in which he argued that the USSR, "with all her mistakes and faults . . . speaks in world councils for the underdog peoples." There was, however, a dilemma for editor Leon Washington. Douglas's Republican opponent, Fred Roberts, was African American. The question of the extent to which American liberalism would revolve around issues of racial pluralism was becoming increasingly politically significant, and would become a major dilemma for proponents of social democracy. Roberts as a member of the California state assembly consistently voted in line with his Republican colleagues against social welfare measures, yet to the *Sentinel* the principle at stake in supporting Roberts was "the right of every American to participate in government, a vote against lily-whiteism in government."[60] Douglas's victory in the election demonstrated that the vast majority of people of color had not returned to the party of Lincoln in the wake of the New Deal, but the issue of race in the campaign raised questions about the future ideological direction of American liberalism that would only intensify as the Cold War invited a debate over the meaning of "freedom" in an American context.

The tension between continuing the promise of the New Deal and recognizing the dangers of communism at home and abroad was beginning to affect the whole Democratic Party. John White has shown the extent of the concern in the Kennedy campaign in Massachusetts, with Kennedy asking an aide how important communism was to the voters in his new district.[61] There was also a renaissance in states such as Maryland of a more anti-statist brand of Democracy, as Senate candidate Herbert O'Conor waged a campaign based on moving to the right of his Republican opponent. O'Conor was another example of a politician using a negative image of the state to legitimize his own stance, arguing that the "most insidious movement abroad today is that which seeks to substitute the guarantee of security for the guarantee of liberty as the prime purpose of our republic. Men who would be free cannot always be secure."[62] O'Conor was one of few Democratic Senate candidates to win in 1946, by a paltry 3,000 votes. The extent to which Democrats would embrace anti-socialism as a qualification of the party's liberalism seemed to relate directly to their support for the growing bipartisan view of foreign affairs. While outlining his support for New Deal measures in his platform, John Kennedy made it clear that he stood for "free enterprise" and "democratic government in a capitalist economy," and that he opposed "communism, fascism and socialism." National health insurance would mean "we would have a totalitarian government." On the question of foreign policy, America "must see to it that [totalitarianism] is never allowed to grow up again. . . . My one regret is that the United States failed to give the leadership which would have made the United Nations really strong."[63]

Even so, the dominant electoral message for northern Democrats in 1946 emphasized the positive legacy of the New Deal and the potential of an ever more ambitious progressive political program. Herbert Lehman, the former governor of New York now running for the Senate, told a friendly audience during his campaign that "the war left in its wake new conditions which threaten to undermine all of the social gains of recent years. The danger did not catch us unawares. . . . A comprehensive program of social legislation geared to postwar problems was laid before the Congress. . . . [President Truman] is entitled to a Congress so overwhelmingly progressive in makeup that no combination of reactionary forces can any longer thwart the nation's will."[64] The New York state Democratic Party platform explicitly endorsed the economic bill of rights drawn up by the NRPB during the war, as well as the maintenance of price controls, federal health insurance, public housing, a Fair Employment Practices Committee and the end of the House Un-American Activities Committee. The list of foreign policy issues in the platform made no direct mention of the Soviet Union, but instead prioritized the United Nations, the Baruch Plan for atomic energy control, the Palestine question, and the status of Italy as a state that had effectively switched sides during the war.

Lehman's address to the CIO national convention in September to mobilize the labor vote set the legacy of the New Deal at the heart of the Democratic Party in the years to come: "There is still work to be done. There must still be an amendment to the Wage and Hour Law. . . . Discrimination in employment because of race, creed or color must be outlawed. There still must be a national health program which will make good medical service available to all—to those who need it as well as those who can afford it. The laborer, and all consumers, must still be protected against the drop in real wages caused by inflationary prices."[65] The Lehman campaign made a conscious decision to tie the idea of equality to the pursuit of social democratic policies rather than purely to a civil rights agenda. A Lehman campaign worker noted after a visit to Harlem that African Americans, he felt, were less impressed by "promises referring to lynching . . . and are more impressed by tangible, constructive plans about raising their life standards and eliminating the social barriers surrounding them than tickling their race pride."[66]

The Democratic campaign in New York in 1946 was the last in which the state's unusual electoral fusion laws were used to their fullest extent, gathering activists from the minor Liberal and American Labor parties, as well as Democrats together behind the Lehman candidacy. Although the growing controversy on the left over communist influence in American politics was undermining popular front cooperation, and had already led to the creation of the Liberal Party as an anti-communist alternative to the ALP in 1944, Lehman's Senate campaign actively sought the endorsement of the left, and championed the cause of a united liberal-left alternative to a Republican party that had grown to dominate Empire state politics in the 1940s.[67] Lehman gratefully accepted the endorsement of the ALP, and also spoke at campaign rallies under the banner of the Independent Citizens Committee of the Arts, Sciences, and Professions and the Women's Division of the National Citizens Political Action Committee, both organizations that would later come under fire for their fellow traveler associations. Anxious to bridge the growing fissure separating anti-communist liberals from popular front bitter-enders, Lehman told the NCPAC meeting that "a just and enduring peace . . . can only be attained on the basis of a full and frank understanding with the Soviet Union." In a radio broadcast shortly before the election, Lehman referred to those arguing against continued links with the USSR as "defeatists," arguing that he wondered "whether they have ever stopped to consider the inescapable and terrifying conclusions which must logically be drawn from the view they prematurely accept."[68] Three years later, when Lehman once again ran for the Senate to replace retiring Senator Robert Wagner, he was forced to recast the experience of the 1946 campaign to fit the new anti-left political climate, arguing in response to Republican challenges that the ALP and its allies had only become communist dominated after the 1946 elections were over, and that during his campaign the party had been "still controlled by a strong anti-communist group." Not only was this manifestly untrue, but it was testimony to the changed political language of American liberalism by the late 1940s. In 1946 Lehman described the ALP as sharing his vision that a "rising standard of living, coupled with real security for all, must become the accepted pattern of American life."[69]

The point here is not that this political strategy was successful in 1946; the Republican Party in fact scored a significant victory in those elections, including in New York, and the liberal promise of the immediate postwar period was never fully realized. Rather, it is clear that progressive Democrats had been committed to an expansive vision of social democracy as late as 1946. They increasingly reoriented their political rhetoric and congressional activity away from themes of economic equality as the Cold War got underway. Herbert Lehman's successful second attempt to enter the Senate, in a 1949 special election, would entail a different ideological emphasis from his 1946 run. In the earlier campaign his years as governor of New York in the 1930s were portrayed as a springboard for further reform; in the 1949 and 1950 campaigns they became halcyon days in which New Deal liberalism had reached its zenith.

Of course the clearest example of the link between interpretations of liberalism and foreign policy views was provided by the argument between President Truman and Henry Wallace as the elections approached. Wallace's Madison Square Garden speech and accompanying letter to Truman resulted in his being sacked as Commerce Secretary in September. The events have been covered in detail elsewhere, but the link between foreign policy critiques and domestic liberalism has not been brought out clearly.[70] Wallace had argued that "Russian ideals of socio-economic justice are going to govern nearly a third of the world. Our ideas of free enterprise democracy will govern much of the rest. . . . Under friendly peaceful competition the Russian world and the American world will gradually become more alike. The Russians will be forced to grant more and more of the personal freedoms; and we shall become more and more absorbed with the problems of socio-economic justice."[71] To Wallace, the pursuit of solutions to problems of socio-economic justice was incompatible with any concept of Cold War. Wallace's view of the Soviet Union, like that of many on the left in America, was unrealistic, harking back to the hard years of the 1930s when the USSR seemed to many to offer more than the debased currency known as capitalism. However, Wallace was not so much concerned with the USSR as with his own country, and with the fact that liberalism seemed to be becoming increasingly preoccupied with anti-communism and less interested in domestic advance. To Truman it was possible to combine a commitment to opposing supposed Soviet designs on other states with a vibrant domestic liberalism. The elections of 1946 were already beginning to test this hypothesis.

Florida forms a useful case study for an examination of the changing political landscape of the United States at mid-century precisely because it formed a political meeting ground between the South and the metropolitan locus of liberal thought in the northeast of the country. Since one of the aims of this study is to attempt to define what constituted "liberal" and social democratic thought in the wake of the New Deal experience, and to examine what impact changing definitions of liberalism had on American politics and society, the fact that Florida was represented in federal politics by one of the most radical proponents of left-wing programs in the country, as well as by more moderate exponents of New Deal democracy, is of great importance.[72] In addition, Florida was a social mix of north and south. George Smathers, recalling the social context of his home state at the time he represented Miami in Congress in the late 1940s, compared "the Miami-Fort Lauderdale area, which is quite liberal," with the north and the panhandle, "bounded on the west side by Alabama and on the north side by Georgia, [where] you've got a totally different atmosphere in terms of the thinking of the people. In the northern part of the state . . . it's sort of conservative. . . . You come on down to Miami, and you have all the people who have moved in from New York City and who have moved in from Chicago, and they are much more liberal in their thinking."[73]

The arrival of the railroad in 1896 and the spectacular land boom of the early twentieth century, particularly the 1920s, had swollen the state's population considerably. The population of Florida increased at four times the national rate in every decade between 1900 and 1950; in 1924 alone the number of registered automobiles increased from 160,000 to 216,000.[74] Wealthy American financiers like Alfred duPont and J. C. Penney were attracted to the state and the entrepreneurial opportunities it provided, contributing in part to a conservative political climate. At the same time, however, population growth also meant the growth of the AFL in Florida and of a markedly more politically diverse populace than in other southern states. Political analyst V. O. Key in 1949 was keen to stress the amorphous, nonprogrammatic nature of Florida politics, but had to note that "no matter how good a spellbinder Pepper is, the fact that Florida's voters sent him to the Senate twice points to the existence of a powerful strain of liberalism within the state."[75] Key also noted that the rapid urbanization of the state had contributed to the "comparatively mild" political treatment of the race issue in Florida. He might have added that the all-white primary had ended in Florida in 1938, and that as a result the large African American population in the poorer, more archetypally Dixie counties of northern Florida had the potential to add to the state's progressive social mix. Half the population of Pepper's home county, Taylor, were black.[76] Florida's politics may have been hard to pin down, but as a result political power was still very much in flux. The racial politics of a southern state fused in Florida with the political influence of the state's immigrant population, often Jewish and committed to the social progressivism of the New Deal. Florida was thus atypical of states beneath the Mason-Dixon line, but still carried the racial baggage of the "solid South."[77]

The campaigns of Florida Democrats for public office in 1946, together with the fact that Senator Claude Pepper still seemed popular both in Florida and in the national press, suggest that the potential for the expansion of the possibilities offered by the expansion of state capacity since 1933 remained strong after the war. George Smathers had helped run the Gainesville part of Pepper's successful 1938 Senate campaign, one of the few bright spots for the liberal wing of the Democratic Party that year, while a law student at the University of Florida, and remained in contact with him after the war to help launch his political career. Once Smathers had decided to take on sitting congressman Pat Cannon in Florida's fourth congressional district, taking in Miami and the Florida Keys, he wrote to Pepper a number of times. In one undated note from early 1946, he told Pepper he had "decided to make the plunge" and asked Pepper to help delay the announcement of a naval station in Key West until after the primary so that Cannon could not benefit.[78] While it was clear from Smathers' campaign that there was plenty of room for debate between himself and Pepper over the future direction of ideological liberalism, his campaign fitted the socially diverse contours of the greater Miami area effectively. His 1946 platform for the primary combined the assertion that "the system of free enterprise and capitalism has produced the highest standard of living on earth and will continue to do so" with the notion that "the government must always maintain the right to intervene on behalf of the general welfare," and that "every person who works should receive a decent and living wage."[79] Smathers saw an opportunity in the political climate of the postwar South to contrast his youthful, pro-New Deal outlook, real or contrived, with the outdated conservatism of his opponent. Smathers, according to the *Miami Herald*, was "representative of the young type of manhood which we have been urging to get into public life and to rejuvenate the political system with [a] newness and freshness of viewpoint and approach."[80]

Such a "fresh" approach need not have been sympathetic to the New Deal; indeed, one section of the Republican Party was gaining strength in 1946 on the premise that what America needed was less government regulation, not more. However, this trend was not readily apparent in Florida, certainly not in Miami, where Pat Cannon attempted to portray himself to the right of Smathers and was soundly defeated at the polls. In one campaign ad Cannon attempted to tie Smathers in with Pepper, an approach that only seemed to help Smathers' cause.[81] The campaign represented the process in the Democratic Party of coming to terms with the legacy of the social and economic reforms of the 1930s and 1940s, involving a discussion of the future parameters of the state. In this debate, Smathers' position was discernible, if not clear. He supported the existing framework of the New Deal. In a debate with his Republican opponent after the 1946 primary, Smathers argued that the New Deal had aimed "to improve the living conditions of the forgotten man, the aged, the indigent, the diseased, the disabled, and the unemployed." Challenging Norman Curtis to name all the New Deal social welfare laws, Smathers asked him in addition to state "which of these laws he approves of and if he disapproves of any, what does he propose as a substitute measure," a clear indication of Smathers' intention to ride into office on the coattails of the New Deal.[82]

The unstable social situation of early 1946, exemplified by the wave of strikes that had paralyzed the nation and prompted President Truman to threaten to draft striking railwaymen into the army, had helped temper the ardor of Democrats like Smathers for further social reform. He stated in a radio speech after the primary election that "people are tired of the many restrictions, controls, excessive bureaucracy. . . . Thus far today certain selfish political factions in this country have capitalized on the maladjustments which resulted from the war in order to further their own interests."[83] This was a clear reference to labor unions, and a warning that the debate over the future of liberalism in America would center around the problem of adapting the social reforms of the depression years to the less obviously urgent social problems of a prosperous postwar nation. Smathers represented a new breed of New Deal liberal who would defend the long-term reforms of the 1930s, and attack the conservatism of the Republican Party, while expressing caution about any further extension of the state's commitment to furthering the political power of specific interest groups.

In 1950, however, when Smathers' political approach to the liberal dilemma had become somewhat different, sections of the press would marvel at the transformation: Smathers "came to the House in 1947 wearing the label of an ardent New Dealer. So far to the left was he supposed to be that when he ran for renomination in 1948, he had to make special efforts to keep an opponent from pinning a Communist tag on him." Stetson Kennedy, a left-wing opponent for Smathers in the 1950 general election and author of *Southern Exposure,* which in 1946 had predicted a positive future for southern liberalism, stated that until the 1950 campaign, apart "from his support of Taft-Hartley and opposition to civil rights legislation, Smathers' voting record has been better than fair-to-middlin', as Southern Congressmen go."[84] Smathers' own political career between 1946 and 1948 bears out this view, showing repeatedly how he defended New Deal policies and attacked Republican anti-statism, arguing in one speech that his party was "working toward a program of full employment, higher wages, housing programs for veterans, ceiling prices . . . health insurance, and many other liberal and constructive measures. Yet the Republicans are fighting each one of these and crying, as usual, 'It will ruin business.' "[85]

Smathers was representative of broad changes in southern politics in the wake of the New Deal. A number of historians have noted the rise of populist liberalism in the electoral arena across the South by 1946, as well as a broadly pro-New Deal voting pattern among southern congressmen except on issues of industrial unionism and civil rights. The defeat of the conservative architect of the House Un-American Activities Committee, Martin Dies, in a Texas primary in 1944, the election of Alabama Governor Jim Folsom and South Carolina Governor Strom Thurmond in 1946 on explicitly pro-FDR platforms, and the emergence of a new generation of civil rights activists galvanized by the gradual recognition on the part of the federal administration and Supreme Court of the race question, were destabilizing conservative hegemony in the South.[86] Such political stances were politically viable in 1946, and help us to understand the evolving ideological form of the center-left in America in the 1940s.

There were already signs that the vitality of the left's reform impulse was likely to wane in succeeding years. The fact that moderate liberals, not just southerners but northeastern liberals like young John F. Kennedy in Massachusetts, conceded the possibility that class based legislation like the Wagner Act might need revision, showed how far the postwar political climate differed from the desperate yet heady days of the mid-1930s.[87] Robert Wagner Sr. himself, together with Pepper and a band of liberals committed to expanding the boundaries of New Deal reform rather than curtailing them, were meanwhile pushing ahead with plans for federal health insurance and continued to lobby for the Townsend pension plan. At the same time, the disintegrating relationship between communism and capitalism across the world after 1946 was rendering Claude Pepper's popular front approach to foreign relations increasingly politically dangerous. He corresponded regularly with a friend in Brooksville, Florida, both making increasingly outlandish claims about the importance of the USSR to world peace. Col. Raymond Robins wrote in one such letter to Pepper in August 1946 that Russia had "held an honorable place in the RESISTANCE OF OPPRESSION . . . in the history of Europe and Asia! . . . And always when the Soviets dominate a situation, the Producers and the Common Man come to the top, and the Possessors and Exploiters are on the bottom." Pepper stated in a letter to Robins that closer ties with the Soviets would be "vindicated by the future."[88] But even as Pepper's own enthusiasm for U.S.-Soviet relations waned as the 1940s progressed, he had little idea of how much the changed international situation would create a political rhetoric that would not only proscribe the development of social democratic policies in Cold War America, but would also destroy his political career and reorient the Florida Democratic Party around the political language of anti-statism.

Rolling Back the State? The Republican Party and the Postwar Order

Already in 1946 the political right were coalescing around the issue of opposition to any extension of the New Deal state, and were using anti-totalitarianism as a weapon against liberal candidates. Such Republicans included John Bricker in Ohio, Ralph Gwinn in New York State, William Jenner in Indiana, and Edward Martin in Pennsylvania. This group stood for the capitalism of the free market, and represented the rejuvenation of private sector business influence in American politics after World War Two. The principal issue for the right in the run-up to the 1946 midterm elections was the challenge posed by organized labor. Ironically, the wave of strikes in American industry, touched off by the General Motors standoff at the end of 1945, provided the perfect theme for an attack on the New Deal state, although it also represented how far the balance of power had shifted away from the right since 1932.

The question of the place for organized labor in the postwar American economy dominated the Republican party's political program in 1946, in both congressional activity and electoral campaigning. Management-labor conflict also dominated the agenda of the U.S. Chamber of Commerce. Congressman Ralph Church (R-Illinois) informed the House in January 1946 that he felt that "the major obstacle to the return to normalcy is the policy of the administration with respect to labor and management. . . . Day by day disastrous strikes are bringing to a standstill reconversion plans." He was not alone in developing this theme in fundraising speeches to local Chambers of Commerce and other business groups, combining the issue of industrial relations with more rhetorically driven appeals to anti-leftism. In a speech to the Highland Park Chamber of Commerce, Church argued that a New Deal politics of interest group pluralism was "converting, if unwittingly nonetheless quite definitely, our American system of free enterprise into a socialistic system of governmental planning and control." Clare Hoffman (R-Michigan) noted that the Roosevelt administration had been "directly responsible for the growth of the CIO and, many think, for the communistic influences within it."[89] As the strike wave gained in intensity in early 1946, with President Truman arguing that some governmental controls over union activity might become necessary, Republicans and their allies gained the confidence to challenge what they perceived to be the specter of social democracy in the United States.

The Republican-led response to the development of a left-of-center network of political activism was based on a two-pronged attack, one taking the form of a bill to rewrite the Wagner Act, sponsored by South Dakota Republican Francis Case, and the other being a concerted congressional push to eliminate the Office of Price Administration. The Case bill aimed to redress what business groups saw as an imbalance in the original National Labor Relations Act by drawing up injunctions against various labor union practices to mirror those applied to management. If enacted, the new law would have applied a wide range of proscriptions to labor organizations that would have limited their ability to challenge corporate hegemony over pay and working practices, proscriptions which included an end to industry-wide bargaining, secondary boycotts, jurisdictional strikes, and, perhaps most importantly, an end to the closed shop.[90] The sheer scale of the industrial strife afflicting America in 1946 pushed even the President into an inherently anti-union stance by April, and allowed congressional conservatives to portray their legislation as moderate and sensible, and labor leaders as "ambitious, power-drunk" and out of touch with the rank and file. When the Case bill passed the House by 230 votes to 106 in May, and when the Senate passed President Truman's emergency control bill to draft strikers in a time of national emergency by 61 votes to 20, it seemed that the growth of a labor-liberal alliance to dominate postwar American politics had been stopped in its tracks. Senator Edward Moore (R-Oklahoma) argued that the "vote clearly reflects the sentiment of the people and the earnest desire of Congress to bring about more equitable and workable labor laws."[91]

In fact an analysis of the House vote on the Case bill demonstrates that the political map of America was polarized, with the 106 votes against the bill coming almost exclusively from Democrats and a handful of Republicans in the industrial northeast, Midwest, and the Pacific west. The New Deal industrial coalition of labor and liberal activists provided 21 votes against the Case bill from New York, 13 from urban, CIO-PAC dominated districts in Pennsylvania, 11 from Chicago and East St Louis in Illinois, and a solid five votes of a possible six (and the sixth was a Republican) from John L Lewis's coal mining heartland of West Virginia. The remaining smattering of pro-labor votes came from New Dealers in urban districts in California (four), Connecticut (four), Washington (three), Wisconsin (four), Minnesota (two), Missouri (three), Massachusetts (two), Kentucky (three), Ohio (five), Michigan (four), and Rhode Island (two), with extra support coming from representatives of states with single CIO districts like Gary, Indiana, and from the odd maverick in Texas, Tennessee, Maine, and Oregon. Four New Dealers from Arizona and Utah also voted against the bill. Representatives of the rest of the country, including all of the south and the Republican heartland of the Midwest and non-urban east, voted in favor. The vote does not in itself tell us categorically where the balance of power rested in American politics ahead of the 1946 elections. More than a hundred representatives failed to vote, a good number of them liberals. In addition, as Ira Katznelson has pointed out, the Republican–Southern Democrat coalition that overwhelmed the New Dealers in the House on the issue of labor relations rapidly unraveled on a host of other socioeconomic issues. On the other hand, a significant number of the 106 who voted against the Case bill lost their seats in 1946 to Republicans, thanks in part to a large drop in the labor vote in urban districts. Anti-statists inside and outside Congress were building a political base in the wake of World War Two, initially on the premise that wartime controls and labor influence over the economy had got out of control. The Cold War would increasingly cast its own shadow over this debate about the future of New Deal pluralism as the decade wore on.[92]

The language of anti-totalitarianism was already permeating into debates over labor relations in 1946. An American Forum of the Air Broadcast in October had the title "Is the PAC a threat or a contribution to America?"; the PAC being the political wing of the CIO unions, dedicated to campaigning against anti-union politicians, particularly in the anti-government wing of the GOP. On the program were anti-statists Senator Joseph Ball (R-Minnesota) and Attorney Louis Waldman, arguing against PAC director Jack Kroll and supporter Dr. Frank Kingdon. Ball argued that the CIO-PAC's "program, if adopted, would mean ever-increasing government control and regulation of the actions and daily lives of individual citizens." Waldman took the argument a stage further: "It is a combination of many left-wing elements together with the Communists and their fellow travelers in and outside of the CIO. . . . Through PAC a large number of Communists and fellow travelers became transformed into 'liberal' and progressive political figures." He argued that the PAC approved of Soviet foreign policy, a charge vigorously denied by Jack Kroll. Thus an advocate of state power was accused of promoting dictatorship, and the suggestion was made that Communists could easily be disguised as "liberals" because their ideologies were clearly related. The PAC program dedicated to the New Deal was, argued Ball, "not liberalism; liberalism means freeing the individual . . . the PAC program is going backward just as Hitler did, just as Stalin is today going backward to the tyranny of autocracy or individual dictatorship." In a Cold War context, anti-statism was increasingly using images of foreign totalitarianism to attack the state, and in doing so, Senators like Ball often seen as isolationists were in fact entering the internationalist mainstream. Ball charged that the PAC opposed the "Truman-Vandenberg-Byrnes foreign policy," implying that all anti-communists must support it.[93]

In their race to gain control of the House of Representatives for the first time since 1930, the Republicans were able to use popular discontent with the Truman administration and its allies to challenge seemingly well-entrenched New Deal incumbents. In the 12th district of California, for example, based around urban, middle, and lower class districts east of Los Angeles, Richard Nixon was chosen as the Republican candidate to run against New Deal Democrat Jerry Voorhis because of his young, modern image as a serviceman new to Republican politics, who would confront problems of postwar reconversion without recourse to governmental controls. A Republican constituency worker urged Nixon to keep to a "philosophy of practical liberalism, practical in that it will work when subjected to the test of sound economics."[94] Nixon could capitalize on popular frustration in his district with the failures of the New Deal state in 1946. Nixon argued in his campaign to oust Voorhis that the "so-called New Deal program, which is neither clear, precise, nor a program, threatens to destroy all democratic processes in our Republic." The New Deal had created a bureaucracy that threatened "to choke off the lifeblood from our economic system." At the same time, however, Republicans had to "recognize that in our complicated, modern economy some controls are necessary."[95] Nixon's campaign against Voorhis dwelt on this basic economic question: "How much will we compromise with the theories of state control?" It was a contrast between the New Deal, whereby "government is responsible for the citizen's well-being" and "will tell him what to do" and the Republican alternative of individual responsibility with state "help where needed."[96] Republicans such as Nixon were feeling their way back into popular favor after the best part of two decades in the wilderness. They were careful not to attack aspects of New Deal philosophy that had become established facets of the political landscape, such as social security, or labor's basic right to bargain collectively. Nixon's speech notes made frequent references to the need to consolidate existing social measures, but at the same time associated American liberalism with an attempt "to smother and impair the most humanitarian concept of all time which is traditional American freedom."[97] In attempting to distinguish in his campaign between his own espousal of the notion of individual opportunity and the "establishment of group controls by the New Deal party, through special minority groups and blocs, banded into voting units," Nixon was preparing the ground for a frontal assault on interest group democracy after 1946, and specifically on the influence of organized labor in American politics. Nixon specifically in his notes for the campaign contrasted Voorhis's "muddled thinking about [a] *mixed* economy" with the vital need to preserve the free market. A "mixed economy" represented to Republicans a certain degree of governmental management, particularly in the case of social insurance, but UDA and CIO visions of a flourishing state sector horrified Nixon and his supporters: "socialization of our institutions I do not favor." According to Nixon, the Democrats were stuck in the mire of depression era thinking when the economy, and with it the American people, had moved on.[98]

The ideological tenor of Nixon's campaign reflected the stake the business community had invested in the Republican party's campaign to capture control of Congress. "Because our business is national in scope, your election was followed with considerable interest," wrote the president of the National Gypsum Company to Nixon after his election to Congress in November. "[s]carcities from strikes, lock-outs, OPA and the many government restrictions have done untold harm to production, now badly needed. . . . The war is over and government spending should be drastically reduced to permit reduction in taxes, so that capital will be left for use in new enterprises."[99] Just as the war had opened up new opportunities and highlighted new challenges for the state, so had it revitalized private enterprise and encouraged representatives of corporate America to lobby aggressively for political representation. Gone were the days when a New Deal cabinet member had attended a Chamber of Commerce banquet and asserted in his diary that he "couldn't help thinking how so many of these great and mighty were crawling to Washington on their hands and knees these days to beg the Government to run their businesses for them."[100] Nixon's notes on "free enterprise" for campaign speeches and leaflets were made with local Chamber of Commerce audiences in mind, contrasting Russian, totalitarian political theories that emphasized "the primacy of states" with the American ideal of "a maximum of self-regulation and a minimum of government regulation. . . . How much will we compromise with the theories of state control?"[101]

The political battle over federal health insurance also demonstrated the ways in which America had reached a political crossroads at the end of the war. Republican congressional election campaigns provided a ripe opportunity for medical lobbying groups to flex their political muscle. In California, for example, Republican Senator William Knowland had to take the sensibilities of the doctors into account when organizing his campaign. The state had undergone rapid political change as war industries sprang up across the west in the 1940s, bringing thousands of new immigrants into California. In 1930, 5,677,251 people lived in California. In 1950 that figure stood at 10,586,223, with no sign of a slowdown in growth. There were a little over four million people in urban areas in the state in 1930; in 1950, more than seven million populated California's cities. There were only 81,048 African Americans in California in 1930. Twenty years later, the census registered 462,172.[102] Aircraft industries in Long Beach and San Diego, munitions plants in Los Angeles, heavy industry in Oakland, were all conspiring to make the state as a whole more receptive to political liberalism than ever before. At the same time California retained its conservative bent with large elderly and private sector management populations in the south and central coastal parts of the state.

A June 1946 report by the Alameda County Campaign Committee for Knowland demonstrates the dilemma facing Republicans when deciding how to balance business interests with the continuing power of interest groups favorable to the New Deal state. Alameda County itself was Knowland's home base, comprising his own city of Oakland and liberal communities such as Berkeley and Piedmont. The Republicans, in the words of the report, needed to coordinate "strong efforts directed to the various racial and professional groups." Committees were appointed to coordinate the campaign among veterans, blacks, women, and ethnic groups such as Portuguese immigrants in Oakland, as well as economic anti-statist groups such as doctors. David Rosen, the Republican worker responsible for the report, highlighted the tightrope being walked by Republicans like Knowland. On the one hand, Oakland Republicans had set up a committee of working class Greeks and mailed 1,000 election cards to African Americans, but at the same time had experienced "some difficulty with the medical group, until I learned of a communication from Senator Knowland to a Dr. Aleson, outlining his position on the Senate so-called 'socialized Medicine' bill. . . . Result, the doctors are going all out for Bill." The Republicans in Alameda had to critique the extension of state power for certain parts of the electorate, while appealing to social groups brought into the New Deal coalition precisely by the expansion of the state.[103]

In the political climate of 1946, and with the Democrats in disarray through internecine divisions, George Malone's Republican campaign in Nevada paid careful attention to the medical lobby, ensuring the first GOP Senate win in the silver state since 1926. During the campaign he came out against the Murray-Wagner-Dingell nationalized medicine plan, despite being a western maverick who bitterly opposed right-wing efforts to rein in organized labor. He proposed a plan endorsed by the local American Legion of setting up a Nevada State system to obviate the need for sending veterans to federally run hospitals. The medical lobby in Nevada and California was jubilant. One doctor wrote to colleagues in Nevada that, recognizing "the possibilities of evil incorporated in the Murray-Wagner-Dingell Bill," Malone had "accidentally stumbled on a sure way of destroying this iniquitous measure. . . . His plan has been submitted to General [Omar] Bradley and will, with minor changes, be approved. With the veterans out of the picture the bill will not pass. So, unwittingly, he has become the outstanding representative in Washington of the medical profession. . . . 'Molly' Malone is scrupulously honest, energetic, affable, and . . . will make an ideal Senator and one who will take a personal interest in his constituents, and particularly the doctors."

Dr. Vinton Muller of Reno also conducted an energetic propaganda campaign in favor of Malone, writing to fellow doctors that "I personally believe it is the duty of each and every one of us to get behind George Malone. . . . It is not our small vote which will count, but that of ours, plus all those we can secure besides. As discussed at our last state meeting, it is high time the medical profession became politically conscious, and began taking an active part in politics. . . . "[104] How far the development of a domestic anti-leftist cold war would further the political ambitions of the medical lobby would become apparent in the years that followed.

Anti-totalitarian rhetoric as a tool to advance a right-wing, private sector political agenda was clearly already in evidence before the height of the Cold War, and indeed had been a feature of American political life since the formation of HUAC in 1938. Still, in 1946, in contrast to later years, foreign policy was not at the top of Nixon's list of important issues. In a letter to an interested correspondent, he ranked foreign affairs fourth, behind government controls, labor legislation, and housing. In addition, he added in the same letter that "on the subject of foreign affairs Mr. Voorhis and I followed pretty much the same line. He definitely came out against the Wallace policy and supported [Secretary of State] Byrnes, and so did I." However, the two candidates' perceptions of the relevance of events overseas to domestic issues differed markedly. While supporting Byrnes' get tough policy with the Soviet Union and his gradual espousal of containment theory, Nixon extended the idea of anti-totalitarianism to a domestic context. In attacking the opposition, Nixon argued that using "the radio and newspapers as daily forums we find the New Deal dispensing the most voluminous propaganda handouts in American history. . . . Let us ever remember—we will not trade off our rights to be represented and heard in Congress to any set of men who seek to suppress and subjugate a people by usurpation and control of our Economic, Social and Political [sic] resources." This was a slight shift in emphasis from a purely economic critique of state power, toward images of the state as being an organ of totalitarianism. The Covina Republican Club took up the same theme in their endorsement of Nixon as their Congressman-to-be: "we conscientiously believe that the American ideals of democracy . . . are in danger of being lost to those who espouse the regimentation of our people, collectivism or communism in some form."[105] In a public debate scheduled with Jerry Voorhis, Nixon prepared to make this a point of difference between them. While stressing the need for a new economic policy, Nixon also stated that the United States as a whole needed to get "behind Byrnes in his stand against totalitarian Russia." That stand included a stand against excessive use of the federal state at home as well as abroad.[106] The Republican commitment to federally sponsored social policy was still ambivalent, and was made more so by the emergence of an aggressively anti-Soviet foreign policy.

John Bricker, running for the Senate in Ohio, argued in a speech in New York that to "appreciate the full significance of citizenship in a Republic, we need only to look at its antithesis. Authoritarian forms of government . . . are a direct negation of the Christian principle. . . . Managed economy, governmental competition with business, restriction of individual enterprise and the growth of collectivism are the inevitable fronts of the authoritarian spirit in government."[107] Linking the Soviet Union to the New Deal, Bricker claimed a Republican Congress would "remove from office all radicals and Communists who have become a part and parcel of the New Deal and who direct its policies."[108] Ostensibly a Republican campaigning on traditional conservative themes of a free market and a society free from an all-powerful state, Bricker's campaign was in fact playing on abstract images of a united, "Christian" Republic and a totalitarian foreign ideology. A powerful state was incompatible with a "Christian philosophy"; the United States was at risk from totalitarianism if it did not reject the New Deal. The CIO in its strong campaign against Bricker in Ohio claimed that as governor of Ohio he had "always chosen to fight on the side of dollars against human happiness," but also that he was associated with a "lunatic fringe" represented by Gerald L. K. Smith and Gerald B. Winrod. A CIO leaflet alleged that Smith in 1944 had nominated Bricker as his running mate "on the anti-Negro, anti-Jewish, anti-foreign born ticket of that outfit."[109]

Bricker's anti-statism represented not only a defense of free market economics as the most efficient way of ensuring national wealth creation, but also a denial of the moral right of government to ensure that diverse socioeconomic and ethnocultural groups obtained a particular standard of living. His association of anti-statism with Christianity and his direct attack on labor unions in the highly industrialized state of Ohio seemed to go hand in hand. Orville Jones of the Ohio branch of the PAC argued that America "is torn between two philosophies. The *Spirit of Reaction* is identified with a desire to return to the old laissez-faire economic practices that resulted in . . . the Great Depression. The *Spirit of Democracy* is the desire to solve our problems on the basis of human values." Bricker was identified with the first philosophy, and with the denial of the state as a force for social equality, racial equality, or economic returns to labor.[110]

Republican House Leader Joseph Martin was also promoting a trend within the party away from the state and toward abstract principles related to opposition to totalitarianism. "What kind of an America are we going to have?" he asked. "Shall it be an America in which individual opportunity will continue to exist alike for all?. . . . Or will we live in an America in which we shall be regimented, . . . an America bound in the chains of some form of Communism, Fascism, or State Socialism?"[111] The Cold War provided concrete examples to illustrate Martin's broad characterizations of un-Americanism. Christian Herter made a distinction in his campaign between genuine liberals and "the fake liberal who is taking his or her pattern from a philosophy completely alien to our conception of free government and who wants to see more government ownership, more government controls, more suppressions of freedom. In fact, all those things which are the exact opposite of true liberalism . . . a dictatorship by a chosen few."[112] The fake liberal was thus not only an actual communist, but also any democratic socialist or left-leaning liberal, and Herter's conception of the left was entirely consistent with the growing "bipartisan" view of foreign affairs. Claire Boothe Luce, although retiring from Congress in 1946, joined the campaign in several debates on Communism in which she associated it with the New Deal state. Her remarks were interesting in that they linked this subject to her recent conversion to Catholicism, comparing the atheist state of Russia to her own faith as an American in God. In one letter Luce stated to a professed atheist that no "first class mind admits to Atheism, with the exception of the Soviet leaders, and in that state, Atheism is in a way the state religion."[113] The right harnessed a strong religious and anti-statist bent in American society, that was also appealed to by those who were at the same time sending out a more liberal message to other audiences.[114]

Congressman Everett Dirksen of Illinois demonstrated in 1946 how a consensus on foreign policy masked the deep ideological implications of anti-Sovietism. In a published booklet he used in the 1946 campaign and for years thereafter, entitled "Communism in Action in the Soviet Union," Dirksen used not personal experience but Congressional Research documentation to create images of Russia which affirmed his own anti-government principles. Most of the study was devoted to living standards in the USSR and the USA, contrasting downtrodden paupers in Russia with the benefits of capitalism in America. In some cases the portrait was seriously limited by its assumption that contemporary America formed an absolute. If, for example, in "the United States we esteem an automobile to be a necessity," the fact that the Soviet Union had few private cars was necessarily unfortunate; an analysis of Russia's public transport facilities, or those of America, was not provided. In a chapter on the use of leisure time, Dirksen remarked that leisure in the USSR "is strictly controlled by the state and the Communist party," as if there were no limits on leisure time in the United States.[115] This is not to pass judgment on the real nature of Soviet society in the 1940s, but rather to argue that in the Cold War a possible rational approach to the role of government in economic affairs in the wake of the New Deal was gradually ceding to a simplistic dichotomy of freedom versus the monolithic left. Such a tendency would grow rapidly in the late 1940s as the Cold War took shape.

In a number of Republican congressional races, however, it was clear that the New Deal and war had shifted the center of political gravity sharply leftward in a way that GOP candidates found hard to ignore. Jacob Javits's successful campaign to win a previously solidly Democratic House district in Manhattan's Upper West Side was very much a product of local factors(he ran against the corruption of the Tammany machine in New York City and won only because he was the candidate of the Liberal Party as well as the Republican Party in a rare case of electoral fusion between unlikely allies)but it nonetheless demonstrated how far the fortunes of the two major political alternatives for the postwar United States remained in flux. Javits argued throughout his campaign that an associative state apparatus comprising government, business, and labor was necessary to ensure economic growth in a mature industrial economy. In a speech during his campaign to a trade association, Javits referred to the need for the state to "undertake a new approach through economic planning." In a letter to Republican right-wing congressman Jesse Wolcott, a major player in the drive to eliminate OPA, Javits called his prospective congressional district "as truly representative as you could find of any urban area. It wants OPA continued." Javits described the 21st district of New York, an area comprising Morningside Heights, the western fringes of Harlem, Columbia University, and the far northwest corner of Manhattan, as having "no extremes of poverty and no extremes of wealth; it has people of every race, color, and creed."[116]

In order to assess the way in which his brand of modern Republicanism would play as the campaign got underway, Javits personally "commissioned the Elmo Roper organization to make a study of political thought among residents of the 21st district for the purpose of determining how closely their thinking paralleled his own." The poll results indicated that Americans in that particular district believed in using the state to solve some of the country's most pressing domestic problems, but that they were also becoming frustrated by the inability of the state and organized labor to resolve the crisis of postwar reconversion. Although 46.5 percent of respondents viewed the provision of housing as the country's most pressing problem, followed closely by high prices, 75.6 percent also endorsed the passage of a law requiring a mandatory cooling off period before a strike could be called. While there was a strong current of opinion expressing at least lukewarm commitment to what was then still the near inviolable concept of a balanced federal budget, only 5.4 percent wanted a balanced budget at all costs, and 39.1 percent were theoretically willing to sacrifice a balanced budget in favor of full employment and adequate national defense.[117]

Javits, a well-respected lawyer who had risen from humble origins in New York's Lower East Side, felt that his ideas of responsible Republicanism that combined a basic commitment to the structure of the New Deal state with an endorsement of the crucial importance of the private sector in the

American political economy was appropriate for the electoral climate of postwar New York City. "Private business has shown its ability to produce goods in vast quantities and to expand and develop the country," argued Javits in a statement in August, "but not to make living standards rise in ratio with increased production, not to avoid depressions. Yet we do not wish to surrender our personal freedoms by permitting political control of our jobs. . . . To plan an economy of plenty, therefore, we must have tripartite action—of employers, employees and government—to make and put into effect our major economic decisions." An example of this idea in practice was public housing, which was "an emergency . . . so great that wartime measures, such as priorities, subsidies, and price controls, should be invoked for residential construction."[118] Javits gained the endorsement of a Liberal Party committed to James Murray's full employment proposals, which it claimed in a statement were "indispensible." But he also reminded the leaders of one local union that "the trades union movement has come to the point where a middle ground is necessary. This middle ground requires . . . that unions shall not use their power to create artificial and uneconomic competitive conditions."[119] Javits was one of many in American politics searching for ways of coming to terms with the New Deal while also challenging the political power of interests that had formed the backbone of the post 1933 political order.

Internecine warfare within the New York City Democratic Party doubtless helped Javits's candidacy, and also lent his campaign a liberal air unrepresentative of the Republican Party nationally in 1946. Sitting Democratic congressman James Torrens lost his primary fight in August to a Tammany Hall regular, Daniel Flynn, by 980 votes, prompting Javits to make political capital out of the affair by asserting that it was "significant that the present Democratic incumbent . . . who voted New Deal consistently, was dropped by the Tammany organization. . . . To believe . . . that [the primary] reflects any attempt by the people to abandon social, economic and political aspirations . . . is to completely misinterpret the intent of the voters."[120] This would explain why there was a significant swing to both the Republicans and the Liberal Party in New York City in the 1946 elections; Tammany Hall was seen as corrupt and unresponsive to social pressures, and so other parties with similar liberal platforms prospered.[121]

Nevertheless, the enormous changes to the landscape of American politics and economy since the beginning of the twentieth century had left their mark more widely on the Republican Party and American conservatism by 1946. Republican Senatorial candidates like Irving Ives of New York, Ralph Flanders of Vermont, and Alexander Smith of New Jersey represented examples of those whose efforts, in the words of one historian, "were aimed mainly at adapting or modernizing American conservatism to account for the tremendous changes in American life that became apparent in the twentieth century."[122]

In addition, as was also true of the Democrats, the extent of anti-leftist activity within the GOP was limited because the question of American relations with the wider world was not yet preeminent in political discourse within the United States. The leftward drift in political thought in Europe and the Antipodes at the end of the war was hardly endorsed in right-of-center circles, yet the right was not yet sufficiently confident of its political clout to make much propaganda use of the world situation. Many Republicans and conservative Democrats increasingly realized that it would be difficult to turn back the tide of the Leviathan state entirely (social security and national security, in particular, were rapidly assuming untouchable status) and made comparatively little reference to the perceived perils of the welfare states being established elsewhere. One maverick Republican congressman, in a letter to liberal Senator Wayne Morse about the promising young Jacob Javits, went as far as to talk positively about the general direction of world politics. Charles La Follette (R-Indiana) stated that he felt Javits would "make a very fine Member of the House, and I think his thinking is closer to yours than mine, because he firmly believes that we can remold our capitalistic economy, whereas I am beginning to think that we must intrude some form of socialistic operation of some of our basic industries before we can create a real democratic state."[123] La Follette may have been atypical, but a glance through the list of successful new Republican candidates for House and Senate in 1946, and a determination of their voting records in the 80th Congress, suggests that the battle over the soul of the Republican Party, like that over the direction of American politics in general, was not yet completely decided.[124]

Henry Cabot Lodge was another example of a Republican Senate candidate who appeared more reconciled to the New Deal than many of his peers. Indeed, Lodge had actually been a Senator from Massachusetts during the New Deal period, but had resigned from the Senate in 1944 to serve in the war. In 1946 he decided to attempt a return to the Senate by running for the seat of conservative Democrat David Walsh. Lodge was quick to stress in his campaign that he would be "in the forefront of those seeking improved working conditions, fair pay and a more fruitful and peaceful relationship between labor and management." In a speech designed for use in front of labor audiences Lodge stated that he had "in the past sought to correct abuses of labor and to prevent exploitation of men, women and children by unscrupulous employers. . . . I will always employ the humanitarian approach toward solution of such problems. But there is one thing which I will definitely not embrace, and that is a reckless series of promises to do this or do that for any group of voters."[125] In other words, whereas the New Deal ideology was a slave to special interests, the Republican Party could endorse the general ethos of liberalism while adopting a more business-friendly approach that would correct some of the perceived imbalances in the American political economy. George Mahoney, a former President of the International Brotherhood of Telephone Workers Union, backed Lodge's campaign, and wrote to union members arguing that because Lodge believed "that government should and can function for the best interests of *all* the people, his candidacy merits your approval and that of every other thoughtful citizen." Andrew J. Walsh of the Plaster Tenders' Union Local of Boston wrote to Lodge on October 23, 1946 assuring him that "as a labor leader I have been with you in all your former campaigns and am still with you."[126] In addition, most labor and ethnic newspapers supported Lodge, including the Italian-American *La Notizia* of Boston and *L'Independent,* a French-Canadian newsletter published in Fall River.

Lodge also benefited from the anti-New Deal record of David Walsh, whose enthusiasm for the Roosevelt years, never overwhelming, had waned considerably with the advent of war. An opponent of greater American involvement overseas and of the extension of the New Deal, Walsh also led many Massachusetts liberals to back Lodge. One such self-described liberal, Conrad Crooker of Boston, decided to seek advice from New Deal cabinet member Harold Ickes on who made the better liberal in Massachusetts. Ickes replied: "I do not believe I could vote for the reelection of Senator Walsh. . . . On balance I would vote for Lodge although with distinct reservations." Crooker was satisfied: "Your letter . . . gives me exactly the message that I want to pass on to our Liberal grouping. . . . [It] might mean the election of Lodge on November 5th."[127]

Certainly polls conducted by Republican strategists seemed to bear out this view, that the convergence of Lodge's ideology and the nature of the Massachusetts electorate would result in a Republican victory. One official poll analysis remarked on "a very marked deterioration in the Democratic position throughout the nation, due to the OPA meat fiasco and other indications of administration bungling. . . . Lodge's war record, his record in public office, and his progressive views also appeal to the voters." The survey reported that only 20 percent of Lodge's supporters in September based their support for him on party loyalty; many were converts from the New Deal. The poll suggested Lodge had a potential 46 percent of the total vote in Democratic Boston, to add to a 67 percent poll in rural Massachusetts, compared to only 38 percent of the Boston vote in 1942. The results of the poll, suggesting Lodge would receive 46 percent of the union vote and a majority in every social category in the state except for the Irish and Catholics, provided evidence that there was much potential in 1946 for the Republicans to capitalize on the unstable political climate engendered by the labor relations conundrum and the collapse of price controls.[128] Foreign policy, by contrast, was expressed only in vague banalities. In one campaign letter, Lodge argued that America had "won the war; we can win the peace. But to do this we must have constructive foreign policy, backed by the resources of a strong America—an America which is thoroughly informed on the facts of the modern world."[129]

The Lodge campaign provided a dilemma for left-leaning Democrats like Florida's Claude Pepper, who in 1946 was one of several liberals arguing for the center and left to be brought together under one party umbrella. Harold Ickes, himself never a Democrat and extremely proud of the Republican Party's progressive past, argued in a letter to Los Angeles Democrat Claude Welch that Pepper's suggestion was "more enthusiastic than realistic," and that "the poll tax states of the south and the big city machines of the north" still controlled the Democratic Party.[130] This was an important explanation of the problem facing left-of-center social reformers and labor leaders at the end of the war: there was still no ready-made vehicle for the left in the United States. Both parties were riven by ideological, factional, and sectional fissures; yet external pressure groups like unions and the UDA did not have the political or financial muscle to rival them.

In addition, the type of Bull Moose progressivism within the GOP that Ickes had cut his political teeth on during and after the 1912 election was very much on the wane in 1946. One factor initially pointing to a potential rebirth of progressivism in the GOP in early 1946 was Senator Robert La Follette Jr.'s decision to disband his Progressive Party, established in 1934, and return to the Republican fold in Wisconsin. The decision, taken at the Progressives' convention at Portage, Wisconsin, in March 1946, divided delegates and observers. The OPA chairman, Chester Bowles, told La Follette that his decision was right given the strength of the two-party stranglehold on American politics, and that "one of the greatest contributions that anyone can make is to work toward the liberalization of the Republican Party over . . . the next few years." Judge R. S. Cowie concurred: "I voted three times for Franklin D. Roosevelt not because he was a Democrat but because he had a program of vital issues. . . . I now believe the Republican Party has awakened to the vast responsibility confronting it and with your and other liberal leadership will make it possible for millions of Republicans like myself to return to their first love with complete self-respect." W. P. Gunson in Milwaukee said that the integrated progressive Republican Party in the city's nineteenth ward contained "as good Liberals as we have in the Progressive Party, and in many cases, I find that they will do more work than our Progressive Boys."[131] La Follette's brand of progressivism, broadly supporting the social and economic advances of the New Deal, and being skeptical of making foreign policy the focus of governmental action, seemed early in the year to be ascendant in Wisconsin, as it had throughout the first half of the century.

There were several reasons why such a prediction turned out to be mistaken. The first was that the new alliance was failing to reach its natural constituency: the poor in both rural and urban Wisconsin. The Republican Party was still seen as reactionary compared to the Democrats. It was, according to a loyal Progressive, "the party of Hoover, Bricker, Mellon and Coolidge . . . the party so barren of liberal leadership that middle-of-the-roaders like Stassen and Morse stand out like curiosities. . . . I shall continue straight ahead, Bob, following the progressive principles in the party of Roosevelt, Truman, and Wallace. They are making a courageous fight." This image of the GOP made it difficult for union leaders to abandon the Democrats for a Republican, and so tended to work to improve the struggling fortunes of the Democratic Party, particularly in Milwaukee. A Progressive worker in Superior complained to La Follette that the "CIO officials are against you without cause or reason. . . . Now, I do not believe that all this opposition to you exists in the rank and file. But this is where it has its bad effect: these leaders are in control."[132]

On the other hand, La Follette did seem to be more liberal than the Republican mainstream, and incurred opposition from the more antigovernment wing of the party. Joseph McCarthy, then a state circuit judge, based his campaign literature for the Republican Senatorial nomination on the fact that he represented the "regular" Republican ticket, who "has the courage to take a Republican stand on specific issues." McCarthy promised the "end of the flood of mistakes, covering up, and incompetence of the New Deal—[the] Re-establishment of good American procedure." In a telegram to La Follette challenging him to a debate, McCarthy charged that La Follette had "by your New Deal voting record done tremendous damage to the people of Wisconsin."[133] La Follette was effectively being crushed between a labor-dominated Democratic Party and an anti-New Deal Republican Party.

The decline of La Follette's influence in Wisconsin was further complicated by the relationship between anti-totalitarianism and progressivism in

1946.[134] If La Follette himself was in large part a supporter of the New Deal policy of using government to iron out social inequality, many of his supporters were not. Dr. F. B. Henderson of Stoughton was not the only Republican supporter of La Follette to state that he, "a stalwart, conservative Republican, split my ticket that I might have the opportunity of voting for you. . . . Your record in the Senate . . . has met in the main with my approval. . . . I also wish to state my opposition to the Wagner-Murray-Dingell [health insurance] bill . . . " A personal friend of La Follette's, John Trautmann, wrote to La Follette that he disapproved of the links to the New Deal, and wanted La Follette to "preserve our American way of life. But—for God's sake—cut loose from any 'crack-pots' like the New Deal—rather 'phew' Deal—produced. GOSH! What a mess they've gotten us in."[135] To support La Follette and yet oppose the principle of state-sponsored health insurance seems difficult to explain, but La Follette's correspondence is replete with such riddles. Progressivism often remained as attached to the same abstract ideal of a rugged, anti-statist America unencumbered by bureaucracy as "regular" Republicanism. One senior state Republican pledged to La Follette responded to a request that he provide ten "Progressive-Republicans" for the primary vote by asking: "What the hell are Progressive-Republicans?. . . . You are either a Republican or you are not."[136]

This fact was brought into sharp relief when foreign policy and anti-communism entered the equation. Up to 1945, La Follette was viewed as an isolationist, and therein lay the reason for much support and opposition to him as Senator. The same Republican who claimed he supported progressivism as a stalwart Republican had said that La Follette's isolationism attracted him. Many progressives also saw a disentanglement from affairs abroad as essential to the vitality of the ideology at home. In a letter to Milwaukee GOP organizer Lester Bradshaw in April 1946, just before the Republican primary, senior Republican Senator Robert Taft stated that he hoped La Follette would win the nomination. "I get on with him very well and would have no difficulty in agreeing with him on social welfare measures. In the long run he will be closer to me than he will be to Morse." Furthermore, Taft stated that he approved of La Follette's skepticism of internationalism.[137]

Now, in 1946, in the light of events overseas and in America with the uncovering of Communist influence there, many more Republicans condemned isolationism. In La Follette's case, this fact led to two notable results: he was attacked as an isolationist by proponents of the state, such as the CIO and the Democratic Party, and, secondly, he himself started shifting toward an anti-communist, internationalist position. Henry Wallace assumed he could count on La Follette as a kindred spirit when in November 1946 after the latter's primary defeat he sent him copies of his letters to Truman and Madison Square Garden speech against directing America's foreign policy against Russia: "There can be only one world. But it must be a world that allows for more than one kind of social and economic organization." La Follette disagreed as anti-communism took hold within liberal sections of the American body politic: "Communist activities in America have become a serious menace to democracy. . . . LIBERALS MUST DIVORCE THEMSELVES FROM FELLOW-TRAVELER ELEMENTS OR THEY WILL BE DISCREDITED AND IMMOBILIZED."[138]

La Follette became a major proponent in 1947 of the Marshall Plan and of the containment of Soviet power. He also had to take into account the views of Wisconsin's large German population, which would mean his views of Germany would have to be very different from leftist progressives such as Claude Pepper, who wanted to see Germany disarmed.[139] In essence, therefore, although McCarthy won the GOP primary by a narrow margin and La Follette's political life was ended, it is unclear exactly how much of a difference his reelection would have made to the emergence of an anti-communist consensus in foreign policy, given the growth of anti-leftist sentiment throughout the American polity.

It was no coincidence that the use of anti-extremist ideology to temper the party's growing liberal element was tied in with foreign policy in the campaign. Knowland argued that isolationism "is a liability of the dead past. It has no place in our world of instant communications, jet speed travel, and the interdependability [sic] of all nations. We can no more return to isolationism than a man can return to childhood, for the world, too, has grown up. . . . The United States wants no partisan foreign policy."[140] That nonpartisan foreign policy specifically excluded calls by Henry Wallace for a coming to terms with Soviet Russia, at least according to Knowland himself. After Wallace visited California to campaign for Rogers and the other Democratic candidates in October, the *New York Times* reported that local Republicans had "leaned heavily on the Communist issue in their campaign speeches." One senior Republican was quoted as saying that "Wallace will help the Democrats out here as much as Mr. Dewey helped the Republicans two years ago."[141] Knowland charged that Wallace had compromised national security in his support for Soviet ideals and his criticism of Truman's foreign policy: "secretary Wallace has succeeded in kicking the props out from under a united American foreign policy. . . . Our very security may depend on demonstrating to the world that our foreign policy is not Democratic, not Republican, but American."[142]

For a foreign policy to be "American" in Knowland's eyes, it had to repudiate the totalitarian left completely, and inevitably would commit the United States to a propaganda war against the USSR in which Communism would be contrasted with a free, anti-socialist alternative in America. What ramifications this would have for the Republican Party's domestic strategy were as yet unclear. It was not surprising, however, that Will Rogers, in setting out a very statist agenda for the Democratic Party in the 1940s, argued that communism and capitalism must "exist on the same planet" or "we'll have a world in pieces. . . . if the Russians get tough, then we must get tough. If they relax, then we can relax. The second policy I advocate is one of cooperation and friendship and communication with the Russian people."[143] Liberals at this time were careful to differentiate between criticism of Soviet tyranny and the condemnation of the left or of Russia in toto.

The Meaning of the Election Results

Whatever one reads into the results of the 1946 elections, it is undeniable that they represented a massive defeat for liberalism in the Democratic Party, and only a partial victory for its Republican variant. The most striking feature of the results is the completeness of the victory for the Republican Party as a whole, outside the south. A brief glance at the Senate results across the nation reveals that not only did the Republicans win every contest outside the south with the exception of Rhode Island, Wyoming, New Mexico, Arizona, Maryland and West Virginia, but also that the size of the GOP margins, and the narrowness of those of Democrats, was remarkable. In Wisconsin Joseph McCarthy took 62.2 percent of the vote, in Michigan Arthur Vandenberg, who admitted to having been in Washington during much of the campaign, took a huge 67.5 percent.[144] The party captured 13 seats to give the GOP control of the Senate, including Pennsylvania, which Edward Martin won by more than 600,000 from New Dealer Joseph Guffey, and New York, won by Irving Ives by 250,000. The House results are even more revealing. The party captured a net total of 54 seats to give Republicans overall control of Congress. The context of those gains was extraordinary. Almost all were in Democratic urban strongholds, areas often seen as having been bought for the New Deal permanently in the 1930s. Three seats fell to the GOP within the Chicago city limits, two of which were in the African American populated south side. Three were in Wayne County, Michigan, the site of the city of Detroit. Javits prevailed in New York's 21st district. Hugh De Lacy's Seattle seat fell to the Republicans. Four gains were made in greater Los Angeles, including Richard Nixon's victory in the 12th. The list goes on—New Haven, Oakland, San Diego, Philadelphia, Milwaukee,

Kansas City, St. Louis, St. Paul, Louisville: all had Republican congressmen in the 80th Congress. The Democrats had been a minority party outside the south since 1938, but now they were all but wiped out in the north, with no seats in Connecticut, two in New Jersey, four in Ohio, one in Minnesota, none in Wisconsin, five in Pennsylvania out of a possible 33, and a post-1928 low of 16 in New York out of a total 45.[145]

More important than the results themselves would be how political groups would interpret them. The social import of the urban results was not lost on the Republican Party, which noted that nowhere "was the Republican sweep more evident than in city districts, which had been a special preserve of the Democrats since the advent of the New Deal. More than half of the districts won by Republicans were in metropolitan areas and they were won because colored voters, labor, war veterans, and other special groups shifted in large numbers to the Republicans."[146] According to the incoming speaker of the House, Joe Martin, the results represented "a vote against political monopoly, communism in high places, subversion in government. It was also a mandate for the Republicans again to rescue the country from the bogs of regimentation, petty tyranny . . . crises and emergencies, and to reduce taxes."[147] One unauthorized campaign letter in California sent out by an AMA member associated state Democratic chair James Roosevelt, son of the late President, with "Hollywood's penthouse pinkos" and "New York's ultra-sophisticates of alien political hue. . . . Like a lot of other young folks in the canopied bed of socialistic daydreaming, Jimmy and Willie [Rogers] stand in danger of becoming hopelessly bedridden and politically mired. . . . That the New Deal is in the last days of its senility should be obvious, unless one is to discount its creaking joints and mummified form."[148] Even if the results of the elections were rather less pivotal than many Republicans wished to believe, they still gave the American right a critical boost to its confidence and political vitality as the 80th Congress opened.

It was certainly possible to argue that the voters had shot the messenger in 1946 rather than the liberal message, blaming the party of Truman for its failure to cope with the economic readjustments of the 1945–46 period. In any case, the conversion of vast numbers of voters to the GOP could be overstated. Although the New Deal coalition of the cities, farmers and the middle class of 1936 had failed to hold together, this was due more to the abstention of 10 million working class votes than to any mass conversion to the Republicans. Many liberals in the party loyal to the New Deal had gone, however, including Joseph Guffey, James Mead, Jerry Voorhis, Ellis Patterson, James Huffman, Hugh Mitchell, and Emily Taft Douglas. Henry Wallace was no longer in the government. Instead, as 1947 got underway, the country would see a new liberalism, committed to a manufactured concept of "bipartisanship" in foreign affairs on the question of Soviet expansionism and to only incremental advances in domestic policy. Both parties in 1946 were increasingly linking domestic and foreign policy in their ideological discourse.

Those on the noncommunist left were dismayed by the results, but were convinced that there was still scope for an ambitious expansion of the New Deal state. James Loeb looked forward to the UDA-sponsored visit to the United States of British government minister Patrick Gordon Walker, scheduled for early 1947, telling him shortly after the elections "how pleased we are that you are going to be able to come to America to make a start on the all-important job of telling Americans, and in particular our fussy liberals, about the dynamic developments in England." Gordon Walker was to speak to labor unions, consumer groups, and local UDA chapters. Interestingly, the general secretary of the National Consumers League hoped that the Labour minister would "be willing to talk on a specific subject such as the Labor Party's program for social security. . . . We would be more interested in having him speak on this subject than on international relations."[149]

The growing chasm between UDA liberals and those committed to Henry Wallace's views on foreign policy was still an issue which left a nasty taste in the mouth of most on the left, and when at the end of 1946 Loeb and his allies decided to create Americans for Democratic Action as a specifically anti-communist alternative to Wallace's Progressive Citizens of America, they still held out hope for a center-left coalition for domestic social reform. The purpose of the January conference to establish the ADA was, in Loeb's words, "to lay the basis for a genuine American non-Communist Left. . . . As it is shaping up, this conference will be perhaps the most impressive gathering of liberals that has come together in America for many years. We shall have the most progressive labor leaders from both AFL and CIO and the top non-labor independent liberals from around the country." However, despite the presence at the conference of symbolic figures of the liberal movement such as Eleanor Roosevelt, Chester Bowles, FDR Jr., and Hubert Humphrey, what Loeb called "the chance of a lifetime" to build a genuine social democracy was already beginning to unravel under the twin pressures of an anti-statist resurgence in Congress and internal fissures on the left over the emerging Cold War.[150] It remained to be seen how this would affect attitudes to the liberal state in both parties in the 80th Congress and beyond.

2. THE 80TH CONGRESS AND CONCEPTIONS OF THE STATE

THE REPUBLICAN PARTY IN 1947 WAS IN A POSITION OF political power for the first time since 1932. The Truman Presidency still controlled the Executive branch, but with 51 Senators and 246 House members the GOP would dominate the legislative agenda in the 80th Congress. The range of domestic issues with which Congress would have to deal was extensive, ranging from labor relations and price control issues left over from the previous year, through a review of the burden of taxation and legislation to solve the housing and health crises besetting the nation. Much of the existing secondary literature on the political history of this period is concerned with the ways in which the Truman administration, Congress, and the American political community in general increasingly shifted the parameters of state-sponsored reform away from direct intervention in the economy in the form of public works, federal control of production, and the like, and toward a more hands-off policy based on manipulation of fiscal policy and the further development of public and private social insurance. It is argued that President Truman and his advisers in the Treasury department, as well as the new generation of liberals in Congress and ADA, were not steeped the ideological heritage of the socialist struggles of the 1920s and 1930s that had formed the political worldview of labor leaders like Sidney Hillman and Walter Reuther. In addition, the leading players in the liberal movement were well aware of the precarious balance of power in American politics, a situation that demanded a less ambitious program of socioeconomic reform. In this climate, what Alan Wolfe termed a "politics of growth," based on the assumption that a sustained period of private sector-led economic growth would iron out inequalities in socioeconomic status, would now come to dominate federal policymaking.[1]

The emergence of the Cold War, and the rhetoric of anti-totalitarianism that accompanied it, effectively killed off tentative efforts begun the year before to shift the center of gravity leftward. In effect, an anti-leftist political discourse came to dominate political debate in the 1947–48 period in a manner that not only provided the right with a powerful weapon with which to influence policy formation, but also changed the political priorities of the center-left in ways not fully developed in the existing historiography. The increasingly widely shared commitment to accepting a federal role in the economy came under challenge not merely from business pressure based on economic concerns. It was also damaged by political appeals to anti-left sentiment in both parties based on the emerging ideology of the Cold War and conceptions of left-wing governments abroad. Imagined concepts of the totalitarian state were not new weapons against the expansion of governmental power. They had not, however, been particularly effective in the wake of the Wall Street Crash, whereas the new ideological climate of the Cold War allowed anti-government forces to capture control of the political debate in both parties. This would create an extra dynamic weakening the liberal evolution of American political discourse, with important ramifications for the transmission of ideologies to the American electorate in 1948.

Contesting the Size of the State: Taxation and the Budget

No sooner had the 80th Congress convened than President Truman's request for a budget appropriation of $37.5 billion touched off an immediate debate over the proper role of the state. The debate was not new, given the fact that government as a share of GDP had been expanding since the 1920s and particularly after the outbreak of the Second World War. The latest increases were particularly large. In 1939, before the war had inflated spending requirements out of all proportion, the U.S. federal government had spent just over $12 billion in total. In 1935, only four million tax returns had been filed. By 1947 that figure had risen to 49.5 million, amassing nearly $40 billion for the state.[2] On one level it is possible to examine political debates over the size of the state in 1947 as a contest between liberal proponents of a redistribution of wealth and those on the right who saw a leviathan state as being economically damaging to the economy. However, the taxation debate in 1947 and 1948, when Congress attempted three times to pass tax reduction bills, also demonstrated that the economic political debate on the merits of taxation was being overlaid by a Cold War debate on the relationship between state power and anti-communism. Anti-statists could associate taxation with moves toward totalitarianism in the public mind, and opponents of communism abroad increasingly saw a liberal domestic agenda as less important than using the taxation power to finance a Cold War.

Many Republicans and some Democrats had been elected in 1946 on a platform committed to a reduction of the heavy tax burden on individuals and business. At the Republican steering committee meeting in November 1946, incoming House appropriations committee chairman John Taber (R-New York) argued that it was "apparent that substantial savings could be made in appropriations on a practical basis which would permit tax reductions which are to come. . . . The steering committee is convinced that a sound governmental fiscal policy is the best way to protect the investment of the people in social security." To that end, Taber and other Republicans on both the House and Senate Appropriations committees proposed a 20 percent across the board cut in income tax, as well as cuts in Truman's budget of between $4 and $7 billion.[3] Many Republicans sincerely believed that there were sound economic reasons for reining in the gargantuan federal government. Lower taxes and less government could stimulate business investment. As Joe Martin put it: "More production, lower prices and better quality increase all real income. . . . It is to that end we intend to stop bureaucratic squandering of the people's money; to balance the budget; to reduce taxes, and to reduce the national debt." Martin also linked taxation policy to the fight against high inflation: "The cure for inflation is production and more production. It is to give the proper incentive to risk capital to invest in business and increase the production of goods and services."[4] The Republicans were developing arguments expressed in 1946, namely that alongside a commitment to state action one also had to manage government effectively for the benefit of the private sector. The state alone could not manage the American economy effectively without free market capitalism.

Many Republicans believed that the aftermath of war had itself proven the case for market solutions to production problems, and that their party was in many ways simply responding to the political changes that had caused the decline of the popularity of New Dealers after 1945.[5] A party dependent on the business world for much of its income had to be aware of views such as those expressed at the U.S. Chamber of Commerce annual meetings in the period. "If we are to look forward to a continuously solvent United States and preserve the integrity of government securities and the private structures dependent on them, we must balance our budget, provide for an orderly reduction of the debt and a decrease of the interest charge," argued a former Congress employee.[6] Industrialist W. E. Clow wrote to GOP

Chairman B. Carroll Reece in November 1947, arguing that "the welfare of this country and success for the Republican Party in 1948 depends on the Republican Party getting this promised *Republican form* of tax reduction passed as early as possible. . . . I have encountered a number of people . . . who are *unfairly* but nevertheless irritated at the Republican Party for its failure to make good on tax reduction." This was but one of many letters from American businesses across the country writing to Republican politicians about the economic basis for tax reduction and the link between antistatism and the party's electoral links with its natural constituency.[7]

A combination of business pressure and the perceived political benefits of general reductions in taxes dominated the debates on the various Republican-sponsored tax reduction bills in Congress in 1947 and 1948. The three bills were almost identical, differing only in their applicable dates of operation.[8] All three passed both houses, the third in March 1948 also overriding the President's veto. It is important to note how approaches to the question of big government were mobilizing political ideologies in the 80th Congress. George Malone (R-Nevada), fresh from his upset victory in the 1946 elections, combined the two economic arguments behind the tax bill in his Senate speech on the issue. "Our ever-expanding economy," he argued, "is dependent on venture capital. . . . We must not continue the high rate of taxation now in effect or we will surely shut off at the source the flow of money necessary to continue our gradual economic expansion." In addition, "taxpayers should now get this reduction which is equivalent to a raise in pay."[9] Senator Gene Millikin (R-Colorado), Chairman of the Senate Finance Committee, reinforced the image, created by the right, of the state having a harmful effect on the very people it was supposed to serve: "the greatest element entering into the cost of goods today is the cost of the federal government."[10] Given the atmosphere of the mid-1940s, when the economy was in turmoil and wages were failing to keep up with inflation, it was scarcely surprising that the economic arguments in favor of tax reduction would pay off.[11]

The arguments of most Democrats and a handful of Republicans against reducing taxes also had a partly economic basis. Republican Wayne Morse, introducing an amendment to predicate tax reduction on the level of economic activity, argued that it was unsound fiscal policy to reduce taxes when the economy was overheating, inflation was rampant, and spending, especially on foreign policy, was rising. Democrat Joseph O'Mahoney (D-Wyoming) also emphasized a growing commitment in liberal political circles to Keynesian ideas of economic management. "If," he argued, "at a time when the people of the United States are in the midst of an inflationary spiral and the national income is increasing because prices are increasing, we deceive ourselves into cutting down the receipts of the federal government, we are only digging the trench holes in which the bomb will explode to destroy our system." Claude Pepper (D-Florida) agreed. Not only was the policy of cutting taxes economically unsound, but it also discriminated against the poorest by granting huge dollar reductions in the tax bills of the wealthiest, destabilizing the economy and creating "economic chaos and another depression in the United States."[12]

Republicans committed to reorienting policy away from a reliance on the state were also divided on this point between a commitment to tax cuts as an absolute and the need for a balanced budget first, requiring cuts of between $4 and $6 billion. William Knowland had managed in early 1947 to pass in the Senate a resolution that at least $2.6 billion should be applied to reducing the government debt, before any tax cuts could take place. In this endeavor he clashed publicly with colleagues such as Millikin, Robert Taft, and Chapman Revercomb (R-West Virginia) who saw tax reduction as an end in itself.[13] All, however, agreed with former Federal Reserve Chairman Marriner Eccles, himself a former advocate of Keynesian measures who had had a change of heart, that "rigid Government economy" and strict controls on wage demands and other inflationary pressures were essential.[14] All believed that high taxes in many ways added to the inflationary spiral and should be reduced. Democratic liberals, on the other hand, countered that tax cuts fueled public spending power at the wrong time, and that lower spending by government would cut much needed programs, such as social security. It seemed that in the 80th Congress the economizers would win the day, but in the context of a public tired of a high tax burden and an improperly balanced economy, rather than any political denial of the need for government.

Almost imperceptibly, however, the nature of debates over the size of the state was becoming subject to other influences beyond the purely domestic and economic, a trend suggested in the context of the recent world war. For liberals determined to oppose a reorientation of attitudes toward taxation and the state's role in the economy, one of the principal arguments was the need for spending on a more assertive foreign policy. Wayne Morse quoted Wendell Willkie as saying in 1944 that the United States had to tax its citizens "beyond any limit that we have hitherto imagined possible." He claimed that America "cannot solve our domestic problems without due regard to our foreign policy. . . . Domestic economic health must provide the foundation for our foreign policy of the future."[15] If America were a nation determined to oppose totalitarianism abroad, domestic policies had to be subordinated to the economic demands of an ideological foreign policy. Joe O'Mahoney argued in the Senate that the government had to "preserve this [capitalist] system. . . . Joe Stalin does not doubt it. At this very moment his policy in Europe is guided by the conviction that the United States is heading for a crash."[16] If America were to oppose Soviet tyranny, the state had to have the resources necessary for an internationalist policy.

The liberalism of these internationalists stressed the theme of freedom from threats from abroad. Democrat Millard Tydings (Maryland) joined this growing centrist consensus on the need for a single American ideology to present on the world stage when he told an audience in Towson, Maryland that Americans were "willing to curtail our own enjoyment of wealth and possessions temporarily in order to restore law and order and reason to this rich and war-torn world. We cannot turn back from this sacrificial action. The risk is too great." Tydings contrasted the "high privilege of being Americans" with the horror of dictatorships and poverty elsewhere in the world. Using images of the world abroad Tydings joined other Democrats and many Republicans in arguing that it was America's destiny to extend American democratic principles abroad and that domestic policy should be little more than a tool to that end. Liberalism was a series of policies intended to project American power abroad, and relied on a series of pictures of "Joe Stalin" and "the tidal wave of that [Communist] ideology." In fact, Tydings was one of a handful of Senators initially to back tax reduction, only to switch votes when it came to overriding the veto because of the international ramifications of a reduced federal income.[17] One of the few Democrats to propose his own progressive plan for tax reduction for the poorest in society, Glen Taylor of Idaho, was also one of the few to oppose this growing commitment to an American anti-totalitarian destiny. Taylor argued that there "is an urgent need for tax relief for the vast majority of the population," calling the attention of Congress to the effects of inflation on purchasing power, and proposing his own plan to raise tax allowance levels on low incomes. While attacking the Republican plan as giving too much relief to the wealthy, Taylor also criticized the growing liberal desire to adhere to Willkie's view that world war had drastically altered the priorities of the state.[18]

The debate over the tax cut in 1947 and early 1948 contained early indications of the administration's growing commitment to dovetail domestic and foreign policy into an overall grand strategy, a strategy that would gather together supporters from both parties in Congress. The tax cut, for example, was one vote on which the Republican-Southern Democrat coalition rested on rather shaky ground. George Smathers explained to his Miami constituents that five items, "all relating to national defense and war costs, comprise 80 cents of every dollar recommended in the president's budget for 1949." Would the GOP majority, Smathers asked, cut "the Immigration

Service, the School Lunch Program, veterans' benefits, the Marshall Plan, or even the national defense. These same men tried it last year, but soon discovered that the government has certain minimum functions it must perform."[19] In a speech at the University of Kansas in April 1948, Smathers outlined his vision of what was coming to be termed Cold War liberalism, stressing the need for foreign and domestic programs that would turn opinion firmly against communism: "At a time when we need low-cost housing for veterans and people in low income groups, [Republicans] refuse . . . because it would cost millions of dollars and jeopardize the tax reduction bill which they promised and must have to win in 1948. . . . A home can turn back a communist idea where a bomb or a bullet cannot."[20] His stance on liberal issues would change markedly as the Cold War progressed, but in 1948 he remained committed to the New Deal coalition in at least some areas.

Liberal coalition politics, however, increasingly hinged upon a commitment to the administration's foreign policy. Jacob Javits of New York, a Republican member of the coalition skeptical of the benefits of a tax cut when the international situation appeared precarious, would later note that "the hallmark of effective political action is the coalition. . . . I look for the rise in power and influence of the liberal Democrat and progressive Republican coalition to counterbalance the ultra-conservative coalition in Congress."[21] Such an accord between the two factions would, however, restrict the future development of a post–New Deal political agenda to the extension of existing measures and the establishment of an ambitious program of aid to western Europe. It was, argued Javits, "the task of the liberal to find the happy medium between [those] who would seek complete state control in providing for the needs of our citizens and those who would provide nothing at all." At the core of the coalition's political outlook when considering the tax cut and other domestic measures was "an interpretation and understanding of the role of the American workers, American investors, American technicians, and American businessmen in the recovery of the world's economy and its stabilization."[22]

Many Republicans knew well that in the postwar era theories of minimal government and low taxation quickly fell by the wayside when foreign affairs loomed large on the national agenda; they had already been fighting to restrict the scope of America's postwar role in the new world order. Twenty-eight Republican Senators out of a total contingent of thirty-six in the 79th Congress had opposed American participation in the Bretton Woods monetary accords. Twenty-five had opposed the extension of the Trade Agreements Act, while 122 Republicans in the House out of 183 present and voting and 18 in the Senate had voted against the loan of $3.75

billion to the British government in May 1946 to help stabilize the British economy.[23] Senator Wayland Brooks of Illinois, spokesperson for Robert McCormack of the *Chicago Tribune* and its isolationist, conservative political outlook, stated on the Senate floor that he opposed the loan to Britain because he was "confident that it will prove to be a gift" that would set the United States on an irreversible course of huge state department budgets and a swollen defense budget. Furthermore, he argued that a right-wing ideology of anti-statism was incompatible with the maintenance by the U.S. government of "a Socialistic experiment in the hands of a party headed by Harold Laski who blithely denounces our form of government and economy at the very time when we are struggling to maintain our system of private enterprise under a truly representative form of government." Brooks saw the multilateral trade and loan arrangements of the Roosevelt and Truman administrations as "part of the Lord Keynes and the New Deal plan for a worldwide WPA project that will lower our American standard of living."[24] William Knowland and Robert Taft led efforts in the Senate, supported by some thirty of their colleagues, to balance foreign spending plans with the financial constraints of a peacetime budget by changing the conditions of the loan, and effort "to prod the administration," in Knowland's words, "into realizing the importance of balancing the budget . . . [and to be] the watch dog of the Treasury in seeing that it does not go out on a spending spree."[25]

This debate over the extent to which Republicans could support the administration's foreign policy agenda when its domestic priorities were compromised continued during the 80th Congress. In February 1947 the Republican majority struck $6 billion from the defense budget. During the tax cut debate Senator Homer Capehart (R-Indiana) asked Joseph O'Mahoney if he and Truman were opposed to tax reduction because "he proposes to spend in Europe the money of American taxpayers which we might save." O'Mahoney replied that he did feel that a Europe-centered American policy to prevent the spread of communism was "the wisest expenditure this country can make." George Malone was not convinced. "If we could determine the fatal fascination of foreign governments for our Government executives, some progress will have been made. Their movements have all the earmarks [sic] of a world WPA. It is about time that we gave our own people and their affairs some attention."[26]

Increasingly, conservatives in Congress were discovering that the innovations in fiscal policy and federal spending that had sprung from U.S. involvement in World War Two were irreversible, and would be yet more entrenched if the United States were to play a part in the reconstruction of the noncommunist world. Senior conservatives and centrists in both parties began to look for ways of constraining the development of a leviathan state while preserving the ability to fund large defense and foreign policy appropriations. The compromises that this endeavor would entail significantly affected the federal government's ability to expand the boundaries of New Deal liberalism, but it also began to shift the focus of American anti-statism away from a preoccupation with small government and low taxes and toward a political perspective dominated by a commitment to anti-communism as a necessary corollary to the institutionalization of the New Deal state.[27]

Partisan political activity continued to involve symbolic disputes over taxation and the size of the state, but increasingly used the rhetoric of anti-totalitarianism to mask a growing consensus over the limits of domestic reform as characterized by the Truman administration's commitment to resist demands on the left for a more ambitious domestic program. Conservative politicians capitalized on the growing anti-communist climate in American politics as foreign policy concerns came increasingly to the fore in 1947. They constructed a political language which saw Americanism as an abstract absolute, threatened by some imagined notion of the state as dictatorship.

The use of anti-Soviet rhetoric to promote a radical right politics was not unique to the United States. A Canadian MP, Patrick Ashby, wrote to Taft setting out the political ethos of the Social Credit party in that country, and soliciting support from Republicans in Washington. The party had been founded in 1935 and had its base in the agrarian western states like Alberta, promoting inflationary monetary policies to help alleviate the agricultural crisis that had beset North America since the late 1920s. Agrarian radicalism was taking on a decidedly anti-statist tone by the late 1940s, partly a product of Canadian regional politics in which outlying provinces felt marginalized by Ottawa.[28] Anti-totalitarianism functioned as a useful political tool for such groups, especially in the wake of the discovery of a Canadian spy ring in 1945. Ashby based his political rationale on a hatred of the extreme left, attempting to demonstrate an affinity with the Republican right across the border. He claimed that "taxation alienates production from its rightful owners and is a method used for the purpose of introducing Communism. See the Communist Manifesto of Karl Marx." Ashby noted that the "Republican victory in the US has given us new hope and we look forward to your leadership in the near future." Interestingly, Ashby tried to broaden the appeal of his party by asserting an anti-government ideological message that spoke to more than impoverished farmers. The fight over the state was, he claimed, "a cultural war to the death . . . the economic war is only incidental." It was important for the Right to "look for cultural affinities wherever they might exist" in the world, and to "get it out of the minds of the electorate that they are collectively sovereign, without limit, over the individual" by abolishing the secret ballot to make all voters responsible for their votes for confiscatory government.[29]

It is important to stress how similar these and other comments by interested anti-statist pressure groups were to statements made in a Cold War context by politicians in Washington of both parties. Government, argued Christian Herter, had "revealed itself as the most powerful and potentially most dangerous lobby of all. It fought . . . every Congressional move to curb its innate urge to expand."[30] Economic critiques of the state were being joined by attacks on the legitimacy of government in toto related to the ideology of anti-totalitarianism dependent on images of foreign regimes. It was clear that the liberal bipartisans were arguing for a larger federal government with which to fight totalitarianism, while the right was looking to shrink government at home in order to stave off statism. Politicians as different in outlook as Malone, Tydings, and O'Mahoney were using the issue of totalitarianism to argue against prioritizing the domestic enlargement of the state. The issue was not yet fully developed in 1947. As domestic anti-government sentiment in America grew, and at the same time the Cold War took center stage, the domestic effects of this trend would become clearer.

The State and Labor: The Case of Taft-Hartley

The field of labor-management relations formed the principal battleground in the 80th Congress over the future of the New Deal impulse in American politics. Given the context of the 1946 elections, it was clear that the drive on the part of business groups and their anti-statist representatives in Congress to readjust the balance of power between management and labor that had been established by the National Labor Relations Act would intensify and gain momentum. Freshman congressman Richard Nixon certainly saw the mandate of his election to Congress in these terms. "The need for long-range legislation in the labor field is just as urgent today as it was on election day 1946, when the people spoke in no uncertain terms," he argued in a newsletter to his constituents in early 1947. In one sense, the tenor of Nixon's regular updates to his district on the progress of the labor law amendments sponsored by Senator Robert Taft and Congressman Fred Hartley (R-New Jersey) reflected the acceptance in GOP circles that the electoral landscape had changed since the 1930s, and that appeals for new legislation had to recognize the role of labor unions in the modern industrial economy. Republican legislators all described the Taft-Hartley bill as an attempt to give more power to individual union members. "It has been said," argued Nixon, "that the Wagner Act was the Magna Carta of union labor. Assuming that such was the case, certainly now is the time that the Congress enacted a Bill of Rights which will give rank and file members of unions a voice in their organizations."[31] Taft himself was careful to cast his public statements on the bill in similar terms: "It was well known that that bill . . . would be enacted if the people voted for a Republican Congress." He defended his drive to take away some of the rights labor unions had enjoyed since 1935, including the closed shop, the right to jurisdictional strikes and secondary boycotts, and the right to deduct automatically union dues from a worker's pay packet, in terms that would gloss over the very real political struggle between the New Deal coalition and the business lobby for control of the postwar American economy: "The Taft-Hartley Act was written for only one purpose—to establish justice and equality in labor-management relations. . . . Countless labor union members have found that it is a good thing for them. . . . The rights of labor are carefully preserved."[32] The Taft-Hartley Act, together with the rash of anti-union-shop initiatives that poured out of State legislatures during 1947, were clearly much more controversial than these statements suggest, but the fact that the provisions of the bill were not more ambitious attests to the changed political landscape of the post–New Deal era, as Republicans adjusted their ambitions in the context of the "Democratic Order" that dominated American politics.[33]

Nevertheless, the enactment of Taft-Hartley represented a stunning blow to left-wing hopes of a development of a social democratic political settlement after the war. The world of business and commerce was predictably in favor of legislation to swing the balance of power away from union bosses and toward management, and built on the groundswell of anti-union sentiment that had swept across the political scene the previous year. The National Association of Manufacturers spent $3 billion in a publicity drive to sell Taft-Hartley to Americans, with full-page advertisements in 287 daily newspapers.[34] The purpose of much of this private sector initiative, including the establishment in 1947 of yet another anti-statist publicity machine, the Industrial Information Institute, was not to contain the New Deal order, but to take the political initiative away from it completely. "Since the beginning of 1932 I have been giving a great deal of my time trying to get the country out of the hands of the New Deal," wrote James Francis, president of the Island Creek Coal Company to Taft in April 1947. Francis testified before the Senate Labor committee on January 30, lobbying hard for the repeal of the Wagner Act and its replacement with what he termed "fair, workable labor laws," which seemed to mean stripping from labor unions most of the rights they had gained since 1935, and especially the right to the union shop and to industry-wide bargaining. One local labor leader in Francis's company asserted that "he does not believe in collective bargaining at all—prior to 1933 his company would not permit its employees to belong to any union, but his company did pay in to the county sheriff's welfare fund to keep the union out of his mines."[35] The 1946 elections had revitalized an anti-New Deal coalition that saw the 80th Congress as amenable to the abandonment of the broker state that had guided the American political economy through the depression and world war.[36]

This frontal assault on organized labor's place in the American political order had, on the one hand, a galvanizing effect on the principal labor organizations and their allies in the Truman administration and in Congress. The CIO and AFL opposed the bill vigorously before the Senate and House committees and in their own publicity drive to mobilize the rank and file. Even Richard Nixon was impressed by the inveterate but by now marginalized figure of UMW leader John L. Lewis, whom he referred to as "by far the most able labor leader who has appeared before the committee. . . . He arose to the occasion in characteristic Lewisian fashion, to the great delight of the throng gathered in the committee room to hear him 'do his stuff.' "[37] More important were the bitterly anti-GOP efforts of the CIO's radio broadcasts such as "Labor USA" on the ABC syndicated network, and the lobbying of even ambivalent New Dealers such as John Kennedy who represented districts where the labor vote could become influential in 1948. In the final analysis organized labor could only count on 83 votes in the House against Taft-Hartley, almost all from industrial states: 18 votes came from New York, including two Republicans, Jacob Javits of Manhattan and John Butler of Buffalo; the rest came from industrial districts in Detroit, West Virginia, western Pennsylvania, California, Ohio, Massachusetts, and Illinois, plus a smattering of maverick New Dealers from states like Texas and Arizona.[38]

Democrats from industrial districts such as Adolph Sabath of Chicago and American Labor Party (ALP) representative Vito Marcantonio of New York led a spirited fight to defeat the measure, but recognized that their efforts would be in vain. Sabath told the House in April that he was sure, correctly as it turned out, "that the Republican vote for the bill will be very nearly unanimous. Of course, they will be joined by some gentlemen from this side who are unfriendly to labor, who have no organized labor in their districts, and who will be swayed by the high-pressure and dishonest campaign carried on for many, many years against organized labor, and whipped up to a new and degrading fever in recent months." But he predicted that Taft-Hartley opened up an opportunity for New Deal liberals to use the issue to mobilize their forces in the 1948 elections and beyond: "I predict that by this senseless action you will give American labor new inspiration to renew the age-long fight for justice and equality and freedom . . . and to expand their membership and their influence as the unorganized majority of workers begin to realize more fully their lack of protection against unjust and vengeful attacks on their economic and political rights."[39]

President Truman saw an opportunity in vetoing the bill to rally organized labor to his political standard in 1948 and to erase the immobilizing drift that had characterized his administration's domestic politics since 1945. "The country needs," he told the American people in a radio address on the day of his presidential veto, "legislation which will get rid of abuses. We do not need—and we do not want—legislation which will take fundamental rights away from our working people."[40] It seemed as though the right turn in American politics in the wake of the midterm election presented an opportunity for American liberalism to mobilize the forces that had in large part absented themselves from the electoral process the previous November.[41]

In many respects, however, the overall drift of American liberalism was in a rightward direction, assisted by a shift in the parameters of left-of-center discourse in the evolving Cold War climate. For one thing, many Democrats even in the north were coming to see the labor issue as an Achilles heel in the light of the lessons of 1946. Freshman congressman John F. Kennedy told a labor audience that in spite of "the strong stand against any changes" on the part of organized labor, "I believe that there will be, without argument from either side, two much needed changes. One, the outlawing of the secondary boycotts, and two, the outlawing of jurisdictional strikes. . . . I myself have reached no final conclusions. . . . Beyond all group interests, above all rights, arise duties to the community."[42]

President Truman himself had outlined the need for new legislation in his 1947 State of the Union message, and in all his pronouncements on the measure was careful to craft his criticisms of Taft-Hartley in terms that explicitly denied a class-based analysis of the labor problem. The President claimed in his veto message that the bill "would go far toward destroying our national unity. By raising barriers between labor and management and by injecting political considerations into normal economic decisions, it would invite them to gain their ends through direct political action. I think it would be exceedingly dangerous to our country to develop a class basis for political action." He added that America could not "be strong internationally if our national unity and productive strength are hindered at home."[43] His administration, in formulating a global anti-totalitarian policy that shied away from left-of-center ideology and required the support of a cross-section of the political spectrum, renounced a politics of class that had become the bedrock of New Deal politics since the late 1930s. Indeed, Truman would readily make use of the restrictive provisions of Taft-Hartley when his Cold War strategy required it in the years to follow.[44]

The shift in political outlook and strategy of the liberal-left movement as a whole can be summarized by an analysis of the changing attitudes of the newly formed Americans for Democratic Action toward both labor and social democratic ideas, as well as the shifting politics of the union movement itself. The establishment of ADA in January 1947 in Washington was, in the words of founder member Reinhold Niebuhr, "to create a climate of liberal opinion which is explicitly and uncompromisingly democratic in purpose," a clear reference to the perceived fellow-traveler credentials of Henry Wallace's Progressive Citizens of America. The preliminary statement of the new group rejected some sort of "simple, inexorable choice between imperialist and fascist reaction and communist totalitarianism." Instead, the group's architects asserted that the "power of government must be adequate to subordinate the exercise of private power to the general welfare, but we must also guard against undue concentration of governmental authority." The "central issue" of contemporary politics was "not between capitalism or socialism, but between those who believe in the inalienable rights of the individual and those who do not." In appropriating the term "liberalism" for an ADA brand of New Deal political action, founder members James Loeb, Niebuhr, Leon Henderson, Chester Bowles, and the like were careful to avoid direct engagement with left-wing ideology when their primary purpose was to rescue the New Deal coalition from damaging associations with the extreme left. "Liberalism is a demanding faith," they argued in a statement produced in advance of the January conference. "Its basis is neither a set of dogmas nor a prescription of specific measures. Liberalism is based on a deep concern for all men, a profound faith in human reason, and an attitude of inquiry." This was a far cry from the popular-front spirit that had mobilized the left behind Henry Wallace's appointment to the Department of Commerce in 1945, or the promotion of the original Full Employment Act. The principal ideological leitmotif of early ADA publicity and correspondence in 1947 was the need "to combat totalitarianism by striking boldly at the conditions of hunger, want, and insecurity which breed desperate political situations."[45]

Americans for Democratic Action remained committed to theories of social welfare and state activity that had taken shape in the United States in the Roosevelt years. Its members also in large part continued to believe that "the British experiment in reconciling political liberty with economic planning is of the highest significance—and that the future of democracy in Europe depends, in no small measure, on its success."[46] However, Patrick Gordon Walker's visit to the United States in early 1947 put the emerging differences between American liberalism and the European left into sharp relief. Ostensibly Loeb and the other organizers of the informal visit saw themselves and the British Labour government as brothers in arms, and described Gordon Walker's speaking tour as an opportunity to discuss "the general subject of British labor's [sic] accomplishments in its first year and a half of its control of the government." A UDA memo told members that "liberals have waited and watched with keen and sympathetic interest this brave attempt to establish democratic socialism. . . . It would be hard to overestimate the importance of this first effort to increase understanding of the British Labor Government."[47] Paul Douglas and Hubert Humphrey were two figures involved in the establishment of ADA in 1947 who initially saw the new organization as reestablishing "the Democratic Party as a progressive force in American politics along British lines, promoting a platform that included a "strong statement requesting [the] establishment of national economic planning. . . . Extension of public health and medical services . . . are fundamentals to [a] liberal platform."[48]

Gordon Walker received an enthusiastic reception from ADA chapters and local labor union groups in cities from Boston to Minneapolis, but his speeches described a political agenda increasingly untenable for a liberal movement engaged in a domestic struggle with the PCA and the extreme left. "The doctrine underlying the policy of the Labor Party . . . has been evolved as a revolt against the assumptions of laissez-faire," he argued. "Labor does not regard the State solely as an evil thing whose powers must at all costs be clipped." Nationalization, for instance, was to Prime Minister Attlee's party "not an end in itself; it fits into a bigger, general scheme. . . . Thus the State will exercise an overriding influence over the whole economy: through its control over credit and taxation; through general directions to nationalized industries; through the conditions imposed upon Boards set up for and by private industries."[49] Americans for Democratic Action, by contrast, although appreciative of the Labour Party's efforts to transform the landscape of British politics, saw liberalism's "essential purpose" in practical terms as "the protection of international security." According to ADA national chairman Wilson Wyatt, ADA's domestic program was predicated upon America's role as "the champion of democratic principles in the world. . . . ADA is pledged to make America the world symbol of progressive democracy. We must be strong at home—free from unemployment and inflation—to be strong abroad."[50]

Labour MP Jennie Lee warned American liberals through an article in *Tribune* that it was dangerous for what she termed, somewhat loosely, "the American Left" to place this international agenda at center stage, to the extent of promoting an irreconcilable split within the movement. Henry Wallace's recent visit to London had generated enthusiastic attention, she claimed, because he had been "wearing the mantle of Franklin Roosevelt, symbolizing those in America opposed to the American Century of Mr. [Henry] Luce and working for the Century of the Common Man." Were ADA members like Leon Henderson and Walter Reuther "so warped with fear and hatred of Communism and Soviet Russia that they give uncritical support to President Truman's foreign policy," even if this meant the collapse of a left-of-center coalition in American politics that had returned FDR to the presidency in 1944? "Must Russia count among its implacable enemies in America not only American reactionaries, but also the bulk of American Liberals, Socialists, and trade unionists?" she asked. She answered her rhetorical question in the negative, while affirming her own party's determination not to make the mistake of the PCA of refusing to recognize the unpalatable truths about the Soviet Union. Implicit in her article, however, was the assertion that American liberals needed to spend less time conjuring up anti-totalitarian slogans, and more time formulating social democratic responses to domestic political and socioeconomic questions.[51]

Even if ADA liberals were broadly thinking along similar lines to their Labour allies in London, often tailoring their political activity to an American political structure that proscribed a frontal assault on anti-statist influence in U.S. politics, the relationship between liberal elites and organized labor in the United States in the unfolding Cold War was rendering the development of an American social democratic movement increasingly fragile. Joseph Lash of the New York chapter of ADA was able to report to Herbert Lehman about "the commitments by labor spokesmen to give real support to the ADA" at the group's national convention in Philadelphia in February 1948 only because the CIO and AFL hierarchy had for the past year been purging labor unions of communists and followers of Wallace's PCA. Lash proudly noted that the "non-communist part of the CIO" was "fully represented on our national Board," and that William Green had "pledged complete cooperation and support to the ADA from the AFL political action and educational setup."[52]

The political price of this alliance of anti-communist liberals was the decline of the political influence of labor unions, whose increasingly introspective and internecine activities have been described in considerable detail elsewhere.[53] One example was Walter Reuther's veto of a merger between the UAW and the Farm Equipment Workers because the latter union was dominated by the far left; Reuther fulminated against what he termed the "united front psychology," renouncing a political strategy that had sustained the American left since the 1936 election.[54] The CIO's growing commitment to the Truman administration's foreign policy represented in one sense the recognition of the perceived benefits to American labor of an integrated world economy in which U.S. foreign aid could stimulate employment opportunities for all, but it also forced organized labor into a Faustian pact with the political language of the American right.

Just as significant was anti-totalitarian liberalism's still-uneasy relationship with organized labor, despite attempts on the part of unions to raze the legacy of their popular front years. John F. Kennedy's role in the investigation by the House Education and Labor Committee into communist influence in UAW local 248 at the Allis-Chalmers plant in Milwaukee was one example. R. J. Thomas, a prominent member of the left-wing faction in the UAW hierarchy who had recently been deposed from his leadership position by Walter Reuther, and Harold Christoffel, the leader of local 248, appeared before the committee in early 1947 when a protracted strike at the plant had unveiled as much discord between factions of the UAW as between labor and management. Kennedy proved to be a worthy ally of Republican anti-union stalwarts like Fred Hartley, Clare Hoffman, and Richard Nixon, and showed up cracks in the Democratic membership of a committee which, on paper, looked to be dominated by the New Deal cohort from the industrial northeast.[55]

Fresh from his labor-baiting performance in Washington, Kennedy addressed the Massachusetts State AFL convention in Springfield in July, arguing that the passage of the Taft-Hartley Act, which he decried as "a calculated and systematic attempt to undermine the collective bargaining process," was partly the fault of the labor movement itself. Organized labor had apparently "lost the public support enjoyed in the thirties." Kennedy felt that this was the result of two factors: "The first factor is that the public believes that communists have gained positions of power in some labor unions. The Christoffel incident shows that this belief is not wholly unfounded. It is of primary importance . . . that Labor itself continue its unrelenting fight to remove communists from positions of control." Having firmly championed his role in the Allis-Chalmers case, Kennedy then in his second point distinguished between union activity and what he termed "the public interest." In the lexicon of anti-communist Americanism that increasingly permeated Cold War liberalism, "private interest must yield to the common good. If Labor is to regain the public support which it has lost there must be a reaffirmation of this principle."[56] It was but a short conceptual leap from such vague conceptions of "the common good" to a concrete attack on a labor radicalism that had helped transform New Deal liberalism in the mid-1930s from a woolly offshoot of early-twentieth-century progressivism into a social democratic impulse akin to developments elsewhere in the industrialized world.

The problem of how industrial unionism fitted into Cold War liberalism preoccupied ADA and Democratic party activists in advance of the crucial 1948 elections. Andrew Biemiller, ADA strategist and former Milwaukee congressman whose left-of-center credentials were impeccable, used the cases of two House special elections in the fall of 1947 to argue that organized labor was rapidly becoming more of a hindrance than a help to the revival of New Deal liberalism in the wake of the disastrous 1946 elections. In Wisconsin's second district, Democrat Carl Thompson came very close to capturing a heavily Republican seat. Biemiller informed the ADA leadership that this was perceived to be mainly because "Thompson himself did most of the speaking, stressing a six-point program in which protection of labor rights was only one of the six points. Monopoly, protection of farm cooperatives, social security, taxation, and housing were the main talking points." Labor's role was restricted to that of "getting its own members to vote and getting them interested in the issues of the campaign." By contrast, the GOP had retained Pennsylvania's eighth district, a seat where Democratic-leaning Allentown was offset politically by its rural hinterland, by a larger than expected majority, a result Biemiller attributed to the role of labor in the campaign. "Probably the worst error made in the campaign was to make the Taft-Hartley bill *the* campaign issue," he argued. "Actually very few people in the district knew about the Taft-Hartley bill and those who did liked it. From the beginning, labor leaders took too prominent a role in the campaign, and for all practical purposes ran it." He concluded his report by commenting that the Pennsylvania campaign had demonstrated that "today the entire liberal cause has been done irreparable harm, locally and nationally, mainly because of Communist activities and because of the mistaken political tactics on the part of labor."[57] In another report to ADA headquarters in November 1947 on the subject of liberal political organization in advance of the 1948 elections, Biemiller returned to the theme of labor's place in a political alliance that transcended class boundaries. "It is essential," he argued, "that . . . we emphasize the common aims of labor and most of the rest of the community, and that we avoid at all costs any feeling of 'labor against the world.' "[58]

Shortly before the 1948 elections, Americans for Democratic Action openly resigned themselves to a Republican victory, and looked in a draft program to their probable post-election strategy. While recognizing the need to engender "unity among all genuinely progressive forces in the nation," including labor unions, the draft document commented disparagingly on the "suggestion that the ADA should serve as the political arm of the labor movement. Such a development is clearly impossible in the present circumstances, and the matter of its desirability is open to question. If ADA were to become the sole political arm of organized labor, and if the rank and file of the trade unions were to become members of ADA in large masses, clearly the non-labor elements of ADA would be completely submerged. This would be to the advantage neither of labor nor of the independent liberals."[59] The division on the left between an intelligentsia and the rank and file was nothing new, nor was it unique to the United States, and represented in part the difficulty of formulating a left-wing program not predicated solely on a Marxist conception of a mass proletariat at odds with the bourgeoisie, a paradigm of limited relevance to America in the 1940s.[60] In part, however, it was a result of the growing reliance of ADA-type liberals on a political program that put class-neutral appeals to anti-totalitarianism before the imperatives of social democracy.

In the case of some congressional Democrats, such as John F. Kennedy, the ADA strategy of integrating the issue of organized labor into a broader political program seemed logical enough. Arthur Schlesinger Jr., who in addition to being a respected Harvard professor and advocate of the New Deal was an ADA member in Kennedy's constituency, wrote on an ADA questionnaire on political strategy in 1948 that Kennedy's district was "a Democratic district as a result of careful gerrymandering. . . . Trade union political activity in Cambridge is practically non-existent."[61] Certainly in some Democratic constituencies there seemed little to be gained from a purely class-based appeal to voters. It was not, however, the whole story. In Massachusetts as a whole the CIO and AFL joined forces with the ADA in 1948 to form the Massachusetts United Labor Committee to coordinate the registration of liberal voters across the state. "This is the first time in the history of the American labor movement that both major labor groups have united in an all-out registration drive," stated a press release on behalf of the new organization in September 1948.[62] In the vast majority of urban industrial constituencies in the northeast and Midwest there remained the possibility of a Democratic campaign based around the concerns of organized labor as well as the professional middle class, both by now wedded to the basic principles of the New Deal state, and in particular Social Security.[63]

Instead, Cold War liberalism managed to tailor its domestic programs toward the promotion of a global anti-communist agenda, contrasting the achievements of American federal economic and social programs with the repression of the Soviet system, while simultaneously marginalizing left-wing discourse, thereby negotiating the treacherous rapids of the American political system. David Plotke is probably right to argue that there was little room in mainstream American politics for a genuine social democratic platform after the war. Still, a commitment on the part of New Deal liberals to establishing "the permanent foundations of a continually expanding economy, free of the shackles of monopoly and the threat of 'boom and bust'" through the expansion of social insurance and the minimum wage could be defended on the basis that it retained the basic nonredistributive ethos of the New Deal while also preserving America from the charge that a "free" economy could not provide for its people.[64] Such a political strategy had little room for a labor movement still wrestling with the question of how it could retain the radical political agenda that had driven its leadership during the war but that was rapidly disintegrating in the bitter struggle over the communist issue. The final draft of the Taft-Hartley bill contained a provision preventing avowed Communists from being union members, a provision supported by the CIO leadership as well as Republicans. Gradually, the encroachment of a foreign policy discourse into domestic legislation was becoming clear.

The gathering of the CIO's California state convention in Santa Cruz in November 1947 demonstrated the confusion that increasingly characterized left-of-center political activity in the early Cold War. An anti-left faction headed by John Despol of the United Steel Workers challenged Bjorne Halling of the leftist International Longshoremen and Warehousemen's Union for the state secretaryship. The reason, in the words of the USW resolution on plans for a third party challenge to Truman in 1948, was the left's support for "the reactionary American agents who, consciously or unconsciously, work for the establishment of a world police state which would deny the individual dignity of man." Despol argued that support for Truman's anti-communist foreign policy was now the key test of members' loyalty to the CIO leadership, which under Philip Murray had endorsed the Marshall Plan and aid to the Balkans. Leftist unions were "one-eyed progressives. They can see with their good right eye all of the defects of rightwing politics but when they turn and look to the so-called extreme left they are blind in the left eye and that good right eye looks into an Alice in the Wonderland [sic] looking glass which simply mirrors their own reflection." Although Despol and others' attempt to engender a modicum of unity among the warring factions in the CIO represented good politics at a time of increasing anti-union sentiment on and off Capitol Hill, the attack on leftist unions blunted organized labor's effectiveness as an organ that could serve to reshape American capitalism and politics. In effect, Despol's arguments implicitly endorsed the ADA release encapsulating the emerging Cold War liberal consensus on the place of interest groups in postwar America. The memorandum stated that "the gravity of the present international situation cannot fail to convince patriotic leaders of our party everywhere that neither imagined rights, private economic interests nor cherished customs of any section of America can remain sacred if they jeopardize the position of our nation in world affairs."[65] A politics of class was inappropriate to the demands of liberal internationalism, which required a united front against Soviet communism. Bjorne Halling survived to fight another day, but the *San Francisco News* observed that the "growing influence of the rightwing faction was apparent at the four day session."[66] Philip Murray's dismissal of Harry Bridges as the CIO's director in northern California in March 1948 cemented the right's control of the state CIO, freeing the leadership from the paralysis of internecine struggle during the 1948 campaign while also blunting the ideological message of labor: that American workers still had much to gain from an ambitious expansion of the New Deal legacy.

Even after the surprise victory of Truman and the congressional Democrats in the 1948 elections, it proved impossible for organized labor and its allies to orchestrate a successful challenge to Taft-Hartley and the might of the private business community at a time when the language of class was forming a progressively less significant part of the political worldview of the American left. Republican maverick George Malone may have been atypical in his vote against Taft-Hartley because he felt that it injected yet more governmental control into the economy. Yet his attack on the notion of class was widely shared, even in liberal circles. Malone argued that federal regulation of labor relations was creating an alien system based on class. "We seem to continually deal with classes in this country," he said in a speech on the Senate floor. "The general public practically never comes into the picture, they are generally ignored. I submit . . . that there are no classes in this country—a ditch digger today may be the manager or the president of the company tomorrow." The state, he contended, in a manner strikingly similar to John Kennedy's address to the Massachusetts AFL convention, was creating class consciousness by alternately favoring one group over another. In a letter to Fellow Nevadan George Wingfield, Malone affirmed his commitment not to "vote to destroy either [labor or management]"[67] In arguing that he believed in "less government meddling, not more," and that he was opposed to "bipartisan combinations" of the right and the New Deal, Malone was arguing against any form of state regulation of American capitalism. In doing so, he was evoking the popular fear of the totalitarian state to attack the extension of government's role as a response to the complex nature of modern capitalism.[68]

Taft referred to Malone's position as "extreme," but a number of prominent Cold War liberals were also worried about the capacity of anti-labor laws to inflame dangerous class antagonisms at a time when the logic of anti-totalitarianism required a united political front.[69] Paul Douglas, prominent ADA liberal and Democratic candidate for the Senate from Illinois in 1948, told an audience in East St Louis in March of that year that Taft-Hartley could have received almost unanimous political backing if it had been divided "into two parts. One of these could have embodied reforms to which virtually every fair-minded man would agree, such as providing that unions as well as employers should be willing to bargain collectively, and that they should publish their financial accounts. The other part could have contained the doubtful sections of the Act."[70] Douglas contended that most congressmen would have voted for the first section, and then more would have voted against the other parts, thus ensuring a better deal for labor unions. In the context of the ongoing deradicalization of labor's political program in the late 1940s, however, the defensive political strategy of liberals like Douglas, who were increasingly turning their attention to foreign affairs, made the realization of a genuine broker state, in which labor leaders would play a significant role, increasingly unlikely.

Protecting the Nation's Health: A Case Study of Anti-Statism

Almost every year since 1939, liberal Senators Robert Wagner (D-New York) and James Murray (D-Montana) had collaborated with several Senate colleagues and with Representative John Dingell (D-Michigan) in an attempt to expand the Social Security system to include a national health insurance scheme, a measure that was gaining political impetus in industrialized nations and, in the United States, that also represented unfinished business from the development and passage of the 1935 Social Security Act.[71]

Much recent scholarship has emphasized the distinctive political and institutional obstacles to the enactment of a public sector response to health provision in the United States. Health care providers were already by the 1940s developing private systems of health insurance for workers and their dependents that narrowed the political appeal of a federal system. In addition, the ideological foundations of New Deal welfare policy stood firmly on an insurance principle that excluded many of those who needed care most while alienating a medical lobby determined to retain control over the financial side of health care provision. The coalition of interests in Congress that formed the bedrock of New Deal legislative activity rapidly unraveled when southern conservatives saw the long-term social ramifications of major health care reform. And labor unions increasingly became drawn to private health care packages as part of a collective bargaining process that guaranteed some sort of coverage for their workers at a time when the state seemed structurally incapable of meeting their needs under a centralized scheme.[72] My purpose here is not to attempt to contest these sophisticated analyses of America's faltering attempts at welfare state building in the New Deal era, but rather to lay alongside them a discussion of the ideological logic of anticommunism that both provided opponents of health insurance with extra ammunition with which to destroy the measure and also increasingly distanced liberal politicians from association with one of the cornerstones of international social democratic thought. Federal health insurance may have been bound to fail in the United States for a number of reasons, but one of the least considered is the steady erosion of liberal Democratic support for social welfare measures that went beyond those established in the 1930s, in order to shore up support for their party caucus in an increasingly hostile political climate.

The political acceptance of state welfare has never been as far-reaching in America as in Europe, but two factors in the late 1940s initially increased the determination of liberals in Congress and in the ranks of labor and the ADA to push for federal health insurance. First, the British Labour government had by 1948 pushed the National Health Service bill through parliament. "In the ten months since the British act went into effect," wrote Hubert Humphrey in the *New York Times* magazine in May 1949, "professional medical opinion (once opposed), the Conservative Party and the British people have provided evidence of the act's tremendous acceptance. . . . The Conservative Party virtually lost the important by-election at Hammersmith before they could reverse their policy and endorse the British Health Service Act." The Committee for the Nation's Health, a medical pressure group formed to support the principle of federal health insurance and to counterbalance the propaganda drive of the AMA, spent much of its meager budget in the period purchasing British Information Service pamphlets on the British NHS for distribution to interested parties.[73]

Proponents of Murray-Wagner-Dingell were under no illusions that they could pass anything like the universal, free at point of service system in operation in the United Kingdom, and remained wedded to the principle of a payroll tax that had so decisively cleared the path for Social Security through the thicket of American federal and institutional structures in 1935. President Truman framed his request for legislation in terms of an American tradition of public aid in a capitalist framework: "A national health insurance program is a logical extension of the present social security system which is so firmly entrenched in our American democracy. . . . An insurance plan is the American way of accomplishing our objective." Still, the President and other proponents of federal insurance felt that they could reproduce the groundswell of support for the project that had proved so compelling in other countries. Truman referred to "numerous polls of public opinion which indicate that our citizens want a comprehensive health program."[74] When in January 1947 a poll in *Fortune* asked whether the federal government "should provide for all people who have no other means of obtaining a living," 72.8 percent said yes; this was a consensus across all social groups. This poll did not ask respondents to be more specific, but another poll in the same publication two months later asked whether social security should be expanded to allow more people coverage. At that time 48 percent said it should be expanded, 32 percent said it should be left as it was, and only 3 percent said fewer people should receive benefits. This hardly represented a ringing endorsement of health insurance, but it is an indication of the shift in popular attitudes toward government after the New Deal.[75]

The second factor behind renewed interest in the insurance issue in 1947 was that the exponential growth in private group insurance plans had exposed the limitations of private coverage. Claude Pepper noted in 1949 that "the growth of voluntary plans has been rapid and I commend them," but noted that private employer-based coverage was still patchy and did not cover many nonunionized workers or the indigent. He argued that the Murray-Wagner-Dingell measure would, as with Social Security, contain a public assistance measure to sit alongside the insurance system for the gainfully employed.[76]

Pepper and other sponsors of Murray-Wagner-Dingell were slow to realize the effects of the growth of private-sector and nonprofit insurance plans in the immediate postwar period on the political feasibility of a federal scheme. As late as 1949 Pepper was still referring to 1946 figures that suggested only three or four percent of Americans had complete coverage, whereas it was clear from the mushrooming number of employee workplace contracts that included health care provision that an increasing number of Americans were prepared to settle for less than comprehensive coverage rather than wait for the administration to manipulate what one historian has termed the "clumsy levers of federalism."[77] The Bureau of Labor Statistics itself noted in late 1946 that the number of workers in privately negotiated health plans had more than doubled in little over a year, to 1.25 million, and that this constituted "a step in the right direction."[78]

Nevertheless, the analytical thrust of the reports prepared for the Committee for the Nation's Health and the Senate Committee on Labor and Public Welfare in the late 1940s and early 1950s was premised on the political opportunity provided by the growth of a fragile and insubstantial private welfare state at the same time as New Deal liberalism was gaining renewed impetus from Truman's decision to move leftward by 1948. Liberal Democrats began to use the perceived deficiencies of the private health insurance system as another means of re-launching a New Deal agenda that had seemed to lose steam after Roosevelt's death. Labor leaders, for example, remained aware of the political value of a commitment to the principle of federal health insurance even as they were accepting the encroachment of a private welfare state into the collective bargaining process.[79]

The Murray-Wagner-Dingell proposal extended the principle of the 1935 Act, levying a 3 percent payroll tax on employer and employee on wages up to $3,600, and providing wide latitude to the states in administration. The public assistance agencies in Social Security would help the needy qualify for coverage, and all Americans, including those excluded from the 1935 Act, would be eligible. Extending the state in this way was one of the principal campaign pledges of many Democrats, including Helen Douglas in Los Angeles and John Blatnik in Minnesota. Blatnik had won a previously Republican district in a bad year for his party by arguing for "a federal housing program; the extension of social security to include all workers; a national health program; an adequate old age pension." He was mindful that although private health insurance was still a relatively undeveloped phenomenon in America, several million Americans would simply not be able to cope without some system of nonprofit health insurance. Blatnik was one of many viewing the government as a more reliable vehicle than private nonprofit organizations for this purpose.[80] In testifying before the Senate Labor committee on the proposed legislation, Social Security administrator Arthur Altmeyer argued that only "a few million persons, probably not more than two or three percent of the population, have what can be termed relatively complete protection against medical bills." To Altmeyer, comprehensive coverage meant protection against the widest possible range of medical expenses, not simply limited coverage for the largest number of people.[81]

The political climate became yet more conducive to some sort of legislation in the field of public health when a number of Republicans also felt moved to support measures to provide public access to health care for those unable to afford private insurance. In contrast to the sponsors of the administration's plan, Republicans tended to view private insurance as the ideal program for wage earners, and instead saw public assistance as a measure that would cover the indigent and thus insulate the status quo from the challenge of political radicalism. Robert Taft, while unable to support Murray-Wagner-Dingell, put forward a proposal of his own, supported by Republican Senators H. Alexander Smith (New Jersey), Joseph Ball, and Forrest Donnell (Missouri). The bill, wrote Taft, would provide "federal financial aid to every state which undertakes to make all-inclusive a plan for providing medical care for all those unable to pay for it and to encourage voluntary health insurance funds in every state." In notes for a speech on health care, Taft wrote that he recognized that "government has an obligation to give free service only to those unable to pay for it." In another speech he argued that it "does not necessarily damn a program to call it socialization. We have long socialized primary and secondary education in the United States. . . . Of course, the difference between the government looking after the indigent and looking after the entire population is a fundamental issue."[82]

Taft disagreed with the insurance proposal as he claimed it would be costly and inefficient, weighing too heavily on all taxpayers. He might have added that the administration's bill challenged the preeminence of private insurance schemes, threatened the power of the medical profession to determine the cost of care through their tight control of the health care market, and would spread the benefits of coverage to large numbers of Americans excluded from the private market on grounds of risk or social status. Taft never admitted to being beholden to the medical lobby, preferring to couch the terms of his opposition to a universal welfare state in abstract ideological terms. In a letter to Senator Ralph Flanders (R-Vermont) he wrote that "the principles which I support will do more good than most of the New Deal ideas of regulation and planned economy. Probably I don't express often enough what my real interest is, because it certainly is not in wealthier people or big business. . . . [Under] a free system we are bound to have much greater inequality than under a socialistic system. . . . I believe . . . that we must accept the inequalities and then do our best to improve the condition of the people at the lower end . . . by direct assistance to health, education, housing and the like."[83] Taft and his supporters tended to criticize the left and "socialization" because they stood in contrast to the Taft vision of an America devoid of cultural and class distinctions but with a limited governmental obligation toward the underprivileged. Socialism tended to "level everybody down rather than up" and would abandon the constitutional safeguards of a federal state.

Henry Cabot Lodge thought that Taft's proposal did not go far enough, and outlined his own ideas on establishing a liberal Republican alternative to Murray-Wagner-Dingell. His plan would "make a free distribution to the needy sick of certain medicines the value of which is proven and which are beyond the financial reach of many persons." Half the funds for state health plans would come from Washington in the Lodge bill, and the scope of the coverage would be greater than under the Taft proposal. Lodge directly linked his idea of a Republican approach to the economic realities of the American capitalist system, arguing that Republican opposition to administration measures was and should only be based on an economic rationale. "Our prime reliance," he argued, "for the well-being of the citizen must always rest on having a private-property economy. . . . But there are chinks which our private property economy does not always reach, and there are certain things which it is more convenient for us to have government do—and government, we hope, will under Republican guidance become an efficient tool to do whatever the people want it to do."[84] A number of Republicans, including conservatives like Styles Bridges (R-New Hampshire) and Frank Keefe (R-Wisconsin) attempted to demonstrate at least a limited acceptance of federal action in social policy by supporting a bipartisan proposal for federal research into heart disease.[85]

It is certainly possible to deny the effectiveness of this feverish legislative activity on social security and health reform; not one of the proposals was acted on in the 80th Congress. There were important economic and institutional reasons why changes in the status quo would be slow in coming. The administration and its supporters' commitment to the insurance principle left out precisely those people who needed state protection the most, while appealing to social security recipients who, although tied to the New Deal through pension and unemployment benefits, increasingly already possessed private health insurance. President Truman argued that in many ways the Murray-Wagner-Dingell plan was potentially far more suited to a free market economy than the Republican alternatives, as the insurance principle would mean the plan would be "far less costly and far more effective than public charity or a medical dole."[86] In fact, however, the development of a private welfare state in the field of health care ensured that federal activity in the 1960s would finally target those outside the reach of the private market: the indigent and retired elderly. Republicans, acting as front men for the AMA, saw the proposal not as insurance but as "the levying of a tax on all the people to bring four or five billion dollars into Washington," which would act as a crude income transfer to those who required health services the most.[87] The decision to take on the private medical community over who should control the financing of private health care provision provoked the enmity of a powerful political lobby jealous of its control over health care financing.

It was becoming clear, however, that the evolution of a political dialogue predicated on the Cold War at home and abroad was helping to embolden the campaign against federal health insurance at the same time as it was dampening the enthusiasm of its supporters. One factor behind a growing distrust of social welfare measures was the increasing importance in political debate of images of the far left as the Cold War got underway. John F. Kennedy made a speech at a Boston medical center in early 1949 in which he argued that there was a great danger of the "resignation of individuals' problems to the absorbing hands of the great Leviathan—the State. . . . The more tasks we choose to do . . . the weaker becomes the possibility that Government will be the master, we the servants." He was concerned that "government is knocking at the door of free medicine to move in and take over." In a draft speech which was, interestingly, not used in this form, Kennedy stated that there "are certain basic concepts fundamental to the American way of life. Our country, founded upon freedom, must remain forever free." He referred to "movements which creep and which at times slither. None of us wants to be cast in the role of a rugged reactionary. . . . And yet the cult of advanced liberalism serves as the goodly exterior for many things which are basically alien to the American way of life." Specifically, Kennedy mentioned "Marxism [which] in its promised distribution of wealth has served only to distribute poverty. There may be some among you who will be disappointed that I do not this evening launch into a specific discussion of health legislation. . . . I prefer to reserve my opinion until hearings are completed."[88] If a Democrat such as Kennedy could not endorse health legislation, equating federal insurance with the growth of an all-powerful state of Soviet hue, there was little hope for America to narrow the ideological gap with Sweden or Great Britain on domestic policy. Kennedy was an early subscriber to the anti-statist language shaping the health care debate, but he would later be joined, whether by conviction or by political prudence, by a significant number of other New Deal liberals.

The increasing reluctance of the Truman administration and its supporters to challenge the dominant anti-left political climate of the 80th Congress was reflected in more than just the rhetoric of individual politicians. Increasingly, proponents of Murray-Wagner-Dingell chose to frame their justification of federal health insurance in terms that explicitly disassociated the plan from other forms of state-sponsored health care. This development was due in part to the Republican victory in the 1946 elections, which had, according to Republican Senator H. Alexander Smith, shifted the "center of political gravity." Certainly it was the case that the *Journal of the American Medical Association*, which had devoted dozens of pages to congressional testimony on the bill during 1946, and which would again come to attach considerable importance to the issue on its editorial pages after the 1948 elections, gave federal health insurance little attention so long as Congress lay in the hands of the GOP.[89] If the administration's bill were to get anywhere in Congress, it would be important for its sponsors to make the legislation seem as unthreatening as possible.

The form that the defense of Murray-Wagner-Dingell took, however, did not simply rest on the tried and tested insurance principle of social security, but in fact was shaped by the assertion that without the administration's plan, the country would inevitably move further left. Liberal Republican Senator Wayne Morse, during Senate committee hearings on Murray-Wagner-Dingell in 1946, had argued that "we who call ourselves 'liberals' are constantly fighting for . . . legislation that sets up minimum economic and social standards that will protect our people as a whole and, in my judgment, protect the preservation of private property economy." Claude Pepper concurred, prompting congressional witness and AFL president William Green to agree that there was "nothing socialistic about" federal health insurance. Social Security administrator Arthur Altmeyer expressed frustration at the AMA's portrayal of the proposal as "regimentation and a form of totalitarianism which is not in keeping with the principles expressed in our Constitution and Bill of Rights." Altmeyer cast federal health insurance as resting firmly in an individualist American tradition: it "might be pointed out that voluntary insurance, as advocated by the American Medical Association, is anything but democratic," as it excluded millions of citizens from access to health care.[90] The debate remained relatively low-key until after the 1948 elections, and thus it was difficult to perceive the extent to which the increasingly antitotalitarian tone of the discussion of health insurance was heartfelt or represented a well-established pattern of rhetorical legerdemain needed to pass even the mildest form of statist policy in the United States. The political power of anti-leftism in a Cold War context in formulating a critique of the Fair Deal would become clearer when the attack on the Truman legislative program gained momentum after the surprise defeat of the GOP in 1948.

Already the Republican majority in the 80th Congress had begun investigating prominent social security bureaucrats in the administration in order to associate the New Deal order with totalitarianism. Representative James Harness (R-Indiana) chaired a House subcommittee investigating a visit to Japan by members of the Social Security Administration and the public health service to investigate health policy in occupied Japan. In a letter to fellow Republican John Taber (New York), Harness argued that the mission by Isidore Falk, Arthur Altmeyer, and other health insurance advocates in the government was dangerous: "The real purpose of the mission is not to assist Japan in working out her basic problems in health and welfare, but to force upon that country a compulsory system of socialized medicine."[91] According to one Texas doctor, New Dealers in the administration in favor of broadening state power were "all known to be advocates of socialized medicine and Communism."[92] To these correspondents, liberalism as defined by the New Deal was synonymous with Communism and the totalitarian state. It was not difficult to make the connection between the dominant message inherent in debates over foreign policy and the reaction in a domestic context.

Anti-statist opposition to health insurance was driven by the American Medical Association and other medical lobby groups, whose members quickly realized the potency of anti-statist imagery at a time of heightened international tensions, and who were quick to make such imagery the centerpiece of their propaganda and public relations campaign. An example of the public-private alliance against the state was Dr. Marjorie Shearon, one of the foremost propagandists in the country on questions of social security and health. She herself was not a medical doctor; she had obtained a PhD in biology from Columbia. She was a major lobbyist, however, on behalf of the AMA and individual doctors, as well as working from 1945 to 1947 for Senator Taft and the GOP policy committee, using her experience as a research analyst for the Social Security Board and other federal agencies in the 1930s. Every month from 1945 onward she gave public speeches against "socialized medicine," as well as sending out thousands of copies of her publication "American Medicine and the Political Scene" and corresponding regularly with Congressmen and lobbyists. The *New Republic* noted that Forrest Donnell had "asked his sharpest questions [on health insurance] from bits of paper passed him by a little woman who sat at his elbow."[93]

Shearon was not only an example of the growing power of anti-statist lobbies such as the AMA, but was also one of many adapting their critiques of state policy to incorporate the language of Cold War. In a speech in 1946 to a meeting of American physicians and surgeons in Chicago, Shearon outlined the development of the state in the 1930s, arguing that the New Deal was "characterized by the infiltration of socializers into the Federal Government." Federal employees like Isidore Falk were promoting a "super New Deal which would bestow universal security based on the principle of 'the greatest good for the greatest number—whether they wanted it or not'. . . . It is evident there now exists a well organized propaganda machine for promoting compulsory sickness insurance legislation. . . . All of Europe which adopted the Bismarckian social insurance laws has finally moved further and further toward the left." In a speech to a group of Republican women, Shearon argued that the "whole scheme is directed toward the furtherance of the Socialist state in the United States." Quoting Canadian Health Minister Ian Mackenzie in a 1943 speech, Shearon concluded that during "the early years of Hitler's regime, the government's medical program was looked upon by many as one of the greatest props of the totalitarian state."[94] Shearon made little attempt to differentiate adequately between socialism, communism, and fascism, or to make a real economic argument as to why such ideologies were unsound. She preferred to create an image of the secret state, filled with bureaucrats devoted to the undermining of American freedom and the introduction of totalitarianism into the United States.

Shearon was an important player in a vast campaign by medical interest groups to associate the state with the totalitarian imagery current since the late 1930s but greatly strengthened by the Cold War. An AMA leaflet containing a list of fifty questions on health insurance for the lay public was indicative of the trend. Question four asked, "Who is for compulsory health insurance?" and provided a list of groups, including President Truman, "all who seriously believe in a socialist state," "every left-wing organization in America," and, naturally, "the Communist Party." AMA chairman Elmer Henderson wrote to all members of Congress in May 1949 arguing that the medical lobby was "going directly to the people on this issue. . . . This is a grass roots campaign in the best American tradition."[95] The *Journal of the American Medical Association* referred to the establishment of the British National Health Service in July 1948 as "the greatest revolution in the practice of medicine that has ever occurred in the world." It was a revolution, however, that the AMA regarded as "the descent into an abyss. Medicine, like all the activities which have made England great, has for centuries progressed on an individualistic system; now it is placed on a socialistic one."[96]

There is direct evidence that the campaign was becoming effective; letters written against the proposals clearly used material contained in AMA and Shearon's propaganda, and Congress could not afford to ignore the growing anti-totalitarian trend. In any case, many in Congress, such as Kennedy and Senator Tom Connally (D-Texas), ranking member of the Senate Foreign Relations Committee, did not wish to ignore it; as bipartisan anti-communists, they could further their own foreign policy agenda by attacking domestic policies seen to be at odds with their anti-Soviet stance. This would assume particular importance when the American Medical Association decided at its House of Delegates meeting in St Louis after the 1948 election to begin amassing a propaganda war chest from a new membership subscription with which to fight the Truman administration and its entire Fair Deal program.

The extension of the anti-statism of the Cold War to domestic legislation applied equally to federal measures to solve the housing crisis or to provide federal aid to education. Again Senator Taft was a prime force behind such proposals, and yet faced criticism from interested lobbies based on theories of socialism and the state. A representative of the building trade wrote to Taft stating he found it difficult to reconcile the Taft-Ellender-Wagner housing bill with "so violent opposition to the so-called National Health legislation. . . . It is difficult . . . to detect a great deal of difference in the socialization of medicine and the socialization of housing."[97] Taft was convinced that opposition to his bill to provide for public housing construction and slum clearance was "utterly and completely unfair and unreasonable," but he was failing to realize the changing nature of opposition to statist projects.[98] There were no fair and reasonable ways of disputing that there were 307,568 unhoused families in Los Angeles alone in June 1947, together with 370,000 in substandard dwellings.[99]

Nevertheless, Herbert Nelson, executive Vice President of the National Association of Real Estate Boards, condemned Taft for seeming to abandon Republican principles. "Businessmen hate the stifling and negative ways of socialism and will tolerate no compromise with it. Senator Taft will never convince them that socializing part of our economy is not socialism. They know that socialism always takes over little by little, never in an overnight move. . . . Advocates of a collectivist economy have no single tool so potent in winning support for their objectives as Senator Taft's name." Specifically dismissing economic arguments against public housing as irrelevant, Nelson argued that even "if the bureaucratic road to production would work, it would cost more in human self-respect than it is worth. . . . Its inability to work is steadily lowering living standards in England, as it has done in Russia."[100] A 1946 cartoon by the same organization showed Taft-Ellender-Wagner as a Trojan horse, crushing private enterprise while providing safe passage for a horde of state employees and leaving the GI behind.[101] Images of the totalitarian state seemed to be proving effective in the late 1940s in domestic as well as foreign affairs; Taft's bill, like that providing federal aid to education, stalled in the House and America had to wait until 1949 before an emaciated public housing bill became law.

The Domestic Cold War 1947–1948

It was ironic that the decision on the part of the Truman administration to attempt to control the debate over political subversion in the United States would enlarge the boundaries of federal activity at the same time as it limited the social democratic possibilities of postwar liberalism. Since at least the mid-1930s Rooseveltian liberalism had included an international dimension based on broad principles of multilateralism. At the same time, the war had demonstrated the need for the administration to deal firmly with the threat of espionage. It is therefore unsurprising that a number of historians have highlighted the Truman administration's desire to use the anti-communist issue in 1947 both to affirm its anti-totalitarian credentials in the face of a resurgent Republican party and to construct a case for building a new international order based on American economic and military power.[102]

The growing importance of the anti-communist issue in American politics served to convince politicians wary of an expanded state that the growth of a federal bureaucracy to combat both internal subversion and totalitarianism abroad was not a development to be emphatically resisted. Clearly Truman's appointment of a Temporary Commission on Employee Loyalty in November 1946 was timed to take some of the sting from the tail of the 1946 election results, and his request in March for a Loyalty Board for the screening of federal employees, together with a package of an extra $24.9 million for the expanded Civil Service Commission and the FBI, served to prime Congress and the American public for the assumption of considerable peacetime overseas responsibilities, initially in the form of aid to Greece and Turkey.[103] In addition, the revelations in the *Amerasia* case and the Canadian spy ring had brought the question of espionage to center stage. "I believe I speak for all the people of the United States," said the President in a statement on the progress of the Loyalty Board in November 1947, "when I say that disloyal and subversive elements must be removed from the employ of the Government." He went on to warn against allowing "employees of the Federal Government to be labeled as disloyal when no valid basis exists for arriving at such a conclusion."[104]

The foundations of Cold War liberalism were completed with the establishment of the Central Intelligence Agency and the National Security apparatus to use American state power to combat the geopolitical expansion of unfriendly states overseas. Although many Republicans remained wary of enlarging state capacity for national security purposes, it was a policy far more easily sold on Capitol Hill than most of Truman's domestic program, and would soon help form a bipartisan alliance of Cold Warriors pulling the Truman administration toward the use of state power for perceived anti-totalitarian ends.[105]

Despite the Justice Department's apparent willingness to cooperate with HUAC to expose key Communists in the United States and to stir up a political atmosphere conducive to the enactment of the administration's foreign policy, the administration did seem to lose control of the communist issue by the end of the decade.[106] However, the development of a political program that fused foreign policy with a domestic agenda emboldened and strengthened anti-communist elements within the liberal movement at the same time as it downgraded their domestic goals. Hubert Humphrey, then Mayor of Minneapolis and according to James Loeb "one of the most promising political figures in the country," was a key figure in the development of Americans for Democratic Action as a sort of political party faction in his native Minnesota, mounting a successful challenge to left-wing control of the Democrat–Farmer-Labor Party in the state. The question of foreign policy was the sole rationale behind the intraparty warfare that broke out in 1947, and provided ADA activists with a cause that greatly strengthened their political muscle in states like Minnesota at a time of mounting international tension.

"The DFL party at the present time is in the control of an undemocratic reactionary group," stated an ADA report on the political situation in Minnesota in 1948, "who in their principles and ideologies represent less than one percent of the people of Minnesota." The report urged that ADA provide "intelligent democratic progressive leadership" to challenge the Wallaceite regulars. Hubert Humphrey provided an explanation of the difference between the "principles and ideologies" of the two factions after being nominated as the DFL's candidate for the Senate in April. The leaders of the DFL old guard, he argued "criticize every aspect of American foreign policy. But they remain strangely silent about the aggressive acts of Russian policy. . . . We too believe in the century of the common man. But we are not prepared to see the century of the common man become the century of the Comintern." ADA supporters, in contrast to those in the DFL promoting "the appeasement of the imperialist aims of international communism," were "neither right nor left. They believe in a militant and vigorous democratic program of the middle" that would consist of "a program of political freedom for ourselves and other people."[107] It was difficult to ascertain how the rival factions within the DFL differed on anything but the question of communism and the Soviet Union, and the increasingly bitter organizational struggle within the party made up in rhetorical fervor what it lacked in ideological specificity.

Although the end result of the internecine battle within the Democratic Party was to weaken the foundations of American liberalism by releasing from the political bottle an anti-communist genie the party could not control, the struggle also had the effect of mobilizing an increasingly politically confident Americans for Democratic Action, whose members downplayed their earlier popular front flirtations with economic planning in favor of an emphasis on their role as anti-communists. "Minnesota ADA has chalked up another political victory," announced the leader of the state's ADA chapter in a report to the national headquarters in Washington in the wake of the DFL party caucuses in April 1948. "On Friday night April 30th, the right wing forces overwhelmed the Wallaceites, commies and other left-wingers." The report noted the dramatic defeats of the far left in county caucuses across the state: in Minneapolis, St. Paul, and Duluth "the great majority of the delegates are labor people, ADA and SDA members and others who have publicly identified themselves with the liberal and progressive movement." It is difficult to pin down the precise meaning of these terms, but one can discern the political program of the ADA group: to eliminate the Henry Wallace faction in the Democratic Party. "The DFL Party in Minnesota has been returned to the progressive citizens who intend to make it the base for a decent, progressive movement and not a sounding board for the foreign policy of the Soviet Union," argued a representative of the local ADA. "ADA has had a striking opportunity to prove the effectiveness of a program of direct political action. What is more, ADA, which can have real influence on a campaign and on a party structure, has unique opportunity in Minnesota to set a pattern for a widespread program of progressivism in politics."[108]

It is true that the vigorous ADA campaign against the hard left in Minnesota and elsewhere revitalized a liberal movement that had been drifting into despair at the beginning of the year over the alleged mediocrity of the President. Despite Michigan Students for Democratic Action member Bob Greene's description of much of the state's Democratic State Convention as "a serio-comic tragedy" during which "the CIO-ADA was kept at arm's length by the regulars," liberal ADA member G. Mennen Williams gained the party's gubernatorial nomination and led his party to a significant victory in the November elections.[109] It is possible, however, to overstate the ideological and political significance of the Democratic resurgence in 1948, given the increasing attention paid to internal security and anti-communism at the expense of an explicit social democratic program, and given the fact that the rejuvenation of New Deal liberalism in the form of the Fair Deal mobilized anti-statist interests with greater political and financial resources than ADA or the Committee for the Nation's Health. Still, the establishment of the national security state in the form of loyalty boards and security apparatus seemed in 1948 to have neutered the Republican resurgence and provided the liberal movement with some much needed confidence and a political program of anti-totalitarianism that legitimized American liberalism in an age of plenty.

The domestic political context of Cold War America made it increasingly difficult for even the most moderate liberal administration to keep control of the internal subversive issue. In 1947 there were yet more exposures of Communists in labor unions, including the Allis-Chalmers crisis and the more general splits within the CIO over Communist Party membership. It was a time in which the interestingly named House Un-American Activities Committee would become a permanent standing committee and would increase its efforts to associate the welfare state with totalitarianism. In 1948 Alger Hiss was unmasked as an alleged agent of the Soviet Union. All these developments stood in the context of the drive for expanded social legislation and the American move into a more active foreign policy role. The growth of anti-communism at home must be set in this context, and must partly explain the derailment of the nascent social democratic impulse in American politics.[110]

Referring to HUAC's treatment of alleged spy Harry Dexter White in 1947, Congressman Emmanuel Celler in a radio broadcast bitterly condemned the nature of the committee's activities, which he claimed had contributed to White's death shortly after his testimony. Congressman John Rankin of Mississippi, whom Celler referred to as "an arch-pretender to white Protestant supremacy, a self-accused Jew baiter," had spoken "of shooting those named as Communists before the committee. Not a member of the committee remonstrated." Celler argued that the committee "attempts to indict or convict on hearsay and incompetent evidence. It seeks to enquire into consciences. It would fashion the American mind into a common mould. All must conform to the political views of the members of the committee. Otherwise, they are subject to this grinding inquest." It was sheer lunacy, argued Celler, to assert treason by using cases from the pre-1945 period when the USSR was an ally: "Russia got all the information she needed simply by asking [the government] for it."[111]

The list of people and organizations under investigation in the 1940s demonstrates the way charges of un-Americanism were employed in defense of the status quo and existing privileged interests. One such case was the Southern Conference for Human Welfare, membership of which included Harold Ickes, Henry Wallace, Joseph Davies, and Frank Graham, all liberals dedicated to the overturning of the social order in the South. The Birmingham *News-Age-Herald* in June 1947 analyzed the committee's attack on the group, commenting on "the slur on liberalism. Note the argument of evil association. . . . It is an old weapon of entrenched prejudice. . . . It is strictly un-American." Ickes wrote to HUAC chairman J. Parnell Thomas (R-New Jersey) the same month, condemning the attacks made on the Conference without a hearing. Ickes had spoken before the Conference in 1946 on the poll tax, "which I take it your committee favors since you have never condemned this particularly un-American activity [but] apparently you do take exception to my having declared against it on a platform that was particularly useful for that purpose." He concluded that he hoped that "one day you and your associates will devote your unique talents to a contemplation of the Fascist theme in America. As I see it, Fascism is our greatest domestic menace."[112]

The proposal in the House in 1948 by Republicans Karl Mundt (South Dakota) and Richard Nixon for a "subversive Activities Control Bill" further highlighted the link between anti-liberalism and anti-communism. The bill ostensibly aimed to prohibit the incitement of revolution or the promulgation of the aims of a foreign power in America, and forced all Communists to register with the Attorney General. Nixon argued that far from "injuring true liberal and progressive movements, the enactment and enforcement of this bill will be an outstanding contribution to such causes in the United States. Every liberal cause which the Communists touch is irreparably damaged by them."[113] Emmanuel Celler disagreed. The legislation would encourage "a Procrustean bed of conformity . . . dictated in the narrow minds . . . of the Un-American Activities Committee." Celler demonstrated how supporters of the British Labour Party could be cited under the Act for supporting the aims of a foreign government.[114]

The statements of J. Edgar Hoover on communism bear out Celler's fears. Declaring that America must stop the Communists from "carrying out their diabolical plot to wreck the American way of life," he included under the subversive umbrella "satellites, their fellow-travelers, and their so-called progressive and phony liberal allies." Under this criterion, half of the New Deal administration would be Communists. Hoover's testimony to HUAC included an FBI report defining Communism as including those who expressed hatred of God, proposed destruction of private property, or advocated "absolute social and racial equality." Questions posed to suspects by HUAC members included issues of atheism and "opposition to our republican form of government."[115] The broad political right was actively seeking to discredit movements for social change through the ideology of Cold War.

The enormous danger for liberalism and the future of the left in America lay in the fact that the social democratic strain of American liberalism emerged from the same ideological mainspring as theoretical communism, in terms of the view of society and the individual's place within the community. As liberal Democrats became more concerned with joining the anti-Communist bandwagon, so their own ideology would be undermined. It was no accident that Joseph Davies had been seduced by Soviet achievements during his time as ambassador to Moscow during the depression, or that Henry Wallace flirted with the notion of a popular front containing communists in the late 1940s. Davies claimed that although he disapproved of the Soviet system, he believed that the two systems were similar in that Americans, too, "were trying to bring about greater distribution of wealth and greater equality of opportunity, economically and socially, for the underprivileged."[116]

American Communist Eugene Dennis in 1945 gave a speech that could have been made by any liberal. He argued that John Rankin "would like to rid our country, not only of Communists, but also of Jews and Negroes, and, of course, of trade unionists," who could all find support from CPUSA principles.[117] Helen Gahagan Douglas in her Democratic Credo speech argued that when "Lenin with the philosophy of Marx and Engels arrived in Petrograd in the midst of a revolt against the czars and the war, there was small wonder that the Russian people followed him who promised bread and freedom. In other words, communism was born out of hunger, slavery, illiteracy, superstition, degradation." So, argued Douglas, was the democratic left in the twentieth century, and the test would be to see which could best achieve "the welfare and security of the people."[118]

Joe Wayne of Los Angeles saw the dangers in the anti-communist crusade in a letter to Harold Ickes after the latter had condemned communism. "There surely must be some little bit of [communist theory] that could be accepted if one is a liberal. . . . " Ickes responded that since communism was totalitarian, the two approaches were "irreconcilable. . . . Perhaps, as a matter of pure theory, a communist could be a liberal . . . but practically, it does not work out that way."[119] Ickes was careful, however, to distinguish the opposition of democratic liberalism to communism from the espousal of an anti-left agenda. In an article in September 1947 he reiterated Helen Douglas' point that the "only way to fight communism effectively is to improve the economic and social conditions that stimulate its growth," a far cry from the definition of anti-communism made by John Rankin or Karl Mundt.[120]

Increasingly, however, liberals were joining the crusade against "subversion" at home. Emmanuel Celler, for example, attacked Karl Mundt's definition of un-Americanism on the House floor and in a radio debate on the future of HUAC, but he did not argue that the committee should be disbanded. Only 12 members of Congress would vote against the financing of the committee in 1950; among them were 10 Democrats, plus Marcantonio (ALP-New York), and Javits (R-New York). The Chairman of Marcantonio's party, David Zeldin, condemned Celler in early 1947 for "red-baiting . . . that did the cause of all liberals and progressives a distinct disservice." At a Brooklyn Progressive conference Celler had "attacked progressive and liberal groups that sought a common front with Communists on certain limited objectives." Celler denied the charge, but defended HUAC and his own condemnation of communists.[121] Celler and most other liberal Democrats faced the difficult dilemma of defending the advance of certain principles of social justice while joining hands with their ideological political enemies, the southern Democrats and Republicans. It would be in the arena of foreign affairs that this alliance would be particularly effective in stifling the advance of liberalism.

3. IDEOLOGICAL INTERPRETATIONS OF FOREIGN POLICY 1947–1948

THE DEVELOPMENT OF AN ANTI-COMMUNIST FOREIGN policy in the United States in the years following the Second World War changed the American political landscape in ways that both empowered and aggrandized the New Deal state apparatus and at the same time strengthened an anti-statist ideological impetus. The historiography of the rise of a Rooseveltian vision of a new American world order from the ashes of conflict, to be gradually eroded by the increasing suspicion of the Soviet Union in Washington and the consequent development of a national security state and a policy of "containment" of the USSR, is voluminous and well known.[1] Less well understood is the way in which proponents of international anti-communism instinctively came to distrust and marginalize a social democratic politics of the left that seemed redundant in the new climate of state building through foreign and defense spending and also had dubious associations with critics of the administration's foreign policy program. The implementation of a Cold War strategy by the "bipartisan" coalition of the Truman administration and its supporters in both parties would encourage by early 1949 a discrediting of alternatives to its anti-Soviet policy on both left and right. Left-wing critics of the administration in the Democratic Party would seal their political fates in the foreign policy debates of this period; Republican anti-statists would lose the battle over significant federal expenditures on foreign affairs but would appropriate the rhetoric of anti-totalitarianism to stage a political comeback at the end of the decade. In the process liberalism and the right would be transformed, and the possibility of increased public support for state projects at home and for friendly left-of-center governments abroad would be significantly weakened.

Four Ideological Approaches to Foreign Policy

Political ideology was central to the formation of responses to events abroad in the early Cold War. It is possible to delineate four broad approaches in this period, and to see the rise of opposition to socialism in terms of which viewpoint would gain most public support during the Truman years. The first approach may be termed the internationalist worldview favored by most in the Truman administration and its supporters in Congress; the second was the preserve of the still significant anti-statist bloc in Congress wary of an enlarged governmental apparatus but pliable on the question of combating world communism; the third was a dwindling but still extant strain of isolationism; the fourth was personified by unashamedly leftist popular frontists like Henry Wallace. Before analyzing specific policy developments in this period and their effects on domestic politics, it is useful to lay out the different political attitudes toward foreign policy after the war, and to assess their relative significance in gaining an understanding of the impact of foreign affairs on the decline of a domestic program of the left in the Truman years.

In many ways the creation of a global political strategy at the highest levels in the Roosevelt and Truman administrations after 1943 defined the terms of state building in the United States for a generation, and renders moot any assertion that the place of the state in the American political economy declined after the war. Nevertheless it is certainly the case that the political priorities of American liberals and planners changed as a result of the globalization of the administration's agenda. A new generation of officials in the State Department and other federal agencies who had cut their political teeth on their country's wartime experience worked assiduously after 1945 to tie a New Deal economic agenda at home to the creation of a world economic system under U.S. control. A carefully calibrated world economy would help to dampen the fires of radical upheaval around the world and prevent the potentially bellicose Soviet Union from assimilating more territory into its sphere of influence. Prominent advisers such as George Kennan, Clark Clifford, George Elsey, Joseph Grew, James Forrestal, Averell Harriman, and Robert Patterson, who all had built up extensive *curricula vitae* in the U.S. foreign service by the end of the war, were architects of a foreign policy that started life as a vision of a world made prosperous under the tutelage of American power and dollars, and which developed into a policy dedicated to the organization of friendly states into an anti-Soviet bloc.[2]

The nature of this policy as set out by a State Department memo in mid-1947 underlined a U.S. commitment to an interdependent world based on American liberal principles of trade and the rehabilitation of war-torn infrastructures, while it demonstrated a growing impatience among State Department officials at the unwillingness of the Soviet government to share American perceptions of the world situation. "The United States believes that its own security, its prosperity, the liberties of its citizens and the survival of their free institutions are intimately related to the survival of the free institutions, individual liberties, and effective national independence of other peoples," asserted the State Department memorandum.[3] The policy, which received wide support in Congress and apparently among the American public, stressed the importance of protecting "national independence" from Soviet aggression, and that countries "able and willing" to oppose Soviet designs on the world would receive substantial American aid. This represented the logical development of the American perspective inherent in the Dumbarton Oaks and Bretton Woods agreements of 1944 and 1945, insofar as the U.S. government wished to reshape the world and sweep away the economic and political blocs that were seen as having helped cause the world conflagration and had worsened the economic crisis of the 1930s. Many saw this policy as an appropriate response to the events in Europe since 1945, when the USSR had betrayed its commitments in the international agreements made at Teheran, Yalta, and Potsdam and had effectively taken control of most of Eastern Europe. In addition, liberal internationalism fitted perfectly into a grand vision for postwar economic growth in the United States through flexible trade and fiscal policies, a policy enthusiastically endorsed in Truman's Council of Economic Advisers.[4]

As early as October 1945 a report by four members of a House Foreign Affairs Subcommittee on a visit to Russia, while stating that U.S.-Soviet relations had not been irreparably damaged, urged "the immediate abandonment of any semblance of appeasement in our own negotiations and relations with Russia."[5] Francis Wilcox, who would become the first chief of staff of the Senate Foreign Relations Committee in 1947, had the year previously helped to compose a memo attacking Soviet foreign policy aims in a tone similar to that of other administration figures like George Kennan and Clark Clifford. It outlined "the nature of Soviet Communism and what we might expect from the Soviet Union in our negotiations with them over the years. We had to understand the kind of opposition we were running into."[6] In effect the idea that the Soviet Union was an aggressive nation and the United States had a responsibility to protect noncommunist states through economic and military aid united many in Congress with the bureaucracy of the federal government. It was a powerful view, or "bipartisan," because it had the full weight of the administration behind it, as well as congressional heavyweights like Arthur Vandenberg and Henry Cabot Lodge, and the media. Republican Senator Irving Ives of New York argued that if his party did not support the administration's program of aid to Europe, "all of Europe, and perhaps the British Isles, is apt to go Communistic within a relatively short time without outside aid. . . . [with] all of Asia and presumably all of Africa; leaving us almost entirely alone."[7] The capacity of the Cold War internationalist perspective to combine a New Deal-style commitment to economic restructuring with an antipathy toward the far left and totalitarianism would help to create a wide acceptance of the policy of containment across the political spectrum, with important consequences for the future scope of ideological debate in postwar America. The internationalist view saw the expansion of Soviet power as deeply inimical to American world interests, and viewed American military and economic support for the non-Soviet world as being of primary importance.

A political commitment to an anti-communist foreign policy was not simply a matter of party politics, which remained a turbulent arena of opportunistic and rhetorical controversy and dissent even as actual opposition to the administration's global agenda dwindled amid the bluster. Cold War liberalism united State Department officials, the administration, congressional liberals, Americans for Democratic Action, and an increasingly significant slice of organized labor in a coalition aimed at promoting the idea of a "Pax Americana" as a way of rescuing the New Deal legacy after the political mauling it had suffered in 1946. Dating the shift in liberal priorities away from domestic affairs is difficult, as ADA liberals made frequent references to both domestic and foreign affairs, but we have already seen how foreign affairs were far from preeminent in the minds of UDA activists before the 1946 elections. The key shift seems to have taken place during the debate over aid to Greece and Turkey. Wilson Wyatt, the national chairman of the ADA, used a speech to the membership in April 1947 to promote the establishment of American strategic power as a force for liberal democracy at home and abroad as an effective call to arms for a listless liberal movement. "Tonight I speak for a new movement of American liberals," he said with patent enthusiasm. He then noted that this movement was "only new in the sense that American liberals have at last established their own organization, free of totalitarian influence and dedicated to the basic American faith in reason, justice and the dignity of the individual."

So the test for the adherents to the spirit of Roosevelt was where they stood after the collapse of the popular front with the formation of the rival ADA and PCA at the end of 1946. For those who chose the ADA route, their "essential purpose," according to Wyatt, was "the protection of international security. . . . The world must act today to ensure the security of nations in the eastern end of the Mediterranean." If Wyatt conceded that he considered domestic issues "equally important," it was in the context of America as "the champion of democratic principles in the world," and thus a nation that "must eradicate the imperfections and intolerances of its own society. ADA is pledged to make America the world symbol of progressive democracy."[8] The ADA leadership fully supported the administration in professing to aim to "combat totalitarianism by striking boldly at the conditions of hunger, want, and insecurity which breed desperate political situations."[9] This vision of a world order based on liberal ideals of social justice and democracy fitted in reasonably well with the administration's growing commitment to creating an anti-Soviet alliance of friendly states, and helped to cement the internationalist consensus driving American policymaking in 1947.

The membership in the internationalist coalition of organs like ADA and the AFL and CIO was important to the growing power of Cold War liberalism in American politics, as these groups would be in part responsible for recruiting internationalist liberals such as Hubert Humphrey, Paul Douglas, and Estes Kefauver to the Senate in 1948 to help shore up support for Truman's foreign policy in Congress. The AFL's newsletter to members, *Labor's Monthly Survey*, devoted its March 1948 issue to declaring the leadership's support for the Marshall Plan and opposition to "soviet aggression in Europe." The editorial stance of the AFL bulletin tied together the Roosevelt-era vision of a new world order through the United Nations with a new commitment to oppose Soviet totalitarianism:

"American workers want an answer to this question: Are the principles of the United Nations to be upheld? To depart from these principles is to step back into the dark ages and permit dictators who ignore law and justice to extend their rule by force and crush out freely elected governments responsible to the people." The newsletter argued that the "free trade union movements of Europe are the only agencies which can liberate the workers from this communist captivity. Today they are showing the workers the falsity of communist propaganda against USA, explaining the Marshall Plan to them, showing them the way forward, reviving their hope, giving them free unions of their own through which they can participate constructively in the task of restoring economic life and rebuilding democracy in Europe."

The AFL leadership saw in Cold War liberalism a convenient way of providing much-needed legitimacy for organized labor in the face of a concerted attack on its privileges from the American right. A vibrant international union movement was portrayed as not only a sure bulwark against the spread of communist influence in Europe, but also a necessary corollary to a properly functioning capitalist system: "Managements who would hamstring free unions," claimed the AFL's *Monthly Survey* in a clear reference to the Taft-Hartley Act, "are playing into the hands of those who would destroy private enterprise. It seems incredible that business men do not realize that Hitler, Mussolini and Stalin got control of industries by first liquidating free trade unions and regimenting labor."[10] With the CIO, under the leadership of Philip Murray, also increasingly coming round to this way of thinking, the combination of labor's concerted opposition to a red tide abroad and business reaction at home seemed a winning strategy in the run up to the crucial 1948 elections.[11]

The powerful forces arrayed behind the Truman administration's unfolding strategic synthesis in foreign affairs presented the Republican opposition in Congress with both a dilemma and an opportunity. On the one hand, the framing of measures such as the Truman Doctrine made it difficult for rightists with impeccable anti-communist credentials to resist administration demands for swollen defense and foreign spending programs despite their commitment to reduce the size and power of the state. On the other hand, the increasingly anti-leftist tone of the administration and supporters in groups like the ADA helped to shift the center of political gravity sharply rightward, leaving the liberal movement fractious and divided just as the Republican Party was using the euphoric atmosphere of the successful 1946 election campaign to paper over the equally palpable fissures among its own variegated constituency. One result was the development of a critique of the Truman foreign policy based on the association of internationalism with the growth of state power at home. Many on the right adhered to this view in Congress and in the country at large, arguing that if America was serious about meeting the Communist threat, it had to ensure it was exporting "American" principles of free enterprise, and also that American government was not substantially enlarged.[12] Some Republicans in this camp were prepared to support the administration's foreign policy on crucial votes while continuing to rail against profligate spending programs and a perceived lack of commitment among administration officials to the combating of communists at home; others were implacably opposed to the administration's policy under any circumstances, hoping to associate Cold War liberalism with the enactment of a massive redistribution of American resources around the world. This view seemed to be at odds with the administration's policy that there was considerable room for maneuver in domestic policy as long as international goals were being maintained. In fact, however, both groups associated the state with extremism in their rhetoric and were growing closer together as the decade progressed.

The anti-statist group consisted of some twenty Republicans in the Senate and a large number in the House, and included Senators Wayland Brooks (R-Illinois), Homer Capehart (R-Indiana), John Bricker (Ohio), and Congressmen John Taber (R-New York), Charles Halleck (R-Indiana) and Ralph Gwinn (R-New York). The political profiles of these figures ranged from traditional Midwestern isolationist conservatives to the group of northeastern conservatives who had formed the bedrock of right-wing Republicanism during the wilderness years of the 1930s.[13]

To conservative Republicans, the 1946 midterm election victory offered an opportunity to wrest the political initiative away from the administration, and so the last thing they wanted was to become enmeshed in the president's foreign policy agenda. When Robert Taft gingerly suggested in October 1947 to the House Ways and Means Chairman, Harold Knutson, that it might be possible to support the Marshall Plan while still managing to cut taxes and scale back the national debt, Knutson's reply was categorical in its frustration at the GOP caucus's inability to take control of the political agenda: "Bob, I continue to cling to the belief that our people are becoming fed up with all these foreign entanglements. Even some of our biggest businessmen are turning isolationist. . . . People with whom I have talked are disgusted with Truman for permitting the dismantling of German plants at the very time he is asking Congress for huge appropriations to rehabilitate that country. . . . By all means, let us stick to our demand that the American people be given more consideration in the future than in the past. We have promised them tax reduction and we must go through with it."[14]

Other Republican doubters, like Taft, were becoming increasingly convinced that the administration was successfully selling its foreign policy to a Republican Party concerned about the power of Soviet Communism. Responding to a strongly worded attack on internationalism from a professor in Texas, Taft argued that he agreed that Truman's foreign policy was flawed, but that as a senior figure in the Senate he did "not desire to promote a major split in the Republican Party." In a letter to former New York Mayor Fiorello LaGuardia he noted that "I don't like this Greek-Turkish proposition, but I do recognize that perhaps we had better maintain the status quo until we can reach some peace settlement with Russia. I don't like to appear to be backing down."[15]

The administration's commitment to opposing the spread of Soviet influence after 1947 posed serious dilemmas for a Republican Party keen to appropriate the anti-totalitarian mantle but wary of committing itself to supporting an administration that seemingly was teetering on the edge of political defeat in the forthcoming elections. Already some Republican anti-statists were discovering that an easy way out was to criticize the administration for not applying the Truman Doctrine elsewhere in the world, and especially in Asia, confident that they would not be called upon to match their rhetoric with cash at a time when the United States was scaling back its support for the Kuomintang in China and its military presence in Korea. In what seemed to be a purely opportunistic letter to America's principal lobbyist for the Kuomintang, Alfred Kohlberg, on the very day Truman announced his plan to assist Greece and Turkey, Robert Taft agreed "that the Greek proposal is entirely inconsistent with the policy in China. If we are going to combat Russian influence, we ought to do it everywhere."[16]

Freshman Congressman Richard Nixon used a similar rhetorical sleight of hand in his regular broadcast to his constituents in California in the wake of President Truman's landmark speech on Greece and Turkey. "I think it essential," he argued, "that a clear cut policy with respect to our resistance to Communism at home and abroad be enunciated by the administration. . . . It seems obvious that our present attitude represents a complete change of policy when we consider all we have overlooked in Romania, Bulgaria, Hungary and the Baltic states. . . . What is the difference between the spread of Communism in China and Red influences in the eastern Mediterranean?" He then tied a domestic political marker to his rhetorical trial balloon on the question of combating world communism, wondering whether the administration was "going to make the same mistake we did in China by sending pinks and fellow-travelers to fight Communism and sabotage our announced program? And, if we are going to attempt to combat Communism in Greece and Turkey, should we not also clean house here at home and remove Communists and fellow-travelers from positions of power in our governmental departments and labor unions?"[17] The bellicose language of the administration on the subject of world communism allowed Republicans like Nixon to import the issue of anti-communism into domestic political debates and call into question the place of the New Deal in postwar politics.

Just as in the case of the internationalist coalition, the anti-statist bloc consisted of a diverse group of political forces whose common agenda masked complex undercurrents of ambiguity and discord. As well as congressional conservatives the anti-administration forces included part of the private business community worried about an expanded state sector and determined to ensure that the construction of a national security apparatus would rely heavily on the private sector. As with domestic policy, however, economic criticisms of the administration's program masked an ambitious anti-statist drive to roll back not just communism abroad, but the New Deal state at home. The group included Herbert Hoover, for example, who argued that aid to Western Europe should consist only of the bare essentials made through private channels. It also included Merwin K. Hart, President of the National Economic Council, who argued before the Senate Foreign Relations Committee that the Marshall Plan was designed "to encourage Socialism, if not Communism, in various countries in Europe." Hart associated the Marshall Plan with "the socialistic policy that seems to have possessed our Administration to a greater or lesser extent for nearly fifteen years. . . . We have a New Deal policy which with slight modifications has been assented to by the Republican Party or by some of its leaders."[18]

Again, Hart's rhetorical bluster, although hardly uncommon in congressional testimony, political debate, and general correspondence on American foreign policy in this period, did not carry the day in deciding the fate of measures like the Marshall Plan. Nevertheless, the late 1940s did see the development of an assertive anti-statist foreign policy agenda that helped to define the ideological parameters of the national security debate. Some Republicans, for example, wished to act on Hart's desire to include Franco's Spain in the Marshall Plan because of its sound anti-communist credentials, and managed to attach such a provision to the House version of the European Recovery bill before seeing it erased in conference.[19] "If we are really serious about checking the menace of communism," argued Senator George Malone of Nevada in a speech to the Colorado Mining Congress in early 1948, "it seems harder to explain why we treat like a step-child the one nation that has successfully resisted communism from the beginning, even though it meant fighting a bitter civil war. Franco of Spain took on all comers from the communist camps and maintained the integrity of Spain. Our people say that we cannot support his type of government because we do not believe in it. This sounds very weak on our part since we do not believe in any of the European forms of government, including England's, yet we have been and are supporting them."[20]

Right-wing politicians, together with industrialists like Robert Wood and H. L. Hunt, wanted to roll back the state in the United States, and were also prepared to use the rhetoric of anti-statism in foreign policy, so as to bring about the end of liberal dominance in U.S. politics. In so doing they would make common cause with other regimes of the right, a tactic that would see its most obvious application later in the decade in China and Korea.[21] Debates over foreign policy would revolve around questions of state power and domestic ideology in the early Cold War, and would contribute to the reassertion of anti-liberal sentiment.

There was some overlap between the attitudes of anti-statists to foreign policy and those of isolationists who had played such an important role in the policy debates in the interwar period. What is important to note here is that isolationism had served as an important brake on the more ambitious plans of State Department officials and internationalist politicians before 1941, and that its diminishing political importance in the Cold War era would have significant repercussions for the future of domestic political strategies. The bond uniting old guard Republicans like Taft, Representative George Bender of Ohio, and George Malone of Nevada with perennial Socialist presidential aspirant Norman Thomas and American Labor Party representative Vito Marcantonio was hardly ideologically consistent, and in some cases was motivated by political considerations unrelated to the foreign policy debate at hand. Marcantonio, for instance, was motivated in his opposition to initiatives like the Marshall Plan because of his continued support for a popular front alliance with Soviet Communism; Republicans, by contrast, were fearful of a powerful state and ever-expanding foreign affairs expenditures. Nevertheless, it is useful to note a certain remnant of isolationist morality in American politics in the late 1940s, and its increasingly marginalized status as the Cold War developed.[22]

The common thread linking these diverse characters, other than a shared commitment to resist incorporation into the bipartisan coalition, was a conviction that the prioritizing of an anti-Soviet foreign policy was allying America with foreign governments committed to political worldviews inimical to American beliefs and interests. As had been true of anti-interventionist sentiment historically, such views could be of the left or the right, and did not mean that opponents of aspects of the administration's agenda opposed an assertive foreign policy in any form. Norman Thomas, for example, was a strong supporter of some sort of Marshall Plan, but opposed the draft and aid to dictatorships in Latin America and southern Europe. Well-known New Deal liberals like Harold Ickes and Helen Douglas balked at supporting the Truman Doctrine because of the less than impeccable democratic credentials of the governments in those countries, but supported United Nations arbitration in the Greek civil war. Radical forces in these countries, wrote Douglas, "had a right, even if some of them were communists, to establish a less autocratic government than they had known in the past."[23] Whether for reasons of political opportunism or genuine conviction, Republicans like Taft also used antipathy toward the totalitarian right to advance their anti-interventionist agenda. Taft asserted that the "American people do not want to become imperialists. They do not want a force prepared to attack every other nation in the world."[24] George Bender argued that the "whole Truman policy is one of military aggression pure and simple and cannot but create more conflict rather than less."[25] He added that the United States had to accommodate "large hunks of the world which have adopted some type of economy other than ours."[26]

In addition, as we have seen, the American government's support for apparently left-wing governments overseas came to form a principal strand of the right's broader critique of the Truman administration and American liberalism. A group of western and Midwestern Republicans in the Senate, headed by Taft and consisting of figures such as Finance Committee Chairman Eugene Millikin, Majority Leader Kenneth Wherry, George Malone, Homer Capehart of Indiana, and Wayland Brooks of Illinois, differed over the exact scale and scope of any desired repeal of the New Deal, but were united in their yearning for a return to a simpler world in which American foreign entanglements were minimal and the responsibilities of the federal government at home were modest. The administration's foreign policy, to these Republicans and a handful of conservative Democrats like Lee O'Daniel of Texas, represented a commitment to the principles of social democracy at home and abroad. The administration was, in the word of Malone, "financing socialist governments whose announced objective is government ownership of property and control of the individual—communist by another name—since the objective is the same."[27] A glance at the final roll call vote in the Senate on the Marshall Plan reveals seventeen dissenting voices, sixteen of which fit into this broad anti-interventionist category.[28] It is therefore hardly surprising that historians have given much greater attention to the administration's perspectives on foreign policy than to the dwindling band of obstructionists in Congress. However, it is important to lay out some of the controversies over foreign policy to show how debates over the size and scope of governmental power had come to dominate the political agenda in the late 1940s.

The final broad political alliance concerning foreign policy was based on the unashamedly leftist platform of former Vice President Henry Wallace and his congressional supporters Claude Pepper, Glen Taylor, John Blatnik, Vito Marcantonio, and Adam Clayton Powell. Historians have tended to marginalize this group, borrowing the perspective of the leftists' opponents at the time, which does not take into account the strong backing Wallace received in early 1948 from stalwarts of the New Deal.[29] Rexford Tugwell, now of the University of Chicago, was a vocal supporter of Wallace, as was Joseph Davies, who remained wedded to the notion of diplomatic cooperation with the Soviet Union well after the end of the war.[30] This group specifically linked its opposition to Truman's foreign policy to support for a left-wing social policy at home, and their marginalization by the bipartisan group also made possible the weakening of its pluralist domestic agenda. All had supported the fight against Nazism, and all saw the effective wartime popular front of western democracy with the Soviets as a remarkable triumph over the evils of the far right.

FDR and Treasury Secretary Morgenthau were themselves early adherents to the leftist view when they drew up the Morgenthau Plan for the dismemberment of Germany. To Morgenthau and others, Germany was a greater postwar threat than the USSR. The legacy of the 1930s and the depression had been partially to legitimize the Soviet Union as an alternative to capitalism; an attack on that utopian far left system was an attack on the left in America, according to Wallace and his supporters.[31] Just as antistatists possessed at least a rhetorical commitment to other regimes of the right, so leftists refused to abandon a diplomatic coalition that included regimes of the far left. They viewed with fear the growing desire after 1945 by Republicans and many in the administration to rehabilitate Germany and break off relations with the Soviet Union. Claude Pepper warned of the "criminal folly committed after the last war, when Germany was rearmed. . . . I had not expected to see international policy based on the maudlin sentiment of those who weep over the sad plight of the convicted criminal while ignoring the victims he maimed and killed. . . . It is the dangerous doctrine of all those who have been seeking for almost thirty years to pit west against east." To Pepper, the bipartisan group was motivated by "hatred for the Soviet Union" and therefore hatred of the left.[32]

Glen Taylor (D-Idaho) in a letter to Harold Ickes reminded him of Henry Wallace's assertion that the USSR felt threatened by western militarism, and argued that "Russia is now firmly convinced that we are bent on total destruction of Communism, by war if necessary. I believe that Communism and free market capitalism can exist in the same world."[33] To the Wallace group, a Cold War abroad meant the end of the promise of the New Deal at home and the rehabilitation of the Right in America. It meant the shattering of the popular front imagery of the 1930s, when the Soviet Union had seemed like a model of progress despite its unfortunate totalitarian bent. British intellectual Harold Laski, a regular feature on the American academic and political scene in this period and another member of the Wallace group, was deeply concerned about the effects of a Cold War on the potential for social reform in America. The U.S. government, he argued:

> "has helped to create an anti-Russian feeling amongst its own people which has reached fantastic proportions, preventing them from realizing that to seek terms of friendship with Moscow is not the same thing as the appeasement of Hitler. . . . In its endeavor to check the spread of socialism, which it regards as hardly distinguishable from Communism, America may break the British Labor Government by offering it economic assistance on impossible terms and cause divisions in

> France and Italy so deep that civil war must follow. . . . [It] is far more important to take steps to safeguard the peace of the world than to protect a form of predatory capitalism which has an almost continuously ugly and evil history. . . . It is all this that makes so tragic the atomization of American liberalism. At the very moment when the world needs so urgently the corrective it could apply to the relentless and impersonal drive of the American economy, there is no organized movement of the left in America to supply it."[34]

Laski, like Wallace and other American leftists, recognized the relationship between domestic ideology and foreign policy, and saw the Cold War as a concerted attack on the Left. It was on this basis that the Wallace group formed the Progressive Citizens of America (PCA) in the wake of Wallace's Madison Square Garden speech in September 1946 in which he had criticized the increasingly anti-Soviet tone of American foreign policy. The twin experiences of the growth of popular front communism in the depression-ravaged 1930s and the wartime alliance had left a legacy of a relatively large Communist Party and a host of high-ranking politicians sympathetic to the potential inherent in a political program of the left.[35] Just as the Cold War was giving rise to a network of political actors and organizations dedicated to policies of resistance to communism at home and abroad, so too had the depression and world war left a legacy of a network of organizations keen to keep alive the flame of the popular front against Fascism and the forces of the right. Among these holdovers from the wartime left were a few recalcitrant labor unions like the Electrical Workers, together with a number of local union branches within the CIO umbrella; New Deal politicians like Claude Pepper and Wallace, who had moved in pro-Soviet circles (including the Council of Soviet-American Friendship) during the war; and maverick political pressure groups such as the Non-Sectarian Anti-Nazi League. The latter organization was a small but well organized New York-based leftist group dedicated to the exposure of what it thought to be pro-Nazi businesses in the United States during and after the war in order to instigate a boycott of those businesses. Underpinning the professed aim of the League was an overarching commitment to a broadly defined politics of the left and a scarcely concealed sympathy toward the Soviet Union as a victim of Nazi aggression.[36]

The PCA was seen in mainstream liberal circles as potentially dangerous to the development of a viable anti-communist liberalism as it brought these disparate forces together as potentially a force to be reckoned with. It also continued to profess a commitment to a politics of the left at a time when

Americans for Democratic Action was shifting focus toward anti-totalitarianism and away from the ambitious plans for domestic socioeconomic reconstruction preeminent until late 1946. ADA founder member James Loeb dismissed the founding of the PCA as a grave mistake at a time when America needed a middle ground between Soviet totalitarianism and Republican reaction, arguing that the inaugural conference "has reaffirmed our doubts that it is real and effective leadership and that it has capacity for growth. . . . It has long been our feeling that the bases must be laid for clearly non-Communist progressivism."[37]

The split in the liberal movement at the end of 1946 clearly had much to do with the question of relations with the Soviet Union. Claude Pepper wrote an article in *Soviet Russia Today* in July 1945 defending Stalin's foreign policy as one of needing to "have friendly states around her borders. Who does not have that policy? Yet have you heard Russia questioning Britain's concern for friendly states across the Channel?" He was quoted the following year as saying that he was "no more pro-Russian than I am pro-Afghanistan. I'm only pro-peace. . . . The failure to achieve Big Three unity is not just Russia's fault. . . . We have got to reconcile Russia's rise with the fall of other nations."[38]

Yet that was not the whole story of the collapse of the liberal coalition in 1947. In the later 1940s it would become clear that the emergence of internationalist anti-Communism would mark the transformation of liberalism, and the decline of a commitment to move beyond the piecemeal ideology of New Deal liberalism. Claude Pepper, for instance, gained a considerable amount of national publicity in the two years after the war in publications ranging from the conservative *Saturday Evening Post* to the more liberal *PM* on account of his status as, in the words of the *New York Times*, "the leader of the extreme left wing of the Democratic Party." Under the headline "Senator Pepper's Emergence As Champion of Left-Wing Groups," the *United States News* reported in June 1946 that he was becoming as much the leader of the Democratic left as Henry Wallace, and that he "remains the spearhead of combative liberalism in the Senate." The periodical *Medical Economics* shared the general editorial feeling of nervous respect pervading the media coverage of Pepper: "Far to the left of such men as Senators Wagner and Murray, Claude Denson Pepper is Congress's greatest anomaly: a radical from the Deep South. . . . He represents, not Florida, but that vague area known as the left—the CIO-PAC, the American Labor Party, and the 'friends of the Soviet Union'." *Newsweek* commented archly in September 1946 that in the wake of Wallace's dismissal the "man in Government on whom the liberal-leftists now counted most heavily was Florida's florid Senator Claude Pepper."[39] It is unclear exactly why Pepper was singled out as far to the left of one of the New Deal's most ardent champions, Robert Wagner, or what exactly was meant by the term "left." It appears that a continued commitment to keep Henry Wallace in the government and to promote the liberal-left postwar agenda of "Sixty Million Jobs" and universal health insurance while simultaneously warning against the dissolution of the wartime grand alliance formed the popular definition of the left in the United States after 1946.

Pepper was not afraid to argue that in the wake of war Americans were not only demanding a program of health insurance and full employment, but that they "are also ready for any change or improvement in the methods of government . . . required to bring such a program to fruition."[40] In his diary in July 1946, he noted that "Britain is showing considerable progress in a year under its socialist government—nationalization of [the] Bank of England, coal mines—now for the future civil aviation, railroads, truck and bus lines, iron and steel. . . . They have enacted [a] housing program and extended social security system and a national health program. That is the direction of things everywhere but here."[41] So clearly Pepper had come a long way since his election to the Senate in 1936 toward viewing the New Deal as the first step on the road to a social democratic politics in postwar America, although his staunch loyalty to the Democratic Party would preclude his participation in the third party challenge in 1948. Still, the logic of the Wallace and Pepper forces combined domestic and foreign policy into a singular desire to retain the popular front vision of a new world order based on left-wing principles that had been common currency in liberal circles in 1945.

The ever-widening rift between supporters of the administration and members of the Progressive Citizens of America and associated critics of American foreign policy raised important questions about the future of left-wing ideas in the postwar United States. For one thing, the left's increasing preoccupation with foreign policy undermined its credibility at a time when events beyond America's shore seemed to point to the impossibility of maintaining an alliance with the USSR. "This desperate cold war has many tragedies," remarked Claude Pepper on hearing the news of Jan Masaryk's death by defenestration in Prague in early 1948, but could not quite bring himself to admit the massive impact of the Czech coup and the end of coalition government there on American views of Soviet foreign policy. It would be August before he began to shift fully into the Truman camp after the defection of a Soviet teacher from the Soviet consulate in New York: "It seems the woman was actually escaping and the case looks bad against the Russians by our standards."[42]

The events in Czechoslovakia, the Berlin blockade, the failure to find a resolution of the German question or the division of Korea, all made alternatives to the emerging policy of containment look increasingly untenable. Secondly, it was difficult to argue with the ADA line that it was perfectly possible to be of the left without being a fellow traveler. The ADA leadership certainly felt in 1948 that "one of the major political issues during the next four years will be the fight for control of the Democratic Party," the outcome of which would "determine whether there will be a genuine labor-supported third party" to carry forward the banner of American liberalism if the Democratic Party remained dominated by southern conservatives.[43] Cold War liberalism was surely about more than the policies of "bipartisan reactionaries," especially since the administration's policies on matters of international security since March 1947 had stolen a march on an increasingly divided and paralyzed right-wing.[44] Yet the development of a new world order based on abstract notions of freedom and democracy debased the language of the left in liberal political discourse and reified the anti-statist concerns of the right even as their influence in foreign policy formation remained limited.

The Truman Doctrine and the Emergence of Anti-Socialism in Foreign Policy

President Truman's decision in March 1947 to press for the authorization of military and economic aid to Greece and Turkey in the wake of Soviet expansion into southeastern Europe and the pressure of communist guerrillas in Greece effectively made anti-communism the central plank of U.S. foreign policy. In his message to Congress on March 12 Truman admitted that the existing governments in Athens and Ankara were not perfect, but argued that the prevention of a communist takeover in either country was far more important to American interests in the region than protesting the existence of an unelected monarchy. The President made a point reiterated many times during the Cold War: if these countries fell, it would only encourage the spread of communism throughout the world. Acting Secretary of State Dean Acheson in his testimony before the Senate Foreign Relations Committee in late March argued that "a failure in these key countries would echo throughout that vast territory [of the Middle East and Western Europe]." Acheson and Under Secretary William Clayton were supported in their assumptions by members of both parties in Congress. Senator Elbert Thomas (D-Utah) agreed with Clayton that if "we succeed in Greece, and then in Turkey. . . . we are better off, Greece is better off, the world is better off, and probably the success here will lead other people into better habits."[45]

In essence, the administration and its supporters in Congress were attempting to develop the international dimension of the postwar Democratic Order, and were using depictions of Soviet aggression to steer a program of economic and military aid to Western Europe through a skeptical Congress. Supporters of the administration believed that only American dollars could render the world economy stable and open to U.S. financial and strategic interests.[46] Senator Millard Tydings (D-Maryland), a leading proponent of the Truman line in Congress, told his constituents in April 1947 that if "nothing is done, it seems reasonable that in many countries struggling to strengthen and re-establish their democracies that Communism will eventually take over." If that happened, Tydings continued, "the tidal wave of that philosophy will rise higher and higher, and in time perhaps spread to other continents."[47] John F. Kennedy argued at the University of North Carolina in April that the U.S. had long believed that "American security would be dangerously threatened if the continent of Europe or that of Asia were dominated by any one power. . . . We have only to look at a map to see what might happen if Greece and Turkey fell into the Communist orbit. . . . The barriers would be down and the Red tide would flow across the face of Europe and through Asia with new power and vigor."[48] The predominant political view was that the Soviet monolith was bent on world domination, no communist supporters could exist in a country like Greece without Soviet patronage, and that the Greek government would be friendly to the United States as long as it was not communist.

Americans for Democratic Action saw the Truman Doctrine as a key test of postwar internationalist liberalism, and mobilized their limited resources behind the administration. James Loeb outlined the logic of Cold War liberalism in a memorandum to local ADA chapters setting out the organization's official viewpoint: "The position taken by the National Conference of ADA on the question of aid to Greece was predicated on the belief that our aid can and should be the instrument of carrying out reforms in the Greek governmental and economic system. . . . we must follow through on the use of our aid, insist on a genuine amnesty, and employ our influence to improve the Greek economy and set it on a firm and healthy basis."[49] In other words, American aid was to be used to isolate parts of the world, especially in Europe, from Soviet influence while simultaneously bringing them into an American economic and political orbit.[50]

Alfred Baker Lewis spoke for ADAers in general when he wrote a statement outlining a less complex rationale behind U.S. involvement in Greece, which was widely disseminated in early 1947, and must have had some influence in generating support for the bill. "Greece is the victim," argued

Lewis, "of aggression by Communists, Greek and foreign, seeking to dismember her on behalf of a foreign government controlled by Communists." He then launched a bitter attack on what he referred to as "totalitarian liberals," otherwise known as the Wallace group described above, for denouncing the Greek government but not "Russian imperialism." He continued that "the best way to make a non-democratic nation democratic is to make it free from the fear of foreign attack, for often the denial of democracy is due to the attempt to gird a nation against foreign aggression." The Greek government was "not democratic but it is far more democratic than the totalitarian dictatorship of Communist Russia. . . . What the 'Truman Doctrine' amounts to is an end to appeasement of totalitarian aggression."[51]

The ADA believed, as did the administration, that until the United Nations could be effective in preserving extant governments free from aggression, the United States should send military and economic aid to both Greece and Turkey. This position was held by political figures across the ideological spectrum, from Alexander Smith (R-New Jersey) and Arthur Vandenberg (R-Michigan) on the right to New Deal Democrats like Truman, Senator Scott Lucas (D-Illinois) and Congresswoman Mary Norton (D-New Jersey). All shared the assumption, however, that the Truman doctrine symbolized a crusade against totalitarianism and an attempt to integrate other parts of the world into an American strategic and economic sphere of influence. Republicans and New Deal Democrats in the bipartisan coalition differed in their attitudes toward the demand management policies inherent in the domestic and foreign agendas of postwar liberalism, and thus had differing views on how far the United States should be expected to support the wider world financially. Of course all assumed an alliance with overseas governments afflicted by leftist thinking; after all, it was the British withdrawal from the Balkans that had precipitated American involvement in the area, and the two governments worked closely together on the new policy. But bipartisan policymaking—with its emphasis on private sector financing of economic assistance, the opening of world markets to American goods, and the diverting of federal public spending priorities to foreign affairs—helped to shift the emphasis of the liberal state away from the ideas of state-managed redistribution of wealth and intervention in the economy, which had girded the framework of the New Deal even if they had never developed fully up to the 1940s.[52]

The administration's foreign policy in the Balkans also served to promote the notion of American capitalism releasing foreign nations from a reliance on the all-powerful state. Throughout the Committee hearings members of the administration attempted to win Congress over by demonstrating the free market principles of the plan, and the fact that it would not be a mere gift to foreign governments. Republicans on the Senate Foreign Relations Committee were intrigued by the proposal, which involved the spending of $300 million for Greece and $150 million for Turkey to ensure not only their military protection but also their economic rejuvenation. Alexander Wiley (R-Wisconsin) asked Under Secretary Clayton how the United States would be reimbursed, and how much of a drain on American resources the project would be. Clayton's argument concluded that if the Balkans should "adopt closed economies, you can just imagine the effect that it would have on our foreign trade. . . . We had exports from the United States last year of over $10 billion."[53] Senator Bourke Hickenlooper (R-Iowa) was unconvinced by this argument, arguing that essentially the plan allowed for the continued subsidizing of a rejuvenated Turkey with no benefit to the United States. Hickenlooper wondered what "the justification is to go into Turkey, because if she cannot support herself now, can she support herself in a competitive world . . . ?" Henry Cabot Lodge, a key member of the bipartisan group supporting the Truman doctrine, also had some economic ideas to add to the debate, proposing an overhaul of the tax structure in Greece to help pay for its defense, and the development of trade relations between Turkey and America.[54]

There was considerable tension between the administration and right-wing Republicans on the economic impact of the plan on the American economy, but in the final analysis there was much agreement on the general abstract principles. Alex Wiley wrote a letter to committee chairman Arthur Vandenberg, questioning the ramifications of continued expenditure on growing spheres of influence around the world, but he voted for the measure with enthusiasm in the final vote. He argued, along with colleagues like Chapman Revercomb (R-West Virginia) that "there is no reason why we should not have subsidiary goals if we are to expend the resources of the American people."[55] These "subsidiary goals" included trade concessions for U.S. companies, and other financial rewards for an American role in defending foreign states from Soviet aggression. Essentially, however, it was possible for New Dealers and Republicans such as Wiley to support the Truman doctrine because it opposed totalitarianism in the Near East while exporting American principles of free markets and supporting anti-left forces. Both ADA liberals and many Republicans were comfortable with the precedent being set for the United States to interfere in the affairs of other nations for ideological reasons, suggesting that both groups would find their ideological differences narrowed by the experience.

The implications of the Truman doctrine for the future of liberalism in America were suggested by the large number of generally sympathetic

Truman supporters who attempted to amend the measure to make it less open to the charge that it was simply preferring one type of dictatorship over another. Jacob Javits (R-New York), who claimed he "swam in the mainstream on foreign affairs," proposed an amendment along with five others to make aid to Greece dependent on the election of a new democratic government. It was defeated by 104 votes to 6, the six including Democrats Chet Holifield and Helen Douglas of California and Karl Mundt (R-South Dakota).

Some liberals and old-style isolationists were also concerned about the consequences of the plan to invest American resources in a civil war abroad. George Bender denounced the Truman doctrine as the beginning of a policy designed to "finance, to sustain, economically, and militarily, any government, anywhere in the world whose overthrow or change might point that nation or people in the direction of Communism." He argued that Americans should differentiate humanitarian and economic aid from the creation of a military shield defending one form of dictatorship from another.[56] Taft also opposed the military aspect of the measure, preferring to fight communism ideologically and economically before attempting to interfere directly overseas.[57] George Malone was another critic on the Republican side who stressed the progressive reasons behind opposition to the Truman doctrine. "Greece," he stated, "entered the war as a Republic, bravely striving to resist a foreign aggressor. She has ended up as a monarchy reigned over by a Hohenzollern Prince without a drop of Greek blood in his veins and occupied by foreign troops, with its administration controlled by foreign sources. . . . the Greek people not only hate the present regime which could not stand without foreign intervention, but they hate the British invaders even more. . . . If there is a better way to build communism than this, I don't know what it is."[58] Harold Ickes also opposed American support for a "German king," and argued that while he would support humanitarian aid to the Balkans, military aid was a mistake. He expressed astonishment at the comments to him by aid administrator George McGhee that "the Greek aid program is not entirely humanitarian in its objectives, but is in the self-interest of the United States."[59]

Henry Wallace attacked the proposal from the left, arguing that it interfered in an internal Greek civil war and wrongly associated the Soviet Union with ideologically committed movements across the world. It was initially difficult to distinguish the critiques of the plan made by Claude Pepper and Glen Taylor from those of Robert Taft or George Bender. Forrest Donnell (R-Missouri) warned Taft of this possibility, arguing that Republican adviser Dick Scandrett was assuming a Wallace line in opposing all military aid to Greece and Turkey. It was necessary to support some military aid, argued Donnell, since "you cannot please the Soviet Union, the domestic Communists, Wallace . . . Pepper and Scandrett. . . . Such persons want our aid to Greece and Turkey limited to plain relief."[60] A research analyst with links to the GOP wrote that the danger for politicians like Taft as well as avowed anti-statist isolationists such as John Bricker was that they would be tempted "to ease the tension with Russia which helps Truman." If such a strategy were adopted, Republicans would be purging "Communists and alleged Communists at home while they appease Stalin abroad. . . . And that is the danger that patriotic Republicans must avoid." If Republicans were obstructing Truman's policies for purely political reasons, then why not point out "the inconsistencies between Truman's policy in Greece and in China"?[61]

The writer was in many respects misinterpreting the nature of the opposition to the Truman doctrine among Republicans. Some were undoubtedly motivated by the machinations of party politics, especially anti-statists determined to obstruct all expenditures abroad. In addition to complex considerations of foreign policy per se, some opposition centered on the party's attempts to reestablish a domestic agenda in the wake of the New Deal, an agenda that would combine a vestigial isolationism and antipathy toward the assumption of an imperial role with a commitment to resist the growth of liberal domestic agenda. Bender told Taft that it was "wrong to let Vandenberg continue to push us into the arms of the Democrats under the guise of this phony bipartisan foreign policy. . . . Instead of an Anglo-American alliance, what we need is a flourishing powerful United Nations. This . . . should be the basis of the Taft plan."[62] A reliance on the UN would allow a scaling down of American defense commitments and, by extension, overall state-sector spending. However, the stark anti-communist message explicit in the Truman Doctrine, and the basic commitment to containing state-sector involvement in American foreign policy implementation, won over a significant part of the GOP, and contributed to the rise of an anti-totalitarian coalition in American politics that left little room for a politics of the left.

The Wallaceite left did in fact go much further than any in the Republican Party in denouncing the program of aid to Greece and Turkey, but well before the 1948 election campaign they represented a politically ineffectual, ramshackle bunch. Glen Taylor proposed riding a horse from coast to coast to protest the plan, arguing that it was "rushing us pell mell into the third, and probably final, world war." In the event Taylor only managed 95 miles, choosing instead a more orthodox method of getting his message across by holding public meetings: "I have asked my audiences to place themselves in the position of the Russians. In other words, how would we feel if the Russians suddenly began dredging the harbors of Mexico . . . and otherwise making military preparations for an unannounced purpose. . . . That is exactly what the United States has been doing in Turkey, and, to some extent, in Greece."[63]

Henry Wallace in early 1948 wrote an open letter to Stalin, proposing a mutual policy of nonintervention in other nations once peace settlements had been reached. The tone and content of the letter is strikingly reminiscent of Roosevelt's communications in the months leading up to his death, in so far as he envisaged the continuation of a policy of strategic negotiation between a concert of nations to develop a peaceful postwar order. Historians are probably right, however, to see a shift in Wallace's thinking between his 1946 New York speech and his foreign policy views leading up to his 1948 Presidential campaign, from a commitment to a policy of realpolitik to one of knee-jerk justification of Soviet policies and a dismissal of Cold War liberalism at home.[64] The shift was not a move from "Realism" to "sentimentality" so much as a reaction to actual policies such as the Truman Doctrine and the later Marshall Plan.[65] Such policies were determining Soviet strategy in the eyes of the left; the administration, far from countering a Soviet threat, was manufacturing it. "Today," argued Wallace in a full-page advertisement for his Progressive Party in the national press, "Americans are asked to support the governments of Greece and Turkey. Tomorrow we shall be asked to support the governments of Spain and Argentina. . . . No people can be bought."[66]

Helen Gahagan Douglas demonstrated how left-of-center concerns about the morality of Truman's foreign policy transcended the sparsely populated ranks of Gideon's Army: although a friend of Wallace's, Douglas was increasingly attracted to the broad coalition of Trumanite liberalism. She nonetheless introduced two amendments to the Truman Doctrine in the House that demonstrated the concerns of many liberals about the direction of American foreign policy. The first, like that of Jacob Javits, linked the provision of aid to the emergence of democracy in the two recipient nations. The second called for a UN or, failing that, a U.S. investigation into "whether the national integrity of Turkey is threatened from any outside source" before providing aid.[67] It was an attempt by Douglas in Congress to reevaluate the rationale behind America's Soviet policy, and to alleviate tension between the two countries. If successful, the left in America would be protected from the destabilizing influence of an anti-communist foreign policy on public perceptions of the democratic left at home. Douglas herself was increasingly becoming disillusioned with Wallace, who did appear to be guilty of the ADA's charge that he "accepts the basic principle that Communists and liberals and progressives can work together in the same organization. . . . Wallace is more and more following the Communist Party line."[68] She did increasingly realize, however, that bipartisanship could remove from political influence those suspicious of the effects of anti-Soviet imagery on the American public's perception of government at home.

The American State and the Recovery of Western Europe

Aid to Greece and Turkey passed both Houses of Congress by lop-sided margins, most having been convinced that the urgency of stemming the perceived Soviet tide was more important than any domestic or imperialist implications. The vote in the Senate demonstrated this fact well. Of the 23 who voted against the plan, only three were on the political Left: James Murray, Claude Pepper, and Glen Taylor. The other 20 were a mixture of anti-statist Republicans and anti-spending Democrats such as Harry Byrd (D-Virginia). Two, Lee O'Daniel and George Malone, were anti-government but also progressive in their view of the need for the prioritization of domestic issues and their awareness of the ironies of American support for governments that were hardly models of the American ideal.

Given the success of the message created by the President's new internationalist policy based on anti-communism, it was hardly surprising that the government would turn its attention to the rest of Europe. The situation was remarkably similar in many ways to that in the Balkans. Western Europe had been devastated by war; its political future was uncertain as Communist groups fed on the economic distress in France, Belgium, Italy, and Austria; its economic recovery could not be guaranteed without the injection of hard currency from the United States. In addition, there was the problem of Germany, divided between the West and the Soviet Union, crippled by the effects of allied bombing, and vulnerable to the appeals of both the hard left and far right. George Marshall chose the end of his own visit to Europe as well as the period immediately following the approval of aid to Greece and Turkey to propose a massive program of economic aid to all of Europe in a speech at Harvard in June 1947. Not only would there be a plan of immediate humanitarian aid to France, Italy and Austria, but also following that emergency plan would come a far-reaching program of economic redevelopment of all who wanted it using private capital and, notably, the American state. The proposal would extend the scope of American government involvement in U.S. economic foreign policy while simultaneously encouraging the growth of private enterprise and denouncing the menace of omnipotent state power.[69]

The administration and its political allies lost no time in constructing the arguments in favor of Marshall's proposal. Tom Connally told a constituent that the proposal was "advanced on the theory that humanitarian reasons prompt the feeding and furnishing of fuel for those in distress at the present time. It is also designed to strengthen the countries of Western Europe to the point where they will resist the spread of communism and thus contribute to their own well-being and security. A hungry and cold man is apt to turn to the illusory promises of communism since he may feel that his own system has failed."[70]

The rationale that the Marshall Plan was a state-inspired form of managed capitalism to protect the people of Europe from the false lure of communism sat well with liberal opinion in both parties. Only by smoothing out the rough edges of capitalism at home and abroad could social justice be achieved and totalitarian alternatives avoided. It attracted support from Republicans struggling to reorient their own party toward an acceptance of this principle, among them Henry Cabot Lodge and Christian Herter, as well as from most liberal Democrats. Marshall added in testimony before the Foreign Relations Committee that without American help Europe would have "no escape from economic distress so intense, social discontents so violent, political confusion so widespread, and hopes of the future so shattered that the historic base of western civilization . . . will take on a new form in the image of the tyranny that we fought to destroy in Nazi Germany."[71] In positing the image of "western civilization," of which America formed a central part, against a Soviet-centered tyranny, Marshall argued that there was more to his proposal than an economic plan for the rejuvenation of Europe.

The wheels of bureaucracy began in mid-1947 to grind concerning problems of procurement and distribution of aid, of how much the American economy could stand, of the relative need of the various recipient states. The Harriman and Krug Committees determined the relationship between provision of aid and the domestic economy, and Francis Wilcox liaised with the State Department to provide members of Congress with detailed economic facts behind the program.[72] Some, however, within the State Department and in Europe itself, agreed that it might be best from an economic standpoint to let events run their course without large-scale American props. But in the final analysis the political reality "involving the futures of all the nations concerned and eventually our own security . . . [requires that] political considerations override all economic considerations."[73]

The key point was that the Marshall Plan was presented principally as a measure to oppose totalitarianism abroad, and thus could represent a way of indirectly increasing distrust of big government at home. Christian Herter, who had led a congressional committee to Europe in mid-1947, argued that the Russians were "still bent on the same policy . . . of wanting to expand their control over nation after nation until they themselves, through a single Soviet state, control all the nations of the world." It was vital to remember that America was "dedicated to the preservation of the dignity of the human individual and completely foreign to their concepts. . . . There is . . . a basic struggle of ideas, and the side which has the strongest and the most active faith in its ideas will prevail."[74] The struggle was thus not within capitalism, but between the ideology of the individual and that of collectivism. The "liberal" consensus on the Marshall Plan was beset by contradictions, setting forth a state-centered solution to the problem of European recovery while implicitly furthering an American consensus on the danger of the omnipotent state for American principles of freedom. This consensus had implications for moderate liberalism as well as for Wallaceite leftists in America. The Marshall Plan debate provided a forum for highly contestable claims like that of Lewis Douglas that America could not lead the "free" world if it was itself subject to the dead hand of the state. Douglas furthermore "distrusted quite seriously the validity" of the British government's view of the UK's economic program since the Labour victory in 1945.[75]

Many on the right used the Marshall Plan debate to argue against the use of federal control over the economy; foreign and domestic ideological battles reinforced each other. Malone was one of several Senators, for example, to attack the arrangements made for the provision of emergency aid to France, Italy, and Austria in November 1947. The $597 million requested by the State Department under the plan would go to the three governments through a revolving fund with an American administrator. Malone argued that the money was being "utilized for the benefit of the governments or groups currently in power," and that goods were not reaching needy people, but were being sold. He also argued that the amount was too large, and that goods, and not credit, should be sent to solve what was being portrayed as a humanitarian crisis. "Many of us believe," he asserted, "that we are not in the business of setting up a WPA in any of the countries of Europe for work-relief purposes." The American contribution, he argued, needed to be economically and administratively sound in order to meet the objective while conforming to Republican principles. William Knowland also argued for the dovetailing of humanitarian impulses with rightist economic constructs.[76] Homer Capehart argued that rather than using the federal government to administer American aid to Europe, America should set up an international Reconstruction Finance Corporation like that established by President

Hoover in 1931 to tackle the depression in America. Capehart, himself a former businessman who had made millions through the sale of jukeboxes before coming to the Senate, argued that his plan would "put these obligations on an American footing. . . . Let us hit [Stalin] with American means, hit him with the free enterprise system. . . . Let us not imitate state socialism and communism in fighting Mr. Stalin."[77]

Marshall and his supporters were arguing the same thing, that their plan would help free enterprise around the world and stop the growth of state socialism and communism, and in fact politicians wrangling over practical domestic issues would grow increasingly united over the essential ideological realities of anti-Sovietism. This debate over the legitimacy of state power in foreign policy was important, though, as it helped provide new ammunition, or new case studies, for the political opponents of the growth of American government. Harold Knutson (R-Minnesota), Chairman of the House Ways and Means Committee, argued in a report to his Foreign Affairs colleagues that in analyzing the Marshall Plan he had looked to Switzerland, as "the Swiss think the way we do," and had consulted a member of the banking sector there. He had reported that there "is no practical way of implementing the Marshall Plan. . . . A crisis is inevitable and American help at this stage will merely defer and aggravate it. . . . The Swiss do not care whether the British government is socialistic or not. What they do care about is the ineptitude of those at the helm and the unwillingness to work prevailing in England." Sweden "is going downhill due to the hash made of the economic situation by the socialistic government there." France "is beyond a shock. It needs a dictatorship as the French have lost the virtue necessary for democratic government." The overvaluation of currencies, the poor administration of the Ruhr, and the unwillingness to pursue free market policies to encourage recovery made the Marshall Plan useless, argued Knutson.[78] Internationalism in America was opening the doors to a new world of overseas examples in the war over state power in America.

As in the case of debates over domestic policy, what seemed to be an economic argument concerning the merits of a proposal like the Marshall Plan in fact masked ideological divisions over the abstract moral value of the state that had been developing since at least the 1930s. Merwin K. Hart, President of the National Economic Council and a confidant of the Republican right, testified before the Senate Foreign Relations Committee and left its members clear on the relationship between anti-statism and the administration's foreign policy. The Marshall Plan, he argued, represented "a continuation of the socialistic policy that seems to have possessed our administration . . . for nearly fifteen years. . . . [It] is un-American and unrealistic." Americanism was an abstract concept of the rugged individual, free from the state. From 1933, "which was marked by the recognition of Soviet Russia by the United States, we began to import wholesale the principles of Marxism, including both Socialism and Communism. . . . We have put more and more of these socialistic principles into statute form." Hart dismissed bipartisanism as "a New Deal policy," and argued that democratic socialism as practiced in Britain and communism were "blood brothers." His solution was to harness the support of Germany and Spain in the fight against communism, deliberately choosing a nation that had a far-right dictatorship or one with a far-right history. "There is no country in all Europe that would make a stouter or more dependable ally for the US than Spain."[79] In his organization's Economic Council Letter, Hart argued that the Plan allowed "the New Deal socialists of the United States (both Democrat and Republican) [to] put over a project to subsidize socialism in Europe."[80]

The growing links between the American far right and fascism in Europe might have appeared as outside the political mainstream, irrelevant to the business of Congress or the recovery of Western Europe. In truth, Hart's words found wide acceptance among right-wingers. Ever since the New Deal, argued many Republicans, the Soviet Union, as well as the democratic left, had grown. "The New Deal planned economy at home was stopped at the election in November 1946," argued Ralph Gwinn (R-New York). "But the State Department continues to operate the New Deal planned economy in foreign affairs . . . and by a fantastic propaganda program, the administration has deceived and frightened the people with threats of communism overtaking Europe. At the same time, it has financed the forces of socialism already in power. . . . " Great Britain had a "Marxist cabinet" that had "led the nation ever further down the treacherous and liberty-killing road of not less, but more nationalization."[81] Gwinn, unlike Hart, actually had an alternative proposal to the Marshall Plan, along the same lines as that of Homer Capehart and centering on the importance of minimizing state involvement. They were two of many using the ideology of Cold War employed in the promotion of the Marshall Plan to undermine the liberalism of the plan's authors.

While the Marshall Plan was passed by large margins in both Houses, many in Congress were beginning to see anti-leftist ideologies resurrected by the growing emphasis on foreign policy in the American polity. George Malone used projects like the Marshall Plan as examples with which to launch an attack on the way in which the American state was operating in the wake of the New Deal. "The so-called Marshall Plan," he argued in an address in Denver, "is the most amazingly brazen and preposterous scheme for a world wide redistribution of wealth that has yet been proposed, even by the socialistic European governments, to level our living standards down to their own." Malone argued that the emergence of the left in Europe had caused a massive flight of capital away from the continent, as private investors feared that they could not invest in countries such as Britain for fear of nationalization or government regulation. European states were thus asking the U.S. government to make up for the lost investment. "We are simply continuing a policy started with Tito in Yugoslavia, financing socialistic governments whose announced objective is government ownership of property and control of the individual—communist by another name—since the objective is the same."[82] Again, we see the characterization of the social democracies as communist, the stark dichotomy between American free enterprise and European socialism, and the implicit attack on the Democratic administration at home as well as abroad. It was not as if Malone was totally ignorant of the situation in Europe; he was part of a Congressional mission in 1947, although his dispatches to his wife and daughter suggest a certain unfamiliarity with the social realities of the "Old World."[83] His strident attacks in the media and in public discourse, however, struck a chord with the public at large less familiar with the world beyond America's borders.

Vandenberg received letters like that from a Stephen Deaver of Berea, Nebraska, arguing that "Truman and his Reds and Pinks . . . have drained our country of oil to train Joe's airforce. . . . Do you know that the Marshall billions will go to complete the communization of England?"[84] A rash of anti-socialist articles and publications followed the Marshall Plan debate. One such book argued that Truman and the Communists were allies and were using the Plan as a way of establishing state control over the economy. Another argued that the "beneficiaries of these handouts are, for the most part, frankly devoted to social systems destructive to the American principle of free enterprise." To right-wing columnist Edna Lonigan, the Truman Doctrine and Marshall Plan represented not the "conflict between the United States and Russia, nor even between Free Enterprise and Marxism. What this political loan portends is another campaign in the now defensive war of Freedom against Statism. This battleground is not in Athens or Moscow, but all around us here at home."[85] The publicity battle went hand in hand with the moves by political figures on the right in Congress to wrest control of the legislative agenda. Attacking Truman's foreign policy measures in a series of speeches, Taft argued that they were "so characteristic of the New Deal," and that far from being bipartisan, "the appeasement of Stalin . . . the betrayal of Polish patriots . . . were not Republican policies," but those of the left and the New Deal.[86] The New Deal had "favored the steady growth of a totalitarian state directing the economic and individual rights of all its citizens. . . . Communists were encouraged to support the Democratic candidate in national elections, and to take over important labor unions."[87] The increasing power of the Cold War in the popular imagination was moving political debate sharply to the right, undermining the promise of a more liberal polity suggested in 1946. In 1948, the right no longer had to come to terms with the state, but could use the Cold War as a stick with which to beat the ideology of Roosevelt.

Because many who had opposed the confrontational character of the Truman Doctrine supported the economic rationale of the Marshall Plan there was less chance of a strong progressive reaction. In addition, anti-communism was as pervasive among Socialists such as Norman Thomas and progressives like Harold Ickes as it was among members of the Republican right. Thomas bitterly attacked Wallace for his opposition to the Marshall Plan, and argued that so "truly do I think Communist totalitarianism 'red fascism' that I should quite literally prefer death to life under it."[88] Many on the left were by 1948 coming to terms with the reality of Soviet dictatorship, and differed from the right only by avoiding the use of this image of totalitarianism as a tool to discredit the liberal broker state. The left also recognized the potential benefits to organized labor of an international union movement buoyed up by the revitalization of managed capitalism with American dollars. Increased productivity in European countries would preserve Western Europe from communism, but would also require a mobilized and democratized labor force that would reinforce the left turn in the politics of the industrialized world since the war. Thus CIO Secretary-Treasurer James Carey lectured the World Federation of Trade Unions on the benefits of American aid for the reconstruction of Europe, and the Reuther brothers traveled to France, Germany, and the UK in 1948 and 1949 to oversee the development of noncommunist unions and the inauguration of the International Confederation of Free Trade Unions as a united anti-communist front for organized labor.[89]

Taft was one of several in Congress to attempt to balance his instinctive bias toward domestic affairs with the need to affirm his anti-communist principles in the foreign policy field. In a speech in Middletown, Ohio, a town which had come up with its own highly publicized foreign affairs platform, Taft argued that he believed in a "strong international association of nations. . . . I have supported the United Nations." He argued for the removal of the veto provision and the handing over of international disputes to its jurisdiction, a view shared by many on the left.[90] He also followed the line that a vastly expanded aid program would have adverse domestic effects: "I am in favor of aid to Europe but not on the basis of any overall global plan, to which we commit ourselves; but only for specific assistance clearly necessary for subsistence, or clearly helpful in increasing production for export." He supported the plan only because of the threat of Soviet expansion westward, and argued that European governments needed to be able to help themselves.[91] George Malone also followed this line, and it is interesting to note that both Taft and Malone were struggling to preserve the Republican right's antipathy toward big government and the New Deal and their vision of a halcyon American past where affairs of the state were simpler, but the growth of a national security state was leaving their political base enfeebled and anachronistic.[92] Malone agreed that humanitarian aid to Europe was necessary, but noted also that it was inconsistent to aim to control inflation at home while "budgeting over a four year period . . . $17 billion [for foreign relief], of which the [Marshall Plan] appropriating $5,300,000,000 is a part."[93] James Kem (R-Missouri) and Taft agreed that foreign programs could "be justified only if it is for our own ultimate benefit, for the benefit of our own people, either as an economic program, or as a political program."[94]

Yet all these critics of the Truman program also argued that the administration had been slow in dealing with Soviet duplicity after the war, and that an assertive, though not necessarily materially generous, foreign policy was essential in meeting the Soviet threat. Slowly but surely, the power of anti-Soviet ideological imperatives was dissolving the opposition to an assertive foreign policy in some form. The Marshall Plan passed the Senate by 69 votes to 17; Republicans opposed to the statist nature of the plan made up almost all the dissenting votes, and Taft joined bipartisan Republicans Vandenberg and Lodge in the majority. The authors of the aid to Europe package had skillfully interwoven a program of American financing of European economic recovery and restructuring with a commitment to force European economies to modernize productive plants, to dismantle closed economic and trading policies, and to open up their markets to American private companies. Administrators would soon bring pressure to bear on the British government to draw its attention away from ambitious social welfare policies in favor of a program of monetary probity in ways that never would have occurred to social democrats in the UDA of 1945. Yet the reality of American dollars relieving Europe's economic distress won over most skeptical leftists in Congress. In short, the administration sold its program both to liberals and a majority of conservatives in Congress and in the private business community.[95] Only one left-wing Senator approved of Wallace's condemnation of the Marshall Plan: Glen Taylor. Claude Pepper and James

Murray, as well as Helen Douglas in the House, voted in favor. Only Taylor and Vito Marcantonio opposed the plan because it divided Europe into two rival spheres of influence and emphasized the fundamental breach between the United States and the Soviet Union and its satellites. The anti-communist consensus in the body politic was well developed by the end of 1948.

Defending America from the State

The desire of the administration's critics to change the direction of policy while supporting its final anti-communist aims characterized other foreign policy debates, notably over the draft and American trade policy, suggesting ways in which leftist thought would fade from American political discourse. The military aspect of the administration's foreign policy represented the first significant American military role in the world in peacetime. Senate Armed Services Committee Chairman Chan Gurney (R-South Dakota) argued on the Senate floor that the new draft and universal military training bill introduced in March 1948 was essential if the administration's anti-Soviet foreign policy was to succeed. He noted that "the Nation's postwar military program originally was formulated in anticipation of a climate far more temperate than has been the case during the past two years."[96] Given the assumption that non-Communist nations, including the United States, had to be protected from a perceived Soviet threat, many felt that the armed services could not be demobilized on a scale normally associated with the end of open hostilities. Voluntary recruitment that had replaced the draft upon its expiry in March 1947 had simply failed to provide the necessary numbers for a policy of Cold War preparedness. As Wayne Morse argued for the internationalist liberals: "We need to pass legislation . . . in order to strengthen our national security so that we can protect this country and other freedom-loving countries of the world in case Soviet Russia proceeds with an aggressive, warlike policy."[97] Under the administration's scheme, all 18-year olds would be required for military training for one year, followed by their transfer to the Reserves. Those in the 19–25 age group would be liable for selective service, or the draft, for two years of service. In addition, the administration proposed the establishment of a permanent security apparatus in the form of a new intelligence service, the CIA. Internationalist policy based on opposition to the Soviet Union was creating its own bureaucracy; how the right and left reacted helped to determine the future direction of domestic ideology during the Cold War.

The draft as finally enacted was in fact rather less ambitious than the plans for universal military training supported at the highest levels in the

Truman administration and the military establishment. The idea demonstrated clearly how far American liberalism had changed as a result of the adoption of a significant global role since 1941. Not only would UMT appeal to Joint Chiefs of Staff keen to possess the ability to mobilize a mass fighting force overnight rather than after a prolonged period of mobilization and training, it also appealed to the President himself as a Cold War liberal tool to promote health and social responsibility among the nation's youth.[98] However, the United States had never before known a peacetime draft, let alone the power of the state to control the lives of all its citizens in such a direct way, and so inevitably the proposal ran into considerable opposition. Anti-statists worried about the development of an omnipotent state joined forces with an assortment of left-wing and progressive activists in Congress, labor unions, church organizations, and farm groups. The Republican leadership in Congress served notice that it was prepared to help steer the draft through Congress in view of the perceived international emergency, made more compelling by events in Czechoslovakia and simmering tensions in Germany, but few in the GOP were prepared to go much further.[99] Thus most debate revolved around the question of a more limited draft law, leading to a broad political acceptance of the foreign policy priorities of the Cold War liberal state under construction in 1947 and 1948.

Among progressives and those on the left there was broad agreement on the dangers of a militaristic state, and these figures joined forces with the anti-statist right to attack the administration's proposals. Republican populist William Langer (North Dakota), an implacable foe of an internationalist foreign policy in any form, argued that the proposed draft would lead to American military obligations across the globe, a burden scarcely justified during world war and certainly not when America was at peace. "The United States," argued Langer, "has grown up all right. We are not merely taking care of the United States any more, but we are taking care of all the continents except Australia." Glen Taylor joined Langer in attempting to block the bill by introducing amendments to abolish segregation in the armed forces.[100] In their attempt to avoid the domestic ramifications of a strenuous foreign policy, Senators like Langer and Taylor made common cause with many on the right uneasy about an enlarged role for the American government in the world. Homer Capehart attempted to stall the bill for 75 days in order to allow the voluntary program time to work. The amendment received 24 votes, including those of right-wingers such as John Bricker and the Wallaceite Taylor. Revercomb argued that compulsory military service established a dictatorship: "Never before in peacetime has Congress been called upon to enact legislation which would compel men to serve in any branch of government, military or civil. . . . This is a free country. We cleave to certain basic principles as fundamental to the life of America."[101]

In the parallel debate on the National Security Act establishing the Defense Department, National Security Council, and the CIA, Edward Robertson (R-Wyoming) argued the government's military program would "create a vast military empire" and that the CIA had "all the potentialities of an American Gestapo. Needless to say, it would be an invaluable asset to militarism." Taft earned high praise from Socialist Norman Thomas for his forthright condemnation of the draft as "contrary to the whole concept of American liberty. . . . In this whole field there is no reason why our approach should not be governed by the same principles of liberty as should guide other government programs. For too long a time the New Deal has taught us that results can only be accomplished by compulsion. . . . . What we need is a highly trained, technical professional force."[102]

It was hard to tell left and right apart on these questions; all were suspicious of the use of military power abroad and saw the dangers of an enlarged federal bureaucracy dominated by the military. They could not match the growing consensus on the need to use the enlarged federal capacity to fight a Cold War, a consensus that united liberal Republicans, Democrats, and most progressives. Only ten Senators voted against the draft, a mixture of anti-government Republicans and Leftists Langer, Dennis Chavez (D-New Mexico), and Taylor. Langer's main point had been that surely the state was intended during the New Deal to promote socioeconomic justice, not support a gargantuan foreign policy establishment. The Cold War encouraged even Taft to back the draft, comforted by the fact that peacetime conscription did not have to go hand in hand with expansive overseas commitments.

Differences between many Republicans and the administration remained over military policy. Many agreed with the assertion that "America, all-powerful in her hemisphere . . . should remain impregnable and invulnerable there" without wasting its strength crusading around the world. This same writer could claim in the same breath that the "godless, brutal, Communist despots of the Kremlin desire world rule" without backing Truman's extensive foreign policy program or agreeing to the sending of forces abroad.[103] The debate over the draft contributed to the enfeeblement of the left inside Congress and out, and helped to establish a consensus on the anti-leftist nature of the American polity. The possibility of a coalition against the elevation of military goals over domestic reform, suggested by the alliance between left and isolationist right in Congress, was stillborn in the atmosphere of 1948.

The Cold War raised other moral questions in the late 1940s that attracted a bipartisan progressive interest, only to be marginalized by the more abstract issue of "freedom" versus "totalitarianism." The concept of an ethical foreign policy that could transcend Cold War issues was not new in the context of Vietnam in the 1960s, but came to the fore in the postwar period on the question of U.S. relations with Latin America. At first glance it seemed as if the Truman administration would continue the policy established at Montevideo in December 1933 of using the Western Hemisphere as a focus for American internationalist action. Secretary of State Edward Stettinius in a letter to the inter-American conference at Chapultepec in 1945 stated that the United States "intends to propose and support measures for closer cooperation among us in public health . . . labor, education . . . and in economic development." Three years later, in Bogota, Secretary Marshall argued that times had changed: "We must face facts. . . . my people find themselves faced with the urgent necessity of meeting staggering responsibilities in Western Europe . . . in Greece and Turkey, in the Middle East, in China, Japan, and Korea. . . . The capital required [for Latin America] must come from private sources, both domestic and foreign."

This shift in American priorities, and the concomitant change in the nature of the inter-American alliance to that of an anti-Communist club made up principally of dictatorships, enraged those outside the bipartisan foreign policy group. An analysis of the 1948 Bogota conference by a leftist observer, Samuel Inman, argued that as a struggle of freedom versus totalitarianism America's South American policy was a sham given the political nature of the continent. President of the conference was Dr. Lauriano Gomez, "one of the most reactionary politicians . . . friend of Hitler . . . twice decorated by Franco." Inman's evaluation of the conference was bleak: "No doubt Bogota marked an important skirmish in the long battle between Democracy and Communism. Why did Democracy, then, suffer its crushing defeat?" Inman argued that "we used the very tactics that play into the enemy's hands, namely: Play partners with the extreme Right, condone dictators, ignore injustice and poverty—then when the people rise in anger and destroy their oppressors, meet and . . . pass resolutions blaming all on the extreme Left."[104]

Republicans joined various leftists in using American policymaking in areas like Latin America as a potential source of embarrassment for the administration. George Bender told Taft that he "was very happy that you called attention to the effect on prices of [Truman's] foreign policy and that subsequently you opposed the armament of the South American dictatorships. . . . Overriding everything else by November 1948 will be this mad foreign policy of military alliances which Truman has let the military sell him."[105] Taft was a lightning rod for neo-isolationist opinion, which, as Taft put it, opposed assuming "the place of the British Empire. . . . We are not imperialists. . . . We have always sided with free governments and hoped they would stay free."[106]

Senator Taft's search for a less extensive program of foreign commitments in keeping with his domestic ideology threw up two difficult questions about foreign affairs in general. The first was that his and Bender's ability to subordinate anti-communism to other ideological concerns was not widely shared, and thus again one must ask whether the Cold War was in fact weakening any possibility of an ideological realignment in the American polity. Henry Wallace and his allies roundly condemned American policy in the Western Hemisphere, but since they were increasingly being associated with the far left in advance of the 1948 presidential contest, it was unwise for any politician with ambition to associate themselves with similar views. If they did they would face a concerted attack by liberals like Truman, Henry Cabot Lodge, Tom Connally and most of the American foreign policy establishment.

The second issue concerned why exactly those who did not associate themselves with the left, such as Taft, would criticize American foreign policy in a way that anticipated "new left" critiques of U.S. foreign policy in the 1960s and 1970s. Rather than the opposition of certain Republicans being purely humanitarian, to a degree it simply reflected right-wing concerns about the domestic effect of an extensive foreign policy. A foreign policy requires taxation and bureaucracy. *Human Events* commentator Felix Morley, a bitter opponent of the left in any form, drew attention to the contradictions in Truman's foreign policy in a similar way to Henry Wallace. Spain, he argued, "will obviously have to be included in the anti-Russian alliance which Great Britain has begun to build, with State Department blessing and support. . . . But we had previously denounced him so roundly as a 'Fascist beast' that it's going to be awkward to get in the same bed with the Caudillo now. . . . With the decision to build a Western European military alliance against Russia, ERP ceases to be primarily a program for economic recovery."[107]

Morley, like many on the right, condemned the Democratic administration for its inconsistencies and its sponsorship of dictatorships purely as a way of attacking a government he did not support, and without prejudicing his anti-leftism at home in the United States. One could be a strong anti-statist and anti-communist in America but a reluctant foreign policy crusader. As the Cold War became more intense, even this division between internationalist liberalism and the right would narrow, as the latter came to appreciate the ways in which abstract anti-communism in foreign policy legitimized their anti-pluralist domestic agenda. This would leave only the electorally discredited left to point to the inadvertent effects of the "anti-communist" foreign policy on domestic attempts to associate American identity with more than simply freedom from socialism.[108]

4. VARIETIES OF LIBERALISM IN THE 1948 CAMPAIGNS

THE ELECTIONS OF 1948 WERE THE FIRST SINCE 1936 TO involve a presidential contest not dominated by the issue of war. As a whole, therefore, the contests at both the presidential and congressional levels could concern the question of whether the New Deal ideology had vindicated itself in the wake of the world conflict. In this light both contemporaries and historians have seized upon the remarkable performance not only of Truman but also of Democrats across the country as evidence of the vitality of liberalism and government-centered policy as the century neared its midway point. Liberal Democrats, they argue, won stunning victories, the hard left in the form of Henry Wallace was utterly discredited through its communist links, and the Republican right faced a strong challenge from liberal moderates who would begin the quest for an appealing candidate in 1952. In addition, Truman's decision to make his assertive foreign policy a central part of his campaign and his ideological credo is seen as a masterstroke, ending once and for all the political wavering over America's response to a very real totalitarian menace.[1] It is true that recent scholarship has placed the Truman victory in more critical perspective, but usually in terms of an inexorable rejuvenation of the private business community in a domestic context.[2]

If one goes beyond the imagery created by the historical participants themselves to analyze the nature of the ideological variants on display in 1948, it becomes clear that the implications of the 1948 elections were deeply ambiguous for the future of proponents of statist liberalism. In the Republican Party the option of reinvigorating the party's progressive past was passed over in favor of a presidential candidate committed to Truman's elusive brand of anti-left liberalism, which was itself an extremely divisive force in the Democratic Party. Furthermore, the defeat of Dewey and of Wallace had the effect in both parties of strengthening the anti-leftist consensus in the American polity that would preclude anything but a piecemeal evolution of the New Deal and an anti-communist foreign policy studded with anti-left imagery. An analysis of both presidential and key congressional races highlights the growing impact of bipartisanship on the weakening of domestic political reform movements in the early Cold War.

Truman, Wallace, and the Future of New Deal Liberalism

The Democrats' strategy of bringing foreign policy to the fore to shore up their domestic electoral position worked well in 1948, and in this sense Henry Wallace's decision to stand as a Progressive candidate for the presidency was a godsend to the President. Yet it hardly seemed so when Wallace declared his candidacy in December 1947. Initially, the Wallace campaign seemed to underline all that was wrong with Truman's leadership of the New Deal project since 1945. The twin themes uniting progressives against Truman were his failure to promote the New Deal beyond its rather insubstantial foundations, and the accelerating anti-leftist direction of American foreign policy. Harold Ickes told Truman directly in March that he had the "choice of retiring voluntarily and with dignity, or of being driven from office by a disillusioned and indignant citizenry. . . . Henry Wallace is not strong because the Communists support him. . . . hundreds of thousands of voters will cast their ballots for Wallace in protest of you."[3] The *New Republic* publicly disavowed Truman's candidacy in April 1948, arguing that he had undermined his own liberal message by a foreign policy "of unending struggle . . . of which [Truman] can only be a prisoner from now on. . . . Lacking direction, we are stumbling toward war."[4] James Loeb of Americans for Democratic Action, a staunch supporter of Truman's Cold War strategy and moderate domestic liberalism, wrote Paul Douglas in March that "the President's stock has dropped so low in recent weeks that it is almost out of sight. . . . My correspondence, my talks with liberal and labor people around the country, all lead me toward the conclusion that the non-communist liberals are terribly handicapped this year because of a lack of dynamism at the top."[5] Before the Democratic convention in July, barely a liberal could be found who rated Truman's chances of winning; many did, however, see Wallace in early 1948 as a powerful articulator of genuine New Deal liberalism and a real threat to the Democratic Party.[6]

The wider significance of the Wallace campaign has often been lost amidst the contemporary and subsequent controversy over its links to the

American Communist Party and its opposition to the Cold War. Wallace himself may indeed have been naïve about the USSR's global intentions; his campaign may have become bogged down by internecine warfare and poor management.[7] Nevertheless, his campaign represented a debate of the future direction of American liberalism. Truman based his candidacy for the presidency in 1948 on the expansion of the parameters of the New Deal, a legacy that historians have increasingly argued to be a political compromise to accommodate the United States' variegated political and social context. He wanted to expand social security, build a limited amount of public housing, and bring labor unions fully into the American economic and political structure.[8] In addition, the Truman administration was by 1948 coming under the influence of a quasi-Keynesian planning movement that was increasingly arguing against direct federal involvement in the economy in the form of capital projects and in favor of limited countercyclical spending and increased reliance on private sector growth to promote general prosperity, a trend symbolized by the Council of Economic Advisers, particularly Leon Keyserling.[9]

The attack on Truman by Wallace supporters who were not Communists was an expression of the widespread frustration in liberal circles at the limited vision of Cold War liberalism. In a radio debate on the subject of the third party, Senator Glen Taylor of Idaho, Wallace's running mate in 1948, argued that Cold War liberalism, in its desire to interlink domestic policy and an assertive foreign policy so closely, was betraying its left-of-center political roots: "Once relieved of the staggering burden of armaments and preparations for war, we could proceed to the tasks necessary to create permanent prosperity here at home." These tasks, in Taylor's view, included nationalization of certain industries and the creation of a welfare state predicated on the principle of universality. The Progressive party convention in 1948 advocated the public ownership of large banks, railroads, electric and gas industries, and those industries where public capital played a vital role.[10] Stewart Martin, chairman of the Maryland Progressives and former special assistant to the U.S. attorney general during the war, agreed that Cold War liberalism was based upon a commitment to anti-left values that could then be exported overseas: "Secretary of Commerce Averell Harriman shocked the Latin Americans at Bogota when he warned that they must create the 'right climate' for private investors if they expect aid from the United States. . . . The bipartisan government speaks for the hidden private government in which we voters have no voice even at election time."[11]

Wallace himself often lost the thread of ideological reasoning amidst windy rhetoric and an obsession with America's relationship with the Soviet

Union. He did, however, represent the ongoing battle over the future direction of the American left which had crystallized in 1946 but had gained intensity and significance as mainstream liberalism shifted its rhetorical and legislative emphasis away from the left and toward a consolidation of existing legislation combined with an aggressive economic and political crusade abroad against the Soviet Union. In his campaign to reorient liberalism back in the direction of the promise of his 1942 "Century of the Common Man" speech, Wallace had the support of a cadre of radical CIO unions with a history of left-wing militancy—the United Electrical Workers, the United Farm Equipment Workers, and the Packinghouse Workers—and southern civil rights activists who had cut their teeth on political battles for democracy during and after World War Two and who were impressed by Wallace's strong commitment to racial democracy. Wallace's southern tour in 1948 cemented a commitment to civil rights spelled out in his December 1947 speech in Tulsa in which he contended that "those who stand in the way of the health, education, housing and social security programs which would erase that gap [between African American and white life expectancy] commit murder. I say that those who perpetuate Jim Crow are criminals."[12] Wallace linked his discussion of civil rights explicitly to an espousal of social democratic policies, and this distinguished his stand from Truman's hesitant commitment to simple desegregation. "Social security, housing, health care, education—these things we can't afford now and can't expect in the future because of the big war budget," complained Albert Fitzgerald, president of the United Electrical Radio and Machine Workers of America and chair of the National Labor Committee for Wallace. He argued in addition that Truman, despite vetoing Taft-Hartley in 1947, was now using its provisions "in a ruthless and aggressive fashion. . . . to keep labor in line."[13] Rexford Tugwell, the most significant Wallace supporter from the Roosevelt administration, argued that the purpose of the Wallace candidacy was to force the establishment in the American political system of a radicalism that had consistently reared its head in the form of third party challenges and popular uprisings, but which had never been able to challenge the dominance of conservative forces in both main parties. "We will force an old party to become progressive," he stated, "or we will push through this new party of ours and replace one of the old ones. . . . If the Democratic Party wants to commit suicide, perhaps we ought not to try to save it."[14]

The American Labor Party's victory in a special House election in the Bronx in February strengthened this belief that leftism could challenge the Cold War consensus. Leo Isacson's majority of over 10,000 votes in a normally Democratic district meant one thing to local Democrats. "It was the silence of Harry Truman," said one precinct captain in the 24th district of New York. "When he came in, he promised to follow in the footsteps of . . . FDR. All he's done is march backwards. I go to my people now, they slam the door in my face!"[15] Isacson himself argued that his victory was specifically "a victory for Henry A. Wallace and the third party—the People's Party." He agreed with Wallace that it represented "a repudiation of the get tough foreign policy" and that working class Americans would not let the Cold War marginalize desperate demands for domestic reform.[16] One ALP campaigner pointed to the 2,000 ALP canvassers on election day as evidence that many voters were sick of talk of the Marshall Plan and voted "against the grim sordidness of slums."[17]

Rapid social change with the migration into the district of some 125,000 African Americans and Latinos had made the area, in Samuel Lubell's words, "an almost perfect example of the new zone of political insurgency developing in our larger cities."[18] Wallace continued to stress the integral link between foreign and domestic aspects of liberalism in his speeches and articles, and the initial reception to his views in the liberal press suggests he was making some headway, even if the unusually politically variegated nature of New York State politics made the region particularly receptive to third parties. In an article on housing Wallace claimed that it was "obvious that a nation which can produce so abundantly for war can meet its peacetime needs, if its government wants to." The Cold War to Wallace was a plot to destroy the New Deal, a big business attempt "to set up an American version of the police state" while seeking "to end all drives of labor for higher pay."[19] The combination of a critique of American foreign policy with a leftist stand on civil rights, labor relations, and social welfare measures in general seemed to have some potency in industrial America in early 1948.[20]

The Progressive Party challenge posed difficult questions for a Democratic Party increasingly determined to make anti-Sovietism one of its principal election planks. Liberal periodicals such as the *New Republic* argued that anti-communism weakened anti-segregationist sentiment in the South, and also remarked on how in other countries moderate social democracy was flourishing precisely because it did not make martyrs out of the far left.[21] It is true, however, that Progressives weakened their cause by often refusing to accept the existence of genuine liberalism in the Democratic Party, a refusal that irritated potentially sympathetic observers. "I wish," said CIO leader and anti-Wallaceite Philip Murray, "that the countless thousands of dollars wantonly wasted by the Third Party could be put into a great effort of the CIO-PAC to gather together the workers. What's wrong with that program?" A CIO local leader in Gary, Indiana, warned ominously that when "the Third Party runs against Ray Madden [D] in Indiana it runs against me."[22]

Wallace had endorsed a host of third party candidates against liberals like Helen Douglas and Sol Bloom.[23] By September many of these Progressives had withdrawn, but the damaging perception of the Wallace group as a hindrance to liberalism, especially among labor unions, was well entrenched by then. Labor was split between Wallace and Truman—Jack Kroll of the CIO-PAC was a prominent founder member of the PCA—but the specter of a Republican victory in the wake of the party's 1946 congressional victory increasingly pushed the CIO into the Truman camp. There was also the perception of a Communist element working at cross-purposes with Wallace to dominate the movement in many areas, and this united most union leaders with ADA intellectuals in a common effort to marginalize the Progressive Party.[24]

It became clear as the year went on, however, that the steady decline in support for the Wallace project was due to his failure to comprehend the effect events overseas were having on domestic politics. In March 1948 Wallace's response to the Communist coup in Czechoslovakia was to muse that it must have been prompted by Soviet fears of the Marshall Plan, a position that many associated with the fact that soon afterward the Czech newspaper *Rude Pravo* praised Wallace's candidacy.[25] When testifying before a congressional committee on universal military training, Wallace argued that Lenin and Stalin had only perpetuated a dictatorship in the 1920s because of "the civil war in which the counter-revolutionaries had been armed and supplied by England, France, the United States. . . . Stalin . . . has determined to modernize Russian agriculture and industrialize without outside financing. In doing so he has, of course, sacrificed many human rights."[26] Wallace did not intend to romanticize Soviet Communism, but rather attempted to demonstrate that as "long as we have a war economy . . . it is impossible to broaden social security, establish a real housing program or develop a medical-aid plan," an argument that would prove to be partially vindicated after the election.[27] In the context of events in Czechoslovakia and Berlin during 1948, however, Wallace's views seemed to imply a return to the appeasement sentiment of the 1930s.

The international background of 1948 gave Harry Truman a way of revitalizing his flagging campaign and of dragging the Democratic Party away from damaging associations with the left. "Although it was not realized until months later," argued Progressive Senatorial candidate Curtis MacDougall, "it was Harry Truman who 'called the shots' during the 1948 campaign."[28] The Truman-ADA strategy at both the federal level and in states such as Minnesota where progressivism was strong was to stress support for the liberal objectives of the New Deal state while simultaneously opposing the far left in all its forms. The Democratic convention, during which ADA liberals like Paul Douglas forced through a civil rights measure endorsed by Truman, marked an astonishing turning point. Whereas in March the *New Republic* was arguing that ADA members "were more interested in political futures than in performing the latter-day functions of Sidney and Beatrice Webb [and] are neither socialist nor committed to native American progressive objectives," in September the same publication was asserting that most Democrats were "liberal," and that the Progressive Party had "isolated itself from the mainsprings of progress. . . . [Truman] has chosen to fight on principles of militant liberalism," principles untainted by a desire to come to terms with Stalin.[29] Pat McCarran (D-Nevada) opposed the increasingly liberal tone of the campaign, but noted that Truman's presidency was being rejuvenated by the likelihood of "an inevitable war just ahead. . . . The Russians will make some move in Germany pretty soon which will call for action by our troops in the American zone. God forbid! But it looks bad."[30] If foreign policy came to the fore, then Truman would be required to lead and his problems as a lame-duck President would end.

Truman after July traveled the length and breadth of the country, portraying himself as the defender of FDR's legacy, and also as his party's champion against the totalitarian left. His nomination acceptance speech in July 1948 contrasted the inclusive achievements of the New Deal with the special interest Republicans who favored "the privileged few and not the common, every day man." Truman condemned the Republican record in domestic policy since 1946, and, in a surprise rhetorical flourish, announced that he would call Congress back in special session in late 1948 to test the Republicans' commitment to liberal reform. He also affirmed his commitment to "leadership in international affairs" and noted that he had encouraged bipartisanship so that "foreign policy should be the policy of the whole nation." Truman pushed to the sidelines all on right and left who argued that his foreign policy was being used to vilify those who opposed his domestic ideology of incremental social and economic reform.[31] The president's message to Congress on civil rights also served to unite progressives behind his campaign banner. A commitment to enforced desegregation was, in the words of Alfred Baker Lewis, "completely in the Roosevelt tradition. It might be wise to say something about the absurdity of Wallace and his Communist supporters charging the President with being reactionary in view of this message."[32] Anti-totalitarianism provided an abstract ideology to legitimize the continuation of liberalism in power when domestic political sentiment was moving away from statist themes. The marriage of the New Deal and an assertive foreign policy ensured a Democratic victory in 1948.

Yet the change in the nature of American liberalism in 1948 with the purge of the Wallace movement had substantial implications for the future of American reform. It became legitimate to associate Wallace with communism, to assert that his supporters were "groups often referred to as the fringe." Remarkably, this "fringe" included "a large percentage of Negroes, university students and white collar workers," backed up by Communists. That African Americans as a group constituted a "fringe" is testimony to the effect of the Wallace campaign on liberalism. A large percentage of Progressive candidates were black; many more were women. Dr. George Cannon, Chairman of the Harlem Wallace-for-President Committee and an African American medical doctor in New York, argued that "Wallace says the things all Negroes want to hear, and not only talks, but acts. . . . You see, the major problem with me is race." He added that he was "not all for Wallace on his Russian stand. . . . That's the major weakness in Wallace's position."[33] The attack on the Progressive party's foreign policy was part of a wider drive by business groups to use Wallace's pariah status to attack his concrete domestic proposals, such as health reform.[34]

Events such as the riot at Evansville during Wallace's visit to the Indiana town also showed the link between political rhetoric and popular antipathy toward the left; very little press coverage discussed Wallace's speech, but rather painted a picture of a radical leftist inciting public unruliness. On April 7, 1948, the day after Wallace's speech at Evansville, the *New York Times* ran a story headed "2 aides hurt in fight at Wallace meeting." The article provided details of the injuries sustained and the violent events prior to the meeting, but gave no details of Wallace's speech, which concerned the nationalization of military aircraft production to prevent war profiteering. On April 10, the same paper detailed Wallace's attack on Evansville College for firing a professor who spoke at Wallace's rally. The lead story that day had been entitled "Colombia battles Leftist mobs burning and looting the capital," coverage which somewhat blunted the impact of the events in Indiana.[35]

Politicians in the Democratic Party faced electoral disaster if they associated with Wallace, a man whose domestic views on civil rights and liberal social policy many agreed with. Wallace lashed out at liberals who refused his help at a Progressive rally at the Commodore Hotel in New York in September, singling out Helen Gahagan Douglas and Chet Holifield (D-California) for criticism. "I guess our friends will vote for Douglas and Holifield but I suspect for fear of offending them, they won't ring any doorbells." Beanie Baldwin, Wallace's right-hand man, argued the same evening that Douglas and Chester Bowles in Connecticut had been forced to repudiate Progressive support. Democrats in Los Angeles had "talked Helen out of filing on our ticket although she agrees with 90% of everything we stand for." Both parties "are out to destroy the Progressive Party because they look upon it as their only real threat."[36]

The remarkable thing was that neither Wallace nor Baldwin seemed to comprehend what was happening to America in 1948. They spoke in confident tones about the strength of their movement, of the fear expressed by their opponents, while across the country liberals were having to repudiate the progressives because of their links with the far left. Add to the domestic ideology a progressive foreign policy designed to restore immediately the Soviet-U.S. alliance of the war years, and one could see the link between the Wallace elite and most ordinary Americans melt away, even in the most deprived of areas.[37] It had reached the stage where a Democrat like John Kennedy, never a friend of the Wallace group, actually condemned Roosevelt's foreign policy in its last months for its attitude toward Russia.[38] The 1948 elections would signal the beginning of the end for public willingness to entertain leftist interpretations of U.S. foreign policy, as well as for a leftist alternative domestic policy for the nation, at least until the 1960s.

Three Republican Candidates

By the beginning of 1948 three frontrunners had emerged for the Republican nomination for president of the United States. Governor Thomas Dewey of New York and former Governor Harold Stassen of Minnesota were both seasoned presidential campaigners, having either received or attempted to receive the nomination since 1940. Both espoused the electoral strategy of self-termed liberal Republicans, accepting broad tracts of New Deal thought, arguing that the Democrats were too corrupt to administer the implementation of their ideology effectively, and embracing the bipartisan foreign policy of President Truman. Assuming that a candidate could receive the greatest number of votes in a pluralist society by being ideologically unspecific, it was clear that both would find it far easier to concentrate on the consensual foreign policy element, and the intrinsic fear of radicalism embedded therein, than to articulate a coherent domestic critique of America's internal weaknesses and problems.

Robert Taft confronted a different dilemma. He was a self-styled foe of the New Deal and of big government, but also clearly felt that he needed to cast much of the Republican Party's postwar record in a relatively centrist light. In addition, he was outside the mainstream on foreign affairs. Taft essentially represented the continuing struggle of the American right and large sections of the business community to roll back the New Deal order, but the growing political power of the Cold War in American political discourse was in fact making the election of a Taft less important to the fortunes of anti-statist interests.[39]

Taft was always the symbol of reaction against the New Deal to a majority of his Republican supporters, and yet the actual nature of that support suggests a conservatism that was populist rather than carefully crafted by the Chamber of Commerce. In his extensive travels across America in late 1947 and early 1948, Taft was inundated with letters and cajoled by supporters associating the state with an assault on their livelihoods. Such letters do not in themselves give us a comprehensive overview of Taft's electoral base, but they do suggest that part of his appeal lay in his apparent opposition to the excesses of governmental power that would become a key theme across the political spectrum in 1948. One supporter in Tucson, Arizona, begged Taft to win so he could curb the "bureaucrats' and "do something that will relieve this unnecessary tax burden on the underpaid laborer. I remain as a Republican in a rotten New Deal state." An elderly couple in Los Angeles responded to a Taft speech in Los Angeles that they "were hardly able to buy anything under OPA. Don't let those Democrats regiment us again. . . . it is a policy of holding up prices and high taxes which cause the high prices."

Occasionally the tension between anti-statism and Taft's popular base would come into the open. A supporter in Phoenix wrote that she had "met a realtor . . . who had said that if Senator Taft is the nominee this man and many of his colleagues would vote against him on account of the housing bill. This man said that the bill would mean ultimate government ownership of housing. I feel that this cannot be correct."[40] To many in America, the state itself was an enemy of the common man, a sentiment Taft was keen to tap into. At the same time, he had co-authored legislation aimed to help reduce social and economic inequality in America, a fact that would cause some disquiet among his natural constituency. The *Chicago Sunday Tribune*, one of his main official supporters, portrayed him as an enemy of overreaching bureaucracy but also as "an earnest public servant who is sponsor . . . of legislation providing millions of dollars for housing, aid to education, cancer and dental research, and a health program to bolster state services."[41] Taft argued for the better management of the state, and appealed to the voter excluded by common perceptions of liberal Republicanism.

Taft's entire campaign attempted to appropriate the mantle of liberalism for his candidacy. In a document setting out his "political credo," he lashed out at the New Deal conception of liberalism as "the philosophy of state control" as opposed to someone who believes "in freedom of thought, who is not a worshipper of orthodox dogma." Arguing that a "higher standard of living is not produced by government handouts," Taft also claimed that "a floor under family requirements is necessary." Taft's campaign had two possible effects on the ongoing debate over the state in America. He could reorient liberalism more around an accommodation of free markets and the profit motive, or he could add to the growing association of the state with dictatorship. Increasingly Taft took the second course. The question, he stated, was between the image of America as having a "government operated by a free people" and "the totalitarian state . . . the kind of state which concentrates in a central government power to direct the lives of all its people, its agriculture, its commerce and its industry."[42] In a speech at Youngstown, Ohio, just ahead of the Ohio primary against Harold Stassen, Taft asserted that "the basic meaning of 'liberal' has always been 'someone in favor of freedom'. . . . Therefore, support of every change proposed is not a test of liberalism but of radicalism. . . . The Republican program has been a liberal program." Pointing to Taft-Hartley and tax reduction as examples of true liberalism, Taft associated Stassen with the Truman-style liberalism that was in fact an attempt to impose "a planned and managed economy." While Stassen would "give us a carbon copy of the New Deal," and "squander his attention on the rest of the world," Taft would "restore American liberties, oust bureaucracy, reduce taxes," and "believes that the safety and welfare of the United States come first." Taft had proved "himself a true liberal with advanced social legislation," but had not supported the more ambitious plans for state action in an "extreme form," which would "lead inevitably to the philosophy of state control and totalitarian government which prevails in Soviet Russia and many other countries today."[43]

Taft's conception of liberalism was highly confused, and, in a Cold War context, liable to be seen as mainstream on the subject of state power rather than radical. His candidacy had the strong support of much of the business community that had done so much to lobby successfully for the passage of the Taft-Hartley Act. One speaker at the NAM national convention shortly after the 1948 election argued that anti-statists like Taft had to make the most of the anti-totalitarian language that was coming to dominate political debate, referring to "the road to statism, tyranny, and slavery" to describe the Fair Deal agenda.[44] Still, Harold Ickes was one of several New Dealers to respect Taft's candidacy. While disclaiming support for any candidate in either party, Ickes told one correspondent that "Taft is both able and courageous and those qualities are worthwhile."[45] Congressman Ben Jensen (R-Iowa) put the right's view of Taft. Mentioning his statist proposals in the 80th Congress on housing, health and education, Jensen argued that "while a lot of people consider Taft a conservative, in reality he apparently wants to put the government into a lot of things. . . . He is well informed, but . . . it seems that about the time we get ready to go all out for him he comes up with some of his very much to the left ideas."[46]

Taft's campaign was openly inciting anti-statist feeling at the same time as it was setting forth programs for using governmental power more effectively for the people. Harold Stassen's campaign, by contrast, aided the decline of liberalism within the GOP by combining an uncertain accommodation of the New Deal with a commitment to an anti-communist foreign policy. His campaign attempted to take the electoral power of the New Deal away from the Democrats and bring it to the Republican Party. In so doing he espoused the anti-communist consensual foreign policy and incited the growth of a Republican right angry at his apostasy from perceived Republican ideals. A top Ohio Republican, furious at Stassen's audacious decision to challenge Taft in his home state, gave a speech attacking Stassen for his failure during the primaries to mention "his trip to Russia a year or so ago, at which he visited with Uncle Joe Stalin. Neither did he refer to his articles on Russia . . . in which—to be charitable—he was none too critical of communism . . . "

The *Tulsa Tribune* termed Stassen "the Henry Wallace of the Republican Party. Like Wallace, he is just nuts about Russia, while the Republican Party is just nuts about America." A typed sheet by a group calling itself the "Anti-Totalitarian Committee" of Wichita argued that "Communists, New Dealers, and other Left-wingers cross party lines to vote for Stassen in the Republican primaries. . . . They are joined by other great 'liberals' such as Pepper, Wallace and Brigadier-General Elliot Roosevelt. . . . The Republicans should awake now to the danger of the ambitious Slav and the danger of totalitarian liberalism."[47]

In his time as Governor of Minnesota from 1938 to1942 Stassen had been known as a liberal Republican, espousing Keynesian economic management and generous welfare policies, but Harold Ickes dismissed him as treating liberalism as "a political coin with which to purchase what he so avidly desires." Stassen had also gained the enmity of organized labor in Minnesota; one labor newsletter said that during his time as Governor "there were wholesale lay-offs and firings of state employees. . . . During Stassen's first term as governor, a very vicious anti-labor law . . . was introduced."[48] As a Republican Stassen was no different from any other candidate in struggling to reconcile the economic marketplace with ideas of social justice and interest group politics.

At the same time, Stassen inadvertently provided ammunition for the Republican right-wing through his foreign policy views. As many of his critics had pointed out, Stassen had been to see Stalin in Moscow in April 1947. The meeting, also attended by Soviet foreign minister Molotov, a Soviet interpreter, Philadelphia GOP leader Jay Cooke, and Robert Matteson of Stassen's staff, was for the most part unremarkable. Stassen asked Stalin if the USSR and the USA could coexist peacefully, to which Stalin replied in the affirmative. Stassen then argued that America's biggest problem was the threat of a depression, which could be staved off by regulating "our capitalism and [stabilizing] our production and employment at a high level without any serious crisis." The fact that Stassen presented a fairly interventionist economic strategy in the context of a visit to the Kremlin was too good an opportunity for anti-statists in America to miss. In their attempt to link the state with images of Soviet dictatorship in the popular mind, the Stassen interview was a perfect tool.[49]

Similarly, Stassen's speech in which he argued that the "British parties, Conservative and Liberal and Labour, are our allies in the fight against totalitarianism. . . . We must not choose between the factions of our friends. . . . We oppose dictatorship and fascism even when disguised as benevolence" was attacked as supporting socialism. Congressman Clare Hoffman (R-Michigan) wondered "whether he is an internationalist, whether the candidate thinks more of the interests of other countries than he does of our country. [People] would like to know whether he is supported by or is under obligation to so-called one-worlders or internationalists."[50] A Republican presidential contender who approved of the administration's foreign policy of entangling alliances with Socialist governments abroad had to be associated with the Left. Stassen's candidacy resurrected long-standing conflicts within the GOP that had surfaced during Wendell Willkie's candidacy in 1940 and recurred in 1944 over the ideological direction of the party. In 1948, however, the growth of anti-Sovietism had given a new lease of life to anti-statism in the party. Stassen's own espousal of Cold War rhetoric against totalitarianism merely added to the anti-statist cacophony of the campaign, and further confused the ideological significance of the winner of the Republican nomination in 1948.

Thomas Dewey, who would win the nomination, faced a very similar problem to Stassen, in that he was a strong supporter of the administration's foreign policy but at the same time was associated with the growth of the state by his espousal of internationalism. He consciously decided to direct his campaign against Truman toward the independent and Democratic voter, leaving the die-hard Republican vote to take care of itself. A Republican

Central Committee survey of GOP candidates had urged that "criticism of the Truman administration should be accompanied by constructive plans. . . . care should be taken that this criticism be not of a type likely to alienate the support of the Democrat and Independent voters whose support we are most anxious to obtain."[51]

The Republicans had not won a Presidential election for twenty years, and were clearly determined to appeal to a wide electoral base in a highly pluralist America, just as they had in 1946. It was no coincidence, then, that the candidates chosen at the party's Philadelphia convention in July to head the ticket were both highly successful governors with a proven cross-party appeal. Dewey had carried New York in 1946 by a vast margin, and Earl Warren as governor of California had not even had a Democratic opponent in his bid for a second term the same year, having won both party primaries. Senator Knowland reminded William Reichel, Chairman of the northern California GOP campaign committee, that "there are over 900,000 more registered Democrats in California than registered Republicans. . . . Every effort must be made to welcome Democrats and Independent voters to come in and join the Dewey-Warren ticket."[52] According to the GOP California survey, the number one issue on voters' minds was inflation, followed closely by "Communism and war with Russia," with "foreign affairs" taking fourth place. Clearly the electoral battle would focus on these issues in 1948, a marked contrast to the campaigns two years earlier.

The strategy of Dewey and Warren would have had to overcome two essential weaknesses in order to have any hope of capturing the New Deal coalition. The first was its failure to match Truman's ability to deal in specifics, preferring to mouth what a GOP post-mortem would term "generalities pleasing but vacuous."[53] The second problem lay in the resultant alienation of the Republican right, which would incite massive divisions in the party for the rest of the Truman presidency. Both developments weakened any possibility of a Republican coming to terms with the state. The campaign to attract a cross-party coalition to the GOP ostracized those with a more definite policy stance, such as Taft, while failing to attract non-Republican voters.

Criticism of the administration was expressed in general terms. The GOP platform pledged a foreign policy "on the basis of friendly firmness which welcomes cooperation but spurns appeasement."[54] In an interview with conservative radio broadcaster Fulton Lewis, Dewey stated that America's foreign policy in 1948 was like trying "to nail a jellyfish up on the wall," and that although Communism was anathema to the United States, it "does not mean we should not use every effort to live at peace with every nation regardless of its form of government."[55] He made no mention whatever of the 80th Congress or of domestic legislation that had been passed, other than in his native New York. In his speeches he tended to argue that domestic policies were not ambitious enough. Social Security, for example, "is not good enough for America. The same needs exist for a higher minimum wage and for a stronger and expanded public health service." Yet he attacked liberalism for so losing "faith in our system of free opportunity as to encourage this communist advance, not hinder it." He called up an image of the Soviet Union where "most of the children . . . unless, of course, they're children of the Commissars—don't have any shoes."[56] While seeming to support the basic principles of the New Deal and the bipartisan foreign policy, he was in effect attacking liberalism through his acceptance of the Cold War imagery of the state and of totalitarianism. Americans needed to "rediscover the essential unity of our people and the spiritual strength that makes our country great. . . . We live in a world in which tyranny is on the march. . . . With mankind as our witness this is no time for doubting the rightness of free governments. This is a time . . . for a great American affirmation."[57]

Dewey, then, had few policies for advancing political liberalism in America, and preferred to vie with Truman for the title of foreign policy champion. Still, however, he incited an anti-statist backlash by Republicans suspicious of a liberal Easterner at the head of the ticket. "What worries me," argued a Texas Republican, "is that the 'Old Guard' seems hell bent on supporting Dewey. . . . I am for TAFT, and no other. If some of the Republican New Dealers get the nomination, I shall fold up and not even vote."[58] Every Republican who associated the bipartisan foreign policy with the expansion of the state bitterly attacked Dewey's candidacy, and united around Taft as the heir apparent. Such a critique of Dewey's approach could come from the far Right or from progressives. Felix Morley wrote to Taft decrying Stassen and Vandenberg for being "wholly uncritical" of Truman's foreign policy. "I assume that Dewey will turn back to his anti-Communist record in order to cash in. But that is Truman's only card now, and the aspirant can't play it as well as the man in power." Morley was one of many arguing that anti-Communist hysteria in foreign policy was damaging the potential for domestic reform. Taft himself argued that "it is most discouraging to have the President so predisposed to believe that Russian governments always desire to conquer the world."[59]

Opposition to liberalism in the Republican Party could take a less progressive form. Robert McCormick of the *Chicago Tribune* told Taft that the "final collapse on Marshall money and conscription was either a surrender to the New Deal or the New Dealers taking over the Republican Party. . . . I take it these eastern internationalists really look upon themselves as English Tories and are inflamed with an energy not understood by the indifferent rest of the country."[60] The debate within the party over the presidential nomination in 1948 revolved around popular perceptions of the state in America, and the place of foreign policy and the Cold War in shaping the development of state power. Dewey and Stassen were seen as proponents of state power, and their espousal of internationalism was seen as just another example of that fact. The effect was to boost the development of anti-statism within the party. The post bag of all candidates demonstrates this. "We need," argued one correspondent, "to worry more about OUR OWN Communists and less as to whether the rest of the world goes Communistic." Another wrote that America would "collapse" if it continued "playing Santa Claus to the world."[61] Dewey and Warren were informed that "parlor pinks in the republican [sic] party have nothing to offer the nation. They died when the Roosevelt administration died. . . . They don't know the New Deal is dead yet."[62] The letter was headed "To Hell with Leftism and Liberalism," and suggests the context of the 1948 campaign.

The End of Reform: Republican Congressional Races

"As Congresses go, the record of the 80th Congress was an impressive one." George Smith's analysis of the 1948 campaign made much of the fact that the GOP had a potentially winning issue, that of the domestic reform undertaken since 1946. Taft in his campaign for the presidential nomination had stressed his positive role in sponsoring agricultural aid, public housing, federal aid to education, and the Taft-Hartley labor bill.[63] House Majority Leader Charles Halleck (R-Indiana) was one of several Republicans to make speeches defending the work of the Republican-controlled Congress as progressive and as establishing "a record of which the overwhelming majority of the American people approve."[64] It was clear even before the Philadelphia convention, however, that many Republicans launching their local and statewide campaigns in 1948 knew that their party was in trouble, and that there would be no repeat of the elections held just two years earlier. Sensing that the public was increasingly seeing the party as anti-government, many Republicans in marginal urban districts stampeded to gain endorsements from major party figures on their positive work in the 80th Congress. Charles Fletcher (R-California), the unexpected 1946 victor in urban San Diego, wrote to William Knowland as early as April 1948, hoping that some of the latter's vote-getting ability would rub off on him in November.[65] In Minnesota, his own party wrote off Senator Joseph Ball in his fight for reelection against the popular liberal mayor of Minneapolis, Hubert Humphrey. An October 1948

Republican field analysis in Minnesota stated that "were the election to be held right now, Ball would unquestionably lose."[66]

Republicans in 1948 were realizing that their party had a definite record in power for the first time since the advent of the depression, and that it did not sit well with all sectors of the American electorate. The Democrats, by contrast, had regained their New Deal luster, but with the vital addition of an anti-communist campaign element that would lessen differences within the national polity on the question of expanding government.

Joseph Ball in Minnesota was one example of a Republican increasingly desperate to associate himself with liberalism in his campaign against Humphrey. An observer of the GOP in Minnesota in 1948 would be forgiven for wondering exactly how politicians and pundits alike were so confident of a Republican victory in the nation as a whole. The Democratic–Farmer-Labor Party in the state had been chronically weak going into the campaign, damaged by the internal battle over communist infiltration, and yet with Humphrey as its new centrist leader it was eating into Ball's support across the state. Bernard Levander, Chairman of the Minnesota Republican central committee, stated in his report to the party in Washington that Ball needed "some speakers. And we need them bad. They should be on the liberal side. Vandenberg, Lodge and Hickenlooper may be out here. . . . Ball's strategy must be that he stands solidly behind Dewey. . . . [His] record on veterans bills and his stand on ECA have hurt him, and on the Taft-Hartley bill he was too extreme." Warren Burger, a GOP attorney in St. Paul who would later be Nixon's choice to lead the Supreme Court, argued that although funding was an issue, "Joe's got to run a better campaign. He has to make the issues." The tone of all Republican activists across the state was reserved, almost pessimistic. Even Harold Knutson's congressional seat in the state was not being taken for granted.[67]

The main problem identified by Republican leaders in Minnesota was that the DFL was successfully portraying itself as a friend of ordinary people and a liberal bastion, but at the same time was anti-communist through its growing commitment to an internationalist foreign policy.[68] Ball needed liberal Republican speakers who were seen as bipartisan, and his negative stance on the Marshall Plan had visibly hurt him. Humphrey, by contrast, was a strong supporter of any measures designed to keep the world and America safe from communism. DFL State Chairman Orville Freeman later argued that the sole factor leading to the remarkable turnaround in his party's fortunes in 1948 was the result of the showdown with the far left, demonstrating that one could be liberal without having any truck with socialism. "From 1946 to 1948 the Communists dominated and controlled the Democratic Party in the state of Minnesota. . . . Henry Wallace came within a hair . . . of being the nominee of the party in this state," he argued. "We learned a little practical politics in that fight. . . . We have high hopes of making real inroads into the Republican state organization which has been dominant for 12 years."[69]

Leading DFL activist Ethel Epstein informed former New York governor Herbert Lehman of Hubert Humphrey's "remarkable campaign against the Wallace forces in Minnesota for the control of the Democratic–Farmer-Labor Party." She felt that this struggle would form the springboard for a concerted campaign against Ball, whose isolationist record would play badly alongside Humphrey's liberal internationalism: "You know the record of Joe Ball. He has been reactionary and isolationist on virtually every issue that has come before the Senate in the past year." Although the National Association of Manufacturers (NAM) was pumping funds into Ball's campaign, allowing him to have a statewide radio broadcast every night, Epstein felt that the Cold War liberal synthesis of foreign and domestic policy in Humphrey's campaign would pay off: "This is *the leading* liberal fight of this election, and the foremost ADA fight as well."[70]

The Cold War was causing a similar shift in the political dynamics in West Virginia. In 1942 Chapman Revercomb had won a Senate seat for the GOP, and in 1946 the party had done the inconceivable and won four of the six congressional seats. The state was one of the poorest in the union, heavily dependent on coal mining as its main source of employment. In 1946 inflation and postwar industrial strife had cost the Democratic Party dear, but two years later Senator Revercomb was all but written off in his bid for reelection. Republican observers saw his support for Taft-Hartley as harmful, particularly in the 5th and 6th congressional districts where John L. Lewis' UMW local 17 "wields tremendous power."[71] Just as important, however, were Revercomb's ties to Taft and his opposition to the administration's Cold War policy, while Democratic challenger and ex-Senator Matthew Neely was a supporter of international anti-communism as well as a New Dealer at home.[72] Revercomb had opposed the draft, opposed the displaced persons bill, and opposed aid to Greece and Turkey. A labor movement highly supportive of Truman's foreign policy could use these facts against him. As in Minnesota, Democrats were using the Cold War and anti-communism to overcome the anti-leftist backlash that had been gaining strength since 1938. Labor unions, in particular, were vocal in their support for bipartisanship as a way of purging communist demons within their ranks. Revercomb's response was to become more and more demagogic, arguing that "Jews are spreading all this propaganda against me" on the question of displaced persons and foreign policy in general, and "it would be a big help if Bob Taft or Homer Capehart could get that pressure taken off from New York."[73] While the Democrats were strengthening their united anti-totalitarian focus, Republicans were deeply divided over how to repeat their success of 1946 in a world that had become very different.

This difference was particularly noticeable in New Mexico, a state where the same Republican candidate stood unsuccessfully for the Senate in both 1946 and 1948. Patrick Hurley had resigned in 1945 as an American envoy in China over the conduct of American policy there, and in 1948 based his campaign to succeed retiring Democratic Senator Carl Hatch on the relationship between liberalism in America and the advance of totalitarianism around the world. A GOP election booklet in New Mexico aimed at veterans associated the New Deal with "Commie infiltration" and the "coddling of Russia" and maintained that the battle in 1948 was that of "Liberty versus the Controlled State." Whereas the "Truman heritage can lead only to the Controlled State," the Republicans believed in preventing "our drifting into a dictatorship and the political commitments of empire."[74] Hurley relentlessly pursued this theme by tying opponent Clinton Anderson's links to the New Deal to the image of an entrenched dictatorship. Throughout 1948 Hurley charged that Anderson, then Secretary of Agriculture, was using federal employees as campaign workers in violation of the Hatch Act. In addition, Hurley appealed to populist sentiment by casting himself as a champion of the common man and Anderson as a millionaire enriched by the patronage of the New Deal state. While Hurley was a war hero and a bitter foe of communism at home and abroad, Anderson had asked in the 1930s for "a State House job and was told to take it out in insurance. He did—a million dollars' worth. . . . He ran relief offices for the New Deal around the west for a few years, finally got into Congress, and in 1945 wound up in Truman's cabinet. He has no record in either war." He had "abundantly enriched [himself] at the public's expense." Now Anderson wanted to "hang on to the teat."[75] Hurley's campaign flooded the state with propaganda alleging that Anderson and the Truman administration had failed the Indian populations of the state through bureaucratic indifference, and tried to build up a coalition among New Mexico's diverse electorate by casting the Democrats as promoters of totalitarianism at home and abroad.

Thus rather than fight Anderson on his terms, Hurley could avoid dealing with economic and social problems by using the Cold War imagery of treachery and betrayal. "Our foreign policy after Yalta," he argued, "fostered communist expansion, totalitarianism and imperialism." In addition, America had "paid for the establishment of a socialist government in England."[76] On the occasions when Hurley did attempt to cast himself as a statist provider for New Mexico, he tended to fail spectacularly. On one occasion Anderson explained to a radio audience that Hurley's plan for state economic development had simply been copied verbatim from a plan put forward in Tennessee. He knew this as the plan included a proposal for "harbor improvements and feeder lines," not a viable idea for a landlocked desert state like New Mexico: "I advise General Hurley that the next time he tries to steal another man's brainchild, he makes sure he really wants all of it."[77]

Hurley's attempt to portray liberalism as a precursor to totalitarianism had little effect on a Democratic Party working hard to set itself to the right of the GOP on the question of Cold War strategy. Anderson as Secretary of Agriculture was a loyal follower of the New Deal line on questions of soil conservation or parity payments to farmers, but confined his defense of liberalism to a defense of existing New Deal programs, never new programs such as health insurance. He combined this with a strong commitment to an anti-Soviet foreign policy. He argued that the "true objective of our foreign policy is the avoidance of another war. To accomplish this, America must be strong and Europe must be strong. . . . Dollars spent today will prevent the spending of lives tomorrow."[78]

Anderson represented a new strand of liberal thought in America which used the changed public perception of foreign ideologies in 1948 to recast events in the past, in this case Hurley's time in China in 1945. At that time Hurley had maintained that the notion of a relationship between Mao and Moscow was overblown, demonstrating to Anderson that "Mr. Hurley was completely misled by the Russians, that he wholly misunderstood their motives and that he could not have been more wrong if he had never set foot on Chinese soil." Anderson's assertion was anachronistic; American perceptions of world communism had not crystallized in 1946, let alone a year earlier. The move was effective, however. In 1948 it was not unusual for a Democrat like Anderson to claim that liberalism was synonymous with anti-Sovietism: "Czechoslovakia has fallen, as did Bulgaria, Yugoslavia, Romania. . . . Other lands are targets. The iron curtain closes quickly. Democracy takes its time. . . . We must become in truth a great force for world peace and freedom."[79]

In a debate with Hurley, Anderson argued that when "Russia's destructive and aggressive policy became apparent, the United States countered by increasing its positive, constructive program for restoring the war-torn nations to economic health and political stability as the surest safeguards of world peace." At the same time, the Democrats were committed, he argued, to popular domestic policies. Although the GOP controlled Congress, had the party "made a serious gesture toward erasing a single one of these [New Deal] laws from the statute books? Not a finger has been lifted. Why? Because a great majority of the people wanted those reforms fifteen years ago and they still want them now."[80] A New Deal ideology supported by a commitment to anti-communism appropriate for a Cold War atmosphere was a difficult strategy for Republicans to counter. Anderson won the Senate race easily, trouncing Hurley by 108,269 votes to 80,226. America's political imagination had changed markedly since 1946, as the approach of the Democratic Party to the 1948 showdown would demonstrate.

The Reshaping of American Liberalism: Paul Douglas and His Political World

In order to understand more clearly the political consequences of the 1948 election for American liberalism, in both ideological and practical terms, it is useful to move beyond the debates of the national campaign to investigate a state race in which the differences between Cold War liberalism and a more leftist alternative emerged particularly clearly and precisely. Nowhere was the decline of the progressive left more manifest than in the selection of a Democrat to run for the Senate in Illinois against incumbent Republican C. Wayland Brooks. Early in the year the Democratic Party saw two front-runners, Carl Sandburg, the famous poet, Lincoln biographer and well-regarded left-wing progressive, and Paul Douglas, an economist and husband of the former liberal congresswoman, Emily Taft Douglas.[81]

It was somewhat ironic that it was the same Paul Douglas who, as a renowned leftist economics professor at the University of Chicago, wrote *The Coming of the New Party* in 1931 as a response to the apparent political paralysis of both main parties as the Depression took hold. He argued that the working class in the United States had to be made to realize "what they stand to gain by using the government as a cooperative agency for collective improvement." He supported labor unionization, nationalization of so-called "sick" industries like coal, and a program of public housing. Douglas was one of many Americans in the interwar period who looked to Europe for examples of social democratic projects that could be emulated on the other side of the Atlantic. "During the last decade," he wrote, "the world has seen in Vienna the most interesting housing experiments of modern times." He also contended that the USSR's experiments in economic planning held lessons for the United States.[82] In 1933, when commenting favorably on Rexford Tugwell's latest work, he mused that the state needed to implement formal economic planning, hoping that "there is a sufficiently strong force outside of capitalism which can control it."[83]

Douglas was steeped in the social democratic tradition within American liberalism as one of the authors of Illinois' first Old Age Pensions Act and its unemployment insurance law, as well as advisor to then Governor Franklin Roosevelt on New York's social security problems. He was an expert on the Social Security Act of 1935, writing a book on the new law and helping to redraft it in 1939. A loyal New Dealer, Douglas also became committed to the world struggle against totalitarianism as a fifty year old Marine in the Pacific theater in World War Two, a struggle in which a shrapnel injury would maim him for life. Douglas in 1948 would date his opposition to totalitarianism in any form to his visit to the Soviet Union in 1927, commenting that "the suppression of human rights in Russia and what I learned about the Russian concept of justice violated my Quaker beliefs." He added, however, that his liberal political ideas acquired in the same period led to a belief that "democracy must be a dynamic and not a static power. If it does not use its own mechanisms to remove the social tensions that arise from time to time, then those tensions will spell the doom of democracy."[84]

In Illinois in 1948, as in much of the rest of the country, the defining issue for Democrats was not the future of the state in American life so much as the extent to which the party and its followers could appropriate the language of anti-totalitarianism that the right had previously made theirs. The principal issue between Douglas and Sandburg was whether one could support Henry Wallace without being a communist sympathizer. Paul Douglas himself told Harold Ickes that Communists in Chicago were "calling the signals for Wallace in this state at least. . . . I welcome this but I think it important that the opposition should be identified and made known."[85] He argued that the Sandburg movement was part of a Progressive Party attempt to take over the Democratic Party and bring its communist fellow travelers into power. Douglas was an active founder member of the ADA, and, like Hubert Humphrey, Clinton Anderson, and most Democrats in 1948, he saw the potential electoral power of a union of New Deal liberalism and Cold War anti-communism. Implicitly linking those supporting his Democratic challengers with Communism, Douglas argued that his left-wing opponents "want to destroy the progressive Center and elect reactionaries because they believe the people would then turn to them."[86] Douglas later stated that once he had the nomination, he concentrated his campaign against Brooks' record on domestic and foreign policy: "I emphasized his opposition to collective security and the United Nations, and to domestic humanitarian legislation as well. And I pledged myself to an exactly opposite course."[87]

Douglas had been able to use exactly the same methods, especially concerning foreign policy, to undermine progressive opposition to his nomination within the Democratic Party. One Chicago liberal set Douglas's ideology alongside that of a majority of the American people, arguing that he was "as vigorously progressive in the field of labor legislation, and inflation controls, as he ever was. . . . I know he supports in Western Europe the democratic socialist parties. On the other hand, there is no doubt that. . . . he seems to be hysterical on the subject [of Russia]."[88] At a time when allegations of spying were beginning to make the headlines, and when the Un-American Activities Committee had reached its apogee of public support, Douglas seemed to have an effective strategy for attacking both the threat of the left and of the GOP in Illinois.

The 1948 battle within liberalism in Illinois represented to the Progressives a litmus test of whether the spirit of the popular front of the 1930s could survive in Cold War America. Chicago progressives were concerned that if Paul Douglas won the nomination, liberalism would be compromised by his endorsement of Cold War imagery. Arthur Wetle wrote to his old progressive friend Harold Ickes that he was "more afraid of Paul Douglas than I am of Brooks. In my opinion, with Brooks the people at least know where he stands." Harry Barnard elaborated on this point: "Paul is not today the same Paul Douglas you and I knew back in the twenties and thirties. . . . In those days, Paul was a liberal. . . . Today, Paul is doing the denouncing of people as un-American. Only recently . . . he said he welcomed the opposition of people who were opposing him, including me . . . who *put Russia first*." [Emphasis original.] Douglas had argued that "we must 'stop the Russians.' . . . he has become a warmonger with respect to Russia. . . . he believes war with Russia is inevitable." Barnard felt that Douglas had "become so emotionally upset over the 'Red issue' that he has strayed far from his earlier liberalism. He sees Communists around every corner. . . . I rank him now among the 'phony liberals,' which I consider more dangerous than frank reactionaries." Barnard, by contrast, believed that aid abroad had to be provided "on a purely humanitarian and economic basis, not on a political basis. . . . I draw the line at helping the present regimes in Greece, Turkey and Spain, etc."[89]

Paul Douglas had himself in his earlier political incarnation as a leftist in the 1920s asserted that the "slopes of imperialism are slippery. Our recent experiences [in Haiti and Santo Domingo] have indicated that America may well be at a point where it must decide whether it shall be an empire or a democracy. It will be difficult for it to be both."[90] Foreign and domestic ideology were for progressives two halves of the same coin, as indeed they were for Cold War liberals. Progressives increasingly believed, however, that the strident pronouncements of politicians like Douglas on foreign policy favored anti-communism over democracy and New Deal liberalism. Several progressives at the University of Chicago claimed that Douglas had stated publicly that if Franco fell the United States would be forced to declare war on Russia, a statement Douglas later denied but which filled many on the left with horror. It is quite possible he did make the comment; two years later he would argue for the dropping of an atomic bomb on North Korea during the Korean War.[91]

The Wallaceites were convinced that Douglas's strong anti-Soviet stance had direct negative ramifications for his domestic views. Their eventual candidate, once Carl Sandburg had withdrawn from the race after coming up against Douglas's vastly superior electoral machine, was Curtis MacDougall, a professor at Northwestern University. A registration law biased against third parties prevented the Progressives from filing in Illinois, but MacDougall stood anyway as a write-in candidate. He argued that he was the only liberal in the race, as he alone opposed "the 'get tough' policy which . . . can only lead to annihilating, atomic war." In addition, because Douglas was so involved in formulating "the Red smoke screen," his domestic platform was politically evasive, failing to spell out how liberalism should develop in the postwar era because Douglas was "not worried about the replacement of New Dealers in Washington by American junkers and cartelists."[92] The fact that a candidate pledged to left of center principles was barred from standing, a proscription welcomed by Douglas and the Illinois Democratic Party, says much about the prospects for social democratic reform in the Cold War era.

In many respects Paul Douglas, in his 1948 campaign and his legislative career in the Senate thereafter, embodied the principles of American liberalism. In a radio speech in May 1948 Douglas contended that Democrats "intend to conserve what we have and in a temperate fashion to push on for fresh progress." He discussed inflation, public housing, social security, and the protection of the rights of organized labor, and argued that legislative action in these areas would "build prosperity and well-being from the bottom up. This is not a radical program, but it is a progressive program."[93] He based his campaign on the assertion that the Progressives and Republicans were essentially in collaboration with each other in Illinois. A vote for the Progressives would help reelect the reactionary Brooks, and then Brooks would continue voting against the administration's foreign policy, effectively voting to allow the Soviet Union free rein in Europe.

Essentially this strategy was the brainchild of the national committee of the ADA, who assumed the role of Progressive slayers while regular Democratic organizations concentrated on attacking Dewey. Franklin Roosevelt Jr.

told the ADA convention in Cleveland in February that Wallace claimed to want "to elect more progressives and liberals to the Congress and Senate of the United States. . . . However, in its practical application, the supporters of Wallace are achieving the opposite effect." This argument, he contended, should be the main weapon of the ADA and its adherents, including Douglas and fellow Senatorial candidate Hubert Humphrey, who was fighting a left-wing insurgency in Minnesota.[94] ADA liberals needed not only to push the achievements of the New Deal era, but also to warn that postwar peace and prosperity was under serious threat from the menace of world communism.

Increasingly, however, the language of anti-totalitarianism was reshaping the political context of Douglas's candidacy. He described the ADA as a "very anti-communist organization of liberals who are trying to develop a middle way between the extremes," and based his whole campaign on that premise.[95] That "middle way," however, increasingly shunned the espousal of statist policies, preferring to frame liberalism in terms of a defense of individual rights in a democracy. A moderate expansion of the New Deal state could sit alongside a commitment to economic aid to the noncommunist world. Douglas was quick to distance himself and his campaign from any association with left-wing ideology. In a memo to his campaign manager in August on proposed subjects for press releases, Douglas discussed the extension of social security, but wrote that the campaign workers must "keep off socialized medicine." In a magazine article in December 1947 he argued that Americans should not be deterred from supporting noncommunist governments in Europe "because these countries may be adopting a greater degree of public ownership than we individually may regard as right and proper."[96]

In September Douglas was forced to repudiate his flirtation with the left in the early 1930s and his support for Norman Thomas, arguing that he was "in no way connected with the Socialist Party," nor had he ever been a party member.[97] He repudiated his own book, *The Coming of a New Party*, arguing that the New Deal had rendered its arguments obsolete, an assertion that would have been hotly contested in liberal circles as late as 1946.[98] The Truman program, Douglas claimed to a gathering of the ADA faithful after the election, was "not aimed at the creation of "stateism' [sic] in any form—not even a welfare state. It is aimed, instead, at removing the impediments to true liberty. . . . To distribute power so that all will have enough to be free and secure and none have so much to be able to oppress others." In a speech to the Liberal Party of New York he contended that just as "rights without duties led to the abuse of an unbridled individualism, duties without rights leads to the rise of 'statism' with all the attendant evils of that Leviathan." He was "wholeheartedly in favor of buying lamb chops but I see no reason why the taxpayer should pay through the nose for those papier-mâché panties that are put on the meatless end bone of the lamb chops."[99] Far more important than social democratic notions of the public sector being experimented with in western Europe were the protection of the limited gains of the New Deal, which in the case of Social Security was becoming almost outside the scope of political discussion, and the defense of rights of individuals through attacks on totalitarianism at home and abroad. The essential basis of Cold War liberalism rested on a synthesis of domestic reform and aid to European countries that had been "putting up a plucky fight against Russian Communism." One former Wallace supporter put it rather more starkly: "The difference between a fumbling, evasive, half-hearted liberalism, and a shrewd, hard hearted, unashamed reaction, may be the difference between saving some fragment of peace in our world and having none at all."[100]

Douglas's decision to direct his campaign toward the theme of totalitarianism represented a shrewd nod in the direction of the shifting local and state politics of Illinois in the early Cold War, and especially toward the powerful demands of Chicago city politics. Anti-communism was fast becoming a rallying cry galvanizing not only the white ethnic communities forming the bedrock of the city's Democratic machine, but also the major players in the African American cultural and political network, who were downplaying their earlier flirtations with popular front radicalism set in motion at the Negro People's Front of 1936. Just as in the case of other African American newspapers like the *Los Angeles Sentinel*, the *Chicago Defender* attempted to maintain its commitment to progressive politics and racial democracy in an increasingly hostile political climate by tempering its espousal of popular front radicalism that had proved so important to the editorship of Robert Abbott.[101] And as in the case of white ethnic communities elsewhere, there was increasing concern in Chicago neighborhoods about the specter of a red tide flowing over Eastern Europe toward the Balkans and the Mediterranean. Paul Douglas certainly sized up the political barometer this way when he decided to devote a significant proportion of his press releases to the subject of foreign affairs, noting that on subjects like the Marshall Plan, Palestine, the United Nations, and the question of "communist aggression" he was "more the Republican candidate on these issues than is Brooks. This is very important but needs to be handled delicately lest I be accused of running out on Truman."[102] Douglas could portray himself as a New Dealer and thereby harness the power of the Democratic machine, while positioning himself to the right of the isolationist Brooks on the question of anticommunism and thus protect himself from the increasingly potent charge of radicalism in the face of an international communist threat.

In the rhetoric of Douglas and the ADA liberals, the Progressive Party campaign was little more than a Communist-inspired attempt to derail President Truman's anti-Soviet foreign policy. Yet candidates like Curtis MacDougall had a political program that at least asked questions about the nature of American liberalism in the 1940s. He accused Douglas of being "strong in endorsement of liberal ideas but weak on specific proposals." MacDougall, both in his response to Douglas's platform published in the *New Republic* and in his own campaign literature and speeches, set out his own vision of what it meant to be left-of-center in postwar America. His policies included the enactment of compulsory health insurance "on which Douglas has made numerous contradictory statements," a long-range public housing program, the repeal of Taft-Hartley, a $1 minimum wage, "a realistic federal tax program based on ability to pay," and the extension of Social Security "to include everyone and increase the average unemployment compensation from $15 to $25 per week." He attached to this statist program a broad commitment to civil rights, supporting a permanent Fair Employment Practices Commission and anti-lynching legislation as well as the end to the Truman loyalty boards and to HUAC. He argued that in foreign policy "the only way to stop the spread of communism is by recognizing the social currents at work in the world," arguing for economic aid to Europe and Asia without programs that were "obviously political, not humanitarian in purpose."[103] Campaign hyperbole notwithstanding, the Progressives seemed to be motivated by more than opposition to Truman's foreign policy; they were formulating a political critique of postwar liberalism, contesting the future of left-of-center politics in the same way as left-wing parties elsewhere in the industrialized world.[104]

In some respects the differences between the professed political views of Douglas and MacDougall were of degree rather than substance. Douglas and Hubert Humphrey both led the fight for a civil rights plank at the Democratic convention in Chicago in July, and both believed that they were among the heirs to the political legacy of the New Deal. Yet their brand of liberalism in 1948 was qualitatively different from that which had lain behind the Full Employment Act or the CIO's vision of a corporate state in 1945. A general commitment to civil rights in the context of the struggle for ideological superiority over the Soviet dictatorship was becoming increasingly more important to Cold War liberals than a statist redistribution of economic resources.[105] The Progressives had woven these two threads of liberal activism together during the 1948 campaign, symbolized by Wallace's tour of the South and his party's repeated commitment to an expansion of the frontiers of New Deal welfarism. Douglas's campaign specifically distanced itself from federal health insurance and the left, and was able to position itself neatly between the virulent anti-statism of Republican Wayland Brooks and the utopian pro-Soviet idealism of the Wallace forces. Douglas and other ADA liberals believed in supporting labor unions, albeit with reservations about restoring the Wagner Act in toto, and in supporting a nascent civil rights movement in the South through a commitment to a Fair Employment Practices Committee, but also in making speeches warning of the Leviathan state in terms which pushed the boundaries of acceptable political debate away from the sort of issues that had occupied the minds of liberal activists since the Progressive era. The Democrats in the 1944 Senate election in Illinois had promoted the concept of "jobs for all" through government activism, contrasting a new era of state-sponsored prosperity with the poverty of the early depression years.[106] Four years later the basic structure of liberalism was represented in Douglas's campaign, but any ambition to push its theoretical possibilities further in the late 1940s seemed circumscribed in the fevered climate of the Cold War.

Rexford Tugwell attempted to mediate between progressives and Douglas, but to no avail. He told Ickes he had managed to get progressives and Wallaceites to agree to forgive Douglas's stand up to that point and to allow him to moderate his views. "But I read in this morning's papers that [Douglas] said 'communists are blackmailing me.' This certainly ends my attempt to conciliate matters. . . . I have found it impossible to go on with the ADA crowd, and in spite of all the disadvantages of a third party move with Wallace as its head, I have decided there is nothing else I can do but go ahead and support him." Ickes felt that the Progressive candidacy in both Illinois and the nation as a whole would be a mistake, but agreed that the ADA was "merely an ineffective Democratic faction," and that he may "be driven in desperation" to back Wallace. "If we have to go down," argued Barnard, "I much prefer that the blame be on the heads of the Brookses. If the blame is on the Douglases, who carry the banner of liberalism, then history will record the absolute bankruptcy of the liberal tradition."

Both Douglas and his Left-wing foes conceptualized their ideology on the basis of the foreign situation; to Douglas the Soviet Union represented the totalitarian bent of the far Left, while Wallace, Sandburg, Barnard, and Tugwell saw "dangerous conflict between two social systems." The need was "to ease the violence which such conflict involves, to bring about peaceful change through reforms and through reasonable yielding on both sides."[107]

Douglas argued that "the Commies have been furious at me for years because I have regarded them as a police state and have said so. . . . I am going down the progressive center between the extreme left and extreme right for what I regard as FDR's policies."[108] The problem was that his definition of these "Commies' and "the progressive center" seemed to be based on his belief that the Soviet Union wished to rule the United States; in deliberately shifting liberalism away from any association with the progressives Douglas implicitly associated the left in general with communism. In so doing, he and most other Democrats were making it harder to create a public opinion amenable to any further expansion in state power.[109]

The Wallace campaign's strident attacks on postwar American foreign policy alienated many who had previously been sympathetic to a challenge to Harry Truman's leadership of the liberal movement. Harold Ickes publicly repudiated the Progressive campaign in October in a statement headed "An Appeal to the Liberals of America." Noting that a vote for Wallace was "a vote for the destruction of the anti-totalitarians of Europe," Ickes branded the Progressive Party as "the most serious attempt in the history of our nation by a totalitarian group to capture and destroy American liberalism" and dismissed its domestic program as "merely an imitation of the Democratic Party program, touched up point by point in a demagogic attempt to outbid everybody for everything." In any case, he continued, the Progressive Party would not even have a domestic platform if it could avoid it: "The chief motivation of the Progressive Party is the promotion of its foreign policy."[110] As Curtis MacDougall points out in his memoir of the 1948 campaign, there was some truth in this assessment. The Cold War had come to dominate the debate within the left over the future of liberalism in ways that significantly downplayed domestic ideological questions concerning the future of social democracy in America.[111]

As in Minnesota, the Democratic Party in Illinois had chosen a Senatorial candidate who could shift the party away from the left and toward a conception of liberalism based on anti-totalitarian imagery. Progressivism had been strong in both states, and in New York, precisely because the contours of that ideology matched those of the constituency in cities like Chicago, Minneapolis, Duluth, and New York. Leo Isacson had won his New York special election, and in 1946 Duluth had elected a liberal Democrat in the form of John Blatnik. Chicago had long been the home of a leftist tradition in American politics, tapping into the liberal conscience of Ickes and Tugwell through its obvious pattern of poverty and deprivation since industrialization. In all these centers, however, anti-communism was more important as an electoral factor. Sandburg did not even stand in Illinois in the face of a concerted effort by organized labor in Chicago and the Democratic machine there to support Douglas.[112] Elmer Benson saw no hope in his prospective Progressive challenge to Humphrey in Minnesota, and withdrew in March.[113] The Progressive Party had found it difficult to find candidates to stand in congressional districts anywhere outside New York City. The Democratic Party could maintain the image of Roosevelt, but could also appeal to an innate anti-communism within the electorate, particularly within the blue collar, ethnic constituencies that tended to vote Democratic.[114] Harold Ickes might complain to Senator J. Howard McGrath (D-Rhode Island) that "there isn't even remotely a moral issue in the campaign," and that "the two parties are disputing between themselves which one has seen the most communists first. . . . As to international affairs, there is no issue."[115] But that was the point: to make foreign affairs an issue, as Taft or Wallace had, was to invite an organized campaign of vilification to which American historiography has contributed. To recognize that a loathing of communism could outweigh support for socialist domestic policies even among union members is to make a significant point about the evolving nature of American politics after World War Two.[116]

Liberalism and the Southern Question

The development of the Americans for Democratic Action over the course of 1948; the campaigns of Paul Douglas in Illinois and Hubert Humphrey in Minnesota; the drive for a civil rights plank at the Democratic convention: all these phenomena pointed toward the growth of a network of liberal political activists reorienting left-of-center political debate around the twin themes of individual freedom, or "civil rights," at home and anti-communism abroad.[117] Both involved the state—in foreign policy commitments or as enforcer of social justice—but both also served to inhibit or deny the need for governmental measures to control economic activity or redistribute income. This liberal network extended across both main parties. Republican liberal Jacob Javits in a letter to the New York *Herald Tribune* shortly after the 1948 elections argued that a modern liberal like himself "believes first and foremost in democracy with constitutional guarantees for the liberty of the individual and for minorities—he is against the monolithic state and the enslavement by it of the mind and efforts of the individual." In a speech to the Liberal Party Institute in New York in 1949 Javits looked to the continued development of a cross-party coalition in Congress, "the rise in power and influence of the liberal Democrat and progressive Republican coalition to counterbalance the effect of the ultra-conservative coalition in the Congress." This coalition would work to enact a permanent FEPC and other civil rights measures, as well as to extend the New Deal in consensual areas like public housing and social security, but would increasingly shy away in the Cold War climate from "an ever-increasing control by government of economic as well as political jobs." Republican liberals offered "a competitive and private economy with government help and cooperation—but not domination. This is all the difference between a drift which could lead to the total state and the development of a uniquely American system to juxtapose to the grim challenge of Communism," a system that would guarantee "the independence of the ordinary citizen's job from the political state."[118] Cold War liberalism could unite Democrats, Republicans, pressure groups like the ADA, and labor unions around the theme of civil rights, "one of the great struggles in the next Congress" without which America "cannot successfully convince the world that democracy is the best plan for society."[119] A world anti-communist crusade thus had a domestic political element that would seek racial justice through legal assaults on discrimination rather than broader state intervention that might seem to offer implicit legitimation of the doctrines of communism or socialism.

The Democratic Party in 1948 was "undergoing a transformation," argued Robert Kennedy of the Chicago *Sun-Times* during the Chicago convention in July. "The party bosses of the North now constitute the left wing. . . . The right wing of the party, of course, comes from the South. . . . Let the reactionaries of the South walk out. . . . The sooner there is real political realignment the better."[120] Paul Douglas was one of a number of activists hastening this realignment through making a "pledge to defend the rights of minority groups against discrimination in employment, in the courts, and at the polls."[121] Evidence of the existence of a liberal network based around the civil rights challenge in Chicago also appeared in a letter from William Benton, then of the State Department and soon to be appointed to the Senate by the ADA Governor of Connecticut, Chester Bowles, to Hubert Humphrey, congratulating him on his election win in Minnesota. Benton had contributed money to Humphrey's campaign, claiming that after his fight to include a civil rights plank, and also to clean the DFL party of communist influence, Humphrey was "already one of the marked men in the Democratic Party. And the eyes of the country are upon you." In an earlier letter Benton noted that Bowles, Leon Henderson, and he were "greatly interested in your candidacy" as the ADA constructed its campaign to revitalize liberalism and challenge the solid South.[122] Humphrey himself would later argue that the main challenge for the Democratic Party in the northern states was "to rebuild our own liberal strength and by doing so we weaken the conservatives in the party. Our fight is not just against the Dixiecrats, by direct action. We win against the Dixiecrats by strengthening our own ranks."[123]

The distinction between North and South, however, increasingly turned on the question of racial democracy, not social democracy. Benton, a strong ADA supporter and Fair Deal liberal, claimed in a letter to have spent "a large part of my life fighting socialism and collectivism in all its forms." In another letter to Harry Truman, Benton congratulated the President on "the way you handled the issue of Socialism—and I agree that the Republicans are dragging out this issue as a 'moth-eaten scarecrow.' "[124] Racial democracy was to be achieved by challenging state-sanctioned segregation in the South, but not by state-sponsored socioeconomic reform. It was a subtle but notable shift from the view expressed in 1937 by Harold Ickes, a keen proponent and sponsor of public works and a welfare state in the New Deal administration, that he had "never dissipated my strength against the particular stone wall of segregation. I believe that wall will crumble when the Negro has brought himself to a higher educational and economic status." Such an elevation, he argued, could only come about with the help of governmental programs, attested to by the presence of de facto segregation in the northern states.[125]

Paul Douglas worried about the consequences of the challenge to Southern conservative dominance in the Democratic Party in the aftermath of the 1948 elections. Speaking at the ADA national convention in Chicago in April 1949, Douglas noted that despite the victory of Truman and numerous liberal Democrats the previous November, still Congress seemed hamstrung by a Southern minority. "We cannot pursue any policy," he argued, "that is likely to aggravate this sectionalism any further. We must continue, at all costs, to seek out where the national interest lies, and fight for it with whatever allies we can pick up in either party or in any region."[126] A key result of liberal Democratic strategy in 1948, however, had been to abandon universal appeals to a broad range of interest groups based on a left-wing interpretation of the New Deal legacy in favor of a politically neutral appeal to American patriotism based on anti-communism abroad and civil rights democracy at home.[127] The attack on Southern political norms that had prompted the formation of the Dixiecrat movement under the leadership of Strom Thurmond had also weakened the power of southern liberals who had come out of World War Two as a force to be reckoned with. As Patricia Sullivan has argued, the ADA never strongly supported groups engaged in direct action against segregation in the South, preferring to enlist the support of elite liberals for a general defense of the emerging "Vital Center" against right and left.[128] The 1948 battle over states' rights in part set the scene for the defeat of liberal stalwarts Frank Graham in North Carolina and Claude Pepper in Florida two years later. It also checked the quiet advance of black voter registration and liberal activism that had been gathering force during the war. The southern bloc in Congress, tied to the New Deal agenda by the lure of federal patronage, had not been hugely illiberal in general on issues other than segregation and organized labor. The shift in the focus of liberalism toward individual rights and away from the pork barrel inevitably put an immense strain on the liberal coalition of the 1930s.[129]

Cold War liberals attempted to synthesize a New Deal domestic program with a commitment to anti-totalitarianism at home and abroad, but in a way that could only alienate southern conservatives. George Sadowski, a New Deal Democrat from inner city Detroit, claimed on the House floor that to any liberal it must be "a fallacy to state that this is a struggle between two ideologies, the Communist ideology and the American democracy. . . . I think there is a third ideology. It is the ideology that is prevailing throughout Europe. It is an ideology that is caught between the jaws of the nutcracker today. . . . represented by so-called Socialist parties in Europe. . . . " Sadowski argued that these countries could not repudiate the left because of the Right's poor response to the depression, but that most "do not want Communism either. . . . We should recognize that ideology." It worked, he argued, in France, Belgium, Britain and the like, and was not so different from New Deal democracy. The response by the ranking Democrat on the Un-American Activities committee, John Rankin (D-Mississippi), demonstrated the right's association of pluralism with communism: "I just listened to the statement here on the so-called socialism of Europe, which is just a shade to the right of communism, which means the destruction of everything that we ever stood for in this country."[130] It was no exaggeration to argue, as Rankin's opponents did, that anti-communism to Rankin was the defense of a social order based on his own political and social beliefs, whether they be the protection of a racial hegemony in the south or economic conservatism.

The limits of Americans for Democratic Action's influence in southern politics were highlighted in Louisiana, where the local ADA chapter in New Orleans put forward one of their own to challenge segregationist congressman F. Edward Hébert in the first district. Hébert, like Rankin, was a member of HUAC and an opponent of Democratic liberalism. Lucille Savoie's campaign also formed part of labor's Operation Dixie to mobilize southern workers, as her office was "staffed largely by union members" in an attempt to extend the political arm of the CIO into the south.[131] Hébert quickly focused his primary campaign on the link between ADA liberalism and the end of segregation, arguing that a broader commitment on the part of northern Democrats to public housing and the like was virtuous camouflage for an attack on the social structure of the south. "The opposition, in this campaign, is dedicated to the complete destruction of States' Rights, and the wiping out of all segregation among the races," he claimed in a rousing radio address to his constituents in August. Noting that Savoie was "the announced candidate of the Americans for Democratic Action," Hébert wondered "who are the Americans for Democratic Action? And for what do they stand? Remember Philadelphia? Remember how the South was trampled on? . . . That means that the Americans for Democratic Action stand for anti-poll tax, anti-lynching, FEPC, and complete removal of barriers between the races. . . . Well, you and I know that I don't stand for that."[132]

Savoie's candidacy was always going to be a long shot in the first district, and she was defeated handsomely, but the effects of the 1948 convention and its aftermath on the New Deal coalition were felt more widely. In the neighboring second district, also based on the city of New Orleans, sitting congressman Hale Boggs was, in contrast to Hébert, a southern New Dealer on most economic issues, and the local ADA supported him. However, the local chapter did not publicly endorse him, as there was "no need, and [we] doubt if he would want us to" at a time when the bitter divisions within the Democratic party over civil rights were starting to make themselves felt.[133] The failure of Operation Dixie and the attempt by Americans for Democratic Action to expand its reach into southern politics exemplified the difficulties inherent in any attempt to change the social dynamics of American liberalism in the late 1940s.

The Meaning of 1948

For anyone who was not a Truman Democrat, the results of the elections of 1948 were a total disaster. Contrary to most expectations, Truman was elected to another term as President by a comfortable margin. Although Truman only narrowly carried states like Ohio, Nevada, California, and Colorado, Dewey won only Maine and Vermont by anything other than tiny margins, and would have lost New York had Wallace not received over half a million votes. Although he came very close to taking California, again Wallace took 200,000 votes that may well otherwise have boosted Truman's margin. For Wallace, the election ended all hope of a third force in American politics. Outside the three largest states in the union his vote barely passed 1 percent of the total, a far less respectable performance than States' Rights candidate Strom Thurmond in the nation overall.[134]

To understand the dynamics involved in the total reversal of the pattern of 1946, it is more revealing to discuss the races at the local and statewide level, which suggests an even greater defeat of Republicans and Progressives throughout the country. In the Senate, the Republicans lost nine of the eighteen seats they were defending, and gained none. The result handed control of the Senate back to the Democrats. In the House, the GOP lost a staggering 75 seats, the worst result for a majority party since the recession year of 1938, when the Democrats had lost 81 seats. In 1949 the Republicans would return to the House with fewer seats than they had had for ten years.[135]

The location and scale of these defeats is also important. Indications in 1946 that the Republican Party might have broken the New Deal coalition were totally dispelled two years later. Every one of the party's urban gains of 1946 were lost, with the exception of the 21st district of New York, which was narrowly held by Jacob Javits. Michigan's 13th district, based on inner city Detroit and won by the Republicans in 1946, gave 62.5 percent of its vote to Democrat George O'Brien in 1948. In Minnesota, not only did Hubert Humphrey capture the Senate seat overwhelmingly from Joseph Ball, but the Democrats also captured three House seats, in Minneapolis, St. Paul, and Harold Knutson's seat in the agricultural heart of the state. Eugene McCarthy's share of the vote in previously Republican St. Paul was 59.4 percent. Humphrey received 729,494 votes statewide, compared to only 485,801 for Ball, the GOP's worst showing in the state since the Farmer-Labor ascendancy of the early New Deal. In Illinois, Paul Douglas demonstrated the weakness of the progressive challenge by trouncing Wayland Brooks on a high turnout; the much-feared abstention of Wallace sympathizers failed to materialize. Douglas received 2,147,754 votes to Brooks's 1,740,026, gaining a plurality downstate as well as in Chicago and greater Cook County. Matthew Neely in West Virginia obtained a majority over Chapman Revercomb of more than 100,000 in a relatively small state, and the Republicans lost all four of their House seats there. Almost every city outside the south had elected Republicans in 1946, and all rejected them just two years later, most by large margins.

The aftermath of the 1948 elections was vitally important for the future ideological direction of both political parties in the Cold War period. The elections touched off a stormy debate in the Republican Party over what had gone wrong, and how the party could regain the initiative it had seemed to gain in 1946. Some saw the fault as lying with those who had abandoned the nascent liberalism of the postwar period and used the 80th Congress as a vehicle of anti-statism. Peter De Vuono, a GOP leader in Chicago's ward 28, a strongly Democratic CIO-dominated ward in a city that had overwhelmingly rejected Republicans in 1948, told Martha Taft that the party had failed to appeal to the working class. Districts like the 7th Illinois district had become "the graveyards of Republican Party hopes." The GOP had not won on a positive program in 1946, but "because of shortages before our economy could be converted to full peacetime production. . . . Some leaders of the Party are still. . . . hoping for something dreadful to happen so that we can sneak into office past a dazed and bewildered people." Since the New Deal, argued De Vuono, the GOP had lost its working class base and its African American support: "Who is left in the Republican Party, the Chamber of Commerce?" The New Deal had given hope to the voters of ward 28, and the Republicans could not use totalitarian imagery to overcome that fact: in "the old days, the only vacation the working man ever got was when he was laid off. Today, he gets a vacation with pay. And he loves it. . . . Do you think he is going to give all this up, because somebody in the Republican Party yells 'Regimentation! Statism'? We Republican precinct captains know better."[136]

Henry Cabot Lodge made a similar point in an article for the *Saturday Evening Post* in December 1948. The Republican Party had to "broaden the scope of its appeal so that there can be no doubt that it is a party for all elements of the people, young, old, rich and poor. . . . It is certainly valueless to have a party in America which stands for an abstract philosophy or dogma—be it conservatism, liberalism, socialism or radicalism."[137] Rather, the GOP should remember its progressive past and propose an effective domestic ideology that would be judged better than the New Deal.

George H. E. Smith interpreted the results very differently in his confidential Republican post-mortem of the elections. Dewey and Warren had "moved on a plane of abstractions too high above the voters' heads." In failing to defend the record of the 80th Congress, the Republicans had sacrificed the initiative to the more aggressive Truman. The party had been "entrapped . . . into a 'Me too' position and otherwise confused the distinctions between Republicans and Democrats. . . . It will be important also for the Republicans to clarify the meaning of . . . true liberalism." Instead of this, Dewey had spoken "like a broken record . . . in generalities pleasing but vacuous."[138] Smith was one among many blaming the liberal bipartisan approach to foreign and domestic problems for the party's defeat. Many outside the Dewey heartlands of New York and the east coast resented the New York Governor and allies like new National Committee Chairman Hugh Scott for their role in the defeat. Iowa National Committee member Harrison Spangler reported that the internecine warfare between rival factions at the annual committee meeting represented at best "a sorry mess and unless the Owlett-Dewey forces can be eliminated, both the party and the country will be greatly harmed. . . . The supporters [of Scott] are really found in Pennsylvania and New York and do not go much beyond that."[139]

Spangler's speech at Omaha decried the Dewey promise of "waste, excessive taxes, arrogant bureaucracy, and socialistic opportunism."[140] The GOP National Committeeman from Massachusetts, Robert Cutler, argued in a speech to the party's national finance committee that America needed a significant change from Democratic rule and its guiding ideology. He argued that "we're going down the same steep path that England has gone—we, the last, the sole, great reservoir of freedom and personal liberty in the whole world—and if this wastage of substance goes on we'll be easy pickings for those bloodthirsty Russian tyrants."[141]

The effect of the 1948 elections had been to shift the balance in the party away from an accommodation with the state and toward using the Truman tool of Cold War imagery to attack the use of state power in America. The Cold War encouraged another dynamic that was damaging both parties' liberal direction after the war. Lodge, Irving Ives, Leverett Saltonstall of Massachusetts, and other Republican "liberals" who backed Truman's foreign policy attempted unsuccessfully in early 1949 to do exactly what Truman had done and isolate or purge progressive Republicans critical of the ideological direction of American foreign policy. Irving Ives appeared on "Meet the Press" in January 1949 to explain his vision for the future of the Republican Party. "We were not trying to liberalize the leadership," he argued in explaining the rationale behind the attempted purge, "we were trying to change it. Insofar as philosophy or ideology is concerned, I don't think there was too much difference . . . in the attitude taken by all of us who are so-called Rebels . . . [and] in the position taken by Senator Taft." Americans needed "economic security . . . under a regime by which they can retain their individual freedom," eschewing the New Deal ideology of big government that would defeat "the very purpose that they're [hoping] to carry out." Ives accepted that Taft was no longer as intransigent a conservative as he had appeared when first elected to the Senate in 1938. He was, however, "the symbol of reaction" by his failure to support the bipartisan foreign policy. Ives' more "modern philosophy" recognized the foreign policy element, while Taft had a program of domestic action, "but it's exactly what he fails to sell" by his association with isolationism. Ives attempted to develop his domestic ideology to contrast with that of Taft, but when pressed by his interviewers he had to confess that he could not. Rather Ives argued that Republican liberalism had to incorporate a strongly anti-communist message. Liberalism among the supporters of Lodge in 1949 had little to do with domestic policy, on which they were unclear, and everything to do with foreign policy. The attack on Taft was an attack on an unwillingness to prioritize anti-communist policies, a reluctance shared not only by Taft, but also by Norman Thomas, and, to a degree, by Henry Wallace.[142] Liberals in the GOP and anti-statists like Spangler were coming together after 1948 on the vital importance of anti-communism as the central principle of Republican ideology.

The Democrats would also reap the whirlwind of the marginalization of anti-Cold War forces. The *New Republic* saw the elections of 1948 as a mandate for "national planning" and "a major welfare program." The election called for a period "as fruitful as the hundred days of 1933."[143] By 1950, such grandiose visions barely appeared in liberal periodicals after two years of piecemeal reform. The rhetoric of the Cold War would form a significant part of the anti-statist attack on a New Deal ideology already weakened by the vibrancy of American capitalism compared to the rest of the world.

Labor unions, the backbone of the liberal movement in the wake of the New Deal, bore the brunt of the shift in liberal priorities. Walter Reuther's negotiations with General Motors in 1948 to establish a guaranteed wage settlement and what amounted to a private welfare state reflected in part his frustration at the limited vision of the postwar American state. Reuther told Paul Douglas that "the inadequacy or lack of federal social insurance programs necessitates our consideration of problems of supplementation of present public provisions and the development of such programs as medical and hospital care and income maintenance during periods of disability." He looked optimistically to the future, observing that any deal with GM "must necessarily be an interim program pending the development of more far-reaching public provisions."[144] Yet in practice as well as rhetoric Democratic liberals were moving away from any sponsorship of an expanded welfare state toward a reliance on private sector growth economics and a commitment to individual equality of opportunity at home and abroad. In 1949 the United States spent 4.4 percent of GDP on social security, less than half the proportion spent in war-ravaged Western Europe. Reuther himself increasingly distanced himself from the language of class as the Cold War came to dominate American political discourse, stating in 1958 that American unionists, unlike their European counterparts, "don't dress our things up with socialist slogans."[145] Reuther was at the center of the Cold War liberal network, mobilizing support for Democratic candidates at the same time as he was helping to purge communists and popular front advocates from labor's ranks.

"Neither of our major political parties has recognized the basic reality of the world swing to the Left," argued progressive anti-Soviet writer Lewis Feuer in November 1948. "American progressivism," he continued, "can develop a constructive . . . policy and at the same time make it clear that it rejects the pattern of Soviet society as the guide for our political thinking." The limitations of liberal policymaking in the 1946–52 period suggest that such a balancing act was far more difficult in the United States than in the war-ravaged democracies of Europe. "The criticism of socialism," argued Feuer, "has become [liberalism's] preoccupation. . . . American progressivism seems to be closing up shop."[146]

5. TRANSNATIONAL PERSPECTIVES AND IMAGES OF THE STATE, 1949–1950

UNTIL EARLY 1949, DOMESTIC AND FOREIGN POLICY DEBATES had in many ways been running in parallel, sometimes crossing paths, sometimes seeming to have little in common. There was always a sense in which both were linked together by the simple fact that both related to ideas of the state. At the midway point of the twentieth century, domestic and overseas policies dovetailed to their greatest ever extent, as the debate over the nature of the state in America reached fever pitch. Two main factors were at work. First, liberal ideas of economic and social development were once again to the fore in the Democrat-controlled 81st Congress in the consideration of changes to the minimum wage and social security, and the development of national health insurance and new agricultural policies. Secondly, American foreign policy was again taking center stage, with events in the Far East as well as in Europe forcing a reappraisal of American aims in the world. These two developments would be brought together by a third factor. American opponents of government-centered policy were increasingly not only using abstract images of foreign states to undermine American liberalism, but were actually traveling to these states for the express purpose of generating an anti-socialist discourse for the American public. Political groups compared American social policy with policies and ideologies developed abroad. By 1950 it was difficult to distinguish between the Republican response to events in China or Korea and the use of a British example to attack the development of an American welfare state. The triumph of Cold War liberalism in 1948 looked by 1950 more like a victory the supporters of the welfare state could well have done without.

"If It is Socialism in England Would It Be Anything Else but Socialism in the United States?"

The Labour government in Britain in the late 1940s held an increasing fascination for the opponents of American liberalism. Internationalism was not merely calling the attention of Americans to the perils of Soviet aggrandizement, but was also opening up the internal workings of foreign states to the close scrutiny of American political élites. The failure of the right in the 1948 elections encouraged anti-statists to look to London for evidence to support their ideology. "I am staying at the Government House, a converted private residence in Mayfair, near Buckingham Palace," wrote Marjorie Shearon in November 1949 in a "confidential" report to readers of her weekly pamphlet, soon to be renamed "Challenge to Socialism." "The place is intended for Socialist officials and Very Important Visitors (like our VIPs). Furnishings, food, and service are luxurious. Of course, this is for Socialist officials. . . . The workers are strictly rationed. . . . Austerity is for the workers, not the leaders. . . . This trip is being made in a search for first-hand ammunition with which to fight Socialism. I wish to be well informed when I testify before Congress."[1] Note the deliberate portrayal of Britain reflecting American perceptions of the Soviet Union; an elite lives in luxury while the masses survive in austerity. As she indicated, Shearon was not a marginal crank, but an important congressional witness on social security and health policy and some-time adviser to the Republican policy committee. On a visit to an NHS practice in Lochinver, Scotland, during her time in Britain, she wrote that she had:

> purchased a goodly supply of [Labour Party] publications. These are on their way to the States by ship. Socialist pamphlets are appealing, cheap, clever, *and frightening*. . . . The Social Security program, combined with a scheme for taxation, constitutes the Socialist dream. . . . In a Socialist society everyone is dragged down to what the person in the lowest place can have. . . . The people are to dress alike, eat alike, and live alike. . . . It works beautifully in Russia, doesn't it, say the Fabians, why not in England? And if in England, why not in the United States say Truman and Lehman as the latter wins a Senate seat by calling for the welfare state."[2]

Shearon was only one of many to use Britain as a vehicle for an all out attack on the New Deal state in the 81st Congress. Articles on the NHS proliferated in medical journals, bearing titles like "Recent Impressions of Medical Practice in Great Britain" and "Medical Scheme Perils US, Cincinnati Physician Declares."[3] The anti-Labour movement in Britain quickly established links with American sympathizers. Factions in the BMA opposed to the NHS received contributions from American pressure groups such as Shearon's Medical Legislative Service.[4] Taft was one of several Senators to receive mail from Britons denouncing the Labour government. One such letter from a doctor in Caterham in Surrey was typical: "I wish to do what little I can to warn the people of the United States to avoid a National Health Service as it has prostituted medicine in Great Britain." Taft responded by asking the doctor to send "all the material available against the plan—letters to the newspapers, magazine articles, evidence of particular abuses, and the like." He then used the Caterham example in his statement to the Senate Labor and Public Welfare Committee on health insurance in May 1949.[5]

Such material was not in short supply; articles appeared weekly in America attacking the British experiment. Congresswoman Frances Bolton (R-Ohio) was one of many in Congress to visit Britain and remark on the "maladministration" of its social programs, that had "largely decreased the personal incentive to work, to produce, and to save."[6] Shearon noted U.S. Federal Security Administrator Oscar Ewing's visit to London, and recounted the "hellish nature of a planned economy" and the "menacing shadow of Government" she had encountered. "The commonest things are unobtainable. . . . Now after one week in England this lay politician [Ewing] has the effrontery to state that the 'national health insurance proposal will be good for America.' "[7]

Much of the transatlantic political traffic on the subject of health care was channeled through the well-financed and increasingly ideologically confident propaganda machinery of the American Medical Association. The AMA executive board and its public relations advisers saw the National Health Service as a useful vehicle to unite the issue of federal health insurance with the broader theme of the development of a totalitarian state, a concept that had been noticeably less significant in earlier political battles over health care. Dr Morris Fishbein, editor of the *Journal of the American Medical Association*, launched a new publicity drive against federal health insurance in December 1948, shortly after the Democrats' surprise victory in the November elections, with a bitter attack in the *Journal* on Britain's health care system. Ostensibly his critique rested on the perceived impracticalities of funding public health out of the public purse, asserting that the "greatest mistake that England made in adopting its National Health Act was its failure to realize that even moderately good functioning of such an act depends on adequate medical personnel and medical facilities. These England did not have." But he then went on to create a dialectic of socialism whereby public health care provision and other social welfare schemes develop "inevitably into a socialized state in which mines, banks, transportation and practically all public services become nationalized." Such an argument integrated the Cold War into an already well-versed anti-statist worldview, suggesting that at "the same time that many of our political leaders oppose communism they move toward communism by embracing socialism."[8] The increasingly tense international situation, and the anger among business and medical lobby groups generated by the 1948 election results, invigorated the campaign to discredit the political legacy of the New Deal by investing vast amounts of money in a publicity drive to associate social democratic liberalism with totalitarianism.

British columnist Don Iddon, writing for the American press, noted the absurdity of the "millstone of mythical misery [that] has to be carried around the New World by any traveler returning from England. . . . Sometimes I wonder if I ever really spent those ten weeks at home. . . . Those were British shops, weren't they, packed with goods and jammed with shoppers? . . . Everyone living here is automatically the target for persistent propaganda glorifying the American way of life and debunking all others." Iddon argued that so endemic was the American glorification of consumer capitalism as opposed to the deprivation of socialist Europe that it had "entered the American consciousness and become almost everyone's reality," despite all indications that the state was increasingly necessary to ensure a more just distribution of economic resources.[9] This was precisely the objective of the American right. The reality of a Labour cabinet minister arguing to a left-wing audience that Britain must "face the facts about the necessity to devote a considerable part of our wealth and resources to arms and defence," sacrificing moves toward socialism in the fight against Russia, was irrelevant to anti-socialists.[10]

Many, like Shearon, Taft, and George Malone, were not particularly interested in the British contribution to the Cold War, but were concerned far more about American domestic policy and the way images of Labour Britain could be used to boost opposition to the Truman administration in America. Thus the line between domestic policy debates and foreign affairs had all but disappeared, and in many ways the term "isolationist" was a misnomer, even for those who opposed Truman's internationalist foreign policy. The Economic Club in Detroit was hardly a haven of pro-Marshall Plan sentiment, but it was happy to invite British author Cecil Palmer to address it on "What Socialism Is Doing to British Freedom."[11] If there was no consensus on an American role in the world, at least everyone could agree on the value of transnational perspectives on American domestic policy.

The 1948 election results encouraged proponents of national health insurance to try to enact their legislation once more in the slightly more sympathetic forum of the 81st Congress. Long-time supporters of the proposal such as John Dingell (D-Michigan) and Senator Claude Pepper (D-Florida) were joined in the new Congress by Andrew Biemiller (D-Wisconsin), who had captured a Milwaukee seat from the Republicans on a platform that had included health insurance, Sidney Yates (D-Illinois), Senators Douglas and Humphrey, and many others. In May 1949 Senator James Murray (D-Montana), new chairman of the Labor and Public Welfare Committee, introduced a bill to "provide a program of national health insurance and public health and to assist in increasing the number of adequately trained professional and other health personnel, and for other purposes." The bill was 163 pages long and dealt with a wide array of health issues, of which insurance was but one part. Its supporters were careful to take into account the ideological climate of the day in promoting federal health insurance. Hubert Humphrey claimed in an open letter to Minnesota doctors that he was "opposed to socialized medicine. . . . The insurance provisions of the bill follow the traditional American principle of social security insurance. . . . I appeal to you . . . as professional people to look at the facts and not at the slogans. . . . All it does is deal with the means of paying the medical bill and assure patients of funds with which they can afford to have medical services. . . . [The] threat of doctor and hospital bills hangs over 80% of our people."[12] S.1679 was joined in the hopper by several other House and Senate plans grappling with the extent to which a federal plan could be consistent with the existing system of medical practice.

The readers of the AMA *Journal* saw their attention quickly drawn to the fact that S.1679's sponsors were not only framing their defense of the bill around the difficult politics of social insurance, striving to guide federal health insurance through a still awkward Congress.[13] The AMA editors also noted "the weird assertion" on the part of congressional witnesses on the bill that the failure to widen health insurance coverage significantly with the help of the state "will lead to governmental control, state medicine and regimented doctors." Indeed, acting Federal Security Administrator J. Donald Kingsley argued before the Murray subcommittee on health that the "real issue is not between voluntary, private health insurance and a national system based on our social insurance experience, but rather between national health insurance and state medicine. I am convinced that nothing short of the social insurance method can prevent the further—and eventually the complete—substitution of state for private medicine. . . . Voluntary insurance has not exactly led to revolution, but neither has it halted the trend toward state medicine."[14]

Kingsley seemed to be arguing that a federal helping hand to enlarge the pool of those with health insurance would prevent an increase in the numbers requiring public assistance to obtain medical care. Senator Humphrey seconded the assertion, arguing that Congress needed "a definition of the word 'socialism'. . . . It is not what we have been talking about this morning. It is state ownership of the means of production and distribution. . . . Now, if there is any socialized medicine in this country, it is to be found in a municipal [public] hospital."[15] New Deal liberalism had always rested in part on the notion of rehabilitating or bolstering the private sector though federal governmental initiatives, but this frantic denunciation of the public sector on the part of representatives of the administration did little to clarify where on the political spectrum New Deal liberalism began and ended in the early postwar era.

Senators Taft, Smith, and Donnell helped to clear up this conundrum somewhat by reintroducing their bill, which specifically argued in the preamble that their Republican alternative "represents certain fundamental beliefs concerning the nature of American government and the principles of government fiscal policy." The administration's desire to levy a 3 percent payroll tax and establish a national system linked to Social Security would, argued Taft, "not only socialize medicine, but will nationalize medicine so that in the end substantially all the doctors will become employees of the Federal Government. . . . [The] book of regulations in England is an inch thick." Having thus tied in the Murray bill to the British experience, Taft argued that his own proposal to provide grants to the states to help the needy obtain emergency medical care and to sponsor voluntary insurance schemes was better designed to protect individual freedom. "We have already extended government operations and control so far that I don't believe we can go much further without letting the government run everything," he continued. "In England . . . there are long queues of people outside every doctor's office. . . . They necessarily get poor treatment."[16] The totalitarian imagery of Cold War pervaded the debate. Taft himself genuinely believed in his alternative plan, which had the support of some fifteen Republican Senators, or more if the supporters of Lodge's more generous alternative were included. Wayne Morse (R-Oregon), the most liberal Republican in the Senate, praised Taft for "making a very constructive contribution in this session of Congress in your endeavor to convince the Republicans in the Senate that they must stand for a constructive program . . . within the framework of our private property economy and constitutional system of government."[17]

The use of Cold War imagery to attack state health insurance would, however, make it unlikely that any reform would be enacted. Marjorie

Shearon wrote to Taft informing him that her crusade against "this whole movement toward State Socialism" would intensify in the run up to the 1950 elections. "Compulsory health insurance will be a major political issue next year. It is a great threat to this country, not so much in itself but because it is one part of the program to nationalize services and industrial enterprises. . . . The Committee for the Nation's Health has its tie in with Communists and Communist front organizations. I don't think you realize how deadly the set up is, how powerful, and how well-financed."[18] She boasted of her massive propaganda campaign that had reached thousands of companies and individuals. Her campaign ran in parallel with that of the vastly influential AMA, which would in 1950 be partly responsible for the defeat of several liberal Congressmen linked to national health insurance. Dr. George Lull of the AMA, in a debate on the plan with Senators Murray and Taft, argued that federal insurance was "based on the tired philosophies of an Old World with health standards far below our own. The plan is borrowed from countries which are politically, socially, and economically on the downgrade. . . . [It] would introduce . . . the poisonous contagion of mass regimentation."[19] An AMA member group in Baltimore published 200 copies of a cartoon booklet for distribution around the city entitled "The Sad Case of Waiting Room Willie," an attempt, according to the AMA Journal, to "dramatize the unfavorable aspects of socialized medicine in a form that is readable, entertaining, and non-technical enough to reach all the voters. Briefly, the story of Willie is a collection of incidents, most of them from factual reports of occurrences under socialized medicine plans in other countries, but all happening to one poor waif, who is really sick but unable to get medical care under the new Utopia because all the doctors . . . are overrun with unsick patients."[20]

The AMA plan used ideological arguments that increasingly formed the backbone of all political commentary on federal health insurance. John Foster Dulles argued that it was irrelevant if statist plans actually worked: "We should consider not merely whether the proposed end is good, but what the process of getting there will do *to* people's character. . . . To socialize the healing profession might, perhaps, make doctors more generally available. But would it not take the soul out of a great profession and turn it into an assembly line process?" Then came the key point in the anti-statist argument that all but ignored the economic theory it professed to follow: "We are engaged in a 'cold war' with Soviet Communism. . . . It is primarily a struggle for souls and minds of men. . . . If health care is best to be found by having government employ doctors and nurses and allocate them to needy persons, then why should those in the world who want better medical care look to the United States for guidance? Socialized medicine already exists . . . in Soviet Russia and elsewhere."[21]

The Cold War had internationalized the debate over health insurance, and by 1950 had killed off any hope of persuading a majority in Congress to back change. If it was associated with the left, it was counterproductive in the world struggle for the minds of men. "There is no 50–50, not even a 90–10 arrangement possible between socialism and freedom," stated congressman Ralph Gwinn. "One or the other must perish utterly. . . . Our socialists propose to continue the march down the road to Marxist serfdom by bribing our doctors to socialize health and medicine from Washington just as the British Marxist government has done. . . . We are at about the halfway stop on the road to total serfdom such as Italian Fascism, German Nazism, and Soviet Communism."[22]

The medical lobby devoted a huge chunk of its financial muscle to controlling the political debate over federal health care. The first step in what would become an increasingly ambitious plan to turn the AMA into an anti-Fair Deal political machine came in December 1948, when the House of Delegates of that organization voted to levy a $25 membership fee with which to fund a propaganda war chest. The official statement of policy outlined at the meeting explicitly listed federal health insurance as "the first and most dangerous step in the direction of complete state socialism." One delegate argued that the "private practice of medicine and thereby the entire structure of free enterprise and the American way of life is in imminent danger."[23] It is unclear how far medical practitioners actually believed in a government plan to turn the United States into a socialist state; the important point, though, is that their publicity drive rested increasingly on that argument. When Clem Whitaker and Leone Baxter of the prestigious Whitaker & Baxter public relations firm were called to address the AMA House of Delegates in June 1949 on the work they had been doing for the AMA to orchestrate a response to the administration's health proposals, both made it clear that the central thesis of their publicity material would be the link between federal health insurance and socialism. This was not merely a rhetorical device, but represented the growing realization on the right that they could become more ambitious in their attacks on the administration at a time of heightened tensions over internal espionage, the Soviet nuclear bomb, and the war in China. The AMA's struggle against the administration, argued Leone Baxter, "can't be ended simply by defeating the Compulsory Health Insurance bills in Congress. The infection goes much deeper than that. Socialization, which has been sweeping the world, has made inroads in America. . . . The people of America are looking across the Atlantic and comparing Britain's government-controlled medical system with the plan proposed here, and they are approaching the conclusion that the plan in its very nature guarantees socialism." She noted proudly that the vast retainer paid by the AMA had enabled her firm to distribute 50,000 copies of an anti-socialization poster to doctors' offices, and that members could "be very sure that the impact of that showing will be felt in the halls of Congress and the White House itself."

The Whitaker and Baxter campaign was significant for more than the money devoted to it; Clem Whitaker's statement that the AMA fight was "a fundamental struggle of free men against government domination," and "probably the most momentous issue which will be fought out before the American people in our lifetime" signified a distinct raising of the ideological stakes of American anti-statism in 1949. The explicit anti-totalitarian language of Whitaker's statement to the delegates that it was "a short step from the 'Welfare State' . . . to the 'Total State', which taxes the wage earner into government enslavement . . . and soon crushes individual liberty" was hardly necessary to convince the AMA delegates about the perceived dangers of federally administered health care, but was designed to disseminate the concept of Democratic liberalism as totalitarianism amongst the public at large.[24] It also represented a way of attracting maximum publicity to the association's decision to take an ever more prominent role in American party politics at a time when anti-leftism was particularly vibrant.

Local spin-off organizations of the AMA were formed in various states where candidates for public office might prove too sympathetic to the Murray-Wagner-Dingell bill. One such group was termed the Allied Medical Arts Committee, a Connecticut-based organization headed by Dr. Thomas Feeney. The Feeney group spent large sums of money in 1950 sending out letters to patients in the state declaring that there were "forces at work in this nation today which . . . would substitute government controlled medicine and all the red tape and inefficiency that inevitably result from a politically dominated profession." Feeney himself wrote to all candidates for political office in Connecticut, demanding their views on the issue and basing his endorsement on their answers. Democratic Senator William Benton was concerned enough to write his own form letter to doctors during his election campaign quoting from his letter to Dr. Feeney opposing "any system or plan whereby the doctor becomes an employee or instrument of the State. I am against any form of socialized medicine or socialized hospitalization."[25]

A doctor friend of Benton's attended a meeting of the Feeney group in September 1950, and reported to Benton that Feeney had "emphasized that the Committee was entirely non-partisan and that its main function was to work toward the defeat of government control of medical practice." Benton's assistant, Phil Levy, was probably right to argue that whatever stand liberal politicians took on the issue, the AMA and its network of pressure groups would "probably continue to badger and oppose" them "because the motivation is 95% Republican politics. All you can really hope to do is convince your fair share of the doctors themselves that the propaganda is a little sick."[26] Feeney went ahead and endorsed Benton's Republican opponent, Prescott Bush, later claiming not to have received Benton's letter condemning the federal plan until it was too late.[27] "I don't think we have to try to find out the effect of the doctors, with their 90,000 letters for Bush," remarked Benton to a campaign worker after his narrow victory in November. "We should start right now trying to prevent it in 1952."[28] The political climate had become particularly clement for the AMA brand of anti-statism when their apparent political opponents were rushing to join the medical lobby bandwagon.

The power of the medical lobby in American politics forced Herbert Lehman into a retreat from support for the Fair Deal in the 1949 special election to fill the unexpired term of veteran Senator Robert Wagner of New York, who was retiring due to ill health, an election Lehman would narrowly win. The Dental Society of New York formed what it termed a "Compulsory Health Insurance Committee" to support Republican candidate John Foster Dulles. "Mr. Herbert H. Lehman," the committee stated in a press release, "pledged himself, if elected, to help carry out the Truman Fair Deal program. 'Socialized Medicine' is an important part of that program." The *Niagara Falls Gazette* noted just before election day in November 1949 that the health care issue "may well be the issue that will turn the scales of the close election contest in favor of Senator John Foster Dulles. . . . Operating as the Healing Arts Committee, doctors, dentists, and druggists are fighting the issue in every section of the state. And if their efforts are as extensive elsewhere as they are in Niagara county, the election returns are certain to show the effects of their work. There is no need for us to point out here the dangers of political medicine. All who can read are aware of its failure in England."[29] One doctor in Buffalo wrote to Lehman's campaign manager, Edward Maguire, informing him of "what is being done by the anti-Lehman forces in the medical profession." Doctors' offices were being flooded with AMA literature, and local medical societies were organizing "telephone squads of wives of doctors to call people to remind them to vote for Dulles . . . because Mr. Lehman stands for state medicine." Dulles' picture appeared on hospital walls complete with dates and times of his radio speeches.[30] President Truman's proclamation in January that the parameters of American liberalism needed to be expanded beyond their depression-era foundations had galvanized private sector interest groups into action against congressional candidates whose election could further that Fair Deal program.

The role of the Cold War in this process took two interdependent forms. First, although private sector campaigns against the expansion of the state were nothing new in the United States, the ideological rhetoric of anti-statism in 1949 was more politically powerful and more strident than during World War Two. Among considerable correspondence Lehman received in 1949 from members of the medical profession, the vast majority adopted the language of Dr. Alfred Lucas of Schenectady: "Nobody can deny that the socialization of medicine would be one step nearer the socialization of everything, or communism. It seems to me that at this time especially we should not be submissive to communistic tendencies, but rather, to adopt [sic] a mode of living in direct antipathy to Russian vandalism."[31] Increasingly opponents of new social welfare measures were adopting the language of anti-Sovietism to advance their cause. Moreover, Democratic politicians like Lehman were increasingly distancing themselves from support of the Fair Deal, and were implicitly narrowing the range of ideological options open to the American electorate. The Lehman campaign moved quickly to isolate medical lobby attacks on their candidate. Lehman wrote a letter to Medical Society of New York president John Keating in October that was published in its official magazine, in which he announced his opposition to federal health insurance. He stated that he believed that "the health of the nation can be protected through cooperation between government, the medical profession and voluntary health insurance plans." In a form letter to anxious doctors Lehman used the anti-totalitarian language of his political opponents, stating that he was "against governmental control of medicine."[32] It was left to a liberal-leaning doctor in New York to warn Lehman that he would "convince no one by a statement like the one you made. You did not say you are against tax-subsidized medicine and that is all [the AMA supporters] need to justify . . . voting Republican, which they do anyway. . . . Do not try to please both sides. There are still more potential patients among the voters than reactionary physicians."[33]

Lehman's campaign did organize itself to defend the banner of New Deal liberalism, but in terms which precluded anything more than the broadening of existing measures. Much of his campaign was devoted to a rebuttal of Dulles' charges that Lehman's 1946 campaign had been associated with communists in the American Labor Party, and to the promotion of Lehman's record in the 1930s as Governor of New York and a supporter of the New Deal. The majority of speeches endorsing Lehman and printed material promoting his candidacy followed the approach of Louis Hollander and

Anthony Froise of the Amalgamated Clothing Workers, who argued that Lehman's "four terms as governor [of New York] constitute the period of greatest social and economic progress this State has ever known."[34] There was a rhetorical disjuncture in Cold War liberalism between the hagiographic depiction of the New Deal era and an anti-totalitarianism which still defended the legacy of FDR but which increasingly downplayed the social democratic promise of American Democracy at the end of World War Two. Lehman adopted the by now standard Cold War liberal rhetorical device of linking the anti-communist struggle to the need to "furnish the world with a striking example of government which is responsive to the needs of all the people" by recognizing "that in a modern industrial society these needs are more complex and varied than in an earlier day." He assailed the Dulles campaign for repudiating Thomas Dewey's moderate platform of 1948 and instead "unfurling the black flag of the 'disaster state' which recognizes no obligation to succor its citizens from the perils of want and insecurity or the catastrophe of depression. . . . [The GOP's] liberal professions have failed to command the confidence of the voter. So today it is making one last try at a program of naked reaction."[35] It was undoubtedly the case that the ideological differences between the two Senate candidates in New York were, as Lehman put it, "clear cut," but that they centered on political maneuvering around the legacy of the New Deal in a Cold War context, rather than a debate over whether there was any future for the sort of social democratic vision that had preoccupied Democrats in 1945.[36]

These state-level contests exemplified the way in which the American Medical Association had assumed a significant political role in advance of the 1950 midterm elections, and had consciously decided to extend its involvement in politics beyond the immediate issue of health insurance. In May 1950 the AMA *Journal* announced that "national compulsory health insurance is a dead issue for this session of Congress," but that because organizations like the CIO and ADA would remain politically active in the forthcoming elections, the AMA should do likewise, and use the momentum it had gained in its battle against federal health insurance to take on the whole New Deal establishment.[37] Incoming AMA president Elmer Henderson's inaugural address was broadcast on syndicated radio, in which he contended, using the Whitaker and Baxter rhetorical blueprint, that the "real objective" of the administration was to "make this a socialist state in the pathetic pattern of socially and economically bankrupt nations of Europe. . . . There is only one essential difference between socialism and communism. Under state socialism human liberty and human dignity die a little more slowly, but they die just as surely!"

This political rhetoric and logic flooded the pages of the AMA *Journal* in 1950, and dominated the San Francisco meeting of the House of Delegates in June. Former AMA president Ernest Irons used the San Francisco platform to launch the association's drive to help defeat Fair Deal liberals in the 1950 elections: "We as physicians and citizens should not relax until, with other patriotic groups in business, on the farm, in the other professions and labor, we shall have rolled back the socialist flood that threatens to engulf our American freedom and our solvency." In October the AMA launched an advertising campaign costing $1.1 million: $560,000 for newspaper advertising, $300,000 for radio spots, and $250,000 to national magazine copy. Some 11,000 newspapers and periodicals carried AMA publicity in the week beginning October 8. The advertising was designed in part "to sell a commodity, voluntary health insurance," but was also intended "to mobilize public opinion in support of a basic American ideal—the principle of individual freedom, as opposed to the alien philosophy of a government-regimented economy." The advertising campaign would use anti-totalitarian imagery of this kind to "bring the issue of government-controlled medicine to a public conclusion," and "to crystallize general public sentiment into concrete public certainty."[38] One member of the Board of Trustees asserted that the "medical profession's nationwide advertising program . . . marked the first time in the history of the United States that a profession, business or industry under government attack has been successful in rallying nationwide advertising support from thousands of unrelated groups, companies and individuals who also believe in freedom and preservation of the American way of life." In the wake of the 1950 elections the editors of the *Journal* would inform their members that they could "rightfully believe [the AMA] exercised some influence in the forming of public opinion concerning these defeated [congressional] candidates."[39] The concerted attack mounted against supporters of the Truman administration stemmed from the administration's continuing support for federal health insurance, but gained both intensity and ambition from the ideological potency of the domestic Cold War.

The result of liberals' unwillingness or inability to fight the powerful AMA drive against federal health insurance left the balance of public opinion firmly on the side of the medical lobby. Of slightly more than half of respondents to an AIPO poll in March 1949 who gave a definition of what "socialized medicine" meant, over half of those identified it as meaning some sort of "government control" of medicine; only 8 percent of all respondents said that it meant that there would be "medical treatment for all." So pervasive was the AMA literature on the proposed bills, and so comprehensive the publicity drive by doctors and their various lobbying groups, it was almost impossible for the general public to be enthusiastic. Only 26 percent of respondents said the Truman plan would improve health care provision; 43 percent said it would damage it, and 19 percent said it would have no effect. 47 percent claimed they preferred the Taft-AMA plan, compared to 33 percent who approved of the compulsory plan. Even among manual workers alone, the AMA voluntary plan won by 40 to 39 percent.[40] Prominent ADA liberal Senator Hubert Humphrey was forced in October 1949 to clarify his position on federal health insurance when he appeared to retreat from supporting S. 1679, arguing that further hearings might be necessary before he could commit to supporting the plan.[41] Clearly the anti-statist campaign against social democracy in America was proving effective, validating the strategy of using anti-communism to set a domestic agenda.

The failure of national health insurance and federal aid plans even to reach a vote in either House did not quite signal an end to attempts to expand the boundaries of state power. The 1949 administration bill to raise the minimum wage to 75 cents and expand its coverage to include parts of the retail sector was unanimously reported out of the Senate Labor Committee, obtaining the blessing of all five minority Republican members Taft, Aiken, Smith, Morse, and Donnell. It was subject to little criticism in either House, most having accepted the ideological basis for the use of the state to regulate the relationship between employer and employee.

Richard Nixon made the interesting claim that the defeat of health measures, the Brannan farming plan, federal aid to education, and the watering down of public housing provisions demonstrated the vibrant link between Congress and a public frightened of increased government legislation in the Cold War.[42] He noted that public opinion would not support a significant extension of government power during the Cold War, the choice being between "England and the US," with the latter symbolizing "freedom" and "the many" as opposed to the dictatorial perils of "socialism." In this speech, designed for his 1950 Senate campaign, Nixon had deleted part of the initial draft, which had stated that "I want a better life for all."[43] America needed to "prove to the world that our system of government and way of life is far superior to anything that any other country has to offer," and so opposed a state commitment to economic equality that would remove a key ideological difference between America and Britain or Russia.[44] A handful of Republicans objected even to the amendments to the Fair Labor Standards Act, again preferring to deal in abstractions rather than economics. W. Kingsland Macy (R-New York) in a letter to his constituents asked "What price the Welfare State?. . . . not in . . . dollars but in concessions, concessions made to what I would call the first of the Four Surrendered Freedoms—Freedom from Want of Individual Liberty." To Ralph Gwinn the minimum wage was "planned economy. It is socialism in any country, including America."[45]

Incremental social reform did continue in the 81st Congress, increasingly supported by Republicans as well as liberal Democrats. A public housing bill was passed in the summer of 1949, albeit stripped of the cooperative housing feature and dependent upon annual appropriations by Congress for public housing projects that were slow in coming. Taft was the main Republican sponsor of this bill, along with Democrat Allen Ellender (D-Louisiana). In one speech Taft went so far as to acknowledge that "to a certain extent it is socialistic in nature. But this question of socialism is a relative matter. . . . I believe that the Federal Government does have a responsibility for preventing the suffering and hardship resulting from extreme poverty at any point in the United States." Taft condemned the opposition to the bill as "indiscriminate and unreasoning."[46] He was caught in the same dilemma as Truman and other liberal Democrats, in that he was condemning anti-statist opposition that he was encouraging in other fields. In Taft's case it was the use of anti-statist imagery to attack health insurance plans and the growth of the bureaucracy; in the case of Truman it was the use of totalitarian imagery to promote foreign policy. "Public housing," argued Ralph Gwinn, "was used as the central highway on which socialist cabinets and parliaments and dictators rode to power in Europe. . . . The various [housing] groups become part of a political machine, dedicated to the idea of state socialism."[47] Gwinn and his allies could not stop the passage of a limited federal housing bill, but they could prevent any real growth in the scope of state power in the immediate postwar period. Between the New Deal and the 1960s the extent of the welfare state would remain within limited boundaries.

Those opposed to the extension of the state in the late 1940s often associated New Deal-era policies with a drift toward socialism, exemplified by the wide-ranging overhaul of the Social Security system during the 81st Congress. Secretary of Labor Maurice Tobin launched a government enquiry in early 1949 into the old age and survivors insurance system, which had not been reviewed for a decade. The Senate advisory committee on social security noted that coverage under the act remained inadequate. Only one-fifth of working people met the eligibility requirements, and those who did received benefits far lower than the average state old age assistance payments. The latter were still by far the most important schemes for providing security in old age despite the administration's determination to replace relief payments with the insurance scheme. The average Old Age and Survivors Insurance payment in 1947 was only $25 per month, compared to state assistance payments of up to $84.72 in Colorado. The committee recommended broadening coverage to include excluded groups, such as the self-employed and farm workers not covered by the 1948 review, the liberalization of eligibility requirements, and an increase in benefits through the raising of the wage base used for levying the payroll tax.[48]

Throughout 1949 and the first half of 1950 the House and Senate Finance Committees wrestled with these issues, hearing from a wide variety of witnesses, debating how much, if at all, to raise the tax threshold from its level of $3,000, and how far to broaden coverage. Walter Reuther of the UAW wrote to the Senate committee members, reminding them that in "the Cold War we are judged by the peoples of the world on our social performance on behalf of our mothers, our young, our infirm, and our aged. . . . I urge you not to pass ammunition to our totalitarian foes."[49] Cold War liberalism laid claim to statist projects previously determined by the ravages of a domestic depression. Business leaders also lobbied Congress, pressing for less liberalization and lower taxes on companies.[50] Most in Congress were, however, resigned to the continuation of the Social Security system as it was, and saw it as a necessary part of the federal state's regulation of the modern economy. Taft, a member of the Finance Committee, agreed with almost all of the Democratic majority's decisions, although in private he wrote that he wished the system could be pay-as-you-go rather than based on a trust fund.[51] By the time of a full vote in July 1950 on the revised and broadened bill, it looked as if state provision of social welfare was firmly entrenched in the American political imagination.

That there would be criticisms of the mechanics of Social Security was hardly surprising. Since the scheme's inception, critics on the left such as Dr. Francis Townsend, author of the ill-fated Townsend Plan, had argued that the system as conceived levied too high a tax on the wage earner and provided too low a return. Advocates of the Townsend Plan for levying a tax on business to finance a flat pension for all were still active in 1950. Townsend's son tried to enlist Taft's support, having seen Taft's criticisms of the trust fund aspect of the administration's bill (HR 6000). Taft was one of many to receive letters from constituents unhappy with the workings of social security. A Mrs. Gerard of Dayton, Ohio, noted that although she and her husband worked, the couple were only entitled to receive benefits on the basis of her husband's salary, an unfortunate piece of social engineering often defended by its advocates as helping to free up a tight labor market.[52] The Townsend Plan did receive the backing of leftist Democrats Sheridan Downey (D-California), Claude Pepper, John Blatnik, Robert Secrest (D-Ohio), and John

Walsh (D-Indiana), among others. One would expect, therefore, given the possible arguments against social security and the alternatives put forward, all of which abandoned the insurance principle, that opposition to HR 6000 would be found mainly on the political left. In reality, most on the left were ready to accept Social Security as an imperfect but necessary Act in a country hostile to more radical alternatives. The far right, by contrast, latched on to alternatives to Social Security with abandon, and attempted to portray the most enduring legacy of the New Deal as the triumph of totalitarianism in America.

Representative Carl Curtis (R-Nebraska) assailed the 1935 Act as "a grossly unsound and inefficient tool for the social security purposes it attempts to accomplish." In a speech on the House floor he made a detailed attack on the bill which would have impressed the most ardent of left-wingers. Emphasizing the unfairness of the current system of distribution, Curtis proposed a flat pension for all and the abolition of old age assistance. Representative Noah Mason (R-Illinois) argued in the House that he preferred the Townsend Plan to HR 6000. Senator Hugh Butler (R-Nebraska) proposed a sliding scale pension based on individual income to be financed by a general tax adjustable with the changing cost of the program. He termed HR 6000 "cruelly unjust to millions of our present aged and . . . so costly to future generations that it might bankrupt the nation morally and economically."[53]

What had caused this minor rebellion by such an unlikely group? One clue lies in the discovery of who helped Curtis draw up the dissenting minority House report on HR 6000, and who helped him "reprint it and sold 19,000 copies for him" in late 1949. "I have come to regard the Social Security Act as the most dangerous law on the statute books," wrote Dr. Marjorie Shearon to Taft, having herself testified against the new bill some months earlier. "It is the backbone of the Socialist State. Not only do the Socialists proclaim the social insurance program to be the very heart of their scheme, but the Communists themselves make this boast."[54] To Shearon, HR 6000 was "a replica of the British National Insurance Law. If it is Socialism in England would it be anything else but Socialism in the United States?" Noting that the British government in 1946 had abandoned the concept of strict social insurance in the funding of the NHS in favor of direct taxation, Shearon saw the same thing happening to Social Security.[55] "Social insurance is neither social, nor insurance," she argued before the House Ways and Means Committee in April 1949. Payroll taxes were "just one more income tax." Her testimony, like those of most of the opponents of the legislation, explained the weaknesses of the insurance principle, and the flaws in its distribution. She was rather more expert than most, having written the economic brief used by New Deal attorney and later Supreme Court Justice Robert Jackson in his defense of the Act in 1937. Behind this rationale, however, lay the main reason why the right was proposing seemingly more liberal ideas for social security for the aged. "Federal officials," she argued, "are working assiduously to impose on this country a program of national compulsory social insurance of the type now in existence in Socialist and Communist countries in Europe and in South America. . . . Other countries are in various stages of transition from 'social insurance' to straight State Socialism or Communism. . . . *The further you go the more deeply you are mired.*" [Emphasis in original transcript]

New Zealand had undertaken such a scheme in 1938, and by 1945 the scheme was consuming 40 percent of all national revenues. Britain provided a similar example. Urging the scrapping of Social Security and the adoption of a direct taxation system less likely to lead to state control of all resources, Shearon made an impression on the committee. "Above all," she argued, "I urge the committee to study the traditional relationship throughout the world between comprehensive compulsory social security programs and either State Socialism or Communism."[56]

Her rhetoric was not enough to stop the passage of HR 6000 by a huge margin in the House, so she turned to the Senate, lobbying not only Taft but also Owen Brewster (R-Maine) and Harry Cain (R-Washington). Social Security was an unholy alliance between the bureaucratic state and Communism. She warned of "more and more links" between "known Communists" and those in the Federal Government who wished "to develop the welfare state." She testified before the Senate Finance Committee, lobbying ranking Republican Eugene Millikin (R-Colorado), but to no avail. The final version of HR 6000 passed the Senate by the astonishing margin of 81 votes to 2, the two dissenters being Harry Cain and Hugh Butler. "There was Senator Taft bearing the banner: 'To vote against this bill would be political suicide'. . . . [All] but two Republicans fell in line like bleating sheep," she concluded, "and blithely gave the country another shove down the primrose path of inflation."[57]

Shearon's attack on Social Security was very much a minority opinion in American politics in 1950. Most on the right were reconciled to a system of social insurance that did not redistribute wealth, and saw in H.R. 6000 a way of including more people and thereby reducing dependence on state and federal handouts. For Cold War liberals social security represented the perfect centerpiece to liberalism in an age of plenty: providing security without resorting to direct federal management of the economy through job creation and capital spending. Wilbur Mills (D-Arkansas) of the House Ways and Means Committee argued that Social Security had become consensual because it did not constitute a "welfare state or is in the direction of a welfare state."[58] Since social security was not socialism, it would not leave liberalism exposed to political attack, as had been the case during and immediately after World War Two, or during the fight for federal management of the health care industry. At the same time, Cold War liberals could use the Cold War as a means of defending and expanding social security, arguing, in the words of UAW leader Walter Reuther, that in "the Cold War we are judged by the peoples of the world on our social performance on behalf of our mothers, our young, our infirm and our aged."[59]

The union between liberal domestic policies and an anti-totalitarian foreign policy was drawing together politicians and interest groups from across the political spectrum into an alliance over issues like civil rights, social security, military spending, and foreign aid. Senator Herbert Lehman, now a leading member of the Cold War liberal network encompassing the ADA and CIO, made it clear that he regarded "the health, welfare, and economic security of the men, women, and children on the home front" as "inseparable from the security and welfare of our boys in Korea, in Germany, Japan, and elsewhere." Yet if America was to win the minds of the non-communist outside world, he had to assert that "I believe with all my heart in a free economy."[60] Therein lay the central dilemma of American liberalism in 1950. Walter Reuther was among those in the labor movement pushing for the development of social democratic solutions to domestic problems such as the lack of adequate health care, but the lack of momentum on the part of Cold War liberals forced him to look to the private sector for help with "the supplementation of present public provisions," beginning what would be a period of decreasing labor radicalism and the downgrading of left-of-center political goals.[61]

A tripartite effort on the part of the Truman administration, the liberal bloc in Congress led by James Murray of Montana, and Americans for Democratic Action to implement the Fair Deal and build on the promise of the 1948 elections culminated in an ADA-led conference on full employment in Washington on July 19, 1949. Members of the administration, the Senate, organized labor, business, and prominent ADAers gathered to showcase James Murray's Economic Expansion Act, a revised version of the Employment Act of 1946 that drew together the various threads of the Fair Deal outlined by President Truman in January. The conference came at an apposite time, as there were strong indications in the summer of 1949 that the U.S. economy was slipping into recession. "We have seen once again," argued Leon Keyserling of Truman's Council of Economic Advisors in his conference address, "that our economy is not self-stabilizing. . . . [America] has become sufficiently conscious of our domestic obligations and our place in world affairs to be satisfied with nothing less than full employment and full production." He was careful to argue, however, that the administration's economic policy had moved away from New Deal planning and capital projects, and from the centralized growth policies that underpinned the original 1945 full employment proposals. The CEA's proposal "should not be misinterpreted to imply vast new efforts in central planning or direction from the top." It centered, rather, around the use of fiscal and monetary policy to engender "wage and price and profit policies of private enterprise . . . geared to the concept of economic expansion." James Murray and his group of sixteen Democratic and two Republican Senators were initially more ambitious in their desire to utilize public works projects as well as fiscal and monetary measures to prime the pump of the economy, but the final statement of the ADA conference downplayed this aspect of the program, stressing the centrality of fiscal policy and the expansion of existing social security measures. The essential goal of Cold War liberal economic policy was now the legitimization of capitalism to the outside world, for if "we fail, Stalin wins; for the yardstick by which the world measures the effectiveness of our way of life is the economic well-being of our people."[62]

Chester Bowles stressed that it was "not enough to go back to the days of the New Deal for the answers" to questions of economic stability and prosperity. The program formulated by Agriculture Secretary Charles Brannan to overhaul government subsidies to farmers represented one aspect of Truman's Fair Deal that did seem to mark a determination on the part of his administration and its supporters to use the legacy of the New Deal as a springboard for more ambitious measures. The administration's new program aimed to cement the coalition of organized labor and farmers that had carried the 1948 election for Truman by replacing the New Deal-era system of parity payments to farmers for restricting production with direct subsidies without price or production controls. James Murray told the ADA conference that the Brannan Plan and his full employment bill were two halves of the same coin.[63] Both would in theory promote increased purchasing power for consumers, including farmers, which would stimulate the economy.[64]

The opposition of southerners and Republicans in Congress, combined with the intensive lobbying of the conservative Farm Bureau, killed the Brannan Plan virtually before hearings had even been held. Many congressmen from rural districts had become attached to price supports, and did not believe it possible to have low prices for consumers and high incomes for farmers simultaneously without significant governmental control over the economy. Senator George Aiken (R-Vermont), who had successfully guided a modified price support bill through the 80th Congress, argued that agricultural policy represented "a fundamental question not only of economics, but of philosophy of government as well. . . . Admitting a definite and serious trend toward state controls throughout the world, it is, nevertheless, unmistakably clear that these nations which have resisted centralized government control are the most prosperous and happiest nations."

The Brannan Plan quickly mobilized Republicans, the Farm Bureau, and conservative business pressure groups into a propaganda drive to associate the Fair Deal state with an imagined extreme left. According to the Iowa Republican state chairman in a press release intended to influence the farm vote in the 1950 elections, Brannan had been "sold a bill of goods by the AAA officials—by government employees in a 'temporary' department which hopes . . . to take over by its subsidies, its iron controls . . . the entire nation's food production." An article in *Human Events* contended that "behind this and other left-wing proposals is a team composed of the CIO, James H Patton of the left-wing Farmers' Union, Under Secretary of the Interior Oscar Chapman and Brannan. Brannan . . . worked his way up in the Farm Security Administration and there received much education from former FSA administrator 'Beanie' Baldwin, who reached his apotheosis as campaign manager for Henry Wallace last year."[65] When this spirited public relations drive coincided with a frosty reception for Brannan by Senate Agriculture Chairman Elmer Thomas and by Senator Clinton Anderson of New Mexico, one of Brannan's predecessors as Secretary of Agriculture, it was clear that just as social security policy had become frozen in the mold crafted in the 1930s, agricultural policy was similarly ossified. The Korean War would stimulate demand for agricultural produce and end the administration's experiments with federal subsidies for farmers that had become politically unwieldy in the 81st Congress.[66]

The important lesson of the Brannan Plan for Fair Deal Democrats, however, lay in the discovery that it lay "in the same class with Communism and socialized medicine" as an issue in the 1950 midterm elections, a proposal "so smeared by the Republican press" that most Cold War liberals were having to denounce what had become a crucial part of Fair Deal statecraft. Kansas Democratic committeeman Carl Rice's assessment of the anti-statist tenor of the approaching elections was widely shared. Iowa Democrats were bitterly divided after selecting Under Secretary of Agriculture and Brannan plan supporter Albert Loveland as their Senate candidate to fight incumbent Republican Bourke Hickenlooper.[67] William Benton in a radio speech during his campaign in Connecticut openly attacked the Brannan Plan as a program of "indiscriminate farm subsidies." His campaign manager urged him to "take [Herbert] Lehman's line and be against the Brannan Plan, just as you have been against 'wasteful farm programs' generally. The Democrats are all running away from the Brannan Plan, and here again there is no advantage in your taking the burden. . . . It is a dead duck."[68] The dynamics of political debates over agricultural policy were complex, but the role of anti-totalitarianism in electoral campaigns followed a pattern. State sponsorship of agriculture through the AAA was by 1949 part of the bipartisan consensus that now shielded parts of the architecture of the New Deal. Yet attempts to extend that New Deal framework offered ample ammunition for anti-statist activists to discredit Democratic liberals at election time.

Social Security was another pillar of the New Deal that had clearly established itself as outside the parameters of ideological debate. Yet the arguments and actions of its opponents were not irrelevant. Their sponsorship of a uniform pension scheme and association of the New Deal state with moves toward dictatorship were significant in the context of the 1950 elections, and permeated every aspect of domestic policy. Debates over the Brannan farm plan or federal aid to education in 1949 follow an identical pattern. In each case, the right proposed alternatives often less economically sound from a "conservative" point of view than the ideas they were opposing. Anti-statists were becoming less and less interested in economic arguments, and more determined to put across a sociological basis for anti-liberalism. It was this that made the foreign policy context so important. The New Deal was portrayed as not simply economically unsound, but as representing the path to dictatorship as seen around the world. Only in the case of Social Security would this argument not have a major impact on the outcome of policy debates. It is now easy to see the importance of the GOP National Committee release of April 1950 entitled "Setback for Socialism: Significance of the New Zealand, Australian, and British Elections of 1949–50." The report analyzed the poor showing of Labour governments in all three countries, with the party losing power in both Antipodean nations and only narrowly holding on in Britain. The results had "greatly encouraged those Americans who believe in the private enterprise method." The report also proved that there were more alternatives to isolationism than agreement with the administration. There was something "more precious than social security or high wages," argued the new National Party prime minister of New Zealand, Sidney Holland. "That is freedom."[69]

A Positive Application of Internationalism: The Case of China

Events in the Far East in 1949 encouraged the American right to expand the use of foreign affairs as an ideological tool with which to fight liberalism at home. It had become increasingly clear by the summer that Chiang Kai-Shek's Nationalist forces faced almost certain defeat on the Chinese mainland.

The right created the impression, using the State Department's recent China White Paper, that a liberal administration had deliberately abandoned Chiang's government, and that it had done so out of sympathy for the far left. As early as February 1948, Richard Nixon in a message to his constituents contrasted American foreign policy in Europe with that in Asia. He argued that the American right must make common cause with anti-communist governments around the world. In Europe, "we say we will oppose the expansion of Communism without regard to the character of the existing governments." America "must be consistent in application wherever the threat or accomplishment of Communist aggression exists."[70]

The Far East represented a clear opportunity for the right to use foreign policy as a tool with which to attack its political opponents, as well as to reshape Cold War strategic policymaking to render it receptive to right-wing ideology. Providing aid to Chiang's forces would entail an alliance with a sympathetic ideology, as opposed to the bankrupt socialism of Western Europe. Just as liberal internationalists were prepared to allow a reasonable degree of latitude in the ideological direction of allied states, particularly in the case of the Attlee government in Great Britain, so right-wing anti-communists and neo-isolationists were prepared to seek alliances with authoritarian regimes of the right who might take over some of the burden of combating communism around the globe. In addition, the Asia-first movement that was developing in the Republican Party was attracted to the fact that Asian regimes like that of Chiang were in political and ideological flux to a greater degree than most European governments, and were therefore in theory more susceptible to American political control. American neo-imperialism in the Far East was hardly new in the late 1940s, but the encroachment of Soviet influence into China and Korea made its application in the Pacific theater much more important to American anti-statists than previously. The emerging representative of this school of thought was General Douglas MacArthur, although his ties to the right-wing establishment in the United States were too tenuous and the right's influence in strategic decisionmaking in Washington too limited to allow his views free expression in the corridors of power.[71]

Many Republicans instantly climbed aboard the Chinese bandwagon, determined to create distance between themselves and a Democratic administration that could be portrayed, however unfairly, as indifferent to the growth of the far left in Asia. House minority leader Joe Martin urged material aid to Chiang, as no American conservative could consider Mao's forces legitimate. America must not "place all our eggs in the European basket. Let us remember that we have friends in Asia."[72] Knowland was a personal friend of Chiang and his wife, and argued forcefully that it would be tragic for anti-communism if Communism should "engulf China and take its five hundred million people behind the iron curtain."[73] Senator H. Alexander Smith, who had in the late 1940s traveled extensively in China and the Far East, argued for a Senate resolution "indicating our support of those courageous Chinese leaders who for many years have maintained their heroic resistance against totalitarian invasion."[74]

Pat McCarran applied the same principle to Europe, stating that "it has become evident that all countries opposed to the common enemy must be recognized as allies. No country has had greater experience in the fight against communism than Spain and her glorious people."[75] The growing recognition of the value of anti-communism to the political right was expanding the possibilities of internationalism. The imagery of totalitarianism could be contrasted vividly with the anti-communism of the right, prompting McCarran and others to push for strong alliances not only with Chiang but also with Franco's Spain as alternatives to Britain's Labour Prime Minister, Clement Attlee, and progenitors of the project to unify the economies of western Europe, Jean Monnet and Robert Schuman. "How would you like to be Communists in a Communist country?" McCarran asked his Nevada constituents. "How would you like your children taught, in school, that there was no God? . . . How would you like to have them taught that there is no virtue except service to the State? . . . My friends of Nevada, this is no day, this is no hour in which . . . to give comfort or consolation to a doctrine that even blinks at human slavery."[76]

This is not to say that all Republicans genuinely wished to appropriate the funds required to support anti-communist regimes in Asia; after all, the congressional GOP had refused to fund the administration's extra-European policies in the 80th and 81st Congresses, culminating in the narrow defeat of an economic aid package to South Korea in January 1950. In the run-up to the 1950 elections, however, the administration's failure to resolve the crises in China and Korea made useful electoral cannon fodder. Taft formed an increasingly important figure within the anti-liberal movement that was busy rewriting the history of the descent of east Asia into chaos after 1945, culminating in the fall of China to Mao in October 1949: "There is not the slightest doubt in my mind that . . . aid to the Nationalist government a few years ago could have stopped Communism in China." Clare Boothe Luce, a member of the American China Policy Association dedicated to supporting the Chiang government, argued that although Chiang's regime was not perfect, it represented a challenge to communism, and had to be supported.[77] Frances Bolton chaired a Foreign Affairs Subcommittee on "National and

International Movements" in 1948 which devoted much of its time to the case of China. "*Chinese Communism is regular Communism.* Its doctrines follow those of Lenin and Stalin. Its leaders are Moscow trained. . . . *The Chinese Communists have followed faithfully every zig zag of the Kremlin's line for a generation.*"[78]

On one level the right's sudden interest in China can be seen as a convenient way to associate the Democratic administration with totalitarianism, thus undermining the political mandate for liberalism received in 1948. Several Far East advisers in the State Department were suspected of links with pro-Communist organizations, including Philip Jessup and Owen Lattimore. Alfred Kohlberg, the enigmatic leader of the American China Policy Association, wrote to Jessup in late 1949 arguing that the Institute of Pacific Relations, to which he and Lattimore belonged and which had helped shape State Department policy since the Second World War, was dominated by "Fellow travelers, Communists, or espionage agents." He noted the membership of Henry Wallace, Carey McWilliams, Theodore White, Lattimore, Philip Jaffe, and various others associated with the left. Kohlberg based his organization on opposition to "the conspiracy that lost Asia to the Communists."[79] Nixon argued that it was not enough to oppose Soviet Russia militarily unless America could "prove to the world that our system of government and way of life is far superior to anything that any other country has to offer." In its "toleration of Communism" the New Deal was failing in this task.[80] Pat McCarran, nominally a Democrat, also attacked the administration for its failure to combat the extreme left abroad. "I cannot explain it," he said, "but the State Department Division of Far Eastern Affairs is definitely soft to Communist China." He argued that Secretary of State Dean Acheson had lied about the amount spent on Chiang since 1945, asserting that only $110 million had reached the Nationalists.[81]

The development of a self-confident Republican-led attack on the administration's foreign policy in the Far East, and the growing power of pressure groups such as Kohlberg's, were changing the balance of power within America. Increasingly marginalized was the earlier Republican attention to domestic affairs and its suspicion of overseas expansion. Instead, Republicans were lining up to join the Kohlberg group or the Committee of One Million group dedicated to the preservation of the Chiang government in China and the defeat of the Communists. Kohlberg called for the declaration of war on Mao's China, and talked of the benefits of a World War III as it would remove Soviet patronage from China, giving the Formosans "the easy task of overthrowing the Communists, no longer armed and led by Russians."[82] More significantly from a domestic point of view, the Far East strategy allowed the Republicans to associate the rise of Communism with New Deal liberalism. Taft and others charted the betrayal of China by FDR in 1944 and 1945, the U.S.-Soviet agreements at Yalta on Polish elections and on Manchuria, and Acheson's desire to back Socialist Britain rather than right-wing Chiang.

The number of Democrats who joined the attack on American foreign policy in the Far East since 1944 demonstrated the political power of anti-communism in a Chinese context. Far from marking the decline of bipartisanship, in many ways China fostered a marginalization of progressivism and domestic concerns after 1948, allowing both parties to find more common ground based on a shared commitment to American globalism.[83] Referring to the 1948 appropriation by Congress of $468 million for China, John F. Kennedy stated that the "end was drawing near; the assistance was too little, too late; and the Nationalist armies were engaged in a death struggle with the onrushing Communist armies. . . . What our young men had saved [in World War II], our diplomats and our President have frittered away." In another speech in October 1949, Kennedy argued that 1949 was "a year of decision. . . . We cling precariously to a cold peace, while all about can be heard the muffled drums of war." Liberalism had to be redefined to shift it away from the "resignation of great problems to the all-absorbing hands of the great Leviathan—the state" that "we in the United States suffer from," and toward the defeat of Communism in the wider world.[84]

As with the right, American liberalism was being redefined by events in the Far East. Senator Paul Douglas quickly proved the point of his progressive detractors in Illinois, arguing that the abandonment of the Far East would allow a Soviet sweep across the world and that "it is clear that we should have at least six million men under arms" in America.[85] To Douglas, Mao's China was "a second Communist police state, as anti-American as the Soviets."[86] Stopping its expansion was at least as important as any extension of American liberalism at home. The membership list of the Committee of One Million Against the Admission of Communist China into the United Nations not only included Republicans like John Bricker and William Knowland, but also New Deal names like Douglas, Hubert Humphrey, Eugene McCarthy, Robert Wagner Jr., and novelist John Dos Passos.

The list of those opposed to the new prioritization of foreign affairs was much shorter, demonstrating the growing weakness of New Deal liberalism at home in a Cold War context. Glen Taylor in a radio debate attacked Knowland's alarmist China policy for failing to distinguish between the strategic aims of different Communist nations, and dismissed Knowland's bill in 1949 for $175 million in military aid to Chiang. "Why, Mr. Knowland, with that amount of money you couldn't buy each Chinaman a bottle of Coca Cola or a stick of chewing gum," he argued, as he criticized the sponsorship of corrupt, undemocratic regimes by the United States.[87] Progressive writer Israel Epstein wrote a book and several articles praising the Communist revolution as a vast improvement on what had gone before, and condemning the United States as being "much like China under the Kuomintang. There is the same suppression of progressive thought coupled with endless self-righteous boasting to hide bottomless ruling class corruption." Such views were for the most part noticeable for their absence, in stark contrast to even a year earlier. The Kohlberg group reprinted Epstein's article as a useful anti-progressive tool with which to recruit more liberals worried by such a train of thought.[88] Events in Asia encouraged the development of a consensus on foreign policy that provided a sympathetic climate for anti-statist rhetoric among liberals as well as on the right.

Developing Cold War Liberalism: Point IV and NATO

Much opposition to the Point IV program to provide aid to developing nations was based upon the premise that the program encouraged the growth of the state. Critics tended to concentrate their fire not on the potential for American imperialism as had been the case in debates in the 80th Congress, but on the extension of government power. The administration often attempted to reassure these critics by playing up the private enterprise participation in the scheme. George Malone claimed that "Point 4 was never a 'plan', but a loosely conceived form of global WPA, trotted out as 'a bold new program', hailed enthusiastically by the do-gooders who think that . . . we should share our taxpayers' money with foreign countries."[89] To Congressman William Lemke (R-North Dakota), taxpayers would in the end be "paying for this lunacy. . . . If we wish to maintain our standard of living, then we must realize that the American farmer and laborer cannot compete with slavery."[90] In 1950, however, the attempt by Malone and his allies to cast their opposition to Point IV in populist terms, claiming that "60% of our own people in the United States of America are not getting along very well," was being progressively weakened by the Cold War consensus. Only 8 Senators voted against Point IV as part of the annual Marshall Plan appropriation, compared to 60 in favor.[91] Free enterprise had to be the guiding strategy behind an administration foreign policy determined to differentiate the United States from the socialist left. Conservative commentator Henry Hazlitt might attempt to argue that the former leader of the American Communist Party had come up with a similar plan in 1944, and that whether or not "the proposals of Point IV stem directly from [Earl] Browder's they embody the same basic collectivist and statist assumptions. . . . International lending *by* governments (or under government guidance) almost inevitably becomes lending *to* governments."[92] In reality, the right was creating a false dichotomy, as in the case of the Far East. Despite domestic indications to the contrary, such as the abortive Brannan Plan and the Murray-Dingell Medical bill, the administration was by 1950 *less* committed to the expansion of liberal ideals than during the New Deal years. The new concept centered on a public-private partnership against the totalitarian left at home and abroad.

The drawing up of the North Atlantic Treaty in early 1949 represented the high point of the administration's anti-communist foreign policy strategy. Its formulation also represented the most significant influence of Republican internationalists on administration policy. The memo in 1948 outlining the weaknesses of the UN Charter as a result of the veto provision and advocating a new Western military alliance to circumvent the paralyzed UN Security Council became known as the Vandenberg Doctrine. Arthur Vandenberg was at least as important as Foreign Relations Chairman Tom Connally in guiding the Treaty through the Senate. The Treaty was significant not only for its acceptance of an American role in defending most non-Communist countries in Europe and Canada, but also for its furthering of a foreign policy attack on communism at the expense of the development of domestic policy. The liberal *Amarillo Daily News* expressed alarm in June 1949 that the Senate might "delay action on the Atlantic Defense Treaty until . . . the President's domestic program receives consideration." Such a policy would symbolize "another triumph of Russia's diplomatic tactics."[93] The United States had to secure peace and unity of purpose in the world first before they could lessen the pressure on Russia and turn inward once more.

Dean Acheson argued that the United Nations had been unable to check the spread of Communism, and that "if the free nations do not stand together, they will fall one by one." Acheson was careful not to portray the new organization as seeking a showdown with the eastern bloc, but its provisions were clear. America was bound by article 3 to supply weapons to member states, and by article 5 to respond in the event of an attack on a member state, though in what way was deliberately left unclear. Article 2 notably asserted that all members of NATO would share the same ideological commitment to freedom as opposed to Communism, whether they be the government of Belgium or the Salazar dictatorship in Portugal.[94]

The NATO agreement symbolized the administration's tacit acceptance by 1949 of what many on the right such as Merwin Hart and Pat McCarran had been pushing for two years: the support of the far right in Europe as worthwhile allies in the Cold War. In addition, the State Department admitted that the Treaty was a new departure in that it did not simply react against actual aggressive actions on the part of the Soviet Union, but worked "against the *fear of aggression* which can seriously impede the establishment of world conditions of peace and confidence." [Emphasis original.] The Vandenberg resolution and the resultant Treaty were "not directed against any country or group of countries; they are directed only against aggression."[95] Under President Truman the United States was now committed to a policy of defending noncommunist nations around the globe. The direction of domestic ideology would thus be vital in defining what types of governments and ideologies were allies of the U.S. government.

The assumption in the proposed Treaty that America would abandon its traditional nonaligned role was enough to revive the old anti-interventionist critiques of foreign policy that were quickly disappearing in the consideration of Asian policy or of the legitimacy of an American foreign role in the abstract. Taft led the Republican doubters in the Senate. His arguments were clearly articulated in his notes and in his Senate speeches. He asserted that the Treaty would provoke aggression instead of deterring it, that it made a farce of the United Nations, that it involved a considerable obligation on the part of the United States, and that it committed America to a foreign policy that may become redundant. In any case, what if a member state's government changed, and it became Communist or Fascist? Forrest Donnell (R-Missouri) concurred. Horrified by the potential for a world war decided at Russia's convenience due to the obligations of article 5, Donnell committed himself to opposing the Pact.[96] Arthur Watkins (R-Utah), normally a supporter of the administration's anti-Soviet policy in the Senate, was also taken aback by the scope of article 5. "My firm conviction," he stated, "is that the Treaty violates the Constitution by robbing Congress of its freedom of action in deciding whether or not this country shall wage war when our allies are attacked."[97]

As in the debate over Article X of the League of Nations Covenant, there was some concern over the scope of American commitments to the wider world as enshrined in treaty law.[98] Taft, Donnell, Watkins, and a handful of other Republican dissenters such as George Malone made common cause once again with Wallace supporters like Glen Taylor, who condemned the Pact as a blatant attempt to reorient American ideology around the simple idea of anti-Sovietism. John Foster Dulles, Taylor argued, "let the cat out of the bag by saying that they had considered in Paris telling the Russians to go jump in the lake, and not even talk to the Russians, so that they, the

American representatives, could keep the liver scared out of us."[99] Taylor found he had much common ground with Taft and Donnell; a GOP national committee report argued that "France, Belgium, Holland, and England are imperialistic powers," and thus America should be concerned with how its arms would be used by Europe. Watkins introduced several amendments to scrap any American commitment to declare war, or to supply arms, which Taylor enthusiastically endorsed.[100] It seemed at first sight that perhaps once more there could be a minority "bipartisan" progressive consensus on the dangers of the administration's military foreign policy.

Opposition to Truman's Cold War policy was, however, changing its character as the national antipathy toward the Soviet Union intensified. For one thing, the Taft group was viewed even less sympathetically in the media and among administration supporters than they had been before. According to the *New York Times*, Taft "backs down before the Russian threats and wishes American foreign policy to conform not to American interests but to the Soviet purpose of keeping the Western democracies divided and disarmed."[101] More importantly, Taft's real reservations to the Treaty were less conditioned by progressivism than previously. Bipartisanship on the question of anti-Sovietism was strengthening in 1949 and 1950, not weakening, as a general agreement at home on the dangers of communism took hold. Taft stated that he would support NATO if there were no commitment to supply arms to Europe, a far cry from Henry Wallace's demand to Taft that "we stop and completely reconsider the entire foreign policy which the Pact expresses."[102] The Republican National Committee Report on NATO drawn up at the suggestion of Forrest Donnell criticized its provisions, but went on to argue that its alternative was "our atomic bombs and the long-range bombers which can deliver them. . . . *A peace can be won by bombing*. . . . Russia, many times larger than Japan, would be more difficult to destroy. But our bombers and bombs are far more effective than those used against Japan. And Russia's targets are vulnerable." The report argued that NATO was not only objectionable for Constitutional reasons, but was unnecessary; a U.S. air shield around the world could do the job of defending the free world against Communism without the need for entangling alliances.[103]

The NATO debate, taking place at the same time as the growing discourse on the Far East, marked the beginning of a Republican commitment to a strong air force and the abandonment of any notion of isolationism in the tense atmosphere of Cold War. As in the Asia debate, one could be an internationalist while still establishing differences of strategy from the administration for political purposes. There were few in Congress still prepared to adopt the rhetoric of progressivism in foreign policy as enunciated by Texas

Methodist minister Arthur Cox. "We are today burdened with expenditures of a military nature that consume more than half our national budget. . . . Can't the members of Congress see that war preparations are making it impossible to achieve the program of domestic reform, for which the American people voted, and at the same time are jeopardizing our political democracy?" he asked.[104]

The answer, both in Connally's reply and in the Senate vote on ratification of the North Atlantic Treaty, was a resounding no, as 82 Senators voted to ratify the Treaty, and only 13 demurred. This was the most resounding victory for the Cold War warriors in America since the beginning of hostilities. Glen Taylor was one of two Democrats to defy the party line, the other being Edwin Johnson (D-Colorado) who had more in common with the Republican anti-statist opponents than with his progressive Democratic colleague. The eleven Republicans were ideologically divergent, some isolationist but most reconciled to an American role in opposing the USSR but simply concerned at the more multilateral direction in foreign policy.[105] By July 1949, the potential for a reassertion of progressive liberalism in both parties, using foreign affairs as a key battleground, was fast declining.

Creating Bipartisanship in Korea

The invasion of South Korea in June 1950 by the North Korean Communists brought into sharp relief the growing sense that the Cold War was allowing the administration a fair degree of latitude in foreign policy while restricting its freedom of action at home. In April 1950 National Security Council officials had prepared the ground for a massive increase in appropriations for strategic purposes with the production of NSC-68, a "battering ram," in the words of one historian, with which the administration could finally scare political waverers and opponents into supporting its ambitious defense spending program.[106] The outbreak of hostilities in Korea pushed most doubters into the administration camp. Senator Styles Bridges (R-New Hampshire), a leading critic of Truman and Acheson's China policy, saw the new Communist threat as holding out the perfect opportunity for a domestic consensus on a response to totalitarianism. America could either "surrender on the installment plan. We postpone war, and we finally become the largest slave state." Or the country could "call Communism's bluff. . . . It is my wish today to . . . [take] a calculated risk . . . of establishing a line in the world. Beyond this line we should announce we shall not permit Russia nor the Communist satellites to penetrate." William Knowland agreed, arguing that if Korea fell, "what hope is there that the chaotic condition in Vietnam can be stabilized, or that world opinion can be mobilized to support the colonial areas of Hong Kong, or Malaya . . . or even India and Pakistan?"

The contrast with the Senate debates even in 1947, let alone in 1937, over America's role in the world is striking.[107] Dissent was all but nonexistent. President Truman was able to announce the sending of thousands of American troops to Korea without more than a whisper of congressional disapproval. Moreover, in the summer of 1950 and again the following year the annual taxation bills were deliberately tailored to provide enough funds for the vast expenditure of the war, limiting opportunities for domestic spending. Cold War liberals Paul Douglas and Hubert Humphrey led the charge for higher taxation with which to pay for the war, noting that after one year the campaign had cost America some $17 billion, of which only $4.5 billion had been met by direct taxation.[108]

The convergence of the right's anti-government philosophy and the anti-totalitarianism of the administration's foreign policy altered the approach of those normally critical of entanglements abroad. On the left, Claude Pepper, fresh from his defeat in the Democratic party primary in Florida in May, accepted the political realities of the Cold War in his reaction to the invasion of South Korea by the communist North at the end of June 1950. On August 31, 1950 he made a speech on the Senate floor, one of his last in that forum, arguing that "hell is not hot enough for those Red criminals who have thrust upon a world still groaning from one war another war," and characterizing communism as "the dungeons of slavery and serfdom, manacled and shackled by a godless tyranny."[109] Even during the primary campaign itself Pepper had clearly come to terms with the changed political realities of America in the Cold War. One campaign leaflet argued that Pepper would, if reelected, "continue to support any and all campaigns aimed at stopping Communism . . . [and will] continue to advocate a fully armed America, strong enough to repulse any danger that may threaten this country from any source or direction."[110] Like many of his liberal contemporaries, however, Pepper discovered in 1950 that belated attempts to combine social democratic policies with a militant foreign policy were not as politically effective as an anti-statist synthesis of Cold War anti-totalitarianism and opposition to the expansion of the New Deal state.

On the right, George Malone tempered his commitment to isolationism, arguing that if America decided Korea and China were important to American security, "then we had better get in. . . . Then, instead of sending a few six shooters into Korea in an attempt to beat Russia . . . let us send there something that will stop the encroachment of one government upon another, not just enough to be of value to the Russians when they capture it." Malone and other anti-administration Republicans like William Jenner of Indiana argued that Korea marked the final realization by Truman of the menace of the far left, and that previously administration policy had been characterized by either sell-outs to Stalin from Yalta onward, or by sell-outs to the left in Western Europe. Malone was "convinced that no one on this floor had the answers as to how it would benefit our Nation to [fund] governments . . . who were already showing signs of socialism or worse."[111]

Previously American policy had been bound to European governments who were to Republicans allied in ideology and in trade to the Soviet Union. Korea marked the beginning of an American unilateralist policy whereby American ideology would be defined less by geopolitical alliances with Europe and more by abstract definitions of anti-communism formed in Washington. This fact alone provided the opportunity for a genuine coalition between the Republican right and Cold War liberals. Taft was another who decided to support American intervention in Korea, charting the shift in administration policy since Yalta. "I have heretofore urged a much more determined attitude against communism in the Far East, and the President's new policy moves in that direction," he stated. "In any event, I believe the general principle of the policy is right, and I see no choice except to back up wholeheartedly and with every available resource the men in our armed forces who have been moved into Korea." Taft went further, abandoning his earlier desire to return America to a peacetime footing in order to concentrate on domestic issues. Instead, he pushed for massive tax rises: "If we are to spend as much as is now proposed on guns, we cannot spend so much on butter. . . . We face a new status of a semi-garrison state, forced on us by the Russian threat. However we got there, now we have to pay for it."[112]

George Malone and other Republicans warned of the dangers of attempting to take on too much around the world, but were no longer opposed to an internationalist policy so long as it had limited and well-defined aims. The idea of a massive air force to project American power around the globe was so attractive to Republicans because it combined a commitment to opposing communism with a unilateralist opt-out clause by which Congress could directly control the scale and arena of American involvement in the world.[113] On the Korean issue, Senator Alexander Smith argued that far from being at odds with State Department policy, all Republicans from himself through to Taft and Herbert Hoover could be "united now with the administration."[114] Taft went further, pushing the administration to guarantee the defense of Formosa and the new Chiang government on the island. In a letter to Harold Ickes, Taft took the contradictory stance of arguing that his support for the war in Korea was forced on him by it being a fait accompli, while at the same time promoting his Formosa plan because it "seemed to me that Formosa was an easy part of the world to defend."[115] Ickes made the interesting point that in the case of Asia it was the administration that had been less internationalist than the Republicans, refusing to include much of East Asia in a U.S. defense perimeter in January 1950. In addition, Acheson rather surprisingly argued that it was not only Communist strength that caused Chiang's fall in China, but also the weakness of the Nationalists, the "total lack of support both in the armies and in the country, and so the whole matter simply disintegrated. The Communists did not create this."[116]

As in the consideration of European policy, events in Asia had an impact on domestic ideology. Until summer 1950 the administration's Asia policy had followed the lines set down by intelligence missions after 1944: Chiang was corrupt, he had lost public support, and most aid programs would inevitably channel funds to the Communists. The right, by contrast, saw a New Deal administration either hoodwinked by or sympathetic to leftist movements, and argued that the Korean incident in June 1950 had finally forced the State Department to reverse its policy. In addition, anti-socialists attacked the perceived harnessing of anti-communism to statist economic projects. An aid bill for South Korea in the House at the end of January 1950 was defeated by 193 votes to 191 by a combination of anti-interventionists and Republicans, such as Nixon, who claimed the bill was useless as it consisted of economic, and not military, aid.[117] He argued that humanitarian legislation both at home and abroad had to give way to a total war on communism. This platform would determine the ideological tone of the 1950 and 1952 elections in America.

"When I Talk About Fighting Communists, I Don't Mean Fighting Communism . . . "

In September 1950, Harry Truman wrote wearily that America was "just going through one of those hysterical stages and we may be better off when we come out of it. The Republicans have usually profited by these waves of hysteria at the time but have lost in the long run."[118] The President was probably right on the second point, but wrong in his claim that America could benefit from the phenomenon often termed "McCarthyism" but which was in fact far more pervasive than such a limited term suggests. The principal aim of those associated with the movement was to purge all those committed to liberalism in either party, and to combat pluralism and social difference in the United States. Again, we cannot view the development of domestic anti-communism in a vacuum. McCarthyism related to the presence of leftists, perceived or real, in the State Department, building on the general suspicion of radicalism in government spawned by Truman's Loyalty Program in 1947.[119] At the same time, anti-communists often associated those promoting big government or pluralism with communism at home, and so the stage was set for an all-out attack on American liberalism similar to that being waged in the legislative arena over agriculture and health care measures. Richard Nixon argued that while liberals like Helen Douglas believed that "Communism grows out of lack of opportunity," the truth was that "almost without exception the Hisses, the Chambers, the Fuchs, and the rest of their ilk, were never denied opportunity. They were educated in private schools, graduated from our finest universities, and held high positions."[120] Anti-communism was far more than an attempt to uncover subversives: it was an attack on the state that would seriously weaken the pluralist future suggested by the elections four years earlier.

McCarthy's revelation in a speech in Wheeling, West Virginia, in February 1950 that he had the names of a large, if unclear, number of Communists in the State Department was a claim that was neither new nor particularly unusual that year. In April 1939, congressman Frank Keefe (R-Wisconsin) had argued that secretly "avowed Communists who have wormed their way into high places in the Government, are now seeking to align us all allies of Communist Russia, and to identify Communist ideals as part and parcel of our future economy."[121] Then, as eleven years later, right-wingers were reacting against both domestic liberalism and a foreign policy they opposed by associating the New Deal state with the far left. McCarthy wanted to "make it clear that when I talk about fighting Communists, I don't mean fighting Communism. . . . [It] wasn't Communism as a theory in the State Department that sold Poland into Communist slavery. . . . It was *particular Communists*—men and women with names."[122]

To McCarthy and his supporters, Communists in America were not ideologues in the abstract, but were those embracing any vision of American society different from McCarthy's imagined portrait of "real Americans" confronting state builders, planners, and their supporters. George Malone asked his constituents what part "did 'poor security risks,' frustrated individuals, homosexuals (91 of whom have been dismissed from the State Department), and other weak administration camp followers play in the formulation and conduct of our Government's policies which led to our present sad state?" What was this unfortunate state of affairs? "People in Washington simply do not think and talk like the rank and file of those good Americans who are the back bone of our Nation. Washington is filled with foreign ambassadors and ministers. . . . In addition, Washington is a haven for those pseudo-Americans who think not as Americans, but as One-Worlders." It was to Malone "always refreshing to get away from Washington and its give-everything-away philosophy and to visit with real Americans."[123]

The Communist charge was increasingly being used to weaken the accommodation with the state heralded by the world war. Frank Keefe in February 1950 joined a number of southern Democrats in using the Communist charge to attack the proponents of a Fair Employment Practices law to eliminate racial discrimination. Vito Marcantonio argued that even if the Communists did support FEPC and oppose a policy of gradualism, that "does not change the validity of opposition to the policy of gradualism because the Communists oppose it. If the Communists opposed nudist colonies the gentlemen would be in favor of them." In this case the link between social conservatism and anti-communism reached farcical levels, with Keefe replying that "your Communist friends advocate them and defend them time and time again. . . . That is exactly what they advocated, nudist colonies."[124]

This debate was taking place at a time when Soviet espionage was of real concern to the United States. Communists, argued FBI Director J. Edgar Hoover in August 1950, "are working behind the masquerade of hypocrisy. For this reason America must be vigilant to recognize Communism for what it actually is—a malicious evil which would destroy this nation."[125] It was clear, however, that the 1950 Internal Security Act, sponsored by Senate Judiciary Committee Chairman Pat McCarran, was influenced by more complex social contexts than simply the spying game. The Act, designed to meet the Communist threat in a similar way to the Mundt-Nixon bill two years earlier, passed the Senate by 70 votes to 7, with almost all Cold War liberals backing what was a bipartisan measure.

Attorney General J. Howard McGrath demonstrated the new parameters of Cold War liberalism when he argued that liberalism "meant freeing the individual from the restraints of the state. . . . Communism is the exact opposite—the unmerciful chaining of the individual to the state; where truth means the will of the ruling elite, freedom the blind devotion to dictatorial command."[126] Members of the Cold War liberal network in the Senate such as Humphrey, Kilgore, Douglas, Lehman, Murray, and Kefauver issued a memorandum to constituents and ADA members urging them that "under no circumstances should loyal and liberal-minded Americans who oppose the Act help the communists or join in organizations with them in their hypocritical attacks against the Mundt-Ferguson-McCarran Act." Senator William Benton's aide Philip Levy noted in October that most of the "liberal bloc" felt distaste toward certain features of the Act but that "they preferred not to vote 'no' on the bill as a whole and run the risk of seeming to be 'soft' on Communists; that they wanted above all to register a vote 'against the Communists.' " Another Benton aide wrote a concerned friend in Chicago that although Benton had voted for the McCarran Act, and had then been absent for the vote on Truman's veto, "he was severely troubled in doing so. . . . Paul Douglas, Hubert Humphrey and other liberals urged him to do so, and joined him on this vote. The argument was that some features of the bill were needed, and on balance these were more important than the remaining bad features."[127]

Most liberal Senators did reverse their position and vote to uphold Truman's veto of the Act, and did later become concerned about the monster they had helped create. The 1950 Act was broad in its terms, not only requiring the registration of all Communists with the Justice Department, but also including provisions for the deportation of Communist aliens and the establishment of emergency detention camps. These camps were for those who "probably will engage in . . . acts of espionage or sabotage." Communists were defined as either being "dominated by a Communist foreign government," or, more loosely, a "Communist front" member who intended to "aid and support . . . the world Communist movement."[128] Yet Cold War liberals, who clearly consulted with each other on the issue and voted as a group, felt that to oppose the Act prior to the veto message would seriously weaken the political clout of Democratic liberalism in advance of the 1950 elections. Bill Benton told Truman that he had voted for the Act "very reluctantly and hesitantly, for reasons involving both Chet Bowles and Brien McMahon," both of whom faced elections in Connecticut in 1950 as Benton himself did. The end result, however, was to shift the political emphasis of liberalism away from social policy and toward anti-totalitarianism. As President Truman himself put it in his veto message: "an organization which advocates low cost housing for sincere humanitarian reasons might be classified as a Communist-front organization because the Communists regularly exploit slum conditions as one of their fifth-column techniques."[129]

Even more significantly, the anti-communist crusade could act as a vehicle for socially exclusive movements. Letters associating communism with Judaism or liberalism were increasingly common. Communism's leaders included Supreme Court Justice "Felix Frankfurter," or "the Jews who constitute the real culprits of the Communist conspiracy," or "Dean Acheson [who] helps dramatize this truth about New and Fair Deal gangsters and traitors." Again, Felix Frankfurter had "made a living out of communism since Sacco-Vanzetti in 1920 [sic]."[130] A Berkeley man argued that the

Rosenberg affair showed "the pressure of the Acheson-Hiss-Frankfurter-Morgenthau treason cult in appointing this loathsome female." He mentioned "the increasing number of arrests and convictions of Jewish spies."[131] Truman vetoed the Internal Security Act, arguing in his veto message that it would "put the Government of the United States in the thought control business."[132] His veto was easily overridden. Anti-communism gave to those contemptuous of the pluralistic strategies of the New Deal the opportunity to purge America of its most liberal elements. In the process the opportunities for the expansion of the state would be severely curtailed. Nothing would demonstrate this more dramatically than the congressional election campaigns of 1950.

6. THE AMERICAN STATE ON TRIAL: THE 1950 MIDTERM ELECTIONS

THE NATURE AND OUTCOME OF THE ELECTIONS OF 1950 could not have been more different from the equivalent midterm campaigns four years earlier. In 1950 the Republican slogan was "Freedom versus Socialism," and this banner may as well have applied to sections of both parties. In contrast to 1948 and, to an extent, 1946, liberalism was on the defensive in 1950, as anti-socialists in both parties linked proponents of the American state to totalitarianism at home and abroad. The campaigns for the House and Senate in 1950 essentially break down into three types for the purposes of this analysis. In the first case, Republican candidates, some of whom had sought election in 1946 under more liberal auspices, undermined New Deal liberalism by associating it with the onset of dictatorial socialism. In the second, Republicans such as Taft and Charles Tobey (R-New Hampshire) struggled to reconcile their ideologically nuanced past with the popular atmosphere of the new decade. And in the third category, the Democratic Party rank and file purged its left flank in an attempt to save the party from damaging associations with the state. The anti-socialist campaign in both parties specifically targeted key liberals who supported efforts to extend state power. Case studies from each category will demonstrate how a combination of anti-government and anti-totalitarian sentiment, melding foreign and domestic policy, was lengthening the distance between popular perceptions of the state by Americans and by their contemporaries in Europe.

Undermining New Deal Liberalism: The Case of California

"Let us prove by precept and example and by our votes on election day that the people of the United States are not going to turn toward any totalitarianism, either Communist or Socialist or otherwise, but that we are going to rely upon the development of a strong and free and intelligent Democracy."[1] Richard Nixon in June 1950 was elected to run as the Republican Senatorial candidate from California, and immediately saw the direction his campaign would take when his Democratic opponent was chosen. Helen Gahagan Douglas, indefatigable defender of the New Deal, opponent of anti-communism when it confused dictatorship with liberalism, had decided in late 1949 that her ideology could be furthered politically only by her election to the Senate. In a radio broadcast early in the campaign, Douglas argued that Californians could "be sure the opposition will distort my record of militant support of the Democratic program of President Roosevelt and President Truman. We can be sure the opposition will misrepresent the reactionary record of my opponent—beside whom Bob Taft is a flaming liberal. . . . I believe that jobs, decent housing . . . are all basic requirements for the protection and spread of democracy."[2] Both hoped to capitalize on the electoral nature of the country's second largest state. Douglas had hoped to challenge Sheridan Downey for the Senate nomination on the basis of her more robust defense of New Deal liberalism.[3]

She had risen to prominence in California Democratic politics on the basis of her involvement in what was coming to be a dynamic left-wing faction in a party traditionally renowned as a cynical patronage machine in a mainly Republican state. Bill Malone, California Democratic chairman who had appointed Douglas state vice-chairwoman in 1940, was a San Francisco Irish political fixer with indeterminate ideological views. Sheridan Downey had seemed radical during his first Senate campaign in 1938, but had rapidly come to a cozy arrangement with state oil interests over the tidelands oil issue and land reclamation. Douglas, by contrast, had revitalized the women's division of the California Democratic Party during World War Two, establishing a strong friendship with Eleanor Roosevelt and using the division as a propaganda machine for New Deal policies. She had then built a congressional career as representative of the poor 14th district of Los Angeles, helping to form a discussion group with other California liberals such as Chet Holifield and leftists like Henry Wallace to formulate a liberal Democratic approach to congressional policymaking.[4]

It was becoming increasingly apparent that the California party was splitting in two even before Douglas's Senate campaign, with organizational fixers like Malone and future Assembly speaker Jesse Unruh in one camp, and ambitious neophyte activists who would form the Young Democrats and, after 1953, the California Democratic Council in the other.[5] Douglas would later claim that Nixon was delighted when Downey announced his intention to retire and Douglas fought off a challenge from Los Angeles *Daily News* owner Manchester Boddy, the candidate of the conservative party bosses, for the Democratic nomination. Nixon thought that Douglas's victory would provide him with the most politically divisive opponent possible in the November election. She rightly noted in her autobiography that the Cold War, and specifically the HUAC hearings in Hollywood and the rise of communism in Asia, had created the ideological space for a form of conservatism in politics that had been notably lacking in mainstream Republican circles under the Warren governorship. The fall of China, and then the outbreak of war in Korea, had shaken the prospects for American liberalism in 1950. "California, always more sensitive to events in Asia than other parts of the country are, was very uneasy," wrote Douglas. "In such an environment of apprehension, a junior congressman who single-mindedly went after spies, traitors and other subversives could quickly be seen as a savior."[6] She might have added that he might also be seen as a savior by Democratic Party conservatives, eager to use the developing right-wing political climate to maintain control of a party that had been shifting leftward since the Upton Sinclair gubernatorial campaign of 1934.

Fulton Lewis was one of the first to note the bitter animosities that a putative Douglas candidacy would arouse, referring in fall 1949 to her "extreme radical tendencies" which would help her "cut deeply into the left-wing vote in South California and the Labor vote all over the State." Nixon, by contrast, preferred to unite California's diverse electorate around his history of opposing the far left. Nixon's GOP primary opponent Raymond Darby barely used the Communist issue in his announcement speech or his primary campaign, whereas Nixon in his fight against subversion had, according to Lewis, "undoubtedly the most brilliant record that has been made by any young congressman in a great many years."[7] The campaign would deliberately be cast as a choice between "freedom" in the form of anti-communism, and the "slavery" of a Socialist state.

Initially in 1949 it looked as though Nixon intended to use his campaign as a vehicle with which to attack what he saw as the excesses of American liberalism. Nixon assured California Republicans that, if he chose to run, "it is my intention to wage an aggressive, hard-hitting campaign against the Socialistic Welfare State policies . . . supported by the incumbent Democratic Senator, Mr. Downey, and by congresswoman Helen Gahagan Douglas."[8] In his speech announcing his candidacy Nixon posed "the choice between freedom and State Socialism. . . . They call it planned economy, the fair deal, or social welfare. It's still the same old socialist baloney any way you slice it." Britain demonstrated "the bleak road of austerity" and "the brink of economic and political chaos" that would result from such an approach. Nixon stood for "the high road which leads to freedom and the realization of the American dream."[9]

This strategy, which would be followed throughout the campaign, was noticeably different in emphasis from that of 1946, when Nixon had felt obliged to portray Republicanism in rather more moderate terms. Even in 1950 Republicans felt bound to restrict their criticism of liberalism in toto. Murray Chotiner, the Los Angeles lawyer who doubled as Nixon's campaign manager, advised Patrick Hillings, Nixon's successor in the 12th congressional district, to use the term "state socialism" rather than any term using the word "labor." The GOP had "enough of a fight against us as it is, without taking on labor unnecessarily. Our campaign policy is not to refer to the 'welfare state' . . . because the Democrats are proudly declaring that they *are* for social welfare."[10] Still, the Nixon campaign recognized that the political atmosphere in 1950 was very different from when Nixon had first run for Congress. His "basic disagreement" with Helen Douglas was that she wanted to "take over various institutions and enterprises in the nation and either operate them directly or control them from Washington." Nixon argued that America had "too much government ownership and control."[11] On one level the California campaign represented a clash over the future economic development of the American state.

In the area of foreign policy, Nixon argued throughout the campaign that Douglas had not supported her own President's program overseas, citing the cases of the Truman Doctrine and aid to Korea. His campaign sent out pink campaign sheets alleging that she and Vito Marcantonio, the American Labor Party congressman from New York, had voted the same way 354 times on both domestic and foreign policy.[12] Douglas herself had in fact introduced anti-communism as a major issue when in the summer of 1950 she had launched her campaign by criticizing Nixon for voting against the economic aid package for Korea in January.[13] In a sense she, too, was distancing herself from her earlier ideological stance. No longer could she argue, as she had in March 1946, that Communism was no threat to America, a statement that, argued Douglas, "had a devastating effect on my credibility," and was used to good effect by her Republican opponents in 1950. Douglas praised the "courageous action" taken by Truman "to halt the forces of Red aggression in Korea," and argued that "Communism's campaign of conquest must end."[14]

Unfortunately her new strategy played right into the Republicans' hands by diverting popular attention away from her policy record and on to anti-communism. "Helen Douglas is trying to portray a new role as a foe of

Communism," stated a GOP strategy plan. "Do not let her get away with it! It is a phony act." Since Korea, it went on, she had voted against the Internal Security Act and the bill to require the Department of Defense to fire poor security risks. Her liberalism was still with her, and could be used against her in the context of the Cold War.[15] "The issue of the conflict between the forces of Communism within the United States and those who are fighting to uphold the ideology of the American way of life will be highlighted in the forthcoming . . . election in California," promised a GOP release. Nixon was the champion investigator on the Un-American Activities Committee; Douglas was "far to the left in her beliefs and actions."[16] Nixon argued that Douglas's domestic liberalism had compromised her anti-communism in foreign policy in the past, and would do so again in the future. If California voters "send my opponent to the Senate," he claimed, "they will cast their votes in favor of the entire domestic spending program . . . regardless of the effect it will have on the defense of this nation against aggression."[17] The *Alhambra Post Advocate* commented on what it termed Douglas's "weird voting record": "While Mrs. Douglas continues to curry communistic favor by her actions on the House floor . . . Nixon is leaving no doubt of his hatred of home front and world communism." It claimed that the Democratic National Committee was concerned about her record "at a time when American soldiers, sailors and marines are dying in the battle against the communists in Korea."[18]

Particularly striking about the 1950 campaign was the Republican determination to associate state-centered liberalism with totalitarianism, a far cry from mere criticism of Douglas for having ignored the Communist threat. According to the Nixon campaign, Douglas *was* a Communist threat. Murray Chotiner and other Nixon organizers decided early in 1950 to recruit the Washington conservative researcher and *Human Events* writer Edna Lonigan to research Douglas's life history in Washington. Her research notes included topics such as "Helen Gahagan Douglas and the Fronts," and "HGD—Candidate of What Party? PCA-PAC-CPA?" Lonigan argued that the CIO's Political Action Committee was a way for Communists to insinuate themselves into public life, and that Douglas was associated with it. The Front's domestic program included progressive legislation like "the industrialization of backward areas . . . aid for farmers, housing, socialized medicine . . . 'democracy' through opposing poll taxes etc." Thus this "PAC program" was by nature "Communist," and if Douglas knew this, "she was willing to help the fifth column."[19]

In a report sent to Nixon, Lonigan argued that the "Communist policy on domestic issues was, like their foreign policy, one variation or another of the

Browder Teheran Plan. It had two main objectives—to get Americans to spend themselves into bankruptcy, and to regiment and federalize our local political institutions . . . and private enterprise. . . . If [Douglas] knew these policies originated in the USSR, she is a Communist." Lonigan argued that the 1945 plan for full employment was advocated by Communist leader Eugene Dennis, and meant when "translated—waste time tinkering with welfare so no one will notice the Soviets rearming." Douglas's fight against Jim Crow and racism was an attempt "to stir up bitter race friction" in order to further social revolution.[20] "I think the pattern can be made very clear," she told Nixon in a memo in July 1950. Six weeks later Nixon himself wrote to Bill Brennan asking him to check some of the Lonigan references so that Douglas's liberal positions could be associated with Communism.[21]

It was clear that Lonigan's material was intended to associate Douglas with the far left by implication rather than by fact, and the Nixon campaign tended to stretch the parameters of totalitarianism to outlandish lengths. For instance, Nixon argued in one speech that if leftists could not obtain revolution by force, liberal tenets such as confiscatory taxation would result in the same result: "Enslavement of the people."[22] Thanks to the domestic ramifications of Cold War, the New Deal was finally coming under effective attack.[23] As Lonigan's material proved, the California campaign was more stridently anti-communist and anti-left than anything during or immediately after the war. "Something unhealthy was developing," wrote Douglas, "a mood of pure hatred."[24]

The right's association of American statism with totalitarianism had a devastating effect on Douglas's campaign. She was forced to argue defensively that the Nixon campaign was "conspiring to sell the welfare of the American people down the river of fear and hysteria for personal ambitions. . . . They are using every conceivable means to confuse and stampede the American people into voting for political poison. . . . For instance, my opponent voted against the National Housing Act in 1949. The real estate lobby said that Act was socialistic. My opponent followed its direction despite the fact that Senator Bob Taft was one of the co-authors of the Act. No smokescreen can obscure these facts." Douglas was caught in the dilemma all liberals faced in 1950; they themselves were stressing anti-communism by highlighting foreign policy, but were suffering in a domestic context from the Republicans' association of the left with communism. "My opponent and I agree on one thing only. We are both opposed to Communism," stated Douglas. She took up her consistent theme that her liberalism meant working for democracy as well as opposing communism.[25]

She repeatedly begged well-known and popular New Dealers such as her friend Harold Ickes and Vice President Alben Barkley to come to California and support her.[26] Her efforts were becoming increasingly desperate, particularly when most senior California Democrats started to drift into the Nixon camp. Her main primary opponent, Manchester Boddy, had attacked Douglas's statist liberalism early in the campaign, arguing that Americans wanted "a sound program that will not turn the country over to the Communists or reduce it to bankruptcy."[27] George Creel, self-appointed head of the "California Democrats for Nixon" that by election day outnumbered Douglas's campaign team, claimed she had "associated herself . . . with twelve organizations . . . cited as Communist and subversive. . . . We do not say that Mrs. Douglas is a Communist. We do say that . . . she has been active for measures and causes that have been either inspired or approved by the Communist Party . . . or the Comintern."[28]

It was clear that the changed political imagination of America had destroyed Douglas's candidacy when the African American newspaper the *Los Angeles Sentinel*, whose main readership resided in Douglas's House constituency, condemned her "weak-kneed stand on the subject of Communism, and its fellow-travellers. . . . The protracted struggle between Capitalism and Communism is . . . affecting all of our national thinking. . . . The future of American Negroes is inexorably related to the future of America itself."[29] At the end of World War Two the *Sentinel*, when discussing local and national politics, had concerned itself almost exclusively with questions of race and domestic liberalism. In 1950 its assessment of the California Senate race contrasted the "airing of shopworn domestic problems" with the two crucial issues of "what to do about Communism (homespun and imported) and our Asiatic policy in the light of Korean developments. . . . A wave of nationalism is engulfing the country, and the Democratic Party everywhere is locked in a 'last gasp' struggle to save its political life." The newspaper renounced its prior support for Douglas's record, and instead condemned "Washington 'do-gooders' who promised us civil rights (which we didn't get), subsidized cradle-to-grave security (which we don't want), and even a 'century of the common man' (whatever that means). Perhaps tomorrow someone will dream up supersonic, super-planned thought control." The editorial policy of the *Sentinel* seemed to be shifting away from the explicit promotion of African American interests through involvement in liberal politics, preferring instead to embrace Richard Nixon's conservative agenda of presenting all Americans as a homogeneous mass that could be treated equally without state intervention on behalf of marginalized groups. Nixon even wrote a letter to the *Sentinel* thanking the daily for its support and reaffirming his belief that "all Americans must band together as never before to resist the infiltration and aggression designed to destroy what you have so appropriately termed 'the American dream'."[30]

The results of the California Senate race in 1950 represented a massive blow for the political left in America, the effects of which would be felt for the next two decades. Of the State's 58 counties, Douglas carried five, of which only three had populations of more than 10,000. She won her largest county, Contra Costa, based on the industrial port of Richmond, by 316 votes, the totals being 44,968 for her to 44,652 for Nixon. Her one comfortable victory was in Solano County, which she carried by 4,004 votes. Elsewhere, Nixon could claim to have done badly if his vote dropped below 60 percent. He broke that total in Los Angeles, where his majority was 319,293 votes. In San Francisco, he obtained 57 percent and a majority of almost 43,000. He took three-quarters of all votes in fast-growing Orange County, and claimed a 20,000 majority in Alameda, normally a difficult battleground in and around Berkeley. The result is even more astonishing when set alongside the actual GOP registration totals in each county. The highest percentage of registered Republican members was 49 percent in Orange County, and in San Francisco the total was only 34 percent and in Alameda, 39 percent. Nixon's victory thus included hundreds of thousands of Democrats, and not only Creel Democrats but African Americans and regular blue collar Democrats terrified by the potential for Communist advance through the American state: 2,183,454 Californians voted for Nixon, almost double the registered GOP total in the State. Only 1,502,507 backed Douglas.[31]

The right's ability to suggest that the moderate and far left formed a totalitarian whole had crippled the descendants of the New Deal. California was by no means the only example, although it was probably the most polarizing, exemplified by Douglas's recollection of what she termed was a "shocking" campaign. "The worst moment, a sight I couldn't shake, was when children picked up rocks and threw them at my car, at me." Raymond Moley, formerly a New Dealer and now a conservative, saw in the campaign a more positive side to popular antipathy toward the left: "The contest between Nixon and Douglas presents the essential domestic issue before the country—the issue of individual freedom as against increasing governmental intervention in economic life." Douglas's "Democratic Credo" was "vague talk about democracy, behind which lurked the reality of a superstate with handouts for everyone."[32]

Undermining New Deal Liberalism: The Case of Maryland

Republican John Marshall Butler's campaign to unseat Democratic Senator Millard Tydings in Maryland in 1950 was somewhat different from the

California example, as Tydings had never thought of himself as a New Dealer and seemed immune from charges that his domestic ideology was a front for totalitarianism and "Un-Americanism." First elected to the Senate in 1926, Tydings came to prominence in the 1930s as a vocal opponent of much of Roosevelt's New Deal, to the extent that he became a prime target of FDR's ill-judged campaign to "purge" right-wing Democrats from the Senate in 1938.[33] "Up to this time," he argued in a 1935 speech attacking the New Deal, "the whole philosophy of the administration, in my judgment, has been to produce less and to increase rather than to decrease the army of the unemployed."[34] He repeatedly pushed for a constitutional amendment to require a balanced federal budget, and warmly welcomed the Taft-Hartley Act in 1947 as a reflection of "the overwhelming desire of the majority of our people for remedial labor legislation that will attempt to remove the causes of labor warfare and promote peace and order."[35] The well-financed and bitter campaign to unseat Tydings in 1950 could hardly have sprung from opposition to his overall political worldview.

In reality, he became a victim in 1950 of his own association with the Truman administration in encouraging an anti-communist consensus on matters foreign but supporting his President in attempting to crush the growth of McCarthyism at home, which he saw as a distraction from the real struggle overseas. The Republican right's serious challenge to Tydings came after he had chaired a Senate Committee investigating McCarthy's charges earlier in the year. His majority report condemned McCarthy's charges of Communists in government, prompting Republicans to seize on the issue as a means of tying the Democratic Party to an image of the bureaucratic state guiding America down the road to Communism. Republican committee member Henry Cabot Lodge argued that the "proceedings often lacked impartiality; the atmosphere was too often not that of seeking to ascertain the truth."[36]

Conservative radio broadcaster Fulton Lewis followed the proceedings of the Tydings subcommittee, pouring scorn on the Maryland Senator's handling of the investigation. He noted that Seth Richardson, the head of the Federal Loyalty Review Board, was "a law partner of Soviet Russia apologist Joseph Davies, who in turn is the fond and indulgent father in law of Senator Millard Tydings of Maryland, who is chairman of the Senate committee which supposedly is investigating the McCarthy charges. Just a big happy family." Lewis noted that one McCarthy suspect who had not been indicted was "a homosexual and a pervert, and spends his time hanging around the men's room in Lafayette Square."[37] Tydings was cast as a captive of bureaucratic liberalism, and liberalism as the defense of social difference seen as anti-American in conservative discourse. A GOP campaign leaflet for Butler's candidacy condemned the Tydings "whitewash," and argued that Americans had "first-hand information of how the Communists took over other countries. . . . With all the excitement over the Tydings' Subcommittee report, do you feel sure in your hearts that our country is not being softened for the same fate?"[38] Republicanism, argued Butler, consisted of "the reaffirmation and strengthening of American principles," and the "self-government that has placed this country head and shoulders above the rest of the world." The Democrats, by contrast, were "wholly committed to the socialization of medicine, agriculture, and industry."[39] It was therefore natural that the administration would be committed to defending federal organs like the State Department from Republican scrutiny.

The Democratic response to the Republican strategy did not leave much hope for a strong defense of the American state. A Tydings campaign leaflet stated that the Democratic Senator had "fought a long and continuing fight against government waste and for economy in government expenditures. . . . He successfully withstood the Maryland Invasion of 1938 and threw back attempts [by FDR] to 'purge' him." Anti-communism in political campaigns tended to encourage anti-statism. Congressman George Fallon, who represented the State's 4th district, based on inner city Baltimore, claimed in a campaign letter that his record in Congress was "that of a conservative Democrat" not bound by the straitjacket of the New Deal.[40]

In fact the Republican attack on Tydings and his Democratic colleagues in 1950 was not designed to create an image of a liberal Tydings versus conservative Republicans. Rather, McCarthyism actually characterized Democrats as part of a privileged elite and Republicans as representatives of a popular will, reversing the dynamic of the New Deal by appealing to anti-communist, rather than economic, concerns. Butler strategists learned from the primary campaign against Tydings by labor radical Davey Lewis, who cleverly cast Tydings as "Milord" Tydings, living in a "mansion" at Havre de Grace, Maryland, with a "royal family."[41] Butler's campaign took a similar line, casting Tydings as part of a New Deal elite "dedicated to socialism for America" by taking taxes from the "little man" and spending them "to destroy" the country.[42] The Butler campaign had the full-time assistance of a massive propaganda machine provided by the *Chicago Tribune* and *Washington Times-Herald*, which provided Butler's unofficial campaign manager, Jon Jonckel, and benefited from McCarthy's personal involvement.[43] Its basic message was anti-government, but it made appeals to the working class as well as traditional Republicans through the lens of anti-communism.

The strategy could not have been much more successful. Democratic county organizers in Maryland were pessimistic when reporting grass-roots sentiment to Tydings in the fall of 1950. Two main issues were bound up together in almost every precinct and county report. The first, as expressed by the county chairman in Howard County, was "the Communist investigation by [the] subcommittee." It was imperative that Tydings "dispel the idea that you 'whitewashed' for Truman." The other issue stressed in Howard County involved "preserving our way of life and avoiding Socialism, reducing unnecessary expenditures wherever possible."

It seemed that the Cold War was as much a domestic war in 1950 as a question of foreign policy, and that anti-communism and anti-socialism were now inseparable. In Kent County the analysis was the same. The party member took "a pessimistic view, but I can see no issues aiding you here today. It seems imperative for something to be done to correct the bad impression resulting from the probe." In Queen Anne's, Tydings was "still very strong. But for some queer reason the McCarthy investigation has hurt you."[44] Tydings received a huge amount of hate mail during the campaign, much of it clearly motivated by Fulton Lewis's broadcasts. These acted as party political broadcasts for the Republicans in Maryland. "You will probably again be using large quantities of whitewash [to] cover up the vivid Reds you are so deeply interested in making as white as snow," stated one correspondent. Another hoped Tydings would "be *badly* beaten—for you are only a catspaw for the Reds." Tydings' own radio attack on Lewis only created a fresh barrage of letters, one arguing that his speech "was admired by Joseph S. Stalin, Hiss etc.."[45] The shift in Republican ideology away from economic appeals to a broad populace and toward a direct attack on liberalism and the Democratic Party generally through the mirage of anti-communism did not go unnoticed. *The Reporter* argued that McCarthyism was diverting American parties from their primary domestic and international roles.[46]

The voters of Maryland in the main thought differently. Butler was declared the winner by 326,291 votes to 283,180, the first time since the 1920s that the Republicans had taken Maryland in a Senate election. Moreover, the scale of the Democratic defeat was impressive. Butler took all the urban counties, winning the city of Baltimore by nearly 18,000 and Montgomery and Prince George's counties, comprising suburban Washington, by large margins. Tydings's victories were notably in the conservative rural counties such as Caroline, Calvert, Cecil, Dorchester, Howard, and Harford. The GOP analysis of the elections noted that in Baltimore, the black vote seemed "to have leaned toward the Republican ticket."[47] In the second congressional district, encompassing several Baltimore city wards as well as suburban counties, Republican James Devereux defeated Democrat William Bolton by just under 3,000 votes, suggesting a large blue-collar shift to the GOP.[48] The post-election Senate investigation into charges of illegal campaigning uncovered "two campaigns within one. One was the dignified 'front street' campaign. . . . The other was the despicable 'back street' type of campaign. . . . which strikes to destroy as suspiciously subversive, rather than simply to defeat an issue."[49] Anti-statism in 1950 meant more than simply anti-New Deal, and was thus often well received by a New Deal audience.

Undermining New Deal Liberalism: The Cold War Liberal Network

Senators Scott Lucas (D-Illinois) and Elbert Thomas (D-Utah) were victims of the power of anti-leftism during this domestic Cold War, as both were strong supporters of the New and Fair Deals in the Senate and had pledged their support throughout the 1940s for the principle of federal health insurance. Both campaigns in 1950 demonstrated the power of totalitarian imagery to further the cause of an economic pressure group, the medical lobby. "Utah presents distinct possibilities in the Senatorial race," stated Republican strategist Vic Johnson in a report to party headquarters in Washington. "Thomas is a school teacher type of fellow, starry eyed in his devotion to the New Deal and Fair Deal philosophies." This was seen as a distinct disadvantage for Democrats in 1950, as opposed to two or four years earlier, and the GOP deliberately chose NAM businessman Wallace Bennett as their candidate for his anti-government credentials.[50] In Illinois the American Medical Association all but commandeered the campaign of Republican candidate Everett Dirksen. The Association spent over a million dollars on a "Message of Freedom" to be published in all major daily newspapers across the United States over a two week period in October 1950, concentrated in States like Illinois and Utah where incumbent Senators were supposedly in favor of "socialized medicine."[51] The message aimed "to reaffirm and solidify public faith in American enterprise through endorsement of voluntary health insurance and opposition to State Socialism." Millions more were spent on radio spots in Illinois linking Scott Lucas to statist projects. John Dingell (D-Michigan) condemned the AMA and its "fellow conspirators who are conniving and conspiring . . . to help kill liberal legislation by defeating those who support the President's Fair Deal program."[52]

These anti-statist tactics were effective in 1950. Lucas was forced onto the defensive, arguing in one downstate community that although Truman was "an intimate friend," Lucas was "against socialized medicine, no matter what they call it, and I'm also against the Brannan Plan."[53] Cold War liberals like

Lucas, William Benton, and Herbert Lehman running for election in 1950 coordinated their electoral strategies to combat the AMA and business-led attacks on their records. "I have collected the actual speeches delivered by a number of liberal Senators who have attempted to meet or head off this medical attack—Lehman, Humphreys and Murray," wrote Bill Benton's campaign manager, Philip Levy. Levy advised Benton to do as Lucas had done and repudiate federal health insurance. Benton himself wrote two campaign workers that when "I was told that Chet Bowles and I were to be pilloried as Socialists" he had asked his contacts at *Encyclopedia Britannica,* his former employer, "to make up a historical summary of past candidates and past issues which have been derided as Socialist." Benton worried that the Democrats had appropriated many left-of-center issues, and that ways needed to be found "in which to twist the material . . . into the lines which I originally laid down." One such issue was the abortive Brannan Plan for granting direct subsidies to farmers. Levy warned Benton that he "should take Lehman's line and be against the Brannan Plan, just as you have been against 'wasteful farm programs' generally. The Democrats are all running away from the Brannan Plan, and here again there is no advantage in your taking up the burden."[54] Liberal politicians were consciously adapting their political strategies to the new political climate, and were reorienting their campaigns toward an attack on Republicans' endorsement of McCarthy and his methods of combating political subversion, rather than the GOP's antipathy toward state-sponsored social welfare.

Still, however, the GOP was able to construct a campaign language that associated Democrats with the far left. Everett Dirksen linked Lucas's domestic liberalism to the Communist issue, arguing that Lucas had "coddled" Communists by holding up consideration of the Internal Security Act and other measures as Senate Majority Leader in the 81st Congress.[55] In a campaign speech at Champaign, Illinois, Dirksen wondered whether it was not "time that we moved in on the Reds in our own country? . . . [Lucas] said nothing about the bungling at Yalta and Potsdam in 1945 where we coddled Stalin and gave him what he wanted and now reap the bitter fruit of this action."[56]

Benton's opponent in Connecticut, Prescott Bush, stated in a radio interview during the campaign that Benton and Connecticut Governor Chester Bowles were "not real Democrats. They are leaders of the left wing which controls the Democratic Party. Chester Bowles is the philosopher, McMahon the spokesman, and Benton is the captive of leftism. . . . They believe in a foreign 'ism'. Sometimes that 'ism' looks like socialism. Often it's close to communism, and those two look very much alike. . . . Whatever it is, this cross-breed 'ism' is not real Americanism. . . . Republicanism will mean what it says, and Democrat will mean left-winger."[57]

Again the question of a domestic economic and social policy was linked to images of domestic and overseas totalitarianism in the context of American-Soviet relations. The Republicans were victorious in both the Illinois and Utah races, and unseated Chester Bowles in Connecticut, failing to unseat Benton by a very narrow margin. It is impossible to say categorically that the GOP was triumphant purely because of the effectiveness of their campaign, although the evidence certainly points strongly in that direction. What is more important to note is that the Democrats consciously distanced themselves from social democratic ideas, and that after 1950 few of the plans of the early postwar era would again be raised in Congress over the following decade.

The approach of the two parties to foreign policy in states such as Illinois and Utah in 1950 suggested that liberalism was in decline not just under an attack from the right, but also because liberalism itself had adopted a similar image of foreign totalitarianism as its central raison d'être.[58] To the Illinois Democratic State Central Committee, the main issue of the election was not domestic reform, but "the maintenance of peace in the world." Lucas's campaign focused mainly on Dirksen's less than wholehearted support for Truman's foreign policy, arguing that he had "jumped back and forth across the fence so many times on international affairs that he can spout both the answers to both sides of the question with equal smoothness."[59] While Lucas was committed to all the anti-Soviet policies of the Truman years, Dirksen was an "isolationist," unwilling to join the crusade for democracy against totalitarianism. The strategy allowed Dirksen the opportunity to attack the "failure" of U.S. foreign policy since 1945. "Mr. Lucas speaks of peace. Well, where is it? The taxpayer shelled out 60 billion for defense and 36 billion for foreign aid in the last five years, and where is the peace? . . . Korea got 110 million in Marshall Plan aid and 356 million in additional economic aid. . . . In China, we spent 225 million of Marshall Plan funds and then the Reds took over."[60]

Both candidates were effectively arguing the same point, coming together on the primacy of anti-totalitarianism abroad, and disagreeing on the methods to be used. The Democrats, however, seemed blind to the effects of their strategy on domestic policy. Bill Benton's campaign team in Connecticut drafted a speech in which he decried Bush's attempt to associate Benton "with that radical apologist for Communism, Claude Pepper." Not content to disassociate himself from one of the most consistent proponents of New Deal liberalism, Benton also wondered in a private memo whether he could "jockey Bush around into a statement of approval of Senator Taft," whose voting record "closely parallels Marcantonio's on many key issues."[61] Pepper and Marcantonio were words of political opprobrium in 1950 even in mainstream liberal circles.

The decision to prioritize anti-communism and brand the Republicans as isolationists was a national Democratic strategy in 1950, taken by Senatorial Campaign Committee Chairman Clinton Anderson and his senior adviser, J. J. Perling. "Can Republican candidates be coaxed to *talk themselves into defeat*?" Perling wrote to Anderson in August. "What is essential is that they be subjected (by one or more newsmen *friendly* to the administration) to several specific questions. . . . What would *they* have done about China? What would *they* do about Korea?. . . . *No matter what the reply, certain segments of voters will be alienated.*" Perling prepared material for Democratic candidates under the heading "Who Heartened the Kremlin?" in which it was argued that Republicans had made the Soviets feel that America was "too disunited to aid the victims of Red aggression." Another release was entitled "Debunking the Republican Manifesto: An Objective Analysis of the Mis-statements, Half-truths, and the Omitted Record Regarding KOREA and CHINA." In an attack on the Republicans, another Democratic election sheet argued that an "*isolationist Congress . . . could destroy the world's hopes for peace.*"[62]

The Democratic campaign's main election material, used extensively not only in Illinois but also in Ohio against Bob Taft and anywhere where a Trumanite Democrat faced a less internationalist Republican, was headed "Who *Voted* to Strengthen the Free World?" The pamphlet argued that Republicans in the main had an anti-interventionist voting record, and were thus unwitting allies of world Communism.[63] According to Anderson himself, Democrats in 1950 recognized "in communism the greatest enemy that free democratic institutions have ever faced. . . . [The Democratic Party] does not stand idly by while the campaign for control over men's minds and for conquest of free soils goes on all over the earth."[64] The 1950 Democratic campaign was Cold War liberalism at its most extreme. The Anderson strategy was to minimize candidates' exposure to domestic issues as much as possible and highlight the party's achievements in terms of protecting the "free world" from "Red Aggression." Thus every candidate from Scott Lucas to hard-left Helen Douglas sought to portray the party as more anti-communist than the Republicans. New Deal policy ideas were "pure political poison" in this context, and tended to be downplayed.[65]

The Dilemma of Republican Liberalism: New Hampshire and Ohio

Senator Charles Tobey (R-New Hampshire) was a typical "Eastern Establishment" figure in the Republican Party, sympathetic to parts of the New Deal and strongly enthusiastic about America's new role in the world. While John McCormack (D-Massachusetts) claimed that Tobey could be beaten in 1950, he could not even get Tobey's name right, which suggested that the latter would not be high on the Democrats' target list in 1950.[66] Instead, anti-liberal Republicans allied to the state's other senator, Styles Bridges, used the opportunity presented by the ideological climate that year to launch their own attack on defenders of federal economic power, including Tobey. Wesley Powell, a New Hampshire attorney and aide to Bridges, was sponsored as a GOP primary opponent for Tobey. The reason for this challenge, argued the right-wing newspaper the *New Hampshire Morning Union*, was Tobey's "Truman Republican record," and his "close affiliation with and subservience to the CIO." In addition, Tobey had deserted the GOP in its "investigation of convicted communists and fellow travellers." The paper recalled Tobey's defense of America's alliance with the Soviets during the Second World War, and his desire in 1946, like that of many other Republicans, to continue to work with Russia as much as possible. "These endorsements of Russia's ambitions . . . no more than four years ago are remindful [sic] of his violent isolationist views before the last war, when he was not in favor of doing anything to stop Nazi Germany in its wild rampage across the world," argued the editorial.[67]

The Powell camp used techniques also employed by Democrats, the CIO-PAC, and many Tobey supporters as well against the Republican right. The anti-Powell forces were using a discourse of symbolism not dissimilar to their opponents; events such as the run-up to Pearl Harbor or U.S.-Soviet relations in 1945–1946 could be completely recast through the distorted Cold War lens. Giving his reasons for abandoning Tobey in favor of Powell, the editor of the *Newport Guardian* contrasted Tobey's progressivism with Powell's concern "with stamping out the seeds of communism which have taken root and threatened to flourish within the very walls of our democracy."[68] Within the Republican Party a struggle to reorient its ideology around an anti-statist theme linked to anti-communism found expression in the 1950 campaigns. Powell was defeated in his challenge, but by the tiny margin of 37,893 votes to 39,203. Liberal Republicanism was coming under increasing pressure in the domestic Cold War for political minds in 1950.[69]

The term "liberal Republican" itself was unclear in a Cold War context, as was "liberal Democrat." The ADA was anything but liberal in its relentless pursuit of Wallace Progressives in 1948, or its espousal of nuclear war against the North Koreans. Thus it was no coincidence that to be a "liberal" Republican one joined what Jacob Javits called a "Republican counterpart to the Americans for Democratic Action."[70] This group, founded in March 1950, called itself "Republican Advance," eschewing "stand-pat negative opposition" in favor of a consensual approach to domestic and international problems. The principal members included Javits, Henry Cabot Lodge, Irving Ives, Margaret Chase Smith, Charles Tobey, and some thirty or so others in House and Senate. Raymond Moley decried the movement as "part of a general plan inspired by the left-wing Americans for Democratic Action to infiltrate both major parties with promoters of more and more government and less and less personal liberty. . . . If the Republican Advance should succeed, which fortunately is impossible, it could well kill the Republican Party."[71]

When one actually reads the summary of the group's principles as drafted by Margaret Chase Smith, it is difficult to see where Moley made the distinction between his beliefs and hers. The main goals of Republican Advance were to reduce taxes, balance the budget, fight deficit spending, attack Communism "here instead of condoning it," establish a "truly bipartisan" foreign policy, and oppose "socialized medicine, socialized farming or hidden taxes." Smith's provision for "smashing the filibuster on civil rights" was the only seriously liberal idea in the whole platform.[72] Republican Advance basically formed part of a congressional political network in both parties dedicated to building support for the Truman administration's foreign policy and support for certain domestic objectives not linked to state intervention in the economy, such as civil rights. As William Benton put it: "Let me be perfectly clear. I am a liberal businessman. I hope I am a businesslike liberal" who would oppose "indiscriminate" state spending.[73] Jacob Javits argued that liberal Republicans believed that the extent to which "government can help the people in the attainment of economic security and increased human satisfaction is far greater than contemplated by conservative Republicans" but limited that role for the state to that of ensuring that "our system of private economy is virile and flexible enough to satisfy far more amply than government alone the aspirations of our people for well-being in the modern day." The key issue for Javits that would build a liberal coalition would be a permanent FEPC, and he called for "an effective coalition of liberal Democrats and progressive Republicans" to fight for that policy in Congress.[74]

Where these "liberals" drew most of their support, however, was through their desire to follow broadly the anti-communist foreign policy set out by the ADA and the administration, and their frustration at the lack of enthusiasm for foreign undertakings exhibited by their colleagues, regardless of the motivations behind such reservations. Thus Republican Advance cast Taft and William Jenner in similar terms, although one was more tractable on domestic policy issues than the other. Margaret Chase Smith was later able to establish a new point of difference with the opponents of Republican Advance by writing her "Declaration of Conscience," opposing McCarthy and his anti-communist campaign. This statement, approving the general principles of anti-communism but condemning McCarthy's methods, was signed by seven liberal Republican Senators, of whom Smith, Ives, and Tobey were founders of Republican Advance and all seven were internationalists concerned about the effects of McCarthyism on a coherent anti-totalitarian foreign policy.[75]

Liberal Republicanism, then, like its Democratic variant, attacked opponents of its foreign policy as isolationists who were aiding and abetting the Red menace. The defense of the state at home was low on their list of priorities. Javits admitted in correspondence that the "struggle for the world between the freedom of the democracies and the totalitarianism of the Communist dictatorships poses a real problem for liberals. Shall all other considerations be cast aside and everything devoted to military preparation and action or shall programs for improving standards of living . . . be continued?" He articulated the logic of Cold War liberalism when he argued that "this dilemma is more apparent than real for both economic improvement and military security are parts of the same struggle."[76] It was not entirely clear, however, in the political climate of America in 1950 that it was possible to campaign successfully for both.

The CIO-PAC dominated campaign against Senator Robert Taft in Ohio was similarly confused in its definition of liberalism. Ostensibly the Democratic Party Campaign Committee's decision to divert so much money and effort into the Ohio Senate race was made on the basis of Taft's sponsorship of changes to the National Labor Relations Act, and his less than liberal record generally. The PAC had singled Taft out in 1949 on the basis of his perceived anti-union stance in the 80th Congress. It was instrumental in choosing State Attorney General Joe Ferguson, a strong supporter of union power who had received CIO backing in his campaigns for Attorney General since 1938, as the Democratic Senate candidate to oppose Taft. The Ferguson campaign stressed Taft's core conservatism, defining it as the promotion of big business interests at the expense of the working man. CIO literature included such slogans as "Taft Wants Taxes on *YOU* not Big Business." The Ohio CIO council's newspaper, the *Ohio Monthly Review,* called Taft and Ferguson "symbols of two worlds. One is the world of poverty, hunger, and despair for the working man and his family. The other is of hope and human dignity. Behind the symbol of Senator Taft are many realities—and all of them are ugly."[77] The Citizens' Committee for Ferguson put out several hundred thousand copies of "The Taft Record," an analysis of his votes in the Senate on all legislation since Taft first entered Congress in 1939. In 1949, the leaflet argued, Taft had been against rent control, "housing," the repeal of Taft-Hartley, and the expansion of public power, to give but a few examples.[78] On one level at least, the campaign to unseat Taft was based on an appeal to the grass-roots union worker in Ohio, who represented a significant proportion of the electorate in industrial cities like Cleveland, Dayton, Toledo, and Akron. According to a CIO cartoon, Taft symbolized the forces of capital, Ferguson the average American laborer, a typical New Deal theme in industrial America.[79]

When the campaign in Ohio is taken as a whole, however, it is remarkable how little attention the Ferguson campaign devoted to domestic affairs. A Democratic organizer in Columbus wrote to Truman's secretary in December 1949, asking for details of Taft's stand on pensions and social security. He was sent a list showing that Taft had cast no negative votes in this field other than his vote against the 1939 amendments to Social Security and his vote against the retrospective coverage of the self-employed in 1948. The issue was not used in the campaign.[80] More often the Ferguson campaign issued literature condemning Taft's opposition to liberal internationalism. "It may surprise you," stated one leaflet, "but Taft votes the Communist line on foreign policy matters. Yes sir, every time Congress was asked to shell out money to fight Communism, Taft was against it. You can take his votes against the Marshall Plan, the arms assistance program—and it fits exactly what the *Daily Worker* approves." The "Taft Record" leaflet devoted far more attention to Taft's votes on foreign policy than domestic legislation; the front cover highlighted not Taft-Hartley, but Korean aid, military aid to Europe, and a "strong Marshall Plan." The cartoon portraying him as a friend of business elites showed him supporting a huge bag of "excess profits" while a soldier entered an aircraft carrying a much smaller bag of "war gear."[81] A campaign leaflet condemned Taft's attacks on the union sponsorship of the Ferguson campaign, arguing that he "really puts his foot in it when he talks about [unions] following 'the party line as do the Communists,' for the *Congressional Record* shows Taft's votes closely parallel those of Marcantonio who so consistently reflects the policy of the *Daily Worker*."[82]

That industrial liberalism fostered by the New Deal had changed since the FDR years was clearly demonstrated by the CIO's bitter attacks on Vito Marcantonio, one of the most consistent champions of union power in the

United States. In 1950, to be liberal was to be utterly committed to a global policy of anti-communism; domestic issues were of lesser importance. In its increasing desire to take a prominent place in the architectural framework of the New Deal Order by acting as the labor campaign arm of the Democratic Party, the CIO leadership had become committed to the administration's foreign policy and its simultaneous rearguard action to preserve the basic blueprint of the New Deal state. As has already been noted, there was a certain logic in organized labor's support for an international order of non-communist unions and friendly anti-communist, often left-of-center, governments. Nevertheless, there is little evidence in the Ohio campaign of any attempt to radicalize the rank and file, or to question the notion of an anti-communist foreign policy superseding the quest for an industrial democracy in which organized labor would take a leading role.[83]

The CIO strategy closely mirrored that of "Republican Advance," and that of the anti-Communist right, who were also committed to a defense of the "average" American against the perils of the monolithic left. The CIO's attacks on Taft were strikingly similar to Butler's tactics against the Democrat Tydings in Maryland; Taft and Tydings were part of a wealthy elite unsympathetic to the dangers posed by Communism to "ordinary" Americans. The CIO also looked overseas in its defense of liberal social legislation. The *CIO News* published an article by Dr. James Howard Means of Harvard Medical School that attempted to debunk the AMA campaign against federal health insurance. Means reported from Britain that the National Health Service (NHS) worked well, exhibiting "no deterioration in the quality of the care provided. . . . We should be grateful to Britain for making this venture."[84] The Ferguson campaign was closely tied to the Democratic leadership in Washington, and thus attempted to portray Democratic liberalism as the defense of freedom against totalitarianism around the world.

Taft thus found himself in something of a dilemma, attempting to portray himself as a domestic progressive to counter the CIO's strategy, while at the same time having to defend his foreign policy record from the same attacks made with good effect against Henry Wallace and the far left. Taft was well aware of the socially varied nature of his home state, and of his very narrow victory by only 7,000 votes over William Pickrell in 1944. His campaign tried to temper his anti-New Deal image. In his speeches and campaign literature Taft argued that while the power of the state was not always the solution to every social problem, "government has the obligation to promote better education, better health, better housing, better security for our people, and equality of opportunity." Specifically, Taft's literature contended that two of the most important domestic measures to pass the Senate in recent years were "the public housing and slum clearance bill and the bill for Federal Aid to Education. *Both* of these bills carry out Senator Taft's humane desire to give equality of opportunity to families, and particularly to their children, who do not have the income to provide a minimum decent standard of living."[85] A Taft leaflet on the minimum wage argued that Taft was behind the 1949 increase of the rate to 75 cents, quoting Claude Pepper as saying Taft was the "KEY man and that it would take the Taft leadership and support to put over the 75¢ minimum." Taft's radio broadcast just before the election listed all of his domestic legislation and proposals. He mused on the reasons behind the CIO's hatred of his candidacy, given that "there are many more conservative Senators than I am in the Senate today. . . . I think it is because . . . I have had definite alternatives . . . to suggest wherever a program really exists. I have gone along with the government in any case where it seemed to me that their program was the proper program."[86]

Taft's campaign cast the candidate as a "friend" of labor and farming groups, and set up campaign groups made up totally of farmers, union men, and business leaders under an umbrella "Citizens' Committee for Taft," totally separate from the Republican Party headquarters.[87] Leaflets emerged setting out Taft's "constructive answer to Socialized Medicine" and his determination to "protect and advance the cause of Negroes."[88] Taft was clearly worried that the CIO campaign would hurt him, but in fact their campaigns were less ideologically polarized in the context of the Cold War than his previous races in 1938 and 1944.

The labor-dominated Democratic campaign gave Taft the opportunity to create a totalitarian image of a sinister labor dictatorship attempting to control and dominate the voting pattern of the rank and file. While most Republicans, and many Democrats and CIO campaign workers, created the symbolic image of pro-Communist elites versus the common man, Taft used a slightly amended strategy. The Taft campaign newspaper for organized labor, *Labor World*, argued that "Communists hate the Taft-Hartley law and so do the union dictators and racketeers." The Republican-oriented *Labor Digest* argued in September 1950 that "alien" labor leaders were insulting their membership by attempting to control their vote and create an un-American class war, whereas Republicans directed their appeal "to the American people *as a people* and not to a lot of selfish splinter minorities. . . . The light is to be turned on Democrat-Socialist evils until all may see them as onrushing threats to our national existence."[89] Republicanism, then, stood for an ill-defined American totality, and liberalism for special interest groups akin to the system known as Communism.

Taft was able, in the fevered climate of the American political scene in

1950, to mount a spirited defense of the Taft-Hartley Act as aiding the struggle of the worker against the unscrupulous labor dictator, supported by common Cold War perceptions of unionism and the state as representing the dictatorial left. A Taft leaflet on Taft-Hartley argued that "the rank and file like it," and that it "protects the worker against dictatorial bosses in both the company and the union."[90] Unions, argued the sister of a California union man, "are out to get control of our government just like they did in England. . . . Truman . . . sure is a pal of Joe Stalin's—when he has broken us then Uncle Joe can take over."[91] There was little difference between this letter and Taft's pre-election broadcast, which argued that the CIO-PAC's purpose "is to enact the socialist program . . . following almost measure for measure that which has been put into effect in Great Britain by the Labor-Socialist Government. . . . Of course, they have a Communist background anyway, most of the PAC people were originally Communists . . . and what they have here is a socialist program as far towards communism as they think the American people will go."[92]

In many ways Taft's record on domestic social programs could not stand up to close scrutiny, and his defense of Taft-Hartley was not based on a script that organized labor could appreciate. His campaign went on the offensive during 1950, using the rhetoric of Cold War anti-totalitarianism to take on the CIO-led Democratic campaign. "I am inclined to think," Taft wrote, "that if this issue is presented in 1950 and 1952, people will reject socialism and the handout state just as they have recently done in Australia and New Zealand. The problem is to present the issue clearly because so few people take an active interest in political principles."[93] Taft discovered a method: present an image of a struggle between Americanism and totalitarianism in a domestic context, using carefully chosen examples from overseas. Such a strategy would weaken his parallel aim to portray himself as a progressive on domestic legislation. To the *Labor Digest*, for example, the minimum wage that Taft himself had defended as his own was "nothing more than a way of paying graft to morons and incompetents." FDR had been "working with Lord Keynes" to become a "dictator and Labor would be his commissars to keep the people in line through a police state." Social Security "has made bums and grafters out of millions of able-bodied persons who would be honest, useful citizens except for it." The paper then explicitly endorsed Taft for maintaining "a vigil over the Truman star-gazing bureaucratic planners."[94]

Ferguson's attacks on Taft's foreign policy also created difficulties for the Republican candidate. Stung by criticism of his foreign policy record by Democrats and the liberal media, Taft made further efforts to join the internationalist mainstream and compromise his residual reluctance to endorse an assertive foreign policy. "Apparently," he wrote to a friend in Hamilton, Ohio, "whenever anyone disagrees with anyone else on any phase of foreign policy, it is fair game to call him an isolationist. . . . I have supported ECA. . . . I have substantially agreed with the President's foreign policy in recent years."[95] At a campaign rally at Dayton in September 1950, Taft argued that there was "no choice today except to build up armed forces sufficient to make it absolutely certain that Russia cannot gain a position from which they might threaten the security of the United States."[96] In an article Taft argued that he had "supported most of the moves undertaken in Europe when I felt that they were effective and well designed. I supported military aid to Greece and Turkey because it seemed to me that these were two points at which Russian military infiltration was possible and perhaps immediate." He then demonstrated how a commitment to an abstract notion of anti-communism abroad could translate directly into a negation of state power at home. "If we want to meet the ideology of Communism we must keep this country strong," he argued. "We cannot adopt the deadening policy of socialism or statism. . . . The decisive struggle today is one of ideas and not of arms. . . . We need to arouse the same religious fervor for the American Doctrine of liberty and free government as the Communists have for Communism."[97] In this ideological atmosphere, it was clear that Taft's commitment to the use of state power was ambivalent at best, but he managed to appeal to a wide range of voters using the unifying banner of Americanism, as candidates like Nixon were doing. Taft took away from the campaign the lesson that "even the American workman will not listen to a class appeal, but proposes to vote as an American citizen first."[98]

Six years after his brush with defeat, Taft cruised to an overwhelming 400,000 vote victory over Ferguson, obtaining one of the best results for a Republican in Ohio in the state's history. Ferguson carried only four counties in the whole state, all by narrow margins. As expected, Ferguson did well in the four industrial counties of Belmont, Lawrence, Jefferson, and Pike. However, he failed to carry Cuyahoga, based on the city of Cleveland, which was usually a Democratic stronghold. Taft took the county by 22,293 votes, having lost it by nearly 100,000 in 1944. Taft carried every rural county, many of which had voted for Truman in 1948, and made astonishing gains to win both industrial Mahoning County, a CIO stronghold, and Montgomery, counties he had never before come close to winning.

Taft had successfully created a nonpartisan coalition of farmers, labor Democrats, and traditional Republican supporters such as the AMA and the Ohio Chamber of Commerce. No other Republican candidate could match him; gubernatorial candidate Don Ebright trailed Democratic Governor

Frank Lausche by some 20 percent, and George Bender's victory in the Ohio at-large House seat over incumbent Stephen Young was far less impressive than Taft's staggering tally. An example is provided by the figures for Cuyahoga County. While Taft was victorious here by over 22,000, Ebright lost the same county by 158,830 votes, and Bender lost by 75,356. Within the Cleveland city limits, Taft received over 40 percent of the vote in one of the most solidly New Deal cities in the industrial northeast.[99]

There was clearly scope for a reorientation of the dynamics of party politics in Ohio in 1950, with the collapse of the New Deal ownership of the vote of organized labor. It was difficult, however, to clarify the actual reasons for this seismic shift. The Taft campaign had visited every Cleveland precinct, stressing Taft's less than reactionary voting record and his commitment to inclusive policies. A report by a polling organization on the Ohio election contended that the "task that Taft faced, and successfully met, was to clarify the fundamental aims of labor legislation designed to protect the public interest."[100] After the result was announced, however, Taft argued that his victory was due mainly to his promulgation of anti-totalitarian ideas, contrasting his views with the Truman program for "government control of everything" and the failure of America's anti-communist policy in Eastern Europe and the Far East.[101] The result "certainly shows that the people of Ohio can make the correct decision on fundamental principles if the case is really presented to them."[102] Lausche's outperformance of Ferguson on the Democratic ticket can also be read in at least two ways. Ebright had been unable to tie the popular and ideologically uncommitted Lausche to totalitarianism as Taft had done to Ferguson, and yet Lausche's vote in blue collar Cleveland seemed also to reflect regular Democratic strength unconnected to the Cold War. It is difficult to know how to read the common view in 1950 that Lausche himself had voted for Taft; did Lausche prefer Taft's less expansive view of state activity, or his association with anti-communism? Taft's commitment to anti-totalitarian "fundamental principles," and his association of the CIO and the Democrats with a campaign with "a peculiar Communist undertone," suggest that the reorientation of American politics was based on the social dynamics of anti-communism, rather than domestic social policy.[103]

Recasting Liberalism in the Democratic Party: From Florida to Idaho.

Nothing better illustrated the change in the general outlook of the Democratic Party between the New Deal and the Cold War than the purge of Senator Claude Pepper in Florida in 1950. George Smathers' announcement in January 1950 to a crowd of some 3,000 people in Orlando that he would challenge Claude Pepper in the Democratic senatorial primary in May seemed at first sight to demonstrate the potency of the Cold War in American politics. In what Pepper termed in his diary a "slashing and gross attack upon me and the Democratic administration," Smathers highlighted the apparent menace of domestic communism in the United States, and portrayed his battle with Pepper as a referendum on whether Americans would "continue up the good road of opportunity and freedom, or will we be led down the dark road of socialism and communism by political Pied Pipers who attempt to buy our ballots with our own Treasury?"[104] The shift in the ideological direction of Smathers' political language in this speech is telling. Referring specifically to the term "liberal," Smathers argued that the term had "been adopted by the radical left-wingers, and they have twisted and disgraced its meaning. We must reawaken to the true meaning of liberalism. Liberalism comes from the word 'liberty'. . . . One is therefore not a reactionary merely because he is opposed to regulation, regimentation, red tape, and big government." This particular definition of liberalism dominated campaign literature and speeches of most Republicans in 1950, and stood in stark contrast to Pepper's contention that "one of the best ways to beat communism is by getting rid of our slums and getting our people into good houses."[105]

The extent to which the Democratic Party's New Deal heritage had come under siege in the frenzied Cold War climate of the late 1940s is demonstrated by the fact that one of George Smathers' original supporters in his attempt to unseat Pepper was President Truman himself. Ever since he had fired Henry Wallace from the cabinet in September 1946 Truman had moved to isolate those Democratic liberals, including Pepper, who, he said, "grasp every opportunity to throw a brick at me or stick a monkey wrench in the Foreign Affairs [sic] machinery."[106]

Both in the disastrous 1948 campaign for the presidency by Henry Wallace and in the 1950 elections, left-leaning Democrats hostile to the direction of American foreign policy since 1946 were removed from political influence. Smathers later recalled that Truman had called him to the Oval Office in autumn 1949 and specifically asked him to run against Pepper in the primaries. The motivation behind Truman's obvious dislike of Pepper, argued Smathers, was Pepper's support for Henry Wallace's approach to foreign affairs.[107] Truman referred to Florida's senior Senator as "that son of a bitch Claude Pepper," and so clearly their mutual antipathy would have serious and deleterious repercussions for the future of left-of-center political thought in the United States. Moreover, Pepper had not only scaled down his support for continued American-Soviet links by 1950, but had also refused to leave the Democratic Party in 1948 to follow Wallace and had gleefully supported Truman's efforts in 1949 to breathe new life into the New Deal coalition through his Fair Deal agenda.[108] Although the Smathers campaign, as Pepper argued constantly during the 1950 campaign, could not use any incident since 1947 to associate Pepper even tangentially with communism, both Smathers and works of historical scholarship maintain that foreign affairs represented the heart of the differences between them. Smathers recalls that he told Pepper that he was thinking of challenging him, and that Pepper would "be amazed at how people over the state are very unhappy with this position that you're taking. People don't like this communist bit."[109]

A closer examination of the organization and rhetorical tenor of the Smathers campaign reveals, however, that the Cold War was a political tool used to dampen popular and political support for Fair Deal programs. Radio commentator Elmer Davis in an April 1950 broadcast on the Florida primary summed up the situation astutely. "Pepper is and always has been a New Dealer," he said. "Smathers used to be, in the main; but if he means what he says . . . he is no longer. . . . Last February in Miami, Smathers talked about raising the banner of Americanism in a desperate battle—for what? White supremacy? No. To keep Joe Stalin and Karl Marx out of Florida? No. A battle for the preservation of free enterprise. And that is what is bringing money into the Smathers campaign in gobs."[110]

The political language of the Florida media (only two out of thirty-eight daily newspapers supported Pepper in 1950), and of the economic interest groups that mobilized to defeat the South's leading New Dealer, was structured to equate social democratic ideology with totalitarianism in the public mind. To the *Jacksonville Journal*, for example, the Pepper-Smathers race was "a strategic and monumental struggle between Americanism and Stalinism. . . . Individual Liberty versus Governmental Grab."[111] The *Tampa Sunday Tribune* attacked Pepper's advocacy of "the 'Welfare State,' which would kill free enterprise . . . socialize industry, and establish an un-American condition of 'statism.' "[112] The nuanced debate over the desirable boundaries of state intervention in the economy and social policy earlier in the 1940s had been replaced by a strident contrast between the defense of "free enterprise" and the promulgation of "statism." Whatever the realities of the size of the American state, that electoral debates had become so polarized seriously limited the possibilities for a vibrant liberalism in the postwar years.

The key interest group supporting Smathers' campaign was the private medical lobby. The campaign to remove from political life all those committed to federal health insurance and the intrusion of the state into medical care formed the link between Cold War and anti-statist rhetoric. One Smathers staff member drafted a long memo on the context of the 1950 campaign arguing that the "words statism, collectivism, and welfare state do not scare the American people" when discussed in terms of the New Deal. However, Smathers could gain mileage by attacking Pepper on "personal grounds. . . . because for three critical years he and Wallace publicly criticized and condemned the Truman foreign policy, thereby aiding and abetting Russian aggression. Such conduct brands him forever as a sorry, unpatriotic American, but a first-class communist."[113] Case studies of foreign statist experiments, and Pepper's support for them, formed the backbone of the American Medical Association's campaign against Pepper, and constituted most of the content of the forty million pieces of literature sent out during the 1950 midterm elections by the AMA at a cost of some $2.5 million.[114]

In Florida, the issue of "socialized medicine," and of the ramifications of liberalism in general for an America engaged in a Cold War with the far left, became the central issue in the Senate primary. One key AMA lobbyist in Florida, Dr. Louis Orr of Orlando, wrote letters to hundreds of wealthy practitioners across the United States asking for contributors to Smathers' campaign. "As you well know," he wrote, "we physicians in Florida have a terrific fight on our hands to defeat Senator Claude Pepper, the outstanding advocate of 'socialized medicine' and the 'welfare state' in America. . . . I feel quite certain that you realize that in eliminating Pepper from Congress, the first great battle against Socialism in America will have been won."[115] In a debate on the *American Forum of the Air* radio program during his primary campaign with Republican grandee Harold Stassen, now President of the University of Pennsylvania, Pepper found himself forced to differentiate between the American contributory proposal, based on extending the social security principle to health care, and the British plan. He did, however, defend social reforms in Britain and Sweden, prompting Stassen to respond that a "Swede in Minnesota lives longer and is healthier than a Swede in Sweden . . . under their semi-socialistic system."[116]

While Pepper had consistently attempted to establish a link between high politics and the electorate through the espousal of social programs and an expanded role for the federal government in the economy, Smathers did the same by associating the state, and, specifically, Pepper, with the defense of totalitarianism. Clearly Pepper's foreign policy views were in reality shaped by his domestic ideology: anti-Sovietism could easily mean anti-socialism and the promotion of the political right in a rehabilitated Germany, or in Spain or Portugal. The Smathers campaign, however, published a cartoon depicting an angry Uncle Sam plucking the gnarled figures of Pepper and

Dean Acheson out of the clutches of Stalin.[117] Florida voters, argued another Smathers advertisement, had a "double duty"; their vote was not just "for Florida" but "for America," a country representing a concept, liberty, opposed to the totalitarian left.[118]

As the campaign got underway, it became clear that Smathers was being used as a tool with which to further the decline of federal power after the New Deal, and to reorient national priorities away from pluralist domestic legislation. A CIO-PAC memo saw the anti-Pepper forces very much in a domestic light. "We face," it stated, "an assault upon the whole pattern of our society—upon unemployment compensation, upon old-age income, public housing, health and education. . . . They are using race hatred and class hatred, character assassination, forgery and falsehood—anything and everything that will confuse the issues and the people."[119] Rather than attack Pepper's foreign policy record for its effects on U.S. relations with other nations, the Smathers candidacy attracted a wealth of anti-socialist pressure groups, including the AMA and the Shearon group, who saw the Cold War as a useful backdrop for a purge of New Deal forces in domestic policy. A group calling itself the "Florida Medical Committee for Better Government" was created for the sole purpose of defeating another advocate of compulsory medical insurance. Physician members of this group paid for Smathers' radio adverts, and conducted letter writing campaigns to their patients. Doctors were, according to a Florida Medical Committee letter after the election, "spending the first three minutes of every appointment discussing the issue of compulsory medical insurance." Many doctors "closed their offices on Election Day and used their automobiles to take voters to the polls. . . . In many of the smaller communities, and in most of the larger ones, doctors' wives did a fine job of ringing every doorbell and calling every number in the telephone book to get citizens registered and to urge them to vote for George Smathers. . . . It is our opinion that no politician running for office in the State of Florida will ever again discount the power of the physicians of this State."[120]

Such power was greatly enhanced by the potency of foreign affairs, specifically images of the totalitarian state. "The issues," argued Marjorie Shearon, who used her pamphlet to aid the Smathers campaign, "are not the usual party issues. Instead, citizens are being asked to decide whether they want as their Representative in Congress a man who consistently favors Russia and the Russian way of life, a man who fights for a Socialist program and who not only associates with subversives, but employs them." Using the technique of associating the state with an elite, remote from popular concerns, Shearon wondered whether his "leftist tinge" was acquired at

Harvard, as "the best way to achieve success in the Federal government is to go through Harvard and turn left." Attacking a Pepper advertisement which called for health insurance, Shearon said it should have been worded: "A vote for Pepper . . . is a vote for Socialism and for federal control of medical care."[121] Felix Morley saw the defeat of Claude Pepper as representing "the repudiation of Democratic Socialism." One Winter Haven resident argued that Pepper "bragged on what Roosevelt, Truman and he have done," but that this strategy was futile in the political climate of 1950. "He will get the vote of the ignorant or sorry white and the negroes," he continued.[122] According to former GOP chairman B. Carroll Reece, Pepper represented "radical elements in Washington" and "alien philosophies of an administration which, if unchecked, will socialize this country."[123]

Republicans, like most economic interest groups, jumped on the Smathers bandwagon in order to attack a driving force behind the furtherance of the New Deal. The chairman of Dade County Republicans wrote to Taft saying that the Smathers campaign had appropriated Taft's name and had left the Republican campaign in Florida without a purpose.[124] In some ways this was hardly surprising: as Republican candidate John Booth was well-aware, Florida was still very much a one party state in 1950, although the Republicans would be able to build on the anti-statist climate of the 1950 election and begin to win public offices later in the 1950s.[125] The President of the Florida Young Republican Club wrote to his members that although the party had its own candidate, "there is no sense in kidding ourselves. The one and only chance is to beat Pepper with Smathers, and we Young Republicans are doing all we can in this respect."[126] One Ohio journalist vacationing in south Florida wrote that "here at Kendall, where a dozen or more former Ohioans live, all of them Republicans, I find they are registering as Democrats. . . . Some of them are making cash contributions . . . and all of them have made themselves available for such campaign 'footwork' as polling, ringing doorbells, and hauling voters to the polling places. . . . My Republican friends here insist that Smathers is just about as close to being a 'Republican' as a federal office holder can be in Florida."[127] An anti-statist network of private sector interest groups, the Republican Party, and wealthy private individuals had harnessed the Smathers campaign as a Cold War weapon against the expansion of New Deal liberalism.

This anti-socialist campaign against Pepper's advocacy of federal power went hand in hand with a campaign associating Pepper with Communism within the United States. An extensive printed booklet entitled "The Red Record of Senator Claude Pepper" was widely circulated in Florida, purporting to be a "documented case history from official government records and original communist documents." Pepper was apparently a member of no fewer than thirteen Communist "front" organizations, including any group associated with civil rights or leftist social issues. As a liberal, Pepper had got "the official nod from Moscow," along with Helen Douglas, Vito Marcantonio, Adam Clayton Powell, and Adolph Sabath. Pepper's proposal to create a national health system had been "prepared under the direction of the accused Communist spy, Charles Kravitsky—Kramer, staff director of Senator Pepper's Committee." Pepper was pictured with Paul Robeson, well-known stage performer and "Negro Red."[128]

Smathers' campaign did not go unnoticed elsewhere. Republican Karl Mundt advised Richard Nixon that he could well use the Smathers technique to offset the power of labor and racial interest groups allied to Helen Douglas. The "Red Record" booklet, Mundt argued, "contributed substantially to the gratifying and emphatic defeat suffered by Senator Pepper in Florida."[129] Anti-communism and anti-statism dovetailed in one piece of Smathers campaign propaganda entitled "Is Senator Pepper a Communist?," which argued that the "literal definition of communism and socialism are almost the same. In substance they are founded on the theory of a 'welfare state'."[130]

The Smathers campaign systematically rewrote the history of the tortuous dissolution of popular front liberalism during and after World War II in order to associate exponents of an expanded New Deal with the far left. According to one newspaper account, Smathers had said that his first "awakening" to the menace of Pepper's radical thought came after Smathers had been discharged from the Marines and "found that Pepper had acted as spokesman for a 'number of Communist and Communist front organizations.' "[131] One of these groups, the Southern Conference on Human Welfare, was a vehicle of prominent New Dealers like Harold Ickes, and represented a drive by New Deal liberals to advance the cause of social democratic liberalism in the South. To attack it was to attack the premises of the New Deal, as Ickes himself had argued in a letter in 1947 to HUAC Chairman Parnell Thomas. Responding to HUAC criticism for having spoken against the poll tax at a SCHW meeting, Ickes assumed that HUAC must favor Jim Crow "since you have never condemned this particular un-American activity [but] apparently you do take exception to my having declared against it on a platform that was particularly useful for that purpose."[132]

Smathers later vigorously denied waging a campaign against Pepper based on the stirring up of racial or class antagonisms.[133] It is clear that by its very nature anti-communism specifically excluded from the social mainstream all those associated with the left and with Pepper, of whom African

Americans were far and away the largest group.[134] The southern racial dynamic in 1950 expressed itself not so much in terms of civil rights directly, but rather in terms of social and economic rights related to the provision of state-centered social legislation. Neither Smathers nor Pepper yet understood the growing pressure for systematic reform in the social relations between African Americans and whites, as writer Zora Neale Hurston noted in an article for the *American Legion Magazine* after the election year fever had died away. Under the heading "I Saw Negro Votes Peddled" she recalled her experiences observing the Florida primary in May 1950, noting that under "the promise of gain, if you can call a dollar bill gain, the inert section of the Negro voters were needled into action and registration." Hurston carefully avoided targeting any one candidacy for criticism, but given the fact that a majority of African American precincts voted overwhelmingly for Pepper, at the very least the Pepper campaign was as fully engaged in such practices as was the Smathers campaign.[135] The campaign to elect Smathers, in turn, produced flyers headed: "A Few Things George Smathers Has Done for the Negro Race," which mentioned allowing people of color attend University of Miami football games and procuring "a complete and almost autonomous police force which operates exclusively in the colored sections of Miami."[136] At one point the two campaign organizations bickered over whether a racist advertisement in *Miami Life* had been planted by the Pepper campaign to discredit Smathers.[137] One of only two newspapers to support Pepper in 1950, the *St Petersburg Times*, ran a story headlined "Rep. Smathers Ducks Negro Meeting When Photographer Appears."[138] Neither candidate openly supported a permanent Fair Employment Practices Commission, and, generally speaking, the issue of striving for a genuine racial democracy in Florida was simply not on the agenda in 1950, nor would it be for another decade.

The 1950 campaign, however, represented the triumph of anti-totalitarian imagery over a New Deal politics that implicitly strove to create economic opportunity for those at the bottom of the socioeconomic ladder, including a majority of people of color. Claude Burnett of the Associated Negro Press, based in Chicago, wrote to Pepper in 1949, arguing that African Americans in general supported Pepper "because of the truly liberal stand which you have taken in public affairs. . . . Word comes to us here that there are forces in Florida who are determined to unseat you at this time if possible. These are the same forces which are against every forward looking social movement and against everything which spells Negro advancement."[139] An African American doctor in Tallahassee wrote in support of federal health insurance, arguing that all "negro laymen and low income white people should be for it. . . . The AMA will not recognize little hospitals like mine and therefore I have lost several hundred dollars on patients who carried Blue Cross and Blue Shield Insurance . . . [as] no benefits will be paid. It is a rotten situation."[140] Thus the anti-statist tenor of the Smathers campaign had serious implications for the development of socioeconomic equality in the South in the early postwar years in both racial and class terms. The focus of mainstream liberalism may have shifted, as Brinkley and Bartley have argued, away from direct intervention in the economy toward social issues like civil rights and a more mature management of world capitalism. Yet the marginalization of the state in political discourse in places like Florida at a time when genuine racial pluralism was barely mentioned in mainstream political circles would leave an enormous gap in American political discourse on issues of race and class.[141]

This argument is best exemplified by a discussion of the way in which the Smathers campaign addressed concepts of racial and socioeconomic pluralism, that is the state-led empowerment of social and class-based interest groups to engender equality of opportunity in the marketplace. In the wake of his election to the Senate in 1950, George Smathers gave a speech to the New York Southern Society, in which he stated that "in recent years there has developed a philosophy which stabs at the foundation of our democratic system. . . . It's a philosophy where future freedom is scrapped for present security. It's the philosophy of group power." This "group power" was the power of labor unions, civil rights groups, and protest organizations to bargain for political rights at the expense of the power of individuals. Smathers argued that the South was a vital region in this struggle because it had proved itself relatively immune from the social democratic bug: "some of them have tried—one rather recently, in Florida and North Carolina—but without success." Those, like Pepper, committed to the type of social democratic reform that attempted to raise living standards of the marginalized in American society, had tried to make liberalism "mean Socialism, regimentation, group dictation."[142] True liberalism, Smathers argued in a radio broadcast during the campaign, "does not pit one economic group against another, class against class, race against race, creed against creed."[143] Yet one could argue that the New Deal, and the later Civil Rights movement, did just such a thing in order to equalize opportunity in American society. The FEPC, a blunt instrument to reduce racial discrimination in the workplace, became in the new world of anti-totalitarian rhetoric a proposal "borrowed lock, stock, and barrel from the 1936 published platform of the Communist Party," or "a vicious wedge with which the reds could pry us loose from certain rights that we, as Americans, hold sacred."[144] Cold War rhetoric in the

Smathers campaign acted as a thin veil covering a battle over the future of the American state and its promotion of socioeconomic opportunity in the postwar United States.

It is difficult to ascertain exactly what direct effects the 1950 Florida primary campaign had upon the voting behavior of the Florida electorate. Clearly it is tempting to ascribe Pepper's landslide defeat to the political power of Cold War and anti-statist imagery. Constituency correspondence to candidates during the campaign is an unreliable guide; indeed, one file of correspondence Pepper labeled the "skunk file," and Pepper often scrawled words such as "crackpot" on letters he received. One such letter, which does at least demonstrate the depth of anti-statist feeling the Cold War engendered, stated that "hell [is] not hot enough for the Wallaces, the Peppers, the Grahams, the Roosevelts, the Achesons, the Hisses, and that horde of New Dealers who used their positions of trust to raise high the bloody hand of the beast in the Kremlin."[145] One cannot discount the sheer weight of correspondence attacking health insurance to Smathers, Pepper, and Spessard Holland in 1950, often using language taken directly from campaign flyers and AMA material. In addition, Holland received enough letters in March 1950 to justify a bulky file for that month alone, but then needed only one file for the rest of the year, coinciding with the end of the Florida primary campaign. Most of the material in the March file takes the form of resolutions adopted by organized pressure groups such as the Lake Wales Business and Professional Women's Club, suggesting that electoral opposition to statist programs had been highly organized and coordinated, and that that was reflected in the election results. The Lake Wales resolution stated that it was opposed to "government control of medical services" because it would "encourage the spread of socialism, which would endanger the rights of our children to the individual freedoms which have been the American heritage."[146]

Slightly more concrete are the detailed polls conducted by the rival organizations during the primary campaign in order to ascertain how electoral strategies should be directed. One such poll, conducted in Dade County on behalf of Pepper's campaign, noted in early March that whereas "Smathers supporters have an unfavorable attitude toward [Pepper] by a 2–1 proportion," Smathers "is not identified with any stands on issues, apparently, and no one seems to have anything against him." The poll noted that pro-Smathers Democrats were in favor of increased social security benefits and higher payroll taxes by 2–1, but did not see Pepper as being more amenable on this issue than Smathers. Although Pepper seemed to have greater support among lower income groups, this trend was not well defined, "just a slight relation of income to tendency to vote for Smathers, a slight positive relation." The poll came to the conclusion that Pepper needed to hammer away at his better liberal record in order to expose Smathers' stand on issues, but admitted to being slightly baffled at the way Smathers had managed to attract even low income whites to his campaign by vilifying Pepper.[147] The general finding of the poll was that Pepper was viewed in a more negative light than Smathers, and given the tone of the campaign, and the top reason given for supporting Smathers—that respondents disliked "Pepper or his program"—it is likely that anti-totalitarian imagery helped to discredit liberalism even among many of those who claimed to support the Fair Deal and Truman.

Making a clear issue between "radicalism and Americanism" seemed to have but one outcome in 1950. Claude Pepper was defeated handsomely across the state as a whole, in a pattern that was becoming familiar in every state where anti-statist political and business groups targeted liberal Democrats. One observer noted that local Democrats "conducting post mortem examinations throughout the state were in almost complete agreement that Smathers' ability to tie FEPC, CIO, and Communism labels on Pepper turned the tide." Doctors, dentists, pharmacists, nurses, and insurance brokers were the backbone of the Smathers campaign against the "Red" menace. Pepper held his labor and minority support in heavily urban, industrial counties such as Escambia and Bay counties, but elsewhere the decline in support for the New Deal was staggering. In Orange County, comprising Orlando and the comfortable northern suburbs, Pepper's share of the vote fell from 54.2 percent in 1944 to 32 percent in 1950. In Pinellas (St. Petersburg), the decline was from 62.6 percent to 46 percent. In Dade, based on Miami and written off by Smathers as too liberal to deny Pepper, Pepper scraped to victory with barely 50 percent. Smathers noted that he had carried more precincts in Miami, but Pepper still retained the loyalty of the poor elderly, African Americans, and those who remembered the New Deal better than the image of Joseph Stalin. The Dade precinct results demonstrate clearly how anti-statism had marginalized New Deal attempts to integrate race and class into an enduring progressive coalition. Whereas in the 1930s the New Deal carried a broad cross-section of socioeconomic strata, in 1950 Claude Pepper carried the 46th, 47th, and 48th precincts of Miami, comprising the African American Liberty City area, by 3,343 votes to 492, and the blue collar lower Miami Beach precincts by 4,635 to 1,070. He lost the precincts comprising wealthy and middle class Coral Gables by 1,592 to 4,424.[148] "In at least one county—Alachua—Pepper's hold on the Negro vote was broken and Smathers carried precincts with heavy colored registrations," remarked one Florida newspaper, although it noted that most other African American areas in Dade, Hillsborough, and Duval counties remained loyal to Claude Pepper.[149] Clearly, though, the New Deal coalition had been replaced by a Cold War coalition, more concerned with anti-leftist credentials than with social policy in Washington.

Such a viewpoint united many rank-and-file union members with the medical lobby. Ironically, given the widely held view that organized labor's contribution to Pepper's campaign hurt him, much of organized labor in Florida itself, such as it was, had its doubts about Pepper. Nothing demonstrated the profound effect of Cold War rhetoric on labor's ability to keep its eye on its own position in the American political arena than a piece in the AFL's *Florida Federationist* in February 1950. It argued that never "in the history of Florida has there been an election where so many vital issues were at stake as in the forthcoming Senatorial campaign." The article then listed only one of these vital issues: the need to protect American freedom "from the danger of Communism."[150]

The CIO was, by contrast, more concerned about the threat to the political clout of organized labor of the anti-statist attack on liberalism in 1950. The CIO *Union Record* in Florida argued that "Florida is at the cross-roads and the issues are duPontism vs. Democracy," a clear indication of the CIO's view on who represented the power behind Smathers' campaign. W. C. Belch, Vice President of the Florida Brotherhood of Railroad Trainmen, told Pepper that his members "are content to have any 'ism', even communism itself, if it is governed by the principles that you have espoused and stood up for these fourteen years."[151] The AFL was stronger in Florida than the CIO, and thus much of Pepper's union backing came from outside the state, as well as from ordinary union members who backed his liberal stand on economic issues. CIO-PAC director Jack Kroll sent envoys to Florida to report back on possibilities of mobilizing workers and minorities behind Pepper.[152]

In many respects the 1950 Florida primary was important because it was part of a significant nationalization of political activity and patronage compared to the nonprogrammatic, personality-driven local state politics described by V. O. Key. The interest groups involved in the Florida primary were national ones: the CIO, the AMA, the Republican Party, a pattern replicated in other states. The battle over the future of American liberalism was a battle for economic control over the resources of the nation, a fact that the AMA and CIO both knew very well indeed. The *St. Petersburg Times* estimated that the Democratic primary had cost at least $2 million. Much of that money had been invested in a political campaign that had sought to tie in Cold War anti-radicalism to domestic anti-statism that would push state-sponsored social reform off the political agenda in Washington.[153] Just as liberal activists were uniting around a limited range of issues, often to do with anti-communism, in organizations like the ADA and Republican Advance, so too were anti-statists forming their own political and institutional alliances. Robert Taft mused privately that "Republicans and many southern Democrats think alike on the basic issues, and . . . perhaps some method can be worked out so that their similarity of views can elect a conservative President." Former GOP national chairman B. Carroll Reece explained his reasons for running for Congress in the party's eastern Tennessee heartland in terms of his opposition to the incumbent congressman's seeming support for "the leadership and principles of radical elements in Washington exemplified by such men as Senator Pepper of Florida and Representative Marcantonio of New York. . . . Republicans and sound thinking Democrats are making the fight to preserve our unique political system against the alien philosophies of an administration which, if unchecked, will socialize this country."[154]

The development of a national campaign to discredit the Fair Deal state not only united Republicans, large sections of the business community, the AMA, and an increasing number of Democrats behind an anti-socialist campaign banner; it also contributed to the development of massive national electoral campaign budgets that the American left, such as it was, was simply unable to match. The races discussed in this chapter exemplify the way in which state-level campaigns attracted the financial muscle, as well as the ideological and political interest, of national-level organizations. Researchers for the *Congressional Quarterly* estimated that at least $10 million was spent to elect the 82nd Congress, an unprecedented sum in midterm elections, although the figures were hard to chart with any exactitude given the rather loose laws on political financial reporting.[155] Richard Nixon reported expenditures on his California campaign of a mere $8,300, although, according to Helen Douglas, California in 1950 "was a garden of Richard Nixon billboards, reported to have cost his backers about $25,000 a month for seven months."[156] The *New Republic* echoed this observation, estimating the total cost of Nixon's campaign as being at least $1.6 million, comprising around 1,400 billboards around the state, extending even into Mexico to catch the tourist trade. "Elect Nixon" billboards, wrote Jean Begeman, "stared at you from almost every corner; and in several instances, Nixon billboards appeared at all four intersections. Nixon had $50 an hour skywriters spelling 'Vote for Nixon' across the heavens." George Creel, of "Democrats for Nixon" fame, was "reported to have been paid $16,000. It was a costly campaign and a dollar-for-dollar one which Helen Douglas . . . could not begin to meet."

In Ohio, Robert Taft declared authorized expenditures of $1,533, and yet forty-five "Taft for Senate" committees "voluntarily reported $425,987.35 in campaign expenditures. In addition, the Republican State Central and Executive Committee of Ohio, the Republican Women's Division and the Ohio Republican Finance Committee registered another $1,639,071.52 in Taft's behalf. The grand total: $2,066,591.87." The CIO, in its most expensive single congressional battle since its founding fifteen years earlier, spent only $250,000 in Ohio.[157]

The pattern of congressional races where significant sums of money were expended relates directly to districts where strong supporters of the Fair Deal were running for reelection or where anti-statist Republicans were hopeful of winning. According to official figures, the costliest House race was in New York's 18th district, where the Democrats, Republicans, and Liberals joined forces to defeat ALP congressman Vito Marcantonio. Another high-spending race was in Nebraska's second district, where the AMA poured large sums into defeating Fair Dealer Eugene O'Sullivan.[158] The national network of forces opposed to any wholesale expansion of the New Deal state were galvanized to mount a well-funded drive to procure a more malleable Congress in 1950; in addition, such forces had a powerful ideological message to broadcast with the aid of that money which allowed for a more ambitious attack on the foundations of American liberalism than had been possible up to that point.

The opponents of an expanded welfare state were greatly assisted by the increasingly obvious fissures in the New Deal coalition. Across America the Democratic Party was redefining its political ideology to conform to the realities of Cold War and the anti-statist attack on big government. In Idaho, Senator Glen Taylor was under siege not only from prospective Republican opponent Herman Welker, but also from his Democratic primary opponents. In a radio broadcast Taylor tied his ideology firmly to the New Deal, arguing that in 1933 the gross personal income of all Idahoans was $115 million, and in 1948, $734 million. "Politicians may argue back and forth all they please and decry the methods of the opposition and call each other socialist and fascist but in the last analysis it is this cash money in your bank . . . which counts, isn't it?" he asked.[159]

A newspaper advertisement for Claude Burtenshaw, the Democrat challenging Republican Henry Dworshak in a second Idaho Senate race that year for a partial term, argued on the other hand that "I believe that any governmental program that does not encourage individual enterprise or increase individual opportunity cannot be justified. Government must be maintained on the local level as much as possible." In another advertisement distancing himself from Taylor, Burtenshaw argued that the state should "not be used to perform any function that individuals or groups can perform for themselves. Many services now rendered by governments are done not because government does them better but because individuals fail to do them for themselves. Greater opportunity would result if business would assume this service."[160]

Taylor's hold on power in his home state had always been precarious, and his defeat was scarcely surprising. Prior to the war he had become reasonably well known across the mountain states as a traveling song and dance man, earning barely enough to get by during the lean Depression years. His political awakening, he later recalled, had come from listening to radical barnstorming Governor Ben Ross in his native state in 1937: "As I sat there a light began to dawn. So this is politics? . . . Ben Ross is an actor. And he's putting on a show for these people. . . . If he can do this and get elected to office so can I, because I can do this sort of thing, too."[161] Running on a platform based on little more than a general sense of outrage at the iniquities of Depression-era America and an espousal of the "production for use" ideas of the likes of progressive businessman King C. Gillette, Taylor burst onto the Idaho political scene in the 1938 Idaho congressional Democratic primary and came a respectable fourth. Two further forays into Idaho's highly individualistic and personality-driven primaries were unsuccessful, Taylor blaming a business-controlled political machine that had locked up primary races in both parties. His approach to politics was nothing if not colorful, riding a horse around the state in the 1942 Senate campaign to drum up support for his candidacy in the remotest of counties. His persistence paid off in 1944, when he beat incumbent Democrat D. Worth Clark by 216 votes in a hotly contested race.[162] But just as the lack of party coordination and discipline in Idaho had allowed Taylor, a relative unknown in political circles, to blaze a trail to Washington, it proved equally easy for his political enemies to initiate a campaign to unseat him, with no significant party apparatus loyal to the incumbent to stand in their way. Clark was keen to avenge his 1944 defeat, and managed to mobilize the state's ramshackle Democratic organization behind him to retire Taylor from active politics. Taylor graciously conceded that his defeat would not prevent him from supporting Clark and Burtenshaw in the two Senate elections in November. "From my observations in Washington it seems to me that as a general rule the Democrats aren't as full of hatred and suspicion as are the Republican Senators and Representatives," he argued in a radio address after the primary.[163]

With Taylor defeated in the primary by Clark, Burtenshaw turned his attention to Dworshak, very much an anti-interventionist on foreign policy as a Senator from Idaho in the 80th Congress, and who had returned to the 81st Congress after the death of freshman Democratic Senator Bert Miller. "Make no mistake," the Democrat told a rally in Blaine County in September, "the unswerving goal of Communism is the complete domination of the world and the total destruction of our way of life, including Christianity. . . . It is a fight to the death between the free peoples of the world and the Communists."[164] This was the new liberal message now that Taylor's New Deal progressivism had been removed with the blessing of most senior Democrats. Republican researcher Vic Johnson commented that Taylor's "existence has become almost a source of personal embarrassment to many people" and that most Idaho Democrats felt that "Idaho is made ridiculous in the eyes of the nation by his antics."[165] Taylor's crime was to be on the political left when anti-left forces were using Cold War imagery to discredit the New Deal. In New York City the pattern was the same, as the two main parties worked together in an unholy alliance to replace Marcantonio with Tammany Hall Democrat James Donovan in the 18th district. In San Francisco, Democratic liberals Franck Havenner and John Shelley found themselves suddenly associated with Communist cells.[166]

Emmanuel Celler shortly after the elections put a brave face on the party's changed fortunes. He noted that in the House the Democrats had only lost 28 seats, leaving them in overall control.[167] In addition, Democrats should not have to apologize for the liberalism of the New Deal. "If we forget that upon our adherence to the New Deal of President Roosevelt and the Fair Deal of President Truman depends the allegiance of the people to the Democratic Party, then we are denying the ultimate source of our strength," he contended. He felt aggrieved that the Republicans had made advances by "seeking to brand all social minded legislation as Communist."[168] Celler failed to comprehend the extent to which his own party had unwittingly aided the rise of anti-liberalism. The Fair Deal and New Deal philosophies were not carbon copies of each other, as the former had incorporated a foreign policy element that encouraged anti-socialism as much as the economic interest group element in the Republican Party.[169] Many Democrats in 1950 played down their party's liberal credentials. Democratic rival to Helen Douglas in the California primary, Manchester Boddy, argued that "I have got to convince a lot of people that we should go slow about the matter of [social] security. There is a danger that we seek for a harbor—call it social security—instead of navigating the stormy seas." This speech indicated to the *Los Angeles Times* Boddy's "basic opposition to so-called Socialist trends in government."[170] Of the names most associated with health insurance or the extension of Social Security or rent control in the 1940s, as well as those critical of the ramifications of anti-Sovietism, all but a handful had been defeated in 1950. Many of these had lost to rival candidates of their own party. Images of totalitarianism at home and abroad had changed the ideological nature of both political parties, with important results for the future of federal domestic and foreign policy.

7. ALL INTERNATIONALISTS NOW:
ESTABLISHING A CONSENSUS ON THE STATE IN THE COLD WAR, 1951–1952

IN THE WAKE OF THE 1950 MIDTERM ELECTIONS AND WITH the intensification of the war in Korea, there was a change in the character of legislation coming before Congress. In the 80th or 81st Congresses as many domestic as foreign policy initiatives had been voted on and adopted. Debates on the Marshall Plan or the North Atlantic Treaty had been accompanied by consideration of social security change, parity payments to farmers, or labor relations legislation. The most notable thing about the 82nd Congress was the absence of a domestic agenda. A glance at a roll call list shows the 1951 Revenue Act as being the only major piece of domestic legislation that year, and that Act was directly related to the funding of foreign policy measures. In 1952, the bill for home rule for the District of Columbia was the main domestic talking point. The rest of the list comprises the renewal of the Selective Service Act of 1948, the bill for authorizing the sending of six troop divisions to Europe, the Mutual Security Act, the Japanese Peace Treaty, and the McCarran-Walter Immigration Act.[1]

Liberalism as defined by Senator Paul Douglas or Congressman John F. Kennedy now revolved around the dichotomy between the non-communist and Soviet-dominated worlds. Furthermore, although among Republicans there still seemed to be some scope for a progressive critique on questions like sending troops to Europe, there was in fact little difference between Douglas and Taft on the primacy of foreign affairs. An anti-totalitarian foreign policy enhanced the power of anti-leftism at home in 1951, encouraging the American right to associate liberalism with dissident social elements in the United States. The nature of political discourse across the political spectrum in 1951 and 1952 would suggest strongly that even if Taft was right in arguing that the New Deal could not be completely repealed, it would not be radically extended either.[2]

The Great Debate on Foreign Policy

The so-called "Great Debate" touched off by President Truman's decision in January 1951 to send further American ground forces to Europe, and to Western Germany in particular, represented the culmination of a gradual shift in American foreign policy over the period beginning in late 1949 with the explosion of the first Soviet atomic bomb and the fall of China to Mao's Communist forces and coming to prominence with American involvement in the Korean War. State Department strategy had clearly taken a more confrontational turn by the time North Korean forces invaded the South at the end of June 1950, symbolized by Acheson's press club speech in January discussing a defense perimeter for Asia, together with the promulgation of NSC-68 and NSC-48. These documents assumed the critical importance of establishing powerful allied states such as Japan, South Korea, and Formosa to sit alongside an economically and militarily revitalized Western Europe as a bulwark against Soviet expansion. The establishment of an Asian defense perimeter would apply pressure to the Soviet colossus at key points around its periphery, and would consolidate the American-centered economic order that had focused on European recovery up until late 1949.[3]

Acheson was well aware that U.S. military power was finite, and also that allied governments in Asia, such as those of Rhee in Seoul and Chiang in Taipei, ought not to be assured of American military assistance should they decide to launch attacks on North Korea or China. Nevertheless, the decision of the communist regime in Pyongyang to attempt to unify the Korean peninsula, and the subsequent temporary collapse of North Korean forces under American pressure in September 1950, led to a concerted effort by the administration in Washington to commit American resources to the anti-Soviet struggle, and to work even harder to create a political consensus on the virtues of an assertive anti-communist foreign policy.

The necessity of forming a broad-based Cold War coalition resulted from the ever-greater demand for resources with which to conduct the war in Korea. The 1950 Revenue Act and the excess profits tax passed the same year effectively marked the end of the domestic Fair Deal, as every cent of extra revenue raised from an increasingly uneasy Congress was swallowed up in the now gargantuan defense budget. In February 1951 the President asked for an extra $10 billion in revenue, the largest supplementary appropriation in the nation's history; Congress awarded him $5 billion in the 1951 Revenue Act.[4] Although the administration lost the guiding force of Senator

Arthur Vandenberg that year, a powerful group of Cold War liberal Senators led by Paul Douglas, Hubert Humphrey, and William Benton sought to pressure their more nervous colleagues into raising the revenue required to fight world communism. The battle involved more than just the war in Korea, as the administration was pushing simultaneously for a large military build-up in Europe.

The center of the great debate in 1951 lay in the widely shared perception in Washington that the Soviet Union was intent on expanding across the world, and that American resources had to be devoted in large part to matters of defense and national security. Paul Douglas argued that "Western Civilization itself is at stake."[5] He wrote a book justifying the postponement of New Deal spending in order to concentrate American resources on a massive arms program. The book called for cuts in domestic programs, as in "wartime we concentrate on guns and cut down severely on butter." America in the 1950s was "somewhere in between" war and peace.[6] In this ideological paradigm, America was an ideal, the USSR a totalitarian symbol of repression and un-Americanism. John Kennedy argued that "every month that goes by when we are so weak and she [Russia] is so strong is dangerous, and we should try to close that gap."[7]

The vital center of American politics, uniting Democrats and many Republicans, could be defined as creating an image of the totalitarian state and establishing a national struggle against that image. Governmental power would be deployed to create a military and strategic structure to oppose Soviet power, and in so doing would stoke the furnace of the American economy without resorting to domestic state planning or pump-priming projects that would siphon funds from the war on totalitarianism. NSC-68 had explicitly linked economic growth to the expansion of the U.S. military, as had Leon Keyserling's article shortly before the outbreak of hostilities in Korea entitled "Planning for a $300,000,000 Economy."[8] On this, mainstream liberalism and the right could agree. As almost all liberals opposed to this development in Washington had been removed from active political life in 1950, the sole opposition to this bipartisan, mainly liberal, group came from the anti-socialist right. This group used a different conception of the outside world and the American state to press for an anti-Communist policy that would see the contest as one at home rather than overseas.

A majority of congressional Republicans supported the administration's Cold War grand strategy, even as they attempted at times to limit the demands for money and manpower. Henry Cabot Lodge in January 1951 moved quickly to establish the basis of a new bipartisanship on foreign affairs. "The public announcement," he argued on the Senate floor, "that a 'great debate' is to be held in the Senate instinctively seems to invite a division of everyone into two groups. Apparently one must be either a 'globalist' or a 'retreatist'. This creates a false impression." There were, Lodge argued, sixteen points of major agreement among Senators. These boiled down to the recognition of an American role in the world, but with the proviso that Congress would always decide the nature and extent of that role. "In all truth," he concluded, "there are no fundamental principles which divide us. There are questions of degree and questions of method—but nothing which really goes to the heart of the matter."[9] He contended that Taft had now decided to join the internationalist bandwagon. Although Taft had serious reservations about the sending of troops to Germany for fear of inciting war, he specifically told Lodge that there was "no reason why the solution of the problem cannot be worked out in an amicable way."[10]

In the House, Edith Nourse Rogers (R-Massachusetts) argued in March that there was a "new" American foreign policy: "Almost lulled into a disastrous sleep, America has wakened at this late hour. . . . No longer will the power and might and force of America permit communism to capture, absorb, and enslave nations just because they are weak. . . . There is little disagreement regarding this new direction of foreign policy. . . . Free civilization cannot afford the luxury of an extended great debate."[11] Rogers was one of many to argue that Congress had been distracted by partisan argument over foreign policy in the past, allowing Russian imperialism to spread westward in Europe, but that now a new moral purpose united the American polity. Both Lodge and Russell Long (D-Louisiana) argued that the structure of the Soviet system meant that in Moscow important strategic decisions were not delayed by democratic debate, so why should not the same be true of America in this time of crisis?[12] Rogers asserted that America should be prepared to go to war with Russia if Moscow did not seek to accommodate itself with American "national principles," defined specifically in the socially exclusive confines of Christianity, "life, liberty, and the pursuit of happiness," democracy, and western justice. It was "unthinkable" to deny the necessity of an all-out struggle against Soviet expansionism.[13]

Taft led a token force of those in the Republican Party still deeply uneasy about the ramifications of sending vast numbers of American servicemen to foreign lands. He did not, however, dispute the ideological imagery of the internationalists. The Soviet Union was a great danger, but ground troops were not the solution. Herbert Hoover, a major critic of American foreign policy in 1951, argued that the war in Korea was proving that "a land war against this communist land mass would be a war without victory." Instead, America should create a "Western Hemisphere Gibraltar of Western Civilization," and allow other nations more room for their own defense. American air power would provide a further defense against Soviet expansionism.[14] Taft wrote a book on the subject, *A Foreign Policy for Americans*, which recognized the "Russian menace" but argued that the solution had to take into account the defense of the United States first and foremost. One review of the book argued that for the most part Taft was as internationalist as anyone else, differing in emphasis rather than in principle.[15]

Paul Douglas attacked Taft's limited vision of a world mission for the United States, arguing that rather than protect itself alone, America should protect "freedom wherever we can." According to Douglas, "the manifestation of Communist aggression in Korea during these last six months is but the showing of the fin of the shark above the water." Characterizing the USSR as a predatory animal, intent upon seizing the world for its own statist dictatorial system, Douglas contended that there "may even be an attack by airborne Russian divisions . . . into Alaska, there to establish air bases from which the continental United States could be attacked. These are no chimeras. . . . They are real possibilities."[16] Douglas argued that Taft knew that air power alone could not be effective in Europe, and that it would in any case destroy the industrial plants and cities of allied countries. There were thus still significant differences between Cold War liberals like Douglas and Republicans like Taft over the nature of American commitments abroad. Both, however, now argued that foreign policy was of more immediate importance to America than domestic issues.

In an August 1950 poll asking respondents whether America should keep out of war or devote itself to halting Soviet expansionism, 68 percent said the latter, with only 25 percent saying America should avoid war at all costs.[17] Taft in October 1951 argued that the Korean War would never have broken out had America not withdrawn her forces in 1948, never mentioning that to keep them there would have broken an international agreement. Significantly, Taft argued that the United States should have remained consistently internationalist after 1945, a considerable reversal of his earlier stance.[18] Again, as in the earlier debate over Asian policy after 1947, Republican calls for a more assertive policy sprang largely from political expediency, and from the luxury of being able to gaze into workings of the State Department from outside. Still, the anti-Soviet imagery dominating American political discourse had shifted even Taft away from his vestigial commitment to avoiding entanglements abroad, and almost silenced any debate there may once have been about the actual nature of regimes like those in Korea. Diplomatic historians now agree in large measure that Cold War strategists in the 1940s and 1950s unwisely discounted domestic political and nationalist concerns in peripheral nations, an awareness of which may well have complicated American Cold War policymaking.[19]

Opposition to bipartisanship now rarely entailed support for the views of Henry Wallace. Dorothy Thompson, a long time critic of anti-communist internationalism, sensed this shift in American attitudes toward foreign policy, arguing that "the majority of Republicans have now joined the Truman War Party." The sending of troops "is the logical result of the Administration's policy to 'deter' Russian aggression wherever it may occur on this globe." She herself attacked the leftist direction of European governments. "There is not a single European government that today has any wide margin of public support," Thompson contended. "The strongest *single* political party in France is the Communist [Party]. . . . In the last elections in Italy, 31 percent voted for the popular front. . . . In France the only 'philosophy' to emerge from the Resistance is 'Existentialism'. It is a sort of atheistic humanism. . . . With nothing else left, they are falling back on a nostalgic conviction of the superiority of European 'culture'. . . . One might cite George Orwell's *1984* . . . and the plays of Jean-Paul Sartre, merely as examples of the prevailing mood." To Thompson, the dominant ideology of Western Europe in her imagination was as alien to American theories of culture and the state as that of the Soviet Union. Thompson despaired that "the 'deter' argument is becoming a 'win' argument" concerning Russia, when American policy should commit itself "irrevocably to the *preservation* of the freedom, culture, and independence of Western Civilization."[20] This "preservation" clearly meant that of a "freedom, culture, and independence" and "Western Civilization" defined in anti-socialist American terms rather than by the "atheistic humanism" apparently dominant in France.

The Great Debate engendered a broader discussion in the United States over the nature of American ideology. A growing consensus over America's international mission would heighten divisions over the direction of domestic policy. George Malone associated the growth of the American Left with alliances with alien ideologies in Europe. In a Senate speech in June 1950, Malone argued that American Marshall Plan aid was "bolstering colonial slavery in various parts of the world. . . . Mr. President, we condemn Russia for her slave camps, while at the same time our Government helps Britain, France, and the Netherlands maintain theirs."[21] America was a unique example of a "free" state, resisting contamination by the failed doctrines of an "Old World" beyond its borders. The discourse was deliberately tailored to attack both internationalism and free trade, two of Malone's most treasured targets, and in this sense represented in part a continuance of a long-established American isolationist tradition.[22]

Malone could use images of abroad current in the Great Debate to construct a critique of the American New Deal state. Malone saw Western European governments as socialist, and thus allied to the Soviet cause. "It is a mystery to many close observers," stated Malone in August 1951, "as to why Russia should want to take over Europe when Europe has been sending Russia everything she needs to consolidate her gains in Eastern Europe and to fight World War III with us. . . . Russia's goal is Asia; and she is utilizing the socialist governments of Europe while the United States is contributing to their support." In supporting Britain since 1945 the United States had preserved "a Socialist, spendthrift government at our expense . . . to preserve a form of government in England and in other countries such as we say we do not want here."[23] Foreign policy concerns broadened America's interaction with conceptions of the wider world.

In some respects the outbreak of the first "hot" war since 1945 created a foreign policy worldview in Washington that transcended traditional ideological boundaries. General Albert Wedemeyer, for example, who would chair Robert Taft's 1952 presidential campaign, was a staunch conservative who believed that the primary goal of American foreign policy in the 1950s was to "check and destroy this world-wide conspiracy which is designed to destroy us, and we shall never succeed in doing so if we dare not take risks," risks that included all-out military action to roll back communism in areas like Korea and China.[24]

Paul Douglas, a Cold War liberal, concurred with Wedemeyer in an address to the American Municipal Congress in December 1950. Had the United States not intervened in the Korean conflict, he argued, Soviet influence would have spread inexorably toward Indo-China and India. In less than two years, "all of Asia would have passed under Communist control. . . . Russian prestige would have risen, western Germany would have lost any will to resist, and would have moved rather quickly into the Communist orbit." Soon, the whole of western Europe would apparently have followed. Douglas supported MacArthur's attempt to move north and repulse Communist forces from the whole peninsula. Furthermore, he approved of the use of Nationalist forces from Formosa, endorsing the view of the Asia-first lobby. Finally, he elaborated on Wedemeyer's lament that the Truman administration lacked the courage to "take risks." Douglas saw no reason "if the atom bomb can be used against the opposing military forces without appreciably hurting our own troops, why we should refrain from its use." Douglas then took rollback ideology to its logical extent: "I have come to the conclusion that the next aggressive act by a satellite should be regarded by us as an act of war and that we should then unleash such power as we have upon Russia itself."[25] Such a perspective did not preclude significant differences of opinion of domestic policy, but it did prescribe a commitment to a national security state that would override domestic concerns.

The heightening of Cold War tensions helped to solidify a right wing determined to oppose the creation of a garrison state at the same time as it pressed for the rollback of communism around the world. The renewal of the Selective Service Act in 1951 to cope with the demands of the Korean War provided an opportunity for the anti-statist right to attack the American state. Representative Thomas Werdel (R-California), best known for his bitter opposition to federal aid to education in 1948, argued that the Fair Deal government had employed "a supreme general staff, modelled after Hitler and the Prussians, seeking military control over industry, labor, all military establishments, the economy, and the press." Werdel asserted that the Pentagon had asked one of Hitler's Chiefs of Staff, Heinz Guderian, to draw up a plan for military expansion in America in 1949. The result would be "military socialism" and an economy controlled by a military high command appointed by New Dealers.[26]

Merwin Hart, far Right publisher of the *Economic Council Letter*, praised Werdel for his comments and argued further that James Forrestal, former Secretary of Defense who had committed suicide in 1949, had been "hounded to death by left-wing commentators and columnists" for opposing the generals' plans. The Democratic administration had betrayed America's allies at Yalta and Potsdam, had refused to ally itself with Spain and other countries that were ideologically "our natural friends," and was run by "the Socialist government of Britain . . . and the Socialist government of France." Truman had dismissed MacArthur from his Korean command in April 1951 because the "Acheson crowd, so greatly under the thumb of Socialist Britain and France, and still shot through with Soviet influence, have had their way. It is a diplomatic victory for Soviet Russia."[27]

The development of this anti-left trend in critiques of the administration's foreign policy was significant, as it demonstrated the shift in the focus of the right's approach to foreign policy away from isolationism and toward a militant rollback position that would come to dominate the approach of the Republican leadership under, for example, Barry Goldwater.[28]

Foreign affairs to this group provided a backdrop for an attack on liberalism at home. Joseph McCarthy, for example, was hardly the model of internationalism his anti-communist image would suggest. In December 1950 he argued that America should abandon the Marshall Plan and concentrate on encouraging the wider world, including Spain and Germany, to arm themselves for a common defense against the totalitarian left. There should be "an army not of American young men but of European young men, including the tens of thousands of Germans and Spaniards who are willing to fight against Communist aggression." In addition, McCarthy worried that a unilateral American assumption of the responsibility for world defense would weaken America in its fight to remain "free" and economically powerful. McCarthy warned that "Russia wants uncontrolled inflation or economic collapse in the United States . . . and that we may have gravely overreached ourselves in economic commitments abroad."[29]

The evolution of a form of conservatism that was militant in its opposition to the left around the world but simultaneously hostile to existence of an international statist machinery to combat totalitarianism assumed importance during a campaign in the Senate to attack the main pillar of the postwar American order: the United Nations, and America's place in international law. Senator John Bricker (R-Ohio) in June 1952 first introduced his constitutional amendment attempting to limit the power of international treaties to constrain domestic legislation. "In our time," argued Bricker, "the power of government has grown at a rampant rate. Whenever the power of government is enhanced, to the same degree human liberty is suppressed."[30] Bricker and allies like Frank Holman of the American Bar Association saw an attempt to abrogate the administration's power to effect treaties that could circumvent full congressional scrutiny as a way of curbing the ability of government to expand. The amendment reflected the palpable frustration in right-wing circles at their inability to control or direct the federal policymaking agenda, and their resentment at the capacity of foreign affairs and questions of national security to dominate governmental activity and to encourage the growth of the liberal state. The challenge to the authority of the President to conduct diplomatic negotiations freely also represented an assertion of congressional authority over policymaking in an age of the "Imperial Presidency."[31]

Eisenhower quickly lost patience with these Republican rebels during the amendment fight in 1953 when faced with the realities of executive power at a time of international crisis; the rebels, by contrast, saw a Republican-controlled Congress and administration as providing the perfect opportunity to wrest control of the Cold War agenda from the heirs to the New Deal legacy. Politicians like Bricker, Malone, McCarthy, and Bill Jenner were Cold War warriors with anti-statist rhetoric, rather than a national security apparatus, as their weapon. In the final vote a less ambitious version of the amendment, proposed by Walter George (D-Georgia), came just one vote short of passage with a two-thirds majority, which demonstrates how keenly many in Congress felt their loss of authority over decisionmaking since World War Two, and how far the dynamic of anti-leftism in the Cold War had rejuvenated debates over the scope and direction of federal power.

Images of abroad directly fed into the domestic wrangle over the scope of state power. A cartoon book entitled "How Stalin Hopes We Will Destroy America" saw liberalism as an ally of Communism by advocating the spending of America into bankruptcy. A white all-American family was depicted discussing inflation over the breakfast table while evil-looking Russians in military uniforms rejoiced at the spending plans of the New and Fair Deals.[32] Liberals such as Paul Douglas might recoil at such tactics, but the intensification of the Cold War, and liberalism's own part in furthering the ideology of anti-totalitarianism, were unwittingly adding to an anti-left campaign spearheaded by the Republican right and business leaders within America.

Domestic anti-socialism as promulgated by Bricker, McCarthy, Werdel, and others was not purely, or even primarily, economic in nature. An ideology that portrayed government as a threat depended on an imagined social reality within the United States, on a definition of America in which government was not required. Thus any social group associated with governmental power was automatically excluded from this definition and vilified. A Christian newsletter headed "America! Return to Constitutional Government! Internationalism is Another Name for Communism!" drew on Congressman John Wood's (R-Idaho) call for America to withdraw from the UN. The United Nations, it claimed, "aspires to control our destinies and use our armed forces and our wealth to further its atheistic One-World Socialism. . . . Doom faces us! There is no alternative now. We either secure the Lord's instant help by meeting the Lord's conditions of day and night crying unto Him, or we become as much the prey of the enemy as the Church of God in China and Russia." Eisenhower, a potential presidential candidate, was "a drinking man" and "a willing tool of the Soviet forces seeking America's destruction" because of his association with the state and his failure to appeal directly to "God's ministers and people."[33]

Again, those outside this Christian-based group, particularly Jews, were associated with Communism. A businessman in Lewiston, Maine, argued that America should "DEPORT ALL THE REDS IN THE USA BACK TO RUSSIA. . . . [The Communists] would . . . institute a WORLD GOVERNMENT IN NEW YORK. . . . The UN is a KARL MARX FRONT. . . . The REDS . . . are working for . . . revolution and slavery for all people but one race that are the REAL RULERS OF RUSSIA, the JEWISH RACE."[34] A Dayton woman wrote that Communists in America operated "under nice names like 'Jehovah's Witnesses,' Youth for Freedom, Youth for Congress, but beware."[35] Anything suggestive of "otherness" or social difference was increasingly being assimilated into the attack against domestic Communism. A Los Angeles woman wrote to Knowland that since he had taken a "patriotic stand on China, you will never get a vote from one of the minorities so it would seem to me that you should vote against the FEPC. . . . You are supposed, in this REPUBLIC, to represent the people of California and you know they voted against this mongrelizing proposal."[36]

There were rumors in early 1952 that Thomas Werdel intended to stand for the presidency for fear that Governor Earl Warren might get the GOP nomination and shift the party away from this flirtation with socio-conservatism. Werdel's abortive campaign was based on "opposition to FEPC, universal military training, prepaid medical insurance, Government housing, and . . . rent control."[37] Werdel was also closely associated with California State Senator Jack Tenney, a local version of Joe McCarthy in his use of an Un-American Committee in Sacramento to unearth enemies of his conservative philosophy. Tenney praised the "Americanism Educational League," founded by John Lechner in Inglewood, California, for leading "the fight on the Pacific coast against subversive propaganda and machinations." Congress needed to "place some 40,000 now on the FBI rolls in protective custody."[38] The identity of these 40,000 was unclear, although a possible idea was suggested by AEL pamphlets with titles such as "Will America Go to the Left?" and "sabotage!," both of which failed to distinguish between liberal pluralism and Communism.[39]

The foreign and domestic imagery of the Cold War was changing the ideological balance of the American right just as it had American liberalism. Social prejudice of the type exhibited by Werdel and Wood was hardly new, and was often unrepresentative, but one striking domestic example of its new power was the McCarran-Walter Immigration Act of 1952. On the basis of this act one historian has argued that the term McCarthyism is better termed "McCarranism" due to the socially exclusive agenda of the new legislation.[40] In a speech to a mining convention in Denver in September 1952, McCarran defended his legislation as an attempt to establish an America strengthened against Communism by being socially homogeneous. "*Just by existing,* we are a deadly danger to the Communist program of world domination," he argued, and "the Communist conspiracy in the United States is still extremely active."[41] Reading the text of the bill that McCarran had defended in these exact terms, it was apparent that all homosexuals and "sex perverts" were a menace to this vision of a free America (section 212(a), subsection 7), as were drug addicts, "aliens . . . seeking entry for activities prejudicial to the United States" (subsection 27), "advocates or members of opposition to all organized government," and those who were "advocates of world communism or totalitarianism." Such people could be deported under the provisions of the Act, or even have their U.S. citizenship revoked (section 349).[42] Despite President Truman's veto of the bill in June 1952, both Houses of Congress passed it by the two-thirds necessary to overturn the veto, suggesting the inordinate power of anti-communist imagery in America in 1952.[43]

Senator Herbert Lehman was one of a handful to condemn the measure as deeply damaging to American liberalism and to the vibrancy of a pluralist American society. "These proponents of the McCarran Act asserted that the purpose of the Act was to get rid of criminals and subversives," he noted. "The trouble is that these men feel that every foreigner is a potential criminal and subversive."[44] The national response to McCarran's new legislation was almost universally favorable, some of it bitterly scornful of Lehman's opposition, aided by the fact that Lehman was Jewish.[45] One letter to McCarran argued that America was "safe for a long time to come from an invasion of unwanted and socially indigestible aspirants to citizenship." Another expressed delight that McCarran had overcome "constant attacks from left-wing, biased newspapers, from certain minority groups and from misguided Americans." Another reads as follows: "Out with Lehman, Humphrey and company! Eventually we will join up with Canada and be a white man's country or go with the mongrel nations 'south of the border' and pass out because of decadence." To American Bar Association Chairman Frank E. Holman, author of the Bricker amendment, the passage of the bill represented "a vindication of your courageous and unselfish leadership in defense of America against the forces of the current internationalism."[46]

Images of otherness abroad could be used to attack internationalism as much as promote it. Social prejudice was by no means new in America, but it was given much wider significance and much more power within the political right than it had immediately after World War II. The constructed image of a "free" America versus a foreign enemy also defined Cold War liberalism, legitimizing a political right with which many Democrats disagreed on key aspects of domestic policy. The crucial elections of 1952 would complete the picture of an American polity transformed by the social imagery constructed by foreign policy debates.

Imagined Ideologies: The Limits of Political Dissent in the 1952 Campaign in America

The various campaigns of 1952 have been widely seen as representing a tumultuous showdown between the forces of liberalism and of conservatism in America. The victory of the Eisenhower forces over Robert Taft in Chicago has been portrayed as a victory of the "middle way" of the former over the anti-governmental stance of the latter. The Democrats, in turn, can be seen as a New Deal-inspired counterbalance to Republicanism's incremental approach to the extension of federal power over social and economic affairs.[47] Both of these views are in fact images created by the parties themselves, disguising a broad and developing consensus based around a constructed fear of totalitarianism. Using different conceptions of an American utopia to appeal to different audiences, American political figures from presidential candidates to congressional hopefuls for the most part sought to cast their opponents as being less concerned about the menace of a totalitarian polity. The language of the campaign was characterized by its similarity rather than by discord, as the attempt by both parties to use anti-totalitarianism as an ideological weapon reached its climax. The end result of the 1952 elections was to center the ideological locus of both parties around foreign affairs for the next twenty years, and to systematize the marginalization of the political left that had begun five years earlier.

Taft and Eisenhower: Constructing a Rivalry

In May 1952, Senator Robert Taft put out a statement outlining the reasons why he should be chosen as the Republican Party's candidate for the presidency at the Chicago convention in July. For fourteen years, he claimed, he had been "fighting as strenuously as I could the philosophy of government that dominated the New Deal and Fair Deal administrations of Roosevelt and Truman." Eisenhower, by this stage the only serious rival to Taft for the nomination, "represents that section of the Republican Party who have practically accepted the general spending control philosophy of the New Deal." Only through Eisenhower's defeat could the GOP "present a clearly defined program of progress within the principles of American liberty." Taft proceeded to define these "principles" by attempting to marginalize all those in the party outside this "program of progress." Eisenhower supporter Paul Hoffman, head of the ECA, was "a full devotee of the spending theory." Ike's supporters in Congress, who had often had cause to praise Taft in the past, had "tended to go along in most respects with the New Deal administration." Eisenhower had "carried out in full the general policies indicated at Yalta" and was "Chief of Staff when Acheson and Marshall worked out the policy of turning over China to the Communists."[48]

Recognizing that Eisenhower was in many ways an impressive apolitical candidate with whom the party could win the November election, Taft adopted a similar strategy to that of the Democrats when faced with an opponent to the left of himself. He characterized Eisenhower as a friend of the New Deal state, and, by extension, as a friend of totalitarianism. In so doing, Taft was increasingly associating himself with the international perspective of Republicans such as Joseph McCarthy, William Jenner, and George Malone, who had never been much concerned with formulating a coherent foreign policy. They were able, however, to associate liberalism with tolerance of the totalitarian left abroad, and therefore at home. Taft decided to rely on a new electoral coalition, one that was becoming more and more powerful thanks to a popular preoccupation with the imagined Cold War. "We must promise the expulsion of the money changers from the temple," he argued. "We can only preserve our liberty by putting into office men and women imbued with a hatred of that totalitarian philosophy of spending and power."[49]

The Taft coalition consisted of two groups. The first was the economic interest group based on the AMA, medical lobby groups, and large and small business, dominating Taft's support correspondence in 1952. Dr. N. Akers of Rialto, California, for example, argued that if Eisenhower won the nomination, America would be ruled by "the internationalist gang of New York and Hollywood—the dastardly clique who engineered us off the gold standard."[50] A San Luis Obispo resident asked Taft "to stop advocating free medical service and free housing. The public is fed up on [sic] communistic and socialistic ideas and want to get back to an American way of life."

Taft's stance on such matters in 1952 was to retain his commitment to limited federal intervention in social policy, but to stress his opposition to any meaningful development of New Deal liberalism.[51] Federal health insurance, Taft argued, "would destroy the independence of the American medical profession. . . . If the service is like most federal services, or like that of Great Britain, it would be pretty poor service."[52] Taft's stand won him the support of a nationwide committee of doctors headed by Dr. Ernest E. Irons of Chicago. Irons stated that the "members of the medical profession have special reasons to respect Senator Taft, and to be grateful to him, for the valiant part he has played in saving our country from the scourge of state socialism." Taft was needed because he could "put an end to the undermining of American principles of freedom and individual initiative."[53] Abstract principles of freedom and Americanism in opposition to totalitarianism served the interests of economic interest groups fearful of the effects of governmental power on their dominance of the marketplace. Cold War imagery could play a significant role in challenging the power of the New Deal philosophy of a welfare state.

A great deal of Taft's 1952 correspondence used Cold War imagery in contesting the power of the federal government. To one Taft supporter, for example, social security was "part and parcel of a Marxian theory, or dogma, put into practice to pull down the masses of the people to a common level—slaves of a despotic government."[54] Representative William Ayres (R-Ohio), a strong Taft supporter in 1952, argued that Eisenhower's victories in the New Hampshire and Minnesota primaries were irrelevant, as both of these states "do not reflect the opinion of the majority of the voters of the U.S." Senator Tobey of New Hampshire, argued Ayres, was "Republican in name only, for he has gone down the line with the New Deal Democrats. This proves my contention that the majority of the voters of New Hampshire are at heart New Dealers." Eisenhower's write-in result in Minnesota "proves how determined they are to do their utmost to leave our country in the hands of the New Deal."[55] In Ayres's view, all Republicans not committed to reducing the scope of federal power were committed to the New Deal; only Taft could unify the party around economic anti-statist principles.

There was, however, a second component to Taft's campaign in 1952 that Taft himself doubtless did not totally approve of. Rather than argue simply that Taft had somehow changed his political philosophy since earlier campaigns, it is more accurate to contend that socio-conservative groups empowered by the Cold War were harnessing Taft's name and image as an anti-statist, real or imagined. Anti-Semitic Christian preacher Dr. Gerald Winrod attached himself to Taft's candidacy, arguing that particular social forces were endangering America. "Anti-Christ agencies expect to destroy us," he maintained in his regular Christian newsletter. Anti-Soviet and anti-Semitic imagery combined in his attack on liberalism: "WE MUST WIN THE FIGHT, OR AMERICA WILL BE A NO BETTER PLACE TO LIVE THAN RUSSIA. . . . This anti-Christ power has its seat in the B'nai B'rith, an international secret organization, composed of Jews. . . . It is not an accident, for instance, that a Jewess writer for Communist publications, like Anna Rosenberg, should be in virtual control of the American armed forces . . . that Felix Frankfurter should be the mastermind behind the New Deal-Fair Deal."

Winrod then turned to Taft and Drew Pearson's attacks on him in early 1952. "We had every reason to expect Pearson to attack us, but with Taft it was different. . . . Pearson was the man who launched the Eisenhower candidacy several months ago. . . . This alone is sufficient to show that Ike was chosen to carry forward the program of international Jewry. Eisenhower is Taft's bitterest foe. . . . Surely [Taft] would be an improvement over what we have suffered over the last few years. He is wise enough to know that the anti-Christ power cannot be successfully resisted by any man aspiring to high office. So when the Gestapo ordered him to denounce Winrod, he denounced!"[56]

Cold War imagery masked a socio-conservative agenda based around the promotion of a form of Christianity and attacks upon Judaism. Taft in this context was perceived as an ally and Eisenhower as an enemy despite Taft's efforts to distance himself from these dissident elements. His association with the concept of anti-communism domestically made him a desirable candidate for a religious right uncertain of how to cast its appeal to the wider electorate. A Christian Nationalist Crusade letter was headed "Ike Drinks to Zhukov: Unbelievable but True."[57] Of course there was nothing "unbelievable" about two allied wartime generals saluting each other, but by 1952 the wartime alliance was a distant memory and instead abstract images of totalitarianism could be used to further a specific social agenda in the United States. A campaign newspaper supporting Taft carried a headline in March stating that "Reds, New Dealers Use Ike in Plot to Hold Power." The paper claimed that a list of Eisenhower supporters "reads like a roll call of Roosevelt-Truman Left wingers recruited from Broadway's theatre and night club belt." The election of Eisenhower would mean "the same Socialist, pro-Communist and appease-Russia policies" as had been pursued under Truman.[58] An anonymous campaign sheet headed "Eisenhower's Record is Pro-Communist," argued that Eisenhower was "for the 'One World Govt.' " Apparently, this concept would "destroy our Constitution, the only bulwark for the freedom of mankind, and would substitute a mixed govt. of Monarchies, Socialist States, Communist States, Democracies and others . . . none with the American ideal of fair play." The sheet backed Taft against Eisenhower's "plot to destroy America" by using all its resources in Korea.[59] The leaflet used images of abroad to construct an American utopia based around Christianity and a minimalist state, to which Taft's name was then attached.

Taft's evolving position on foreign affairs contributed to his appeal to the far right. The chairman of his national citizens' committee was General Albert C. Wedemeyer, formerly leader of the American forces in China and a strong advocate of a positive Asian program. In Wedemeyer's words, Taft was "neither an isolationist nor is he an internationalist. He is a realist. . . . Abroad we have pursued policies that have lost the peace in both Europe and Asia. . . . I am supporting Senator Taft because he can and will turn our country away from socialistic trends and will restore the free competitive economic system which made America great."[60] Taft's wavering position on foreign affairs was perfect for the right; he was opposed to profligate spending abroad, particularly on left-wing projects, but was militant on the subject of air power and stopping communism. Taft claimed that the administration and its GOP supporters were "the new isolationists. They would abandon most of Europe and most of Asia to Russia and adopt a purely defensive policy. . . . I made it clear . . . that I was in favor of definitely notifying Russia that if they attacked any of the [NATO] nations, they would find themselves at war with us, a Monroe doctrine for Europe. That certainly is not isolationism."

Clearly Taft had rewritten his earlier foreign policy ideas for the 1952 campaign, as he knew isolationism was not an option in the fervent atmosphere of the Cold War. He also linked foreign policy specifically to the domestic ideological struggle, arguing that "we can only achieve victory by winning the battle against communism in the minds of men. . . . If [Americans] are willing to take a definite, overwhelming stand against the trend toward totalitarian government, we can set out on a crusade and spread the doctrine of individual liberty throughout the world."[61] This was a rather different approach to his earlier agreement with Norman Thomas that America had to combine the development of the state at home with an ethical foreign policy committed to more than just blanket anti-communism. Now Taft claimed that the Truman government had ignored "our good friends in Central and South America," which presumably included the governments of Getulio Vargas in Brazil and Juan Peron in Argentina.[62] By the end of 1952 Taft decided to move from the Finance Committee to the Foreign Relations Committee in the Senate, a move welcomed by the internationalist mandarins as signaling his acceptance of the evolution of anti-communist foreign strategies since 1947.[63] Taft's more militant stance had the principal effect, however, of strengthening his appeal for conservative groups using anti-communism as a shield for domestic attacks on pluralism and on the state.

The Eisenhower campaign attempted to portray itself as more inclusive and moderate than that of Taft, but in reality was also committed to using anti-socialist arguments to undermine the Democrats, and even to attack Taft. The four issues identified in an Eisenhower strategy document were inefficiency, corruption, high prices, and high taxes. Liberalism was based on "political expediency" in contrast to Eisenhower's "business-like program designed to stop the spiral of inflation." Truman's foreign policy had "bungled us into a stalemate war."[64] An Eisenhower-Nixon campaign letter issued by the Italian American Committee for Southern California argued that "this administration's unprincipled foreign policy has humiliated and betrayed America before the decent peoples of the world, and has lost behind the iron curtain 600,000,000 free human beings, stripped of every vestige of dignity and liberty."[65] An Eisenhower leaflet argued that the Republicans "cannot save the country until we drive the New Dealers out of Washington. . . . [Eisenhower] is disturbed at the enormous expansion of the Federal

Government and at the declining power of the States." The subheadings in the leaflet were interesting, dealing with "Freedom," "Religion," the "American system," "Free Enterprise," "American Democracy," and "War."[66] Eisenhower campaign manager Sherman Adams, Governor of New Hampshire, attacked Taft before the convention for supporting federal aid to the states in several fields, causing Taft to contend that he had "always vigorously pointed out that health and welfare services should not be socialized by the state, or locality, or federal government. . . . [but] I think that we have a job to do in eliminating hardship and poverty in the United States."[67]

Each campaign manipulated the same conceptual and linguistic themes, primarily based on fears of the totalitarian state, in order to cater to a perceived popular mood. In addition, when Eisenhower did capture the Republican nomination in July, he was inextricably linked to a specific political party, which did not change its ideological message simply because Eisenhower was at the head, and not Taft. A GOP campaign report on the Americans for Democratic Action argued that "the ADA consistently supports big spending programs, government controls and suggests the government as a 'cure-all' for all evils. They are fanatical on the subject of civil rights and even go so far as to propose that the United States Government show proof of disloyalty before removing the offender from his government job. Throughout their existence the ADA membership have consistently defended Communists and the Communist movement although frequently professing their opposition to this particular form of totalitarian government." The document referred darkly to a "liberal-labor alliance . . . to effect the Marxian program they espouse and promote."[68]

Representative Adam Clayton Powell (D-New York) noted that both parties had back-tracked on civil rights compared to the 1948 platforms because of a need to pander to Cold War political priorities.[69] The political right was united around a general opposition to leftist economic and social issues as the ideological Cold War intensified. A Republican booklet for GOP candidates argued that the Democrats' policies would lead to "socialism," a "collectivist state—which means the end of individual freedom. . . . Britain is now suffering the agonies of the dope addict in trying to withdraw from her Socialist follies."[70]

Once Taft left the presidential ring in July, the socio-conservative and professional interest groups simply fixed their flag to Eisenhower's running mate Richard Nixon instead. According to one far-right newspaper, the secret fund incident that threatened to destroy Nixon's campaign in September was a plot by "Reds, New Dealers, ADL—B'nai B'rith forces. . . . The *New York Post* . . . led this attack. . . . The editorial was written by Dorothy

Schiff who is the granddaughter of Jacob Schiff, the strong financial power behind the Jews who launched the Communist revolution in Russia in 1917." The New Deal had attempted to appropriate Eisenhower's campaign, it continued, but found that "something went wrong and . . . they could not control Nixon . . . and he continued to blast Communism and the New Deal in his speeches."[71] The Cold War for the Republican Party had become as much a direct attack on federal power and on social inclusiveness as a foreign policy struggle against the USSR.

Reconfiguring Democratic Liberalism

To the political right, then, Adlai Stevenson was a leading ADA member dedicated to the furtherance of "national and international socialism." His "service with Alger Hiss and Dean Acheson began in the State Department on the 24th day of February 1945. . . . when the blundering about Poland . . . laid the foundation for the loss of Eastern Europe behind the Iron Curtain."[72] Stevenson's own campaign made such charges ludicrous, as he centered his own campaign on combating totalitarianism. He and Truman both were careful to defend domestic liberalism. Truman argued in Tacoma in October that Republicans had used the term "socialism" to attack "every advance the people have made in the last twenty years. . . . 'socialism' is their name for anything that helps all the people."[73] However, Stevenson tempered this theme by adopting the ADA language of the Cold War. He referred to the "ancient struggle between freedom and tyranny, which is renewed in every generation, [and] is critical in ours. And the most important single event in our history is that it is our turn to be freedom's foremost champions." He attempted to create a liberal alternative to conservative anti-communism by claiming that the state could be used as a weapon for removing economic injustice that could lead to communism, an idea the Republican National Committee termed "one of the most pernicious fallacies of our time."[74]

Cold War liberalism had reached its apogee, as exemplified by a letter to Stevenson from Chester Bowles, founder member of the ADA and now American ambassador to India. Bowles argued that the United States had to commit itself to supporting the economic and military stability of the entire noncommunist world. If India, for instance, "goes under . . . south-east Asia will be doomed and Japan will be brought under almost impossible pressures." Bowles argued that if the United States allowed such an event to happen, "Bevanism would rapidly increase, a spirit of compromise and peace at any price would quickly spread through Europe, and tens of millions of people now on our side would become convinced that they had bet on the wrong horse." The Truman foreign policy of containment had to be "filled out, expanded and clarified."[75] Stevenson's campaign followed this strategy. The Italian-American Division of the Democratic National Committee targeted Italian Americans with mailshots in English and Italian in which the only domestic issue mentioned was "prosperity" due to New Deal reforms. The rest was devoted to the Marshall Plan and what it had done for Italy.[76]

The domestic dimension to Stevenson's campaign was carefully crafted to avoid any direct association with statism. Bill Benton congratulated Stevenson in April on his assertion to *Newsweek* that "I don't like subsidies, doles, or interference with free markets, free men, and free enterprise." Benton wrote that it was "a great phrase and I hope you will keep hammering it." The principal theme of the Stevenson campaign was individual freedom, a concept that could apply equally to domestic and foreign affairs. To ADA liberals like Bill Benton the main thread of modern liberalism was civil rights, not social democratic collective rights, and thus he strongly supported Stevenson's choice of Senator John Sparkman of Alabama as his running mate as "a first step down what is going to prove a long, tough and hard road—selling to the South the need for federal legislation in the field of civil rights."[77]

Hubert Humphrey argued that the liberal movement still needed to remember the backbone of its political strength: "the militant support of the great rank and file of the people—the farmers, the workers, the minority groups. These are our forces. They represent our Divisions in this political battle. Right now these Divisions are not up to combat strength. Sure, we have the endorsement of the AFL and the CIO, but the important thing is to have the militant, enthusiastic support of the rank and file member." Yet the political context of the appeal to these New Deal forces had changed since the 1930s, and the main body of opinion in the party was coming increasingly to embrace the view that would be articulated by a leading congressional liberal later in the decade: "The Democrats need a new line. As somebody said, we have run out of poor people."[78] The party's research division prepared material for candidates entitled "Two Decades of Progress: Some Statistics," "Our Successful Battle Against Communism," and "Twenty Years of Civil Rights Progress."[79] There was no mention of labor law reform, health insurance, or state involvement in economic planning beyond helping other countries to remain free from communist domination.

In part the shifting dynamics of American liberalism were the natural result of the logic of containment theory with its emphasis on antitotalitarianism and individual freedom. In part they represented a defensive response to the political power of conservative political forces. "The President's earlier specific recommendation of National Health Insurance was not included in his messages to Congress in 1952," wrote Philip Levy to Bill Benton, outlining the political context of the latter's reelection bid in Connecticut. "Neither the Murray Bill nor any other national health insurance bill was introduced in the Senate during the 82nd Congress. These recent actions were quite deliberate, and were designed to take the steam out of the largely political drive of the AMA. . . . The degree of withdrawal from all-out national health insurance presents tough political decisions which Governor Stevenson himself will have to face on a national level."[80]

The Nation argued that Stevenson's strategy was "an unfortunate concession to current hysteria." That assessment was borne out by a memo from Democratic National Committee member Stephen Mitchell to local party groups telling them to counter the Republicans' attempts to recruit doctors and professionals on the basis of the "socialized medicine" issue. Stevenson himself countered the GOP strategy by saying that he was "as opposed to socialized medicine as any doctor in this country, just as I would be as opposed to socialization of my profession of the law." Eisenhower's "attacks on health insurance and the so-called Brannan Plan are interesting but obsolete," argued Stevenson in a campaign speech. "Neither is in the Democratic platform or recommended by the Democratic candidates."[81]

The liberal strategy was to defend the state and the New Deal while talking the same anti-communist language as their opponents, particularly on foreign affairs. The 1952 campaign was focused less around ideological difference, and more around interest groups promoting a particular candidate and attempting to secure the mantle of Americanism and anti-communism. The Korean War was to Stevenson "a crucial test in the struggle between the free world and communism," the latter based not in Korea itself or in China but in the Kremlin.[82] Cold War liberalism was by 1952 a well-oiled machine, a network of political actors primed to defend each other from phenomena such as McCarthyism while themselves promoting anti-statist political discourse. "No thinking American would advocate—and I would certainly oppose with all my strength—any program to socialize medical care or hospitalization, or to make our doctors employees or instruments of the state or National Government," wrote Bill Benton to the secretary of the Connecticut State Medical Society during his election campaign. This was the same Bill Benton who had made his political name pushing for the censure of McCarthy in the Senate as early as 1951. The language of that letter was deliberately crafted to reflect the anti-communist hysteria of the moment, and was both a political move to counter the threat posed by the medical lobby, and also a sincere attempt to recast American liberalism as the true guardian of personal freedom in the Cold War era.

Earlier in the campaign Benton sent two emissaries to see if the Feeney group that had caused so much trouble in 1950 could be persuaded to stay out of the race in 1952. Dr. Feeney was noncommittal, but acknowledged that any statement that Benton was "unalterably opposed to socialized medicine would be welcome to the doctors."[83] Stevenson and his liberal allies maintained their commitment to New Deal pluralism, but were unable to give it expression in the context of the right's successful attempt to link liberalism with communism in the Cold War, a war that Stevenson genuinely felt needed to be waged. Both Stevenson and Benton went down to defeat in 1952, Benton arguing that Cold War liberals could not out-McCarthy McCarthy. He asked his party contacts in Wisconsin to help him counteract the negative effects of his attacks on McCarthy, noting that New Haven Democratic congressman John McGuire "is positive that my attack on McCarthy is hurting me greatly throughout the state" and especially among Irish Catholics.[84] There were strong social and ethnic cross-currents that Benton and others seemed unable to counter, but what is just as important is that liberals did not attempt to counter them with statist ideas, but rather with the same language of freedom and individuality as their opponents. Liberal anti-communists cast their conception of freedom in very different ways to those on the right, developing, for example, their point that a politics of civil rights was essential if the United States was to stand as a symbol for the free world. Just as during World War Two, however, mainstream liberals tied their plans for a postwar order to established, anti-left modes of political discourse, limiting the potential scope of political and social change.[85]

The Decline of Liberalism in Congressional and Gubernatorial Campaigns in Massachusetts and California

Christian Herter's campaign for the governorship of Massachusetts in 1952 exemplified perfectly the contradictions inherent in Cold War "liberal" Republicanism. Democratic Governor Paul Dever had captured the State House from the Republicans in 1948 and held it in 1950 by portraying the GOP as "conservative" and "reactionary" in contrast to the New Deal record of his own party. Herter used his own moderate record in Congress to contest this charge.[86] In addition, he sought to contrast liberal Republicanism with the corruption and waste of the Democratic administration, and to link Democratic liberalism to the inefficient bureaucracy of totalitarian governments. The Democrats, Herter claimed, "plan a campaign to throw dust in people's eyes, so that the public cannot see the mink in the nation or here at home. . . . We . . . will expose their inner rottenness, and we will present affirmative, sound and humane policies to meet current problems."[87]

Herter cited Archbishop Cushing to the effect that America "has been travelling the road toward state socialism for several decades." He stated that the "blueprint" for political liberalism was "drafted 100 years ago by the father of communism, Karl Marx."[88] Bay State Republicans were able to use the highly factional and organized structure of the Massachusetts Democratic Party to create a portrait of a political dictatorship akin to the Soviet model. A Democrats for Herter group in Boston claimed to be rebelling against a party "that would herd ordinary individuals like you and me into a virtual political concentration camp. . . . The inevitable result of this type of superimposed big and beastly government is . . . an uprising of the forgotten, neglected, and downtrodden individual." Herter, in a speech for this group clearly not written by himself but endorsed by his campaign, urged these rogue Democrats not to "believe that I don't know what some of you have been going through since you have made your own personal choice of freedom from regimented domination."[89] Republicanism proposed a "middle-of-the-road course" as opposed to "the planned economy of socialism." The GOP campaign's portrayal of "bossism" was remarkably similar to its image of the "Russian bear issue" and "the extension of Communist slavery."[90] Dever was "power drunk with authority," just as the Soviet leaders represented "a bureaucracy run by a Politbureau [sic] of ruthless Red ideologues."[91]

Herter also claimed that liberal domestic programs made the waging of a Cold War more difficult, and that liberal Democrats were guilty of indirectly damaging the anti-communist cause. He and Dean Acheson had met earlier in 1950 and, Herter claimed, had agreed that, on the question of balancing social spending and waging the Cold War, it "was certain that both could not be done." Herter contended that domestic and foreign policy priorities were "incompatible . . . and . . . the American people must choose to which of the programs they wish to give priority. . . . My last word to [Acheson] was that I hoped that if Joe Stalin did not come through with his assistance in precipitating crises which would wake the American people to the situation that he himself would not hesitate to create the crises himself."[92] Herter caricatured a bloated state bureaucracy in Massachusetts not only as totalitarian but also as a genuine menace to American Cold War strategy.

The campaign in Massachusetts for the Senate seat held by Republican cold warrior Henry Cabot Lodge demonstrated the changed parameters of American ideology. Lodge had not only been a Republican liberal in the Senate, but had also been a strong supporter of the administration's assertive anti-Soviet foreign policy. This created a dilemma for the ideologically similar John F. Kennedy. Both used the mantle of liberalism as a tool to attract a diverse sociological coalition to their candidacies. "I have," argued Lodge in a television speech during the campaign, "struggled hard and publicly against reactionary elements in both parties. . . . I intend to go on voting to protect the citizen as regards his home, his wages, his savings and his need to be sheltered from the fears of unemployment and the insecurity of old age. These things are not a monopoly of one party." Ten days later he took up the same theme in another television address: "Government can be helpful in the field of shelter, diet and medical care. . . . We are in an era in which the federal government plays a tremendous part in the national economy."

Arguing that the American state was in 1952 a major client of some of America's largest industries, Lodge claimed that anti-statism was economically unsound. He then made an assertion that could have come from Adlai Stevenson or Helen Gahagan Douglas: "We must always have a social program so effective that communism can never get a foothold in America."[93] In a speech aimed at wooing blacks and other cultural and ethnic groups in the State, Lodge came out strongly for civil rights, noting that Kennedy had expressed his support for the McCarran Act, while Lodge had voted against it.[94] In front of a labor audience in Boston, Lodge argued that the "world situation should not be used as a pretext to give up consideration of measures which will lead to social progress, and which will lead to the betterment of the life of the citizen." The federal government "should provide free diagnostic clinics, including X-ray service, furnish periodic health examinations for all school children, and make available to those who cannot afford expenses—medicines—free of charge." As long as America conducted its governmental affairs "in such a way that the communist leaders in Russia can point to us and say that we don't really mean what we say . . . we are in a very weak position."[95]

Lodge focused his campaign on endorsing almost every aspect of the New Deal, from the minimum wage to federal direction of prices and production in times of crisis, and attempted to combine this argument with a commitment to a strong anti-Soviet foreign policy. As a Cold War liberal, Lodge saw any commitment to a liberal domestic social agenda as being conditioned by the need to present a specific image of America to the outside world. Any electoral strategy in early 1950s America had to focus not only on the socioeconomic demands of the electorate, but on meeting the perceived menace of communism as well.

In many ways Lodge's 1952 campaign was almost a carbon copy of his strategy six years earlier, with slightly more emphasis on anti-Sovietism and on his liberal record. Unlike in 1946, however, Lodge's campaign was singularly unsuccessful. His supporters quickly came to a consensus on the principal reason. Kennedy had successfully moved to the right of Lodge on the Cold War issue and had thus been able to attract the support not only of traditional New Deal Democrats but also of right-wing Republicans disturbed at Lodge's liberalism and his management of the Eisenhower campaign. A September 1952 poll suggested that Lodge was running some 90,000 votes behind Kennedy in Boston, a city Lodge had carried easily in 1946. "Kennedy runs very well and Cabot very poorly with the 'upper income' group of voters—who are relatively few and predominantly Republican," the poll argued. It suggested that this interesting fact might "reflect the bulk of the Taft deflection [sic]," and that Republicans bitter at Taft's failure to win the nomination were turning on Lodge.[96]

The contours of liberalism were being inverted by the imagery of the Cold War; Kennedy was far more popular than Lodge among the Republican right. Massachusetts GOP leader Basil Brewer came out for Kennedy, prompting Lodge to argue that Kennedy was a disciple of the political right by welcoming Brewer's "views against progressive legislation."[97] A group calling itself "Independents for Kennedy" received the public support of right-wing *Chicago Tribune* editor Robert McCormick. A Boston Republican wrote to Taft saying he intended to back Kennedy because of Lodge's liberalism and his failure to oppose the expansion of government. "I think Lodge is a blooming sissy," he wrote. "I am sick and tired of blue blood Senators with no red blood. [Leverett]Saltonstall [the state's other senator] isn't so bad, but Lodge stinks. . . . Did you ever hear Churchill not criticizing the opposition in government or advocating such a policy?"[98]

A personal friend wrote to Lodge after his defeat in November by 70,737 votes out of almost 2.5 million cast, stating that his "first reaction . . . was that the Irish Catholics of Boston had cut you. Further study would indicate that this isn't so . . . because (Thank God) they didn't vote for Dever. It can only be concluded that the Taft die-hards waited their opportunity."[99] The final results in staunch Republican Barnstaple, on Cape Cod, seem to bear out this view. Although Lodge carried Barnstaple as a whole by over 2,000 votes, his margin of victory was far smaller than Herter's over Dever in the gubernatorial race, or Saltonstall's in the 1948 Senate race. Edward Kelly, the Democratic Party manager in Barnstaple, told Kennedy that his performance was excellent, and "indicative to everyone of the tremendous strength that you would have" if Lodge were not the candidate, given his strong record.[100] In the 8th congressional district, based on the towns of Medford and Malden in the Boston suburbs adjoining what had been Kennedy's own

Congressional district, Kennedy ran ahead of Republican Congressman Angier Goodwin, who was reelected. Kennedy received only 2,028 fewer votes than Lodge in this Republican district, and carried a majority of the towns in the region.[101] Lodge was not only having trouble securing the support of the various elements of the New Deal coalition, but was also lagging among traditional Republican groups.

It is possible that Kennedy's success among upper income and Republican groups was due mainly to the legacy of bitterness resulting from the Republican convention in Chicago. The nature of Kennedy's campaign suggests that this was not so. Rather, Kennedy was using Cold War imagery to move the focus of American liberalism sharply to the right, just as had been the case nationwide in 1950. At first sight Kennedy, like Lodge, called upon the legacy of the New Deal to provide a framework for his candidacy. "It was the Democratic Party," he argued in a television broadcast in October, "which first saw the need for the exercise by the federal government of its powers on behalf of the individual."[102] Kennedy's campaign was aimed directly at traditional Democratic groups: blacks, ethnic groups, the working class.

The tenor of the campaign was not primarily focused on the New Deal, however, or even on domestic affairs at all. The Democratic campaign in Massachusetts in 1952 followed word for word the rhetorical technique used by the Republican right. "I think it is significant," Kennedy told an AFL audience early in the campaign, "in these days of anxiety about communistic trends to recall that Samuel Gompers and Peter Maguire years ago were confronted with a problem just as menacing as communism, the trend towards a Socialism that would have destroyed the American system of private enterprise. . . . I am well aware that the government has a job to do in the war against alien philosophies. That is one reason why I am anxious to be a part of the great Senate of the United States."[103]

Kennedy's campaign strategy was a response to the growth of anti-communist sentiment in a Cold War context. His supporters produced booklets of material for use in Kennedy's live debate with Lodge in Waltham in October, in which foreign policy and anti-communism were the overriding themes. The booklet argued that if Lodge took the Democrats to task for ballooning taxes and federal deficits, it was a fact that over "85¢ of every dollar . . . will go for defense, for aid to our allies and for paying the cost of licking Hitler and Mussolini (and Japan)." If Republicans brought up the concept of a "socialized health program," Kennedy should not support the idea but simply accuse Republicans of having no plan at all.[104]

In all his speeches Kennedy attacked Lodge's record on foreign policy, arguing that Lodge had been "wholly oblivious to the Soviet threat" and that

Lodge had been too willing to support the less successful aspects of Truman's foreign policy. Bipartisanship was a liability in 1952, and Kennedy did not hesitate to attack President Truman in his attempt to reorient liberalism in a more hawkish direction. Lodge had "voted 14 times against attempts to reduce these [foreign policy] expenditures to a more realistic level" and had "never raised his voice about the appeasing Administration policy in China and the Far East." Kennedy blamed the State Department categorically for the "loss" of China, and argued that "all non-essential spending should be curtailed."[105] A Democratic report on Lodge's contradictory voting record is more an example of American liberalism's loss of direction by 1952 than a genuine portrayal of Lodge's double standards. It argued that he had "proposed first a cooperative attitude, then a strong-armed attitude toward Russia," and that he was "unwilling to accept responsibility for errors" in the bipartisan foreign policy supposedly backed by Kennedy.[106] It was easy to see why Kennedy had much appeal in Republican circles in 1952.

Kennedy followed traditional Democratic rules in focusing his campaign on distinct ethnic audiences in Massachusetts. In 1952 the aim of an ethnic strategy was not to unite the generally less economically fortunate behind a New Deal candidate, but rather to use images of the overseas world to attract ethnic groups to Kennedy's Cold War campaign. A list of issues affecting "nationality groups" was drawn up. The issues were all concerned with events in the countries of origin themselves. The Italian group could be attracted by issues such as the return of Trieste to Italy, the removal of the war guilt clause from the 1947 Italian peace treaty, and the "fear of Communism" in Western Europe. Issues concerning the German population of Massachusetts included the continuation of Marshall aid after 1952 and the "fear of Soviet occupation of Western Germany as a step to 'unite' Germany." The list continued along the same lines for a wealth of ethnic groups, from Poles to Jews to Russians.[107] A Kennedy campaign letter composed on behalf of the "Albanian American Citizens Committee for Kennedy" argued that his record "shows that he has a great sympathy and understanding of the problems of smaller nations and has a deep hatred of atheistic Communism."[108] There was no mention of domestic policy in the letter.

Kennedy's contribution to a campaign tape made jointly with Congressman John Fogarty (D-Rhode Island) on the subject of Ireland provides a stark example of using images of foreign states to further a domestic political campaign. Kennedy's main reason for opposing partition, he claimed, was the "realization of the threat that a divided Ireland offers to our chances in the world struggle against Communism. In the event of open war with Russia, a divided Ireland would present a real difficulty in setting up the defense of Western Europe. . . . [Britain's] position is exactly the one which by professed and declared viewpoint the democratic powers condemn in cases where the Soviet Union has sneaked into countries where there are a local majority of Communists. . . . No nation has fought longer or harder for freedom and the democratic way of life than the Irish."[109] The mythologizing of the world beyond America's borders formed the principal component of Kennedy's campaign, and the main result was to shift his candidacy away from New Deal liberalism. The most enduring fact was that this strategy was seen, correctly, as viable; that Irish Americans would be as concerned with Communism as with unemployment or even Irish nationalism.

Konrad Sieniewicz, Secretary General of the Polish Christian Labor Party, based in New York, told Kennedy that Polish Americans would be swayed by assurances that American policy would "liberate Poland and other nations now under the Communistic yoke" and that "the security of Poland after its liberation will be guaranteed."[110] Kennedy built a powerful coalition in 1952 encompassing traditional Democratic labor groups in Boston and Springfield together with cross-class groups fearful of Soviet totalitarianism. The result was to ally Kennedy liberalism with anti-governmental forces in the Republican right, and to portray Lodge as a representative of the administration forces that had failed to repel Communism. What this Communism actually represented was unclear, but as it was on the left it by definition would make it harder for liberalism to include any aspects of left-wing ideology in America. During the campaign Kennedy wrote to Paul Douglas praising his book on governmental economy and asking for more details on how government could be reduced. It was, he argued, "a tremendously important issue."[111]

In California in 1952 an anti-liberal Cold War consensus was indicated by William Knowland's victory in both the Republican and Democratic primaries. The Democratic Party was in complete disarray in the aftermath of Helen Douglas's disastrous 1950 Senate campaign, and San Diego congressman Clinton McKinnon was unable to rouse his party against a senator who had been a strong advocate of aid to China and of the Korean War. McKinnon had emerged as his party's front runner mainly because of his anti-communist and ideologically ill-defined views, in direct contrast to Douglas's militant liberalism. Even so, he received a million fewer votes than Knowland in the Republican primary, and 333,325 fewer votes than Knowland in his own primary in a state in which cross-filing was permitted. Knowland carried every county in both primaries with the exception of McKinnon's home county of San Diego, many by 2 to 1 margins. Thus in a state where Democrats had a clear lead in party registration, there would in

1952 be no Democratic candidate for Senator. In a bizarre twist, the Progressive Party filed for inclusion on the primary ballot, and their candidate, Reuben W. Borough, received 5,258 votes in an unopposed primary, thereby becoming Knowland's sole opponent in the general election. Knowland in the Republican primary had received 1,341,170 votes, and in the Democratic primary, 966,881 votes. Thus a senator who had received a total of 2,308,051 primary votes faced an opponent chosen by 5,258 Californians to represent the forces of the political left. The possibility of a political mandate for an expansion of governmental power in California seemed barely possible before the campaign had even begun.[112]

Knowland's campaign strategy before the June primaries helps to explain his ability to appeal to a massive cross-class, cross-party section of the California electorate that would hold at the general election. As early as June 1951 Knowland met with a group of senior California Republicans at the Biltmore Hotel in Los Angeles to plot his reelection strategy. All, including campaign manager Murray Chotiner, congressman Norris Poulson, and GOP State Chairman McIntyre Faries, agreed that Knowland was stronger than ever, and that Democratic heavyweights such as congressman Clair Engle preferred to wait for him to retire than take him on. One GOP worker present remarked that he had been impressed by Taft's campaign in Ohio in 1950, and urged Knowland to "make a concentrated effort to talk to 'rank-and-file' in as many industries as possible throughout California." The issue to bring before these traditionally Democratic voters was not, however, the question of low pay, or labor relations policy, but the question of foreign policy. It was Knowland's "conviction that the international situation was the central, basic, key issue." All domestic issues, such as high taxes and economic controls, revolved around foreign affairs.[113]

A typical Knowland primary campaign speech would highlight perceived failures in foreign affairs, arguing that American "policy in China was responsible to a large degree for the loss of 400,000,000 friends in China to the Communist world [while] those who participated in the decisions were promoted and praised." Then a discussion of domestic issues would highlight the "greater and more rigid controls" that were pushing "American business, agriculture, and labor toward the precipice of state socialism."[114] A GOP campaign manual stated clearly that the party "*must* appeal to Democrats to support Bill Knowland." This was not to be done by appropriating the Democrats' liberal mantle, but rather by portraying McKinnon "as a supporter of the Truman spend-spend-tax-tax program." Knowland, meanwhile, was "recognized as an outstanding authority on international affairs." It was preferable for GOP workers not to "mention the opposition unless you are asked about him. Our job is to re-elect Bill Knowland, not advertise his opponent."[115]

The Knowland campaign chose to focus popular attention on perceived links between liberalism and the extreme left. A pamphlet was distributed aimed at factory workers entitled "So the Fair Deal Lost" which, according to a representative of the Chicago-based publisher, was "designed to educate the rank and file on the benefits of the Free Enterprise System. This series is sold to the boss man for distribution to his employees. . . . While this one particular brochure has a strong political slant, the reception from both employer and employee . . . is most enthusiastic." The booklet analyzed the 1950 elections and attempted to show popular dissatisfaction among the working class with the Truman Presidency and American liberalism in general.[116]

Foreign and domestic policy debates became indistinguishable, and shifted Knowland away from the more government-friendly electoral stance he had adopted in earlier elections. Knowland's managers were simply following the party's national strategy, one designed to recognize that "the average American is a HUMAN BEING—A PERSON WHO REACTS TO EMOTIONAL APPEALS. . . . a fearless ATTACK, ATTACK, ATTACK technique. . . . The election will be won by the candidate who can sell himself to the HOUSEWIFE, THE NON-ORGANIZED WORKERS AND THE CARD-CARRYING, DUES-PAYING UNION MEN AND WOMEN. . . . ONLY SHORT, HOT COPY WILL WIN THE VOTES OF THE MASSES. . . . LONG, INVOLVED 'THINK CLASSICS' WILL WIN. FOR THE OTHER FELLOW."[117] By creating a portrait of a Cold War at home and abroad against the state, Republicans could sidestep difficult ideological policy issues and create a broad electoral coalition in which the electorate's self-interested economic concerns were subordinated by a fear of totalitarianism.

Reuben Borough attempted in vain to counter this strategy and create a clear ideological distinction between progressivism and Republicanism that would attract traditional Democrats to his expressed left-wing banner. In an open letter to the Democrats of California Borough argued that a vote for Knowland would be an endorsement of "the all-out corruption of Chiang Kai-Shek and his American henchmen in the iniquitous 'China lobby', and the all out application of the McCarran and Smith Acts toward destruction of our American liberties." Borough's alternative program was genuinely radical, advocating immediate American withdrawal from Korea, a national health service, federal aid to education, and the repeal of Taft-Hartley together with the revision of the Wagner Act.[118] His first major statement after the primary actually used and defended the term socialism: "I shall clash with Senator Knowland all along the line. I shall clash with war hysteria. I shall clash with his anti-labor bigotry. I shall clash with his conspiratorial enmity against civil liberties and the Bill of Rights and his hatred of socialism and political progress generally. In this final campaign I expect wide support from the workers, everywhere."[119]

In a country other than the United States a radical campaign might have secured wide support, particularly among labor groups and minority ethnic populations in Oakland, Los Angeles, and San Diego, as well as the relatively poor agricultural region around Fresno. In California in 1952, however, the self-described Socialist endured one of the worst defeats in American political history in a normally competitive state. Knowland's winning majority of almost 3.5 million votes has never been surpassed in California. He received almost 4 million votes, dwarfing Richard Nixon's 2 million two years earlier. Borough received 542,270 and failed to carry a single county. In industrial Contra Costa county, a Douglas stronghold in 1950, Borough received 17,578 votes to Knowland's 102,704. In San Francisco Borough received 42,865 votes; Knowland accrued 246,416. In Los Angeles, Borough seemed to do well in gaining the support of more than a quarter of a million people, but Knowland received 1.6 million votes there, and more than 11,000 people in the city's south side wrote in the name Helen Gahagan Douglas rather than vote for Borough.

The anti-liberal tide swept all before it. San Francisco Democrat Franck Havenner, repeatedly a victim of rumors associating him with communism, was defeated after almost twenty years in the House by Republican William Mailliard. John Baldwin came only 2,000 votes short of winning the sixth district from Democrat Robert Condon, a district based on industrial Richmond and heavily Democratic Solano County. Faced with a conflict between "radicalism" and Republicanism, every conceivable category of voter cast their vote for the Republicans. Most House Democrats in California were reelected, but all had Cold War images and disassociated themselves from the Borough campaign.[120] Borough's campaign reflected the state's radical past, recalling the memories of the Upton Sinclair campaign of 1934 or Sheridan Downey's defeat of William Gibbs McAdoo in 1938. Less than two decades later, Cold War images of totalitarianism in the popular mind had killed radicalism in California. It would be many years before it would return, even after the Democrats recovered their political might in the Golden State in 1958.

Political Consensus and Division in 1952

"The profound national issue that goes by the name of Senator Joseph R. McCarthy has now come close to producing an open break in the ranks of the Republican Party," argued national columnist Joseph Alsop in August 1952. Knowland was told by his assistant, George Wilson, that Taft ally Tom Shroyer had said that "the feeling in Ohio is still pretty bitter as a result of the decision of the Republican convention. . . . They would, of course, vote for their friend John Bricker, but would refrain from voting for the presidency because they saw little difference between the two candidates."[121] It was certainly easy to detect differences in the approach of Republicans such as McCarthy and Jenner from that of Lodge. In the main, however, the differences represented factional discord rather than clear ideological division. Taft represented to many the conservative face of Republicanism, in contrast to Eisenhower's liberalism, but in his letter to Everett Dirksen in August 1952 setting out his shopping list of demands to Eisenhower, Taft was less than obstructionist. He asked for a commitment to a $60 billion budget in fiscal 1955; he demanded that Paul Hoffman and Thomas Dewey be excluded from government, and that Taft-Hartley be retained, with an appeal "direct to the union members." If Eisenhower agreed to this, "I would be glad to campaign vigorously for the ticket, and urge everyone to go along."[122] It was thus not difficult for the Taft forces, as Alsop put it, "to get General Eisenhower to run as a sort of pseudo Robert A. Taft."[123]

Eisenhower's speech in Everett, Washington, in October attacked "disloyalty" and asked why "do we have to worry whether there are disloyal persons in high places?"[124] There was little difference between Eisenhower's image of pro-communist corruption in government and Jenner's attack in his campaign in Indiana on corruption, war, "crushing taxes and spiralling inflation."[125] Internecine Republican warfare in Connecticut over the failed attempt by right-winger Vivien Kellems to obtain the Senate nomination revolved around personalities as much as ideology.[126] Clearly popular perceptions of candidates could vary; to one Connecticut Republican Ike was "a bed-fellow with New Dealists who jumped him from Lieutenant-Colonel to 5-Stars. . . . McCarthy just isn't Ike's kind."[127]

In the final analysis, no Republican argued in 1952 for the extension of governmental power, and no such candidate won election. In cases where Democrats were victorious, as in the cases of John F. Kennedy, Stuart Symington, Henry Jackson, and Mike Mansfield, all put anti-communist foreign policy above domestic reform. Occasionally an American would express dissatisfaction with the imagery of anti-totalitarianism. A Miami correspondent rebuked Clare Boothe Luce for using a television broadcast to berate Stevenson for his weakness on the Communist issue, asking her to clarify her term "the free world." "Where is that free world, Mrs. Luce? In Spain under the Fascist boot of Franco? In Portugal under the Jesuitical tyranny of Salazar? . . . In Argentina? In Santo Domingo under Trujillo? In Cuba? In South Africa? . . . This hypocrisy nauseates me."[128] In the main, however, Stevenson spoke for all those outside the Republican-dominated political mainstream when he told Clinton Anderson that "our enterprise was doomed from the start" in 1952.[129] The election results of 1952 may have been ambiguous from a party point of view, as the Republicans swept the Electoral College in the presidential election but struggled to gain a majority in the House and Senate. Ideologically, though, 1952 marked the high point of the anti-left consensus in America strengthened, intentionally by the right and unintentionally on the part of liberals, by portrayals of the world as under threat from the totalitarian state.

CONCLUSION

THE COLD WAR, THE STATE, AND POST NEW DEAL AMERICA

CLAUDE PEPPER'S POLITICAL CAREER DID NOT END WITH his ignominious defeat in the 1950 Florida primary. Having briefly flirted with the idea of moving to a state more receptive to political liberalism, such as New York or California, he eventually decided to remain in Florida and to attempt to unseat senior Senator Spessard Holland in the Democratic primary in 1958.[1] Such was the furor over the race question that year in the wake of the tumultuous events of the previous four years, beginning with the *Brown* decision and culminating with the Southern Manifesto, that Pepper's much trumpeted political comeback died when the results came in. Holland was re-selected as his party's candidate with a majority of 87,000. To Pepper there was no doubt what the result meant: Holland had received "two-thirds of his majority in the smaller counties of the state due to the fact that in the latter half of the campaign he took the strongest possible position for segregation, and in denunciation of the Supreme Court, and in offering to get the Supreme Court decision repealed by legislation, and attacking labor. . . . The situation in the South is utterly tragic respecting the race situation."[2] Indeed, the independent "Citizens Committee for Holland" during the primary campaign circulated material warning of the danger posed by Pepper's candidacy as an "ultra-liberal and pro-Communist. . . . Pepper will get the solid 'bloc vote' of the minorities, which is a long advantage in an off-year election."[3]

It was certainly the case that the perceived specter of racial integration in states such as Florida in the wake of the 1948 Democratic Convention and the Supreme Court interventions of the 1950s had helped to mobilize Southern conservatives in an organized movement to stymie efforts to promote large-scale social and political change.[4] It is also true that Pepper was, and Holland had been in his first Senate campaign in 1946, a moderate on matters of racial integration who preferred to raise questions of the distribution of economic power in terms of class and social mobility rather than race. In this respect Pepper was an old-style New Dealer, a political operator who negotiated the treacherous rapids of America's socially and politically complex governmental system by tackling some issues and sidestepping others. The New Deal had been premised on an adaptation of the nation's social and economic structure within existing political, institutional, and constitutional boundaries. Yet by the 1960s much of this steady work to build the political foundations for a more ambitious form of social welfarism had foundered on the rocks of Cold War anti-left political activity and institutional, private sector antipathy. Instead, private sector dominance of the American socioeconomic structure remained relatively secure, and American liberalism increasingly turned on questions of social inclusiveness within the existing framework of American institutions; the question of the status of various interest groups came to lie alongside the redistribution of wealth as a priority for liberal activists, with important consequences for the ability of liberals to push their agenda in the face of concerted Southern white opposition to social change.

The advances in state-led reform of American social welfare provision and racial equality in the 1960s might make much of the foregoing seem highly problematic. If organized labor was by the 1960s a shadow of its former self of the Depression era in its capacity to shape and articulate demands for the reordering of the balance of political and economic power, surely the Great Society years altered the landscape of social policy and raised questions of racial, gender, and sexual pluralism in ways just as useful to the advance of equality, if not more so, than a simple transfer of economic resources from one ill-defined socioeconomic group to another?[5] Had not the combination of governmental organization and private sector innovation to create a national security apparatus and a private sector welfare system proven to be the motor behind American economic growth in the postwar era, rendering wartime popular front conceptions of a social democratic state quaint and impractical?[6] Did not the Great Society programs provide targeted welfare that circumvented the institutional obstacles to universal welfarism that had stymied attempts by 1940s planners to enact more ambitious social welfare programs?[7] In any case, had there ever been an attempt in mainstream political circles after 1933 to promote a social democratic agenda for the American people, given the fact that the avenue of social insurance chosen during the New Deal period differed in scope and generosity from the welfare states under construction elsewhere?[8]

I have attempted in this study to establish that the political imagination of Cold War anti-statism contributed to the waning of a reform impulse that had gathered strength in the early 1940s from America's participation in the war and the domestic socioeconomic changes that had ensued. I have also aimed to chart the shift in political priorities of liberal activists by the early 1950s toward interest group pluralism at the expense of a broad-ranging critique of the nation's economic and class structure. It was not the case that there were simply two binary alternatives for those who termed themselves "liberals": piecemeal economic reform of the New Deal or a challenge to the social structure of American society, particularly in terms of civil rights. There was, briefly, a synthesis of these variant strands of left-of-center rights-based politics, centered around the development in the early 1940s of a politically confident labor movement and a network of left-wing political activists in the Democratic Party and in pressure groups like the Union for Democratic Action. This particular political discourse stressed questions of the redistribution of wealth, consumer rights, and civil rights as part of the same package.[9] By the end of the decade, ideas of social democracy lay outside the mainstream political arena, effectively cast as the preserve of the extreme left, communists, and fellow travelers associated with the failed Wallace candidacy in 1948. The American right, already supported by a fair degree of financial muscle, capitalized on the change in the ideological climate of the postwar United States even as the international Cold War forced conservatives to wrestle with the thorny problem of how to fight communism without enlarging the power of the state.

This analysis of American policy debates and election campaigns during the presidency of Harry Truman is intended to add another dimension to the existing historiography on postwar American political development. The present study sits alongside the literature on the political and institutional constraints circumscribing leftist political activity in the postwar years, and the theoretical literature tentatively outlining the parameters of American liberalism, but does not directly contest the theses expressed therein. My aim has been to show in general terms the link between Cold War ideology and the distinctive pattern of political change in postwar America. Often the analysis has painted in broad strokes a pattern that is subject to almost infinite complications and qualifications. For example, politicians like Paul Douglas did not necessarily associate their espousal of racial pluralism with a seismic shift in their political worldview. Claude Pepper may have been a good example of a leftist in mainstream politics, but this does not mean he was entirely clear about what that meant or how far his principles were consistent with the political realities. Nevertheless, an awareness of the important change in the center of political gravity in the United States in the early Cold War period helps us to put other studies of the weaknesses of American liberalism in their immediate historical context.

If it is true that American liberalism has increasingly been concerned, broadly speaking, with interest group rights at the expense of a critique of the larger American political economy, and that the private sector right effectively won the battle over the expansion of the New Deal beyond the development of existing structures and policies, it leaves open the question of where this leaves our understanding of U.S. political development in the second half of the twentieth century. The consequences of the rise of antistatism in the American body politic after the war were dramatic and far-reaching. For example, the large majority of the labor movement who opted to rely increasingly on collective bargaining agreements with the private sector for the achievement of welfare-related goals did not do so simply because it was the better route, but because the state-centered political route was fast becoming a political liability in the climate of Cold War. Similarly, Cold War liberals did not consciously choose to align themselves more closely with elements on the right because they felt kinship with them, but because Cold War anti-totalitarian rhetoric and policy inevitably led to a narrowing of ideological options open to politicians. The question of why labor governments in the United Kingdom and elsewhere met this problem more successfully than their peers in the United States is one that must draw on theories of political culture outside the scope of this study, although I have suggested some points of comparison and contrast that highlight differing contemporary views of the object of moderate leftist politics as being partly responsible. The idea current in much of Europe that social democracy or Laborism relied on a concept of community that stressed redistribution of wealth and universal access to social capital—education, health, security—increasingly sat at odds in the late 1940s with the Cold War liberal emphasis in the United States on the concept of individual freedom in which rival communities of interest groups strove for integration into private sector capitalism.[10] In one sense differences of political culture and institutional structure had always entailed differences of approach to such problems, but the window of opportunity in the immediate postwar period for the extension of popular front left-wing politics to the United States shows this explanation to be inadequate.[11]

The effect of the Cold War was to allow the right to blur the distinctions between variants of leftist thought, and to reorient liberal ideas of equality around the notion of freedom from totalitarianism and the gargantuan state. "We Americans have got ourselves into an institutional knot," argued

Robert Lynd in 1948. "Somehow we must break this fearful fixation on ourselves and this denial of alternatives." America had to redefine "the concept of democracy, which we are rapidly destroying by making it synonymous with capitalism."[12] Cut away the rhetoric supporting the image of a "Cold War" between two diverse social systems, and one perceives instead a political war over the future direction of American government and its impact on social change in the latter half of the twentieth century.

NOTES

Introduction: Ideologies of the State in Early Cold War America

1. Aaron Friedberg, *In the Shadow of the Garrison State: America's Anti-Statism and Its Cold War Grand Strategy* (Princeton: Princeton University Press, 2000); Michael Hogan, *A Cross of Iron: Harry S Truman and the Origins of the National Security State* (Cambridge: Cambridge University Press, 1998); Anthony J. Badger, "State Capacity in Britain and America in the 1930s," in David Englander, ed., *Britain and America: Studies in Comparative History, 1760–1970* (New Haven: Yale University Press, 1993), 295–306; Margaret Weir, Ann Shula Orloff and Theda Skocpol, eds., *The Politics of Social Policy in the United States* (Princeton: Princeton University Press, 1988); Otis L. Graham, *Toward a Planned Society: From Roosevelt to Nixon* (New York: Oxford University Press, 1976); Alan Brinkley, *Liberalism and Its Discontents* (Cambridge: Harvard University Press, 1998); Alan Brinkley, *The End of Reform: New Deal Liberalism in Recession and War* (New York: Knopf, 1995); David Plotke, *Building a Democratic Political Order: Reshaping American Liberalism in the 1930s and 1940s* (Cambridge: Cambridge University Press, 1996); P. Evans et al. eds., *Bringing the State Back In* (Cambridge: Cambridge University Press, 1985); Theda Skocpol and John Ikenberry, "The Political Formation of the American Welfare State," in R.F. Thomasson, ed., *Comparative Social Research*, vol. 6 (Greenwich, CT: Jai Press, 1983).

2. UDA memorandum on the planned visit to the United States of Labour minister Patrick Gordon Walker, November 7 1946, UDA/ADA papers, Cambridge University Library, reel 7, section 98.

3. See Ira Katznelson et al, "Limiting Liberalism: The Southern Veto in Congress, 1933–1950," *Political Science Quarterly* (Summer 1993): 283–306 for the argument that southern Democrats broadly supported New Deal reform in areas other than civil rights and labor rights.

4. Helen Gahagan Douglas, "My Democratic Credo," March 29, 1946, Harold Ickes MSS, Library of Congress, Box 55, Helen Douglas file.

5. This question is often posed in works which examine European state building. See, for example, Tim Tilton, *The Political Theory of Swedish Social Democracy Through the Welfare State to Socialism* (Oxford: Oxford University Press, 1990): viii, 280. Tilton examines Swedish social democracy as a distinct ideology, and argues that this method of analysis provides more answers to why Sweden developed a

sophisticated state sector than institutional or transnational factors. I intend to examine American political developments in the immediate postwar period in a similar way.

6. See Brinkley, *The End of Reform*; Elizabeth Fones-Wolf, *Selling Free Enterprise: The Business Assault on Labor and Liberalism, 1945–1960* (Urbana: University of Illinois Press, 1994); David Mayhew, *Placing Parties in American Politics: Organization, Electoral Settings, and Government Activity in the Twentieth Century* (Princeton: Princeton University Press, 1986); Meg Jacobs, "'How About Some Meat?': The Office of Price Administration, Consumption Politics, and State Building From the Bottom Up," *Journal of American History* 84, no. 3(December 1997): 910–941; Katznelson et al., "Limiting Liberalism: The Southern Veto in Congress, 1933–1950," 283–306.

7. John Foster Dulles address to the American Political Science Association, December 28, 1949, Christian Herter MSS, Houghton Library, Harvard University, folder 1362. See also Friedrich von Hayek, *The Road to Serfdom* (London: Routledge, 1945).

8. See Richard Hofstadter, "The Pseudo-Conservative Revolt," in *The Paranoid Style in American Politics and Other Essays* (Boston: Jonathan Cape, 1966); Alan Brinkley, "The Problem of American Conservatism," *American Historical Review* 99 (April 1994). A fascinating account of the ways in which the American right attacked social difference and left-wing thought as expressed in federally funded art projects in the early Cold War is provided by Jane De Hart Mathews, "Art and Politics in Cold War America," *American Historical Review* 81 (October 1976): 762–787.

9. See Alan Brinkley, *The End of Reform*; James Patterson, *Congressional Conservatism and the New Deal* (Lexington: University of Kentucky Press, 1967); Colin Gordon, *Dead on Arrival: The Politics of Health Care in Twentieth-Century America* (Princeton: Princeton University Press, 2003); M. J. Heale, *McCarthy's Americans: Red Scare Politics in State and Nation, 1935–1965* (London: Macmillan, 1998).

10. The historiography on this subject is an ever-expanding field. See Alan Brinkley, *The End of Reform*; Alonzo Hamby, *Beyond the New Deal Harry S. Truman and American Liberalism* (New York: Columbia University Press, 1973), and his masterly "The Vital Center, the Fair Deal, and the Quest for a Liberal Political Economy," *American Historical Review* (June 1972): 653–678, which remains the classic exposition of the view sympathetic to the Truman administration and Keynesian politics. A much more critical account is provided in Alan Wolfe, *America's Impasse: The Rise and Fall of the Politics of Growth* (New York: Pantheon, 1981), and in Robert Griffith, "Forging America's Postwar Order: Domestic Politics and Economy in the Age of Truman," in Michael Lacey, ed., *The Truman Presidency* (Cambridge: Cambridge University Press, 1989), 57–89. See also the excellent essays in Steve Fraser and Gary Gerstle, eds., *The Rise and Fall of the New Deal Order, 1930–1980* (Princeton:

Princeton University Press, 1989). Some recent scholarship that has stressed the inevitable importance of the private sector in post-depression America includes Aaron Friedberg, *In the Shadow of the Garrison State* and Patrick Reagan, *Designing a New America: The Origins of New Deal Planning, 1890–1943* (Amherst: University of Massachusetts Press, 1999), epilogue.

11. See Nelson Lichtenstein, *Walter Reuther: The Most Dangerous Man in Detroit* (Urbana: University of Illinois Press, 1995); Steve Fraser, *Labor Will Rule: Sidney Hillman and the Rise of American Labor* (New York: Free Press, 1991); Mike Davis, *Prisoners of the American Dream: Politics and Economy in the History of the US Working Class* (London: Verso, 1986). Meg Jacobs develops this "decline of liberalism" thesis in terms of consumers as well as labor in Jacobs, "'How About Some Meat?'." Two studies less critical of the role of organized labor in politics after 1945 are Taylor Dark, *The Unions and the Democrats: An Enduring Alliance* (Ithaca: Cornell University Press, 1999), and Kevin Boyle, *The UAW and the Heyday of American Liberalism, 1945–1968* (Ithaca: Cornell University Press, 1995). See also Elizabeth Fones-Wolf, *Selling Free Enterprise.* For an analysis of the role of anti-communism in postwar American politics, see Steven Gillon, *Politics and Vision: The ADA and American Liberalism, 1947–1985* (New York: Oxford University Press, 1987); Michael Heale, *McCarthy's Americans.*

12. Examples of literature on institutional constraints on state building include Ira Katznelson and Mark Kasselman, *The Politics of Power: A Critical Introduction to American Government* (New York: Harcourt, Brace, Jovanovitch, 1987); Theda Skocpol, "State Structure and the Possibilities for 'Keynesian' responses to the Great Depression in Sweden, Britain, and the United States," in P. Evans et al., *Bringing the State Back In* (Cambridge: Cambridge University Press, 1985).

13. Richard Freeland, *The Truman Doctrine and the Origins of McCarthyism: Foreign Policy, Domestic Politics, and Internal Security, 1946–1948* (New York: Knopf, 1970). See also Ellen Schrecker, *Many Are the Crimes: McCarthyism in America* (Princeton: Princeton University Press, 1998).

14. In failing to differentiate adequately between anti-communism and a fear of the state *in toto,* some observers have made the same misjudgment as many at the time. In the early Cold War, anti-communism was almost a given outside the CPUSA itself, but only rarely did those committed to using government as a tool for social justice see the danger of a position that was often a code for a broader attack on social difference or on the Left as a whole.

1. The Dynamics of Postwar Politics Before the Cold War

1. See Edwin Amesta and Theda Skocpol, "Redefining the New Deal: World War II and the Development of Social Provision in the United States" in Weir, Orloff, Skocpol, eds., *The Politics of Social Policy in the United States* (Princeton: Princeton

University Press, 1988), 81–122; Alan Brinkley, *The End of Reform: New Deal Liberalism in Recession and War* (Cambridge: Harvard University Press, 1995).

2. Joseph Martin Address to Lincoln Day Banquet of House and Women's Republican Club of Washington, D.C., February 7, 1946, in Joseph Martin MSS, Joseph Martin Institute for Law and Society, Stonehill College, Massachusetts, Box 63, file 113; Christian Herter Broadcast over WHDH Network, October 22, 1946, in Christian Herter MSS, Houghton Library, Harvard University, Cambridge, Massachusetts, folder 1196.

3. Two excellent studies of the international linkages between reform and planning movements in the first half of the twentieth century are Daniel Rodgers, *Atlantic Crossings: Social Politics in a Progressive Age* (Cambridge: Belknap Press, 1998), and Patrick Reagan, *Designing a New America: The Origins of New Deal Planning, 1890–1943* (Amherst: University of Massachusetts Press, 1999).

4. So called "state-centered" analyses of the development of social policies in the United States and elsewhere abound. See Theda Skocpol and Kenneth Finegold, "State Capacity and Economic Intervention during the Early New Deal," *Political Science Quarterly* 97, no. 2 (Summer 1982): 255-278; see also essays in Peter Evans et al., ed., *Bringing the State Back In* (Cambridge: Cambridge University Press, 1985); Theda Skocpol and John Ikenberry, "The Political Formation of the American Welfare State in Historical and Comparative Perspective," *Comparative Social Research* 6 (1983): 87–148. More recently, Daniel Rodgers has put American political reform into its international context, showing how reformers outside the apparatus of the state as well as inside it helped to shape an international dialogue of reform. His story ends in World War Two; mine continues into the postwar years. See Rodgers, *Atlantic Crossings*.

5. Joseph Lash memo to UDA New York chapter board meeting, September 4, 1946, UDA/ADA papers, Cambridge University Library, reel 13, section 210.

6. Paul Sifton to Ralph Wolf, February 12, 1945, UDA/ADA papers, reel 6, section 91.

7. James Patterson, *Congressional Conservatism and the New Deal: The Growth of the Conservative Coalition in Congress, 1933–1939* (Lexington: University of Kentucky Press, 1967).

8. See David Mayhew, *Placing Parties in American Politics: Organization, Electoral Settings, and Government Activity in the Twentieth Century* (Princeton: Princeton University Press, 1986); Ira Katznelson, "Considerations on Social Democracy in the United States," *Comparative Politics* (October 1978): 77–99; Ira Katznelson et al, "Limiting Liberalism: The Southern Veto in Congress, 1933–1950," *Political Science Quarterly* 108, no. 2 (Summer 1993): 283–306.

9. Claude Pepper and Hays Gorey, *Eyewitness to a Century* (San Diego: Harcourt Brace Jovanovich, 1987), 149. For details of the make-up of Congress in the 79th

Congress, see *Congressional Directory*, 79th Congress, 2nd session (Washington DC: US Printing Service, 1946).

10. Vinson to Wagner, May 30, 1945; George Outland to James Loeb, December 1, 1945, UDA/ADA papers, reel 6, section 91.

11. Outland testimony, June 21, 1945, UDA/ADA papers, reel 13, section 233.

12. Minutes of UDA executive meeting, October 24, 1946, UDA/ADA papers, reel 13, section 210. The committee included Loeb, Saul Padover, Ethel Epstein, and Joseph Lash.

13. See Meg Jacobs, "'How About Some Meat?': The Office of Price Administration, Consumption Politics, and State Building from the Bottom Up, 1941–1946," *Journal of American History* (December 1997): 910–941. Jacobs argues that it was only when the OPA failed to live up to its wartime record after the war that this large state organ lost public support.

14. Paul Porter to UDA meeting, New York, March 22, 1946; FDR Jr. to UDA members, January 1946, UDA/ADA papers, reel 13, section 229. See Elizabeth Fones-Wolf, *Selling Free Enterprise: The Business Assault on Labor and Liberalism, 1945–1960* (Urbana: University of Illinois Press, 1994).

15. Walter Reuther to Bernice Kandel, May 24, 1946, UDA/ADA papers, reel 7, section 94; Reuther speech at UDA dinner for Wallace, January 29, 1945, UDA/ADA papers, reel 16, section 289; Emil Rieve speech to Town Hall meeting in support of Henry Wallace as Secretary of Commerce, February 26, 1945, UDA/ADA papers, reel 6, section 93. For an analysis of the left-wing political vision of CIO industrial unions at the end of World War Two, see Nelson Lichtenstein, *Walter Reuther: The Most Dangerous Man in Detroit* (Urbana: University of Illinois Press, 1995), chapter 12; Kevin Boyle, *The UAW and the Heyday of American Liberalism, 1945–1968* (Ithaca: Cornell University Press, 1995), especially chapter 2; Steve Fraser, *Labor Will Rule: Sidney Hillman and the Rise of American Labor* (New York: Free Press, 1991), chapter 18.

16. *ILO Official Bulletin* 26, no. 1 (June 8, 1944).

17. See Patrick Reagan, *Designing a New America*, 218–219.

18. James Loeb to Jerry Voorhis, April 12, 1946 and April 23, 1946, UDA/ADA papers, reel 7, section 94; Leon Henderson to Town Hall meeting for Wallace, February 26, 1945, UDA/ADA papers, reel 6, section 93.

19. *UDA London Letter*, July 26, 1946, August 15, 1946, November 15, 1946; UDA/ADA papers, reel 16, section 308.

20. Three useful analyses of social democracy in Britain and Sweden are John Campbell, *Nye Bevan and the Mirage of British Socialism* (London: Weidenfeld and Nicolson, 1987); Martin Francis, *Ideas and Policies Under Labour, 1945–1951: Building a New Britain* (Manchester: Manchester University Press, 1997); Tim Tilton, *The Political Theory of Swedish Social Democracy through the Welfare State to Socialism* (Oxford: Oxford University Press, 1990).

21. UDA memorandum "On the German Problem in the Light of Soviet Policy," November 23, 1946, UDA/ADA papers, reel 7, section 95.

22. Jennie Lee, "Comment on Wallace," *Tribune*, April 29, 1947, ADA papers, reel 16, section 288.

23. James Loeb to Matthew Connelly, May 7, 1946, UDA/ADA papers, reel 6, section 92.

24. Elizabeth Fones-Wolf, *Selling Free Enterprise*, 34, 35.

25. Claude Pepper diary entry, July 21, 1946, Claude Pepper MSS, Pepper Library, Florida State University, Tallahassee, Florida, S439/2/3.

26. *Congressional Record*, 79th Congress, 1st Session, September 28, 1945, 9115; ibid., 2nd session, February 8, 1946, 1138–1139.

27. The ten opponents of the Full Employment Act in September 1945 were Douglass Buck (R-Delaware), Harry Byrd (D-Virginia), Peter Gerry (D-Rhode Island), Chan Gurney (R-South Dakota), John McClellan (D-Arkansas), Eugene Millikin (R-Colorado), Edward Moore (R-Oklahoma), Lee O'Daniel (D-Texas), Edward Robertson (R-Wyoming) and Kenneth Wherry (R-Nebraska). See *Congressional Record*, 79th Congress, 1st Session, September 28, 1945, 9153.

28. See, for example, Robert A. Taft MSS, Library of Congress, Washington, D.C., Box 878, OPA file; Box 875, inflation file; Box 877, NLRB file.

29. GOP Background Materials, "What Shall Our National Labor Policy Be?" (1946), Taft MSS, Box 1288, Stassen file 1945–8 1 of 3.

30. AIPO Poll, October 2, 1946, in *Public Opinion Quarterly* 10, no.4 (Winter 1946): 632. The full question reads: "Do you think it makes much difference which party wins the elections for Congress?"

31. AIPO Poll, August 3, 1946, in ibid. (Fall 1946): 423–424. The question reads: "What do you think will be the most important problem facing this country during the next year?" Inflation was by far the most popular issue. 46% cited it first, ahead of the 20% who said food shortages and a mere 10% who said the problem of peace and foreign affairs.

32. Joseph Davies, *Mission to Moscow* (New York: Simon & Schuster, 1941), 358; Sumner Welles, *The Time for Decision* (Cleveland: World Publishing, 1944), 315. This chapter is headed "The Constructive Power of the USSR." For an analysis of the link between radical thought, including praise of the USSR, and the New Deal, see Richard Pells, *Radical Visions and American Dreams: Culture and Social Thought in the Depression Years* (New York: Harper & Row, 1973). See also John Steinbeck, *A Russian Journal* (New York: Viking Press, 1948); Rexford Tugwell, *The Battle for Democracy* (New York: Columbia University Press, 1935).

33. Confidential notes of interview between Pepper and J. Stalin at the Kremlin, September 14, 1945, Pepper MSS, 204A/77/10.

34. Charles Parmer interview with Pepper, nd, 1945, audiotape, Pepper MSS, AV

A(291); Claude Pepper, "Hands Across the Elbe," *Soviet Russia Today*, July 1945, Pepper MSS, 201/16/10.

35. Another good example is the singer and actor Paul Robeson, who saw in the USSR a socially and racially equal society during his visits there in the 1930s and 1940s. See Martin Bauml Duberman, *Paul Robeson* (London: Bodley Head, 1989), especially chapters 10, 11, and 15.

36. Helen Gahagan Douglas, "My Democratic Credo," March 29 1946, Harold Ickes MSS, Library of Congress, Box 55, Helen Douglas file.

37. That there was an opening for a more social democratic political agenda in liberal politics in the 1940s based on the idea of social pluralism, that is the empowerment through government action of disenfranchised interest groups (labor, minorities, the economically deprived), is examined in much of the literature cited in the introduction to this study. Especially useful is Patricia Sullivan, *Days of Hope: Race and Democracy in the New Deal Era* (Chapel Hill: University of North Carolina Press, 1996), especially chapter 7; Meg Jacobs, "'How About Some Meat?'" 910–941.

38. Smathers platform 1946, Smathers MSS, Box 96, platform file.

39. Smathers speech at Hadassah, FL, May 27, 1946, Smathers MSS, Box 96, speeches, non-political 1946 file; notes on Cannon speech at Miami, April 26, 1946, Smathers MSS, ibid., opposition file.

40. "Spessard L. Holland's Announcement of Political Principles in Connection with His Race for US Senator," 1946, Spessard Holland MSS, Special Collections, University of Florida, Gainesville, FL, Box 229, platform file; Holland campaign speech, Bartow, March 8, 1946, Holland MSS, ibid., speeches 79th Congress, 2nd session file. Three out of four Democratic primary candidates for the Senate seat of the late Charles Andrews could be termed New Deal populists, although one of the three, former Congressman Lex Green, was a race-baiter. See Holland MSS, Box 228, Lex Green file.

41. Holland speech to the Florida Chamber of Commerce, Miami, December 3, 1946, Holland MSS, Box 229, speeches 79th Congress 2nd session file; Holland announcement of political principles, Box 229, platform file.

42. See footnote 8. Meg Jacobs remarks on "the extent to which scholars have overemphasized concern with anti-communism to the exclusion of price controls" in the 1946 elections. See Jacobs, , "'How About Some Meat?'"941.

43. Rogers speech to Lowell Business and Professional Women's Club, Edith Nourse Rogers MSS, Schlesinger Library, Radcliffe College, Cambridge, Massachusetts, Box 13, folder 168; Celler speech over WLIB radio, May 27, 1946, Emmanuel Celler MSS, Library of Congress, Washington, D.C., Box 536, Pre-1948 and Undated Speeches file.

44. Jacob Javits with Raphael Steinberg, *Javits: The Autobiography of a Public Man* (Boston: Houghton Mifflin, 1981), 110.

45. AIPO polls, September 18, and August 18, 1946, *Public Opinion Quarterly* (Winter 1946): 640 and 618. The second question reads: "Do you think the UN should be strengthened to make it a world government with power to control the armed forces of all nations, including the US?"

46. Ickes to Julia Ann Coe, April 15, 1946, Ickes MSS, Box 83, Russia 1946–51 file. Coe had argued that anti-Soviet hysteria was a British plot to harness American support for its own imperial interests, testimony to the continuance of foreign policy views common before the war. See also Ickes MSS, Box 78, Claude Pepper file for more correspondence on the USSR, including the April 1946 issue of Southern Conference of Human Welfare's magazine, *Southern Patriot,* which devotes itself to a tribute to Senator Claude Pepper and his leftist foreign policy views.

47. M. M. Odil to Ickes, September 9, 1946; Ickes to Odil, September 16, 1946, Ickes MSS, ibid.

48. UDA foreign policy statement, October 28, 1945, UDA/ADA papers, reel 13, section 228. It is vital to note that in early 1946 the United States had not categorically cut off aid to the USSR. See Pepper, "An American Policy for Peace and a New World," March 20, 1946, Ickes MSS, Box 78, Claude Pepper file. See George C. Herring, Jr., *Aid to Russia, 1941–1946: Strategy, Diplomacy, the Origins of the Cold War* (New York: Columbia University Press, 1973). The debate over the loan to Britain in May 1946 shows how economic and other issues unrelated to anti-Sovietism, such as anti-British feeling, still had considerable relevance in foreign policy discussions in this period.

49. "Her district is a cross-cut of America," wrote *The New Republic* in 1948. "The Mexican population is its largest single element. Its Negro community is the largest west of Chicago. It has Polish and Russian Jews, Italians, French, Chinese and Japanese. Its contains great estates around Lafayette Park. . . . And it contains "skid row," with its grog shops, flophouses, and salvation missionaries. . . . some of the worst slums on the coast." See Douglas article, *New Republic* (September 20, 1948): 10.

50. JFK speech to Young Democrats in Pennsylvania, August 21, 1946, John F. Kennedy Pre-Presidential MSS, JFK Library, Boston, Box 94, Boston office speeches file.

51. 1946 JFK platform, JFK MSS, Box 99, Platform file. John White produces evidence that Kennedy was very concerned about Communism in 1946, but my point is that it did not yet get in the way of democratic liberalism among Democrats. See John White, *Still Seeing Red: How the Cold War Shapes the New American Politics* (Boulder: Westview Press, 1997), 45.

52. JFK MSS, Box 73, B file 1 of 2.

53. Helen Douglas to Herbert Lehman, January 25, 1944, Herbert Lehman MSS, Lehman Suite, Columbia University, New York, Helen Douglas special file 222. For

an in-depth study of Douglas see Ingrid Winther Scobie, *Center Stage: Helen Gahagan Douglas* (New York: Oxford University Press, 1992), and also Helen Douglas's autobiography, *A Full Life* (Garden City: Doubleday, 1982).

54. Helen Douglas, "My Democratic Credo," March 29, 1946, in Ickes MSS, Box 55, Helen Douglas file.

55. Douglas to Ickes, October 2, 1946, Ickes MSS, Box 55, Douglas file.

56. An example is his promise if elected to "support an adequate pension system under which our unemployed citizens past sixty years of age shall receive a sufficient annuity as a matter of social right and without the degrading 'means test' that is now required." Rogers interview, October 20, 1946, Knowland MSS, Bancroft Library, University of California, Berkeley, Box 86, Miscellaneous file.

57. Douglas to Ickes, October 31, 1946 and September 11, 1946, Ickes MSS, Box 55, Douglas file.

58. Glenn M. Anderson, California Democratic State Central Committee, Analysis of California election returns, November 1950, Clinton P. Anderson MSS, Library of Congress, Box 1052, California file.

59. Republican Central Committee Research Division Report, Jan 16, 1947, Knowland MSS, Box 87, file 1.

60. *Los Angeles Sentinel*, September 26, 1946; October 3, 1946; October 31, 1946.

61. White, *Still Seeing Red*, 45.

62. See Harry W. Kirwin, *The Inevitable Success: Herbert R. O'Conor* (Westminster, MD: The Newman Press, 1962), 413. Unfortunately, O'Conor's papers were destroyed in a basement flood.

63. Kennedy platform 1946, JFK MSS, Box 99, Platform file.

64. Herbert Lehman speech to Liberal Party conference, September 18, 1946, Lehman MSS, speeches 1946 file C235–12.

65. New York state Democratic Party platform, 1946, Lehman MSS, C235/11; Lehman address to CIO convention, Lake Placid, September 14, 1946, Lehman MSS, C235–12.

66. Leon Savage to G. Backer and P. Weinstein, October 27, 1946, Lehman MSS, C235/9A.

67. A useful account of the emergence of the New York Liberal Party and the turmoil on the left at the end of World War Two is provided in Steven Fraser, *Labor Will Rule*, chapter 17.

68. Lehman address at Hunts Point Palace on the ALP, October 7, 1946; Lehman speech at ICCASP meeting, September 29, 1946 and October 20, 1946; Lehman speech to Women's Division, NCPAC, September 24, 1946; Lehman radio address, NBC, October 26, 1946, Lehman MSS, C235–12.

69. Lehman to John Foster Dulles, October 17, 1949, Lehman MSS, C235–17; Lehman address at Hunts Point Palace, Lehman MSS, C235–12; Steven Fraser, *Labor*

Will Rule, chapter 17. Fraser argues on page 519 that the Communist party was by 1943 "too potent a force, not only in the ALP but in the CIO, to alienate."

70. See Alonzo Hamby, *Beyond the New Deal: Harry S. Truman and American Liberalism* (New York: Columbia University Press, 1973), 132–133; Mary Sperling McAuliffe, *Crisis on the Left: Cold War Politics and American Liberals* (Amherst: University of Massachusetts Press, 1978), chapter 1.

71 . Wallace Madison Square Garden speech, September 12, 1946, Taft MSS, Box 612, Foreign affairs 1946–7 file.

72. There is a growing literature on the importance of Florida politics in representing broader national trends, and on important political figures such as Pepper and Smathers. See Tracy Danese, *Claude Pepper and Ed Ball: Politics, Purpose, and Power* (Gainesville: University Press of Florida, 2000); Brian Crispell, *Testing the Limits: George Armistead Smathers and Cold War America* (Athens: University of Georgia Press, 1999).

73. George Smathers Oral History, interview with Donald Ritchie, Senate Historical Office, Washington, D.C., 1989, 42.

74. See Danese, *Claude Pepper and Ed Ball*, 13; chapter one details the socioeconomic development of Florida in the early twentieth century in some detail.

75. V. O. Key, *Southern Politics in State and Nation* (New York: Random House, 1949): 99. Chapter 5 of this work is entitled "Florida: Every Man for Himself," and is a lucid contemporary summary of the loose-knit political organization of the Sunshine State in the 1940s. See also David Mayhew, *Placing Parties in American Politics*, 120–121.

76. Key, *Southern Politics in State and Nation*, 85; Danese, *Claude Pepper and Ed Ball.*, 51.

77. Numan Bartley provides an excellent discussion of the southern context to liberalism's travails in the 1940s in *The New South, 1945-1980* (Baton Rouge: Louisiana State University Press, 1995), especially 64–73. See also Samuel Lubell's classic study of postwar US politics, *The Future of American Politics* (London: Hamish Hamilton: 1952), chapter 6, especially 120–121, which deals with the North Carolina and Florida primaries of 1950.

78. Smathers to Pepper, nd 1946, Pepper MSS, series 204A, box 48, folder 1. See also Smathers letters to Pepper approving his political stance on issues and asking for support in ibid., 204A/48/6; 204G/1/9; 204G/1/20.

79. George Smathers congressional platform 1946, George Smathers MSS, University of Florida, Gainesville, Florida, box 96, platform file.

80. *Miami Herald*, May 2, 1946, in Pepper MSS, 204G/1/20.

81. Cannon advert "The Cat's Out of the Bag! *Now* It Can Be Told!," Pepper MSS, 204G/1/20.

82. Smathers debate notes, Smathers MSS, series II, box 96, radio speeches, general election 1946 file.

83. Smathers WIOD speech, October 30, 1946, Smathers MSS, series II, Box 96, radio speeches 1946 file.

84. Robert Riggs, "It Is the 'Free State' or 'Jail State' Is the Theme of Pepper's Opponent," *Pittsburgh Courier-Journal*, nd, Smathers MSS, Series III, Box 111, unnamed file 1; Stetson Kennedy, "KKK Drives to Defeat Pepper," *The Daily Compass*, February 27, 1950, Smathers MSS, ibid., Photostats envelope 1. For a brief discussion of *Southern Exposure*, see Numan Bartley, *The New South, 1945–1980*, 36.

85. Speech at Springfield, IL, nd, to veterans group, Smathers MSS, Box 96, speeches non-political 1946 file. See also the other files in this box for liberal speeches between 1946 and 1948, especially his speech to the National Young Democrats Convention in Cleveland, November 13, 1947, in ibid., general speeches file.

86. See Patricia Sullivan, *Days of Hope: Race and Democracy in the New Deal Era*, chapters 7 and 8; Ira Katznelson et al, "Limiting Liberalism," 283–306; Michael Klarman, "How Brown Changed Race Relations: The Backlash Thesis," *Journal of American History* (June 1994): 81–118; Walter Edgar, *South Carolina: A History* (Columbia: University of South Carolina Press, 1998), 517; Anthony Badger, "Whatever Happened to Roosevelt's New Generation of Southerners?," in Robert Garson and Stuart Kidd, eds., *The Roosevelt Years: New Perspectives on American History, 1933–1945* (Edinburgh: University of Edinburgh Press, 1999), 122–138; Numan Bartley, *The New South*, chapter 2; William D. Barnard, *Dixiecrats and Democrats: Alabama Politics, 1942–1950* (University, AL: University of Alabama Press, 1974), chapter 2.

87. See JFK speech on the Taft-Hartley bill to the Holy Cross Club of Worcester, MA, February 18, 1947, JFK MSS, Box 93, labor speeches file. He stated that he had "reached no final conclusions" on the bill, bitterly opposed by Pepper and the liberal left, and said that beyond "all group interests, above all rights, rise duties to the community," a clear attack on the principles of interest group pluralism.

88. Raymond Robins to Pepper, August 1, 1946; Pepper to Robins, July 26, 1946, Pepper MSS, 201/130A/1. Robins had headed the American Red Cross in Russia at the time of the Bolshevik revolution in 1917, and had been active in the Bull Moose movement in 1912, standing as its Senate candidate in Illinois in 1914. His pro-Soviet views dated, rather like those of John Reed and other Americans in Russia in 1917, from his first-hand experiences of the revolution.

89. *Congressional Record*, 79th Congress, 2nd session, January 14, 1946, 9, 30.

90. There is a large and stimulating literature on postwar labor relations, which includes Melvyn Dubofsky, *The State and Labor in Modern America* (Chapel Hill: University of North Carolina Press, 1994); Nelson Nichtenstein, *Walter Reuther: The Most Dangerous Man in Detroit*; Steve Fraser, *Labor Will Rule*, chapter 18.

91. *Congressional Record,* 79th Congress, 2nd session, January 17, 1946, 100; June 4, 1946, 6196.

92. A roll call on the Case bill is provided in the *Congressional Record,* 79th Congress, 2nd session, May 29, 1946, 5946. For details of House districts and their representatives, see *Congressional Directory,* 79th Congress, 2nd session, July 1946 (Washington DC: US Government Printing Office, 1946). For a lucid analysis of congressional voting patterns in the 1940s, see Ira Katznelson et al, "Limiting Liberalism," 283–306.

93. American Forum of the Air transcript, October 15, 1946, Taft MSS, Box 304, AFA file.

94. J. Spencer to Nixon, December 17, 1945, Richard Nixon MSS, Nixon Library and Birthplace, Yorba Linda, California, SP5. Henceforth this source will be referred to under its official library reference, RN yl.

95. Campaign sheet "Destination: Congress" by 12th District GOP, RN yl, PPS 1.121a; Nixon speech to a Lincoln Day dinner, Pomona, California, RN yl, PPS 208.3.

96. Nixon speech notes, RN yl, PPS 208.35.1.

97. Speech file, March 1, 1946, RN yl, PPS 208.3A.

98. RN yl, PPS 1.121a; PPS 208.23.

99. Melvyn Baker to Nixon, November 20, 1946; this and other business endorsements of Nixon can be found in RN yl, PPS1.233–272.

100. *The Secret Diary of Harold L. Ickes: The First Thousand Days, 1933–1936* (New York: Simon & Schuster, 1953), 31, entry for May 4, 1933. For a discussion of the relationship between business and the state in the 1930s, and its legacy, see Colin Gordon, *New Deals: Business, Labor, and Politics in America, 1920–1935* (Cambridge: Cambridge University Press, 1994).

101. RN yl, PPS 208.35.3.

102. U.S. Bureau of the Census, *Statistical Abstract of the United States 1957* (78, edition, Washington, D.C., 1957), tables 19, 18, 27.

103. William Knowland interviews, "California Republican Politics in the 1930s," in Earl Warren Oral History Project, Regional Oral History Office, Bancroft Library, University of California, Berkeley, volume II, Earl Warren's Campaigns, introduction and 20, 25. The latest biography of Knowland, which tends to focus on his conservatism in later years, is Gayle B. Montgomery and James W. Johnson, *One Step From the White House: The Rise and Fall of Senator William F. Knowland* (Berkeley: University of California Press, 1998).

104. Dr. Miley B. Wesson of San Francisco form letter; Dr. Vinton Muller to Dr. J. LaRue Robinson, August 23, 1946, George Malone MSS, Nevada Historical Society, Reno, Nevada, 1946 correspondence file.

105. Nixon to Nathan Pratt Hause, January 21, 1947, RN yl, PPS 1.460; Campaign sheet "Destination: Congress," RN yl, PPS 1.121a; Covina GOP statement, RN yl, PPS 1.219.

106. Voorhis debate notes, RN yl, PPS 208.10.

107. Bricker to the Lenten Forum at Madison Avenue Presbyterian Church, NYC, March 13, 1946, in The *New York Times*, March 14, 1946, 3.

108. *New York Times*, October 22, 1946, 21.

109. CIO leaflets "Dollars v. People—Which Side Are You On?" and "Operation Bricker," Taft MSS, Box 879, PAC 1946 file.

110. Orville Jones to Ministers and church leaders of Ohio, October 29, 1946, Taft MSS, Box 879, 1946 PAC file. Note that the PAC and the left also appealed to churches in the election campaign. Although there were few forums at this time for a serious discussion of the political ramifications of a multicultural and multi-class society, labor unions provide one example. Race-based organizations would provide another. Bricker's form of anti-government thought denied the need for either, as to do otherwise would be to accept the need for significant state involvement in social and economic policy.

111. Martin address February 7, 1946, Martin MSS, Box 63, file 113.

112. Herter broadcast October 22, 1946, Herter MSS, folder 1196.

113. John Davis Lodge to Luce, October 14, 1946; Luce to John Davis Lodge, October 22, 1946, Clare Boothe Luce MSS, Library of Congress, Box 123, Li-Ly file; Clare Boothe Luce to Robert Teller, September 22, 1947, Luce MSS, Box 145, Te-Thom file.

114. The widespread social conservatism and suspicion of otherness in the United States of that period is illustrated by the vast amount of correspondence with Luce from around the country after her conversion. Most of the letters were unfavorable, casting Catholicism in a remarkably similar light to Communism—a foreign doctrine alien to American principles. Luce was bemused by the vitriol, but was more at home with it where anti-communism was concerned. See Luce MSS, Boxes 123, 124, 130, 145.

115. Dirksen to Luce, November 29, 1946 with accompanying details of the booklet, Luce MSS, Box 540, Dip-Dis file.

116. Jacob Javits address to the National Paper Trade Association convention, Chicago, October 19, 1946; Javits to Wolcott, July 18, 1946, Jacob Javits MSS, SUNY Stony Brook, series 5, subseries 1, box 1.

117. Elmo Roper poll, Javits MSS, 8/2/17; Javits press release summarizing poll results, October 2, 1946, Javits MSS, 5/1/1.

118. Statement of program by Javits, August 5, 1946, Javits MSS, 5/1/1. See also Jacob Javits, *Javits: The Autobiography of a Public Man* (Boston: Houghton Mifflin, 1981).

119. "Liberal Party program for full employment"; Javits to Tool Oweners Union, October 15, 1946, Javits MSS, 5/1/1.

120. Javits statement on the Democratic primary, August 22, 1946, Javits MSS, 5/1/1.

121. Jacob Javits discusses this point at length in his autobiography. See Jacob Javits, *Javits*, especially page 92.

122. John Malsberger, *From Obstruction to Moderation: The Transformation of Senate Conservatism, 1938–1952* (Selinsgrove, PA: Susquehanna University Press, 2000): 13.

123. Charles La Follette to Wayne Morse, September 24, 1946, Javits MSS, 5/1/1.

124. John Malsberger has undertaken some of this work in his *From Obstruction to Moderation*, chapters 4 and 5, although the analysis is somewhat two-dimensional in places. See also Clyde Weed, *The Nemesis of Reform: The Republican Party During the New Deal* (New York: Columbia University Press, 1994) for a discussion of a slightly earlier period.

125. Speech to Lithuanian voters, Lodge MSS, Box 4, file 1; Labor speech, ibid.

126. Mahoney to union members, Lodge MSS, Box 4, file 5; Walsh to Lodge, ibid.

127. Crooker to Ickes, October 19, 1946; Ickes to Crooker, October 23rd 1946; Crooker to Ickes, October 28, 1946, Ickes MSS, Box 71, Liberals file.

128. Opinion Research Corporation, Princeton, NJ, report, 'The 1946 Campaign, Massachusetts, September 1946', published October 14, 1946, Lodge MSS, Box 4, file 1.

129. Campaign letter, September 16, 1946, Lodge MSS, Box 4, file 8. In addition, in his speeches to ethnic groups Lodge used the experience of war to appeal to their attachments to homelands: "I will do my utmost to protect human rights and human freedoms from imperialism and aggrandizement, whether it be Nazi, Fascist or Communist." See Lodge MSS, Box 4, file 1.

130. Ickes to Welch, October 19, 1946, Ickes MSS, Box 71, Liberals file.

131. Bowles to La Follette, March 21, 1946, La Follette MSS, Library of Congress, Box C533, B file; Cowie to La Follette, March 19, 1946, La Follette MSS, Box C533, C file; Gunson to La Follette, LF MSS, C533, G file. See Patrick Maney, *"Young Bob" La Follette: A Biography of Robert M. La Follette, Jr., 1895–1953* (Columbia: University of Missouri Press, 1978).

132. Henry Berquist to LF, March 24, 1946, LF MSS, C533, B file; W.R. McCabe to LF, April 24, 1946, ibid., M file. The Republican Party was generally seen as the enemy of organised labor by union leaders, if not the rank and file; the 1946 Case bill in Congress aimed to regulate labor unions more closely, and was a mainly Republican measure.

133. Leaflet "Vote the Regular Republican Ticket!," LF MSS, C533, G file; McCarthy to La Follette, C533, M file.

134. See Michael Paul Rogin, *The Intellectuals and McCarthy: The Radical Specter* (Cambridge: MIT Press, 1967): chapter 3.

135. Henderson to LF, April 19, 1946, LF MSS, C533, H file; Trautmann to LF, Ibid., S-T file.

136. Walter Neilson to William Hobbins, June 3, 1946, ibid., N file.

137. Taft to Bradshaw, April 11, 1946, Taft MSS, Box 751, Political file 1944–51. This view of Taft is somewhat unconventional, but in later chapters Taft will assume an important role in attempting to fight off an anti-statist consensus on all domestic policy based on a conception of foreign affairs.

138. Wallace to LF, November 8, 1946, LF MSS, Box C24, Wallace file; La Follette article in *Colliers* Magazine, February 8, 1947, "A True Liberal Turns the Light On Communism," LF MSS, Box C25, T-Z 1947 file.

139. See Karl Brandt to LF, October 14, 1946, LF MSS, Box C534, B file.

140. Knowland undated foreign policy speech, Knowland MSS, Box 87, campaign material file 2.

141. *New York Times*, November 3, 1946, 18; October 23, 1946, 17.

142. *Los Angeles Times*, September 20, 1946, section II, 1.

143. Rogers speech on foreign policy at the Palace Hotel, San Francisco, September 17, 1946, Knowland MSS, Box 86, 1946 Campaign file.

144. Vandenberg confided to Taft that "this is a rather novel experiment I am trying—namely, a Senatorial campaign without *any* personal appearances." See Vandenberg to Taft, October 29, 1946, Taft MSS, Box 874, 1946 foreign policy file.

145. Republican National Committee Research Division Report, The Elections of 1946, November 1946, Lodge MSS, Box 4, file 7. For Congressional district maps see US Congress, *Congressional Directory*, 79th Congress, 2nd session (Washington: US Government Printing Office, 1946), 779–829.

146. "The 1946 Elections—A Statistical Analysis," Republican Party Research Division, November 1946, Knowland MSS, Box 86, file 1.

147. Martin speech to GOP national committee, undated 1946, Martin MSS, Box 63, file 113.

148. Form letter of Dr. Carter Harrison Downing of San Francisco, July 26, 1946, Knowland MSS, Box 86, Senatorial Campaign file.

149. James Loeb to Patrick Gordon Walker, November 9, 1946; Elizabeth Magee to James Loeb, November 20, 1946, UDA/ADA papers, reel 7, section 98.

150. James Loeb to Patrick Gordon Walker, November 26, 1946; James Loeb to Daniel Hoan, Wisconsin Liberal League, November 27, 1946, UDA/ADA papers, reel 7, section 98. See Steven Gillon, *Politics and Vision: The ADA and American Liberalism, 1947–1985* (New York: Oxford University Press, 1985) and Mary Sperling McAuliffe, *Crisis on the Left: Cold War Politics and American Liberals, 1947–1954* for detailed treatments of these themes.

2. The 80th Congress and Conceptions of the State

1. The literature on this subject is enormous, and is discussed in the introduction, but some key works are Alan Wolfe, *America's Impasse: The Rise and Fall of the Politics of Growth* (New York: Pantheon, 1981); Alan Brinkley, *The End of Reform: New*

Deal Liberalism in Recession and War (New York: Knopf, 1995); Nelson Lichtenstein, *Walter Reuther: The Most Dangerous Man in Detroit* (Urbana: University of Illinois Press, 1995); Kevin Boyle, *The UAW and the Heyday of American Liberalism, 1945–1968* (Ithaca: Cornell University Press, 1995); Robert Griffith, "Forging America's Postwar Order: Domestic Politics and Political Economy in the Age of Truman," in Michael Lacey, ed., *The Truman Presidency* (Cambridge: Cambridge University Press, 1989), 57–88.

2. US Treasury Department figures quoted in *Congressional Record*, vol. 93, 80th Congress, 1st Session, May 5, 1947, 4487; July 12, 1947, 9278. For a useful analysis of the taxation policies of the state during the New Deal, which throw extra light on the above figures, see Mark Leff, *The Limits of Symbolic Reform: Taxation Policy in the New Deal* (Cambridge: Cambridge University Press, 1984).

3. Minutes of the House GOP Steering Committee meeting, November 14, 1946, Martin MSS, Box 63, file 113.

4. Joe Martin speech to the annual meeting of the Pennsylvania Manufacturers Association, Philadelphia, February 25, 1947, Martin MSS, Box 63, file 114; Martin to the 17th annual meeting of the New Jersey Taxpayers Association, Newark, January 9, 1948, Martin MSS, Box 63, file 115.

5. A forceful exposition of this thesis that the war rehabilitated the private sector politically can be found in Murray Rothbard, "The New Deal Monetary System" in Leonard P. Liggio and James J. Martin (eds.), *Watershed of Empire: Essays on New Deal Foreign Policy* (Colorado Springs: Ralph Myles, 1976).

6. Address of Marcellus C. Shield, former clerk, House Appropriations Committee, to US Chamber of Commerce 36th annual meeting, Washington, D.C., April 28, 1948, Knowland MSS, Box 148, 1948 appropriations April/May file.

7. W. E. Clow to B. Carroll Reece, November 18, 1947, Taft MSS, Box 892, Taxes 1947 file. For an analysis of private sector pressure to cut corporate taxes, see Elizabeth Fones-Wolf, *Selling Free Enterprise: The Business Assault on Labor and Liberalism, 1945-1960* (Urbana: University of Illinois Press, 1994), chapter 2.

8. Revenue Act 1948, in Wallace White MSS, Library of Congress, Box 58, legislative file. The Republican bills reduced all income taxes by fixed percentages, from 30% on lower incomes to 10% on the highest. They allowed income splitting on joint tax returns and increased individual tax allowances to $600. A person paying $400 in taxes to the federal government in 1947 would see a new total in 1948 under the bill of $332, on top of the allowance changes and other provisions.

9. *Congressional Record*, vol. 93, 80th Congress, 1st Session, July 18, 1947, 9277.

10. Ibid., 9261.

11. In the Senate vote on July 14, 1947 on the first bill, 60 Senators backed the proposal and only 32 opposed it. Of the 32, only two, William Langer and Wayne Morse, both liberal mavericks, were Republican. Twelve Democrats, most from the

south, joined the Republicans. More than 300 Congressmen also backed the bill, some 65 of them Democrats, and the House overrode Truman's veto on all three occasions. The Senate was a few votes short, the vote on overriding the veto in July 1947 being 57 votes to 36.

12. *Congressional Record*, July 18, 1947, 8762; 8788; 8803.

13. Ibid., February 26, 1947, 1528–1535.

14. Marriner Eccles, "The Current Inflation Problem—Causes and Controls," Statement before the Joint Committee on the Economic Report, November 25, 1947, *Federal Reserve Bulletin*, vol. 33, No. 12, December 1947, 1457.

15. *Congressional Record*, July 12, 1947, 8765.

16. Ibid., 8797.

17. Tydings Address at an "I am an American" meeting, Towson Lodge, November 28, 1947, Millard Tydings MSS, McKeldin Library, University of Maryland, College Park, series II, subseries 1, Box 2; radio broadcast, April 13, 1947, Tydings MSS, Box 7, April 1947 file. For the vote tallies on tax reduction, and Tydings' reasoning, see *Congressional Record*, July 18, 1947, 9282.

18. Taylor press release, November 29, 1946, Ickes MSS, Box 86, Glen Taylor file.

19. Smathers letter to a newspaper, probably the *Miami Herald*, February 2, 1948, Smathers MSS, Box 96, general speeches 80th Congress file.

20. Smathers speech at the University of Kansas, April 3, 1948, Smathers MSS, Box 96, speeches 1946 file.

21. Remarks of Jacob Javits at the Liberal Party Institute, nd, Javits MSS, 1/1/2.

22. "The Case for the Republican Liberal," Javits MSS, 8/2/3; Javits campaign press release, September 13, 1948, Javits MSS, 1/1/1.

23. See Richard Freeland, *The Truman Doctrine and the Origins of McCarthyism: Foreign Policy, Domestic Politics, and Internal Security, 1946–1948* (New York: Schocken Books, 1970), 77; *Congressional Record*, 79th Congress, 2nd Session, May 10, 1946, 4806. Sixteen Democrats in the Senate also voted against the loan to the UK.

24. *Congressional Record*, 79th Congress, 2nd Session, May 1, 1946, 4269.

25. Ibid., May 9, 1946, 4718.

26. *Congressional Record*, 80th Congress, 1st Session, 8798; 9277–9278.

27. See Julian Zelizer, *Taxing America: Wilbur D. Mills, Congress, and the State, 1945–1975* (Cambridge: Cambridge University Press, 1998), especially 86–87; Aaron Friedberg, *In the Shadow of the Garrison State: America's Anti-Statism and Its Cold War Grand Strategy* (Princeton: Princeton University Press, 2000).

28. See Paul Fox, ed., *Politics: Canada* (Toronto: McGraw-Hill Ryerson, 1982), 319–320.

29. Patrick Ashby MP to Taft, June 2, 1947, Taft MSS, Box 885, Communism file.

30. Christian Herter, "Our Most Dangerous Lobby," *Reader's Digest* (September 1947): 5–10, in Herter MSS, file 1203. Note the way in which the state was presented

to a mass audience by politicians as a danger regardless of the economic or social benefits of actual policies.

31. Richard Nixon newsletter "Under the Capitol Dome," nd 1947, RN yl, PPS 208 (1947): 6.

32. Taft statement at the panel discussion of the State Bar of California meeting at Santa Cruz, September 12, 1947; Taft address at the Philadelphia Bulletin Forum, March 9, 1948, Taft MSS, Box 672, Labor 1947 file.

33. The term "Democratic Order," and the thesis underlying it (that New Deal liberals managed successfully to maintain the liberal impulse in an unfavorable political climate by accepting some moderate erosion of their political agenda) are developed in David Plotke, *Building a Democratic Political Order: Reshaping American Liberalism in the 1930s and 1940s* (Cambridge: Cambridge University Press, 1996): chapter 8.

34. Elizabeth Fones-Wolf, *Selling Free Enterprise*, 43.

35. James Francis to Taft, April 5, 1947; Hans E. Kinney, president Local 7075 UMW, to Taft, February 2, 1947, Taft MSS, Box 676, Labor file 2 of 4.

36. The development of anti-unionism as a dominant strain in postwar U.S. politics is the dominant theme of the extant historiography on this subject. See Melvyn Dubofsky, *The State and Labor in Modern America* (Chapel Hill: University of North Carolina Press, 1994); Nelson Lichtenstein, *Walter Reuther*: chapter 13; Kevin Boyle, *The UAW and the Heyday of American Liberalism, 1945–1968*; David Plotke, *Building a Democratic Political Order*: chapter 8; Ira Katznelson et al., "Limiting Liberalism: The Southern Veto in Congress, 1933–1950," *Political Science Quarterly*, Summer 1993.

37. "Under the Capitol Dome," April 4, 1947, RN yl, PPS 208 (1947): 15.

38. *Congressional Record*, 80th Congress, 1st Session, June 20, 1947, 7489. See the analysis of the Republican-southern Democratic coalition on labor issues in Ira Katznelson et al., "Limiting Liberalism." For a discussion of the CIO's efforts to mobilize opposition to the bill, see Elizabeth Fones-Wolf, *Selling Free Enterprise*, 44.

39. *Congressional Record*, 80th Congress, 1st Session, April 15, 1947, 3418.

40. Truman radio address, June 20, 1947, *Public Papers of Harry S. Truman*, 1947 volume (Washington: GPO, 1963): item 121, page 299.

41. See David Plotke, *Building a Democratic Political Order*, 240–241. He notes that Oscar Ewing, Truman's Federal Security Administrator, observed that Truman needed to "convince the various groups of voters that President Truman was pitching on their team." See also Stephen Amberg, *The Union Inspiration in American Politics: The Autoworkers and the Making of a Liberal Industrial Order* (Philadelphia: Temple University Press, 1994).

42. JFK speech at the Holy Cross Club, Worcester, Massachusetts, February 18, 1947, JFK MSS, Box 93, Labor speeches file.

43. Truman veto of the Taft-Hartley Labor Bill, June 20, 1947, *Public Papers of Harry S. Truman*, 1947, item 120, page 297.

44. See Nelson Lichtenstein, *Walter Reuther*, 262.

45. Reinhold Niebuhr to Herbert Lehman, November 19, 1946; Preliminary and Provisional Statement of Principles, November 15, 1946; ADA Statements on foreign and domestic policy, December 19, 1946; ADA foreign policy program for the national convention, March 29, 1947, Lehman MSS, ADA special file 17a.

46. ADA foreign policy program, March 29, 1947, Lehman MSS, ADA special file 17a.

47. James Loeb to Patrick Gordon Walker, November 26, 1946; UDA memorandum, November 7, 1946, ADA papers, reel 7, section 98.

48. Hubert Humphrey to James Loeb, January 4, 1947, ADA papers, reel 7, section 105.

49. Patrick Gordon Walker speech notes, ADA papers, reel 7, section 98. For letters detailing PGW's reception in liberal circles, see Eugenie Anderson of the Minnesota DFL party to Loeb, January 28, 1947; Johannes Hober of the Philadelphia ADA to Nathalie Panek, February 5, 1947, in ibid.

50. Wilson Wyatt speech, April 8, 1947, ADA papers, ibid.

51. Jennie Lee, "Comment on Wallace," London *Tribune*, April 29, 1947.

52. Joseph Lash to Herbert Lehman, February 24, 1948, Lehman MSS, ADA special file 17a.

53. See Nelson Lichtenstein, *Walter Reuther*: chapter 14; Kevin Boyle, *The UAW and the Heyday of American Liberalism*: chapter 2. See also Steven Gillon, *Politics and Vision: The ADA and American Liberalism, 1947–1985* (New York: Oxford University Press, 1987), chapter 1, for a discussion of the development of ADA and anticommunist liberalism in 1947 and 1948.

54. Nelson Lichtenstein, *Walter Reuther*, 267.

55. Ibid., 258–259. Of a Democratic minority membership of ten, six were northern New Deal liberals from New York, Michigan, Massachusetts, Indiana, and Pennsylvania. Of the four southerners, only one was overtly anti-New Deal: John Wood of Georgia, although all four voted for Taft-Hartley.

56. JFK speech at AFL State Convention, July 31, 1947, JFK MSS, Box 95, AFL 1947 file.

57. Andrew Biemiller, "Observations and Conclusions on Special Elections in Wisconsin and Pennsylvania," October 6, 1947, Lehman MSS, ADA special file 17b.

58. Andrew Biemiller, Notes on Political Organization, November 27, 1947, ADA papers, reel 29, section 20.

59. "A Political Program for Liberals," November 1, 1948, ADA papers, reel 106, section 3.

60. For some useful perspectives on this conundrum, see Christopher Lasch, *The*

Agony of the American Left (Harmondsworth: Penguin, 1973); Michael Kazin, *The Populist Persuasion: An American History* (New York: Basic Books, 1995).

61. Arthur Schlesinger ADA questionnaire, 1948, ADA papers, reel 106, section 12.

62. Massachusetts United Labor Committee press release, September 20, 1948, ADA papers, reel 106, section 12.

63. See Nelson Lichtenstein, *Walter Reuther*; Ira Katznelson, "Was the Great Society a Lost Opportunity?" in Steven Fraser and Gary Gerstle, eds., *The Rise and Fall of the New Deal Order, 1930–1980* (Princeton: Princeton University Press, 1989), 185–211.

64. David Plotke, *Building a Democratic Political Order*, 254.

65. *San Francisco News*, nd 1947, *Oakland Tribune*, November 27, 1947, 8; John Despol speech at Santa Cruz convention, November 1947, ADA papers, reel 31, section 38; ADA release, nd, ibid, reel 31, section 36.

66. *San Francisco News*, November 27, 1947.

67. Malone speech in Senate, July 26, 1947 and June 27, 1949, Malone MSS, clippings file; Malone to Wingfield, May 19, 1947, George Wingfield MSS, Nevada Historical Society, Reno, Nevada, Box 51, Malone file 1947.

68. *Congressional Record*, June 23, 1947, 7527.

69. *Congressional Record* reprint, May 9, 1947, Wingfield MSS, ibid.

70. Paul Douglas press release, March 4, 1948, ADA papers, reel 106, section 7.

71. The *New Republic* remarked that all "over the world, governments based on widely differing ideologies are coming to recognize the responsibility of the state in this matter." *New Republic* (May 3, 1948): 14. See Gosta Esping-Andersen, *Three Worlds of Welfare Capitalism* (Princeton: Princeton University Press, 1990); Margaret Weir, Ann Shula Orloff, Theda Skocpol, eds., *The Politics of Social Policy in the United States* (Princeton: Princeton University Press, 1988); Daniel Levine, *Poverty and Society: The Growth of the American Welfare State in International Comparison* (New Brunswick: Rutgers University Press, 1988); Raymond Richards, *Closing the Door to Destitution: The Shaping of the Social Security Acts of the United States and New Zealand* (University Park: Pennsylvania State University Press, 1994); Jacob Hacker, *The Divided Welfare State: The Battle over Public and Private Social Benefits in the United States* (Cambridge: Cambridge University Press, 2002). Two classic studies of the fight for federal health insurance in the United States are Daniel Hirshfield, *The Lost Reform: The Campaign for Compulsory Health Insurance in the United States, 1932–1943* (Cambridge: Harvard University Press, 1970); Monte Poen, *Harry S. Truman versus the Medical Lobby: The Genesis of Medicare* (Columbia: University of Missouri Press, 1979).

72. The above represents a very brief summary of a vibrant and intricate area of historical scholarship, best summarized in the following: Colin Gordon, "Why No

Health Insurance in the United States? The Limits of Social Provision in War and Peace, 1941–1948," *Journal of Policy History* 9, no. 3 (April 1997): 277–310; Alan Derickson, "Health Security for All? Social Unionism and Universal Health Insurance, 1935–1958," *Journal of American History* (March 1994): 1333–1356; Jacob Hacker, *The Divided Welfare State,* chapters 4 and 5.

73. "The Case for National Health Insurance," *New York Times* magazine, May 8, 1949; British Information Service pamphlets and bulletins of the CNH, Pepper MSS, 201/93/1.

74. *Congressional Record,* May 20, 1947, 5655; Truman message to Congress, May 19, 1947, Taft MSS, Box 639, Health 1946–7 file.

75. See *Public Opinion Quarterly* (Spring 1947): 162–163; ibid. (Summer 1947): 310. The *New Republic* cited a 1944 poll which found that 82% of those questioned supported plans "to make it easier for people to get medical care." See Helen Fuller, "Playing Politics with the Health Issue," *New Republic* (May 3, 1948): 19.

76. Claude Pepper radio broadcast on health, May 2, 1949, Pepper MSS, 201/93/1.

77. Claude Pepper radio broadcast, May 2, 1949, Pepper MSS, 201/93/1. The term comes from Colin Gordon, "Why No Health Insurance in the United States?", 296. In 1946 fewer than one million workers benefited from workplace negotiated plans; by 1950 that number stood at 7 million, and by 1954, 27 million. See Jacob Hacker, *The Divided Welfare State,* 232.

78. Boris Stern, Bureau of Labor Statistics, "New Horizons in Industrial Health and Welfare: Labor and Management at the Conference Table," *Journal of the American Medical Association (*hereafter *JAMA)* (November 30, 1946): 760–761.

79. Alan Derickson, "Health Security for All?" As late as 1951 George Meany of the AFL used the defeat of federal legislation in health matters as a key issue with which to launch a new voter registration drive. See Meany speech, November 1, 1951, Pepper MSS, 201/93/1.

80. John Blatnik, on the CBS Review of the 80th Congress, July 29, 1947, RN yl, PPS 208 (1947): 49.5.

81. Arthur Altmeyer testimony before the Senate Committee on Education and Labor, April 4, 1946, *JAMA* (April 20, 1946): 1172.

82. Taft, "What Should Congress Do About Health?," June 5, 1947; Taft Speech to Wayne County Medical Society, Detroit, October 7, 1946, Taft MSS, Box 639, Health 1946–7 file.

83. Arthur Watkins to Dr. Glenn E. Snow, March 24, 1947, Taft MSS, Box 652, Housing 1947 file 1 of 4; Taft to Flanders, November 27, 1947, Taft MSS, Box 891, Senators Correspondence 1947 file.

84. Lodge Lincoln Day address, Lincoln Club, Louisville, Ky., February 12, 1947, JFK MSS, Box 113, tax reduction file. See also Lodge proposals for a federal health assistance plan, Lodge MSS, Box 37, files 3 and 6.

85. Hearings before a Subcommittee of the Senate Committee on Labor and Public Welfare, 80th Congress, on S.2215, "to provide for research and control relating to diseases of the heart and circulation," April 8, 1948, Taft MSS, Box 643, Social Security 1945–6 file. The bill would have provided federal funds to chosen hospitals for research purposes. It is possible to find a number of such limited measures, and the byzantine nature of U.S. Congressional politics prevents us from reading too much into them, but a general trend away from blanket anti-statism in both parties can certainly be observed.

86. Truman to Congress, May 19, 1947, Taft MSS, Box 639, Health 1946–7 file.

87. Taft statement, June 5, 1947, Taft MSS, Ibid.

88. JFK speeches April 25, 1949 and to Mass. Health Conference, February 19, 1949, latter not given, JFK MSS, Box 93, Health speeches file.

89. "Senator Smith of New Jersey and Medicine," *JAMA* (May 10, 1947): 147. I examined every issue of the *Journal* between 1946 and 1950, and noted a slackening of interest during the two years of the 80th Congress, with the exception of coverage of the British NHS.

90. Senate Education and Labor Hearings on federal health insurance reproduced in the *JAMA* (May 4, 1946): 45, and ibid., (April 27, 1946): 1179. The editor inserted editorial comment into the congressional committee reports to demarcate the AMA's official stand on the plan. Of Harold Ickes's testimony, for example, the *Journal* notes that it "revealed a lack of knowledge by Mr Ickes of current activities in the field of medical care." See *JAMA* (May 4, 1946): 39.

91. Dr. Walter Ford to Connally, June 4, 1947; Lillian Byrd to Connally, September 20, 1947; Connally to W. L. Clifton, March 22, 1948, Tom Connally MSS, Library of Congress, Box 183, Compulsory Sickness Insurance file; James Harness to John Taber, September 9, 1947, Connally MSS, Box 183, Socialized medicine in Japan file. There were many more such letters in the Connally archive alone from 1947 onwards, contrasting markedly with more pro-government polls prior to mid-1947.

92. Dr. J. C. Terrell to Connally, October 20, 1947, Connally MSS, ibid.

93. Helen Fuller, "Playing Politics with the Health Issue," *New Republic* (May 3, 1948): 20. Fuller referred to Shearon as "a former government employee and a personal crusader against 'socialized' health insurance plans," who was "rated by some as even more effective than [the] well-organized pressure boys" of the AMA, although Joe Lawrence, the AMA's full time Washington representative, "was one of the highest-paid lobbyists last year."

94. Marjorie Shearon, "Blueprint for the Nationalization of Medicine," to Annual Meeting of the Association of American Physicians and Surgeons, November 8, 1946; "Socialized Medicine" speech to Republican women, undated, Taft MSS, Box 639, Health file 1946–7. The speech to the surgeons' conference was also published in 1947 and distributed to doctors and interested parties across the land—the very

language used is identical to that in the letters to politicians such as Tom Connally. See also Shearon, "Research Material and Professional Services Available to Medical Associations, Chambers of Commerce, and Other Groups Seeking Advice about Plans to Nationalize Medicine"; or Shearon, "Digest and Critique of the First Wagner-Murray-Dingell Bill," November 28, 1945, Taft MSS, ibid.

95. AMA leaflet, "The *Voluntary* Way is the American Way: 50 Questions You Want Answered on Compulsory Health Insurance Versus Health the American Way"; Elmer Henderson to members of Congress, May 23, 1949, Taft MSS, Box 643, national program 1949 file 1 of 3.

96. *JAMA* (August 7, 1948): 1331.

97. Robert H. Morris to Taft, April 5, 1946, Taft MSS, Box 649, Housing 1946 file.

98. Taft notes on Housing, Taft MSS, Box 651, 1947 file 3 of 3.

99. "Facts on the Housing Shortage in Los Angeles, June 1947," Report of the Joint California Senate-Assembly Committee on the Housing Problem, April 9, 1947, Taft MSS, Box 651, 1947 file 1 of 3.

100. National Association of Real Estate Boards press release, October 21, 1947, Taft MSS, Box 652, Housing 1947 file 3 of 4.

101. NAREB cartoon in its publication *Headlines*, February 1946, Taft MSS, Box 649, Housing 1946 file. Similar arguments were made concerning Taft's proposal for federal aid to the poorer state for school education. Herbert Hoover and Dwight Eisenhower both argued that federal intervention would lead to the state control of children's thought. The latter, in a letter to right-wing Republican Ralph Gwinn (R-New York), argued the measure was "yet another vehicle by which the believers in paternalism, if not outright socialism, will gain additional power for the Federal Government." See *Detroit News*, June 15, 1949, Taft MSS, Box 535, Education 1948–9 file.

102. See Richard Freeland, *The Truman Doctrine and the Origins of McCarthyism* ; Aaron Friedberg, *In the Shadow of the Garrison State*; Ellen Schrecker, *Many Are the Crimes: McCarthyism in America* (Princeton: Princeton University Press, 1998); Athan Theoharis, *Seeds of Repression: Harry S. Truman and the Origins of McCarthism* (New York: Quadrangle, 1971); Francis Thompson, *The Frustration of Politics: Truman, Congress, and the Loyalty Issue 1945–1953* (Rutherford: Fairleigh Dickinson University Press, 1979).

103. Letter to the Speaker of the House of Representatives Requesting Appropriations for the Employees Loyalty Program, May 9, 1947, *Public Papers of Harry S. Truman*, 1947, no. 89; Freeland, *The Truman Doctrine and the Origins of McCarthyism*: chapter 3.

104. Statement by the President on the Government's Employee Loyalty Program, November 14, 1947, *Public Papers of Harry S. Truman*, 1947, no. 222.

105. Rhodri Jeffreys-Jones, "Why Was the CIA Established in 1947," *Intelligence and National Security*, 12, no. 1 (January 1997).

106. Freeland, *The Truman Doctrine and the Origins of McCarthyism.*

107. James Loeb to Arthur Naftalin, Humphrey's secretary, November 13, 1946, ADA papers, reel 7, section 105; "Political Plans of the Minnesota ADA," ADA papers, reel 106, section 1; radio address of Hubert Humphrey, April 23, 1948, ADA papers, reel 106, section 1.

108. Report on Minnesota DFL precinct caucuses, April 30, 1948, ADA papers, reel 106, section 1; ADA report "Direct Political Action Pays Off," June 22, 1948, ADA papers, reel 106, section 5. See also Steven Gillon, *Politics and Vision,* chapters 1 and 2.

109. Bob Greene to National SDA Political Committee, nd, ADA papers, reel 106, section 13.

110. JFK to Mass. State AFL Convention, Springfield, Mass., July 31, 1947, JFK MSS, Box 95, AFL convention file. See Nelson Lichtenstein, *Walter Reuther*: chapter 12; Athan Theoharis, *Seeds of Repression*: chapter 5; Ellen Schrecker, *Many Are the Crimes,* passim.

111. Emmanuel Celler speech on Freedom House Forum, WEVD radio, September 1, 1947, Celler MSS, Box 20, Internal Security, printed material file.

112. *Birmingham Herald* extract in *Citizens in Action* news sheet of SCHW, June 27, 1947; Ickes to Thomas, June 27, 1947, Ickes MSS, Box 90, HUAC file 1947.

113. Nixon Washington Report, May 13, 1948, RN yl, PPS 208 (1948): 23.2.

114. *Congressional Record* reprint, May 18, 1948, Celler MSS, Box 20, Internal Security printed material file.

115. Hoover speech to the American Legion, San Francisco, September 30, 1946 with accompanying material, Taft MSS, Box 513, Communism file 1945–1947.

116. Joseph Davies, *Mission to Moscow* (New York: Simon and Schuster, 1941), 358.

117. Eugene Dennis speech at Madison Square Garden, September 18, 1945, Taft MSS, Box 513, Communism file 1945–1947. It would not be overly cynical to dispute the motives behind a Communist espousal of pluralist principles; left-wing sympathizers Irving Howe and Lewis Coser do an impressive hatchet job on the party in Howe and Coser, *The American Communist Party: A Critical History* (New York: Praeger, 1957). My point, however, is that in supporting the HUAC approach to the CPUSA, liberals were indirectly criticizing their own beliefs.

118. Douglas, "My Democratic Credo," March 29, 1946, Ickes MSS, Box 55, Helen Douglas file.

119. Wayne to Ickes, Jan. 20, 1947; Ickes to Wayne, Feb. 1, 1947, Ickes MSS, Box 52, Communism file.

120. Quote from Ickes's article in Louis Becker to Ickes, September 24, 1947, Ickes MSS, Communism file 1947–50.

121. Zeldin to Celler, February 20, 1947; Celler to Zeldin, February 24, 1947, Celler MSS, Box 20, HUAC correspondence 1947–9 file.

3. Ideological Interpretations of Foreign Policy, 1947–1948

1. I can only summarize the vast historiography of American foreign policy strategy in the late 1940s: Melvyn Leffler, *A Preponderance of Power: National Security, the Truman Administration, and the Cold War* (Stanford: Stanford University Press, 1992); Aaron Friedberg, *In the Shadow of the Garrison State: America's Anti-Statism and Its Cold War Grand Strategy* (Princeton: Princeton University Press, 2000); Michael Hogan, *The Marshall Plan: America, Britain, and the Reconstruction of Western Europe, 1947–1952* (New York: Cambridge University Press, 1987); Bruce Cumings, ed., *Child of Conflict: The Korean-American Relationship, 1943–1953* (Seattle: University of Washington Press, 1983): especially the introduction.

2. See Melvyn Leffler, *A Preponderance of Power;* Gabriel and Joyce Kolko, *The Limits of Power: The World and United States Foreign Policy, 1945–1954* (New York: Harper & Row, 1972); Richard Gardner, *Sterling-Dollar Diplomacy in Current Perspective: The Origins and Prospects of Our International Economic Order* (New York: Columbia University Press, 1980).

3. U.S. Department of State, "The Development of the Foreign Reconstruction Policy of the United States, March–July 1947" (Washington: U. S. Government Printing Office, 1947); Truman address to the Canadian Parliament, June 11, 1947, Taft MSS Box 612, foreign affairs 1946–7 file.

4. See Aaron Friedberg, *In the Shadow of the Garrison State,* 110. Friedberg argues that Keynesian growth management took a more strongly internationalist turn in 1949 after Leon Keyserling displaced Edwin Nourse as chairman of the CEA, but its theoretical underpinnings were in place well before then.

5. Report on a visit to the USSR by Frances Bolton (R-Ohio), Karl Mundt (R-South Dakota), Joseph Ryter (D-Connecticut) and Thomas Gordon (D-Illinois), October 1945. Publication of this delicate report was withheld until June 1946. Taft MSS, Box 612, foreign affairs 1946-47 file.. The report was published in *US News,* June 28, 1946, 63–70.

6. Francis Wilcox Oral History Interview, October 1984, Senate Historical Office, Washington, D.C.

7. Irving Ives radio broadcast, December 4, 1947, Taft MSS, Box 893, aid to Europe file.

8. Woodrow Wyatt speech, April 8, 1947, ADA papers, reel 7, section 99.

9. ADA foreign policy program for the national conference, March 29, 1947, Lehman MSS, ADA special file 17a.

10. AFL *Labor's Monthly Survey,* March 1948, Patrick McCarran MSS, University of Nevada at Reno, Box 14, Marshall Plan file.

11. See Nelson Lichtenstein, *Walter Reuther: The Most Dangerous Man in Detroit* (Urbana: University of Illinois Press, 1995), chapter 12; Kevin Boyle, *The*

UAW and the Heyday of American Liberalism, 1945–1968 (Ithaca: Cornell University Press, 1995), chapter 1. For a broader analysis of the importance of organized labor to the Cold War internationalist coalition, see Taylor Dark, *The Unions and the Democrats: An Enduring Alliance* (Ithaca: Cornell University Press, 1999).

12. See Aaron Friedberg, *In the Shadow of the Garrison State* for a sound exposition of the thesis that the congressional GOP was able to limit the scope of the national security state in the late 1940s and also to encourage the use of the private sector in providing finance and materials for the Cold War while endorsing the basic strategy of anti-Sovietism.

13. See Clyde Weed, *The Nemesis of Reform: The Republican Party During the New Deal* (New York: Columbia University Press, 1994); John Malsberger, *From Obstruction to Moderation: The Transformation of Senate Conservatism, 1938–1952* (Selinsgrove, PA: Susquehanna University Press, 2000).

14. Robert Taft to Harold Knutson, October 31, 1947; Knutson to Taft, November 3, 1947, Taft MSS, Box 892, taxes 1947 file.

15. Taft to Oliver Radkey, May 31, 1947, Taft MSS, Box 887, foreign policy file; Taft to La Guardia, April 18, 1947, Taft MSS, Box 887, Greece file.

16. Taft to Kohlberg, March 12, 1947, Taft MSS, Box 887, foreign policy file.

17. Richard Nixon, "Under the Capitol Dome," March 14, 1947, RN yl, PPS 208 (1947): 9.

18. Herbert Hoover to Arthur Vandenberg, January 18, 1948, Connally MSS, Box 106, Hoover file; Merwin Hart testimony to the Senate Foreign Relations Committee, January 24, 1948, Connally MSS, Hart file.

19. See correspondence in Connally MSS, Box 180, Spain in ERP file.

20. George Malone address at the Sow-Belly Dinner, Colorado Mining Congress, February 7, 1948, J McDonald MSS, 98–05/VI/2.

21. This thesis is forcefully expounded in Bruce Cumings's introduction to his edited volume: *Child of Conflict: The Korean-American Relationship, 1943–1953*, 9.

22. See Ronald Feinman, *Twilight of Progressivism: The Western Republican Senators and the New Deal* (Baltimore: Johns Hopkins University Press, 1981); Justus Doenecke, *Not to the Swift: The Old Isolationists in the Cold War Era* (Lewisburg: Bucknell University Press, 1979). As will be suggested later, Cold War liberal internationalists by the end of the decade were attempting to establish a link between right wing politicians like Taft and the leftist fellow traveler Marcantonio in order to discredit them at election time.

23. Ickes to Taft, June 14, 1948, Ickes MSS, Box 86, Taft 1948–51 file; Helen Douglas, *A Full Life* (Garden City: Doubleday, 1982), 254.

24. Norman Thomas to Taft, March 15, 1948, Taft MSS, Box 896, foreign policy 1948 file; Taft speech to the Denver Lincoln Club, February 14, 1948, Taft MSS, Box 616, foreign policy 1948 file 2 of 3.

25. Bender to Taft, July 14, 1947, Taft MSS, Box 615, foreign policy 1947 file 1 of 3. Bender is a vital figure in Congress espousing a moral foreign policy from a Republican standpoint. He is quoted at length by Ronald Radosh in his *Prophets on the Right: Profiles of Conservative Critics of American Globalism* (New York: Simon and Schuster, 1975): chapter on Taft.

26. Bender quoted in Radosh, *Prophets of the Right*, 159.

27. Malone address to Colorado Mining Congress, Febraury 7, 1948, McDonald MSS, 98–05/VI/2.

28. *Congressional Record*, 80th Congress, 2nd Session, March 13, 1948, 2708ff. The seventeenth vote was that of Glen Taylor (D-Idaho), whose views on foreign policy are described below.

29. See Alonzo Hamby, *Beyond the New Deal: Harry S. Truman and American Liberalism* (New York: Columbia University Press, 1973), *passim* for an example.

30. Melvyn Leffler, *A Preponderance of Power*, 32–33.

31. John Morton Blum, *Roosevelt and Morgenthau: A Revision and Condensation From the Morgenthau Diaries* (Boston: Houghton Mifflin, 1970): chapters 21, 22. Blum argues that Morgenthau's main objective, which changed little between 1944 and 1945, was to ensure "a cooperative and friendly Russia, a liberal community of democratic nations in a world free from war." Blum, *Roosevelt and Morgenthau*, 559. Wallace himself called in 1948 for "a foreign policy based on understanding with Russia." He argued that supporters of the administration's line "prefer war with Russia to settlement of differences in a peaceful way." See Wallace, "Why I Choose to Run," *New Republic* (January 5, 1948): 5–10.

32. Pepper speech "Where is the Republican Party's Foreign Policy Taking the United States?" February 5, 1947, Taft MSS, Box 616, foreign policy 1947 file.

33. Taylor to Ickes, November 4, 1947, Ickes MSS, Box 52, Communism file.

34. Harold Laski, Passages from articles in *The Nation*, 1947, Taft MSS, Box 602, ERP 1947 file.

35. Mary Sperling McAuliffe, *Crisis on the Left: Cold War Politics and American Liberals, 1947–1954* (Amherst: University of Massachusetts Press, 1978); Richard Pells, *Radical Visions and American Dreams: Culture and Social Thought in the Depression Years* (New York: Harper & Row, 1973); Richard Pells, *The Liberal Mind in a Conservative Age: American Intellectuals in the 1940s and 1950s* (New York: Harper & Row, 1985); Steven Fraser, *Labor Will Rule: Sidney Hillman and the Rise of Organized Labor* (New York: Free Press, 1991); Fraser Ottanelli, *The Communist Party of the United States: From the Depression to World War Two* (New Brunswick: Rutgers University Press, 1991); Robin Kelley, *Hammer and Hoe: Alabama Communists During the Great Depression* (Chapel Hill: University of North Carolina Press, 1990).

36. The papers of the Non-Sectarian Anti-Nazi League are held in two archives at Columbia University in New York under call number MS Coll/NSANL 14/10–11.

37. James Loeb to Daniel Hoan of the Wisconsin Liberal League, November 27, 1946, ADA papers, reel 7, section 98.

38. *Soviet Russia Today*, July 1945, Pepper MSS, 201/16/10. The periodical had a Communist editorial line. See also *New York Times Magazine*, November 3, 1946, Pepper MSS, 201/16/1.

39. *New York Times Magazine*, November 3, 1946, Pepper MSS, 201/16/1; *United States News*, June 7, 1946; *Medical Economics*, October 1946; *Newsweek*, September 30, 1946, Pepper MSS, 201/16/2. See also *Saturday Evening Post*, August 31, 1946, Pepper MSS, 201/16/3; *PM*, June 1, 1947, Pepper MSS, 201/16/6; *New York Times Magazine*, May 20, 1945, Pepper MSS, 201/16/10.

40. *New York Times Magazine*, May 20, 1945, Pepper MSS, 201/16/10.

41. Pepper diary, July 21, 1946, Pepper MSS, 439/2/3.

42. Pepper diary, March 10, 1948; August 13, 1948, Pepper MSS, 439/2/5.

43. Draft ADA program, "A Political Program for Liberals," November 1, 1948, ADA papers, reel 106, section 2.

44. Pepper diary, March 5, 1948, Pepper MSS, 439/2/5. See Richard Freeland, *The Truman Doctrine and the Origins of McCarthyism* (New York: Schocken, 1970); Alonzo Hamby, *Beyond the New Deal.* Aaron Friedberg demonstrates how anti-statism influenced the development of U.S. foreign policy in this period, but admits that the dominant process was the development of an American global policy that most anti-statists had little power to prevent. See Friedberg, *In the Shadow of the Garrison State.*

45. US Congress, Senate Committee Hearings, 80th Congress, Senate Library, vol. 816, (1947): 10, Assistance to Greece and Turkey, March 25, 1947, 24, 81.

46. David Plotke, *Building a Democratic Political Order: Reshaping American Liberalism in the 1930s and 1940s* (Cambridge: Cambridge University Press, 1996): chapter 10; Melvyn Leffler, *A Preponderance of Power*; Jack Snyder, *Myths of Empire: Domestic Politics and International Ambition* (Ithaca: Cornell University Press, 1991).

47. Tydings radio broadcast, April 13, 1947, Tydings MSS, series II, subseries 1, Box 7, April file.

48. JFK speech, April 1, 1947 reprint in *Congressional Record*, JFK MSS, Box 94, Greece and Turkey file.

49. James Loeb memo to ADA chapters, April 19, 1947, ADA papers, reel 7, section 99.

50. See Gabriel and Joyce Kolko, *The Limits of Power: The World and United States Foreign Policy, 1945–1954* (New York: Harper & Row, 1972), 2 for the argument that the administration's aim was "to restructure the world so that American business could trade, operate, and profit without restrictions everywhere."

51. Alfred Baker Lewis statement, enclosed with letter to Ickes, April 9, 1947, Ickes MSS, Box 58, Greece 1946–52 file.

52. See Alan Wolfe, *America's Impasse: The Rise and Fall of the Politics of Growth* (New York: Pantheon, 1981); Aaron Friedberg, *In the Shadow of the Garrison State*. David Plotke argues that it is impossible to see a decline in the influence of New Deal liberalism after the war because it had never been hugely ambitious in the first place. This view ignores the considerable upswing in left-of-center ambition in elements of the New Deal coalition between 1942 and 1946. See Plotke, *Building a Democratic Political Order*, 295. For an alternative perspective, see Patrick Reagan, *Designing a New America: The Origins of New Deal Planning, 1890–1943* (Amherst: University of Massachusetts Press, 1999).

53. U.S. Congress, Senate Committee Hearings, 80th Congress, 816, 1947, 10, 81–82.

54. Ibid., 87, 34.

55. *Congressional Record*, vol. 93, 80th Congress, 1st Session, March 20, 1947, 2286–2287.

56. Bender speech in House of Representatives, March 18, 1947, Taft MSS, Box 615, foreign policy 1947 file 3 of 3.

57. Taft notes on future foreign policy, undated, Taft MSS, ibid.

58. Malone press release, April 21, 1947, Joseph McDonald MSS, 98–05/VI/1.

59. Ickes to McGhee, November 29, 1947, McGhee to Ickes, November 25, 1947, Ickes MSS, Box 58, Greece file.

60. Donnell to Taft, March 16, 1947, Taft MSS, Box 615, foreign policy 1947 file 2 of 3.

61. Memo from Christopher Emmet to Benjamin Stolberg, March 25, 1947, Taft MSS, ibid.

62. Bender to Taft, July 14, 1947, Taft MSS, Box 615, foreign policy 1947 file 1 of 3.

63. Taylor to Ickes, November 4, 1947, Ickes MSS, Box 52, Communism file.

64. Wallace to Stalin letter May 17, 1948, Ickes MSS, Box 91, Wallace 1946–8 file. For views on the nature of FDR's Soviet policy, see Adam Ulam, *The Rivals: America and Russia Since World War II* (New York: Viking Press, 1971), chapters 1 and 2; Robin Edmonds, *The Big Three: Churchill, Roosevelt and Stalin in Peace and War* (London: Penguin, 1992). For a view of the shift in Wallace's opinion on foreign policy after the war, see Hamby, *Beyond the New Deal*, 203–204. See also John Culver and John Hyde, *American Dreamer: A Life of Henry A. Wallace* (New York: Norton, 2000).

65. Alonzo Hamby, *Beyond the New Deal*, 203–204.

66. "Henry Wallace Answers President Truman," *Washington Post*, March 20, 1947, 24. See also Wallace, "Count the Cost!" *New Republic*, April 12, 1948, 9.

67. Amendment text in Ickes MSS, Box 55, Helen Douglas file. See also Helen Gahagan Douglas, *A Full Life*, 254.

68. ADA memo, May 31, 1947, Ickes MSS, Box 91, Wallace 1946–7 file.

69. The role of the American state in fostering European economic recovery is stressed in Michael Hogan, *The Marshall Plan: America, Britain, and the Reconstruction of Western Europe, 1947–1952* (New York: Cambridge University Press, 1987). Alan Milward provides a slightly different view in his *The European Rescue of the Nation State* (London: Routledge, 1992).

70. Connally to E. H. Styron, January 31, 1948, Connally MSS, Box 180, Marshall Plan file 2 of 2.

71. U.S. Congress, Senate Committee Hearings, 80th Congress, Senate Library, vol. 850, part 1, 1948, 1.

72. See the detailed reports by Wilcox and Charles Dewey for the Senate Foreign Relations Committee and the Joint House-Senate Committee on Foreign Economic Relations on the Marshall Plan, Connally MSS, Box 105, ECA file.

73. Statement made by Lewis Douglas, U.S. Ambassador to London, in minutes taken by Christian Herter during a meeting between Douglas and Herter, September 3, 1947, Herter MSS, folder 888a. Douglas argued that the Labour government in London was determined to get by alone if necessary, and resented American calls for it to abandon its statist experiments. Without American help Britain would abandon its imperial commitments, "which would obviously be moved into by Russia in one form or another."

74. Herter draft of an article "U.S.-Soviet Relations," Herter MSS, folder 1238.

75. Douglas meeting with Herter, September 3, 1947, Herter MSS, folder 888a.

76. *Congressional Record*, vol. 93, 80th Congress, 1st Session, November 26, 1947, 10899–10900; 10917. The amendments were defeated, but in the case of a reduction in the amount of aid the defeat was quite narrow: 30–56. Most of the 30 Senators believed in limited government, and in limiting the scope of foreign policy spending to enlarge the role of the federal government in the economy.

77. Ibid., vol. 94, 80th Congress, 2nd Session, March 11, 1948, 2519–2520.

78. Knutson report on Marshall Plan to House and Senate Committees dated October 29, 1947 and submitted January 5, 1948, Connally MSS, Box 107, Knutson file.

79. Hart testimony to Senate Foreign Relations Committee, January 24, 1948, Connally MSS, Box 106, Hart file.

80. Quoted in Stanley K. Bigman, "The 'New Internationalism' Under Attack," *Public Opinion Quarterly* 14 (Summer 1950): 235–261; 259. Bigman's article deals with an array of right-wing and anti-Semitic attacks on the state in the foreign policy arena by right-wing journals and newspapers. Much of it shares many characteristics of European Fascism. The basic premise of anti-liberalism was taken up by many on the right in mainstream politics, and was encouraged by foreign policy initiatives of the liberals themselves.

81. Gwinn, "The New Plan for European Recovery" in his report to his constituents, February 25, 1948, Taft MSS, Box 238, 1948 Miscellany—Material on ERP file.

82. Malone address at the Sow-Belly Dinner, Colorado Mining Congress, Denver, February 7, 1948, McDonald MSS, 98–05/VI/2, Malone correspondence, 1948–51.

83. Correspondence from Malone to his family, October-November 1947, Malone MSS, 1947 correspondence file. These letters include rather wide-eyed accounts of luxury hotels, and a trip on a train in Germany which he referred to as the "Goering Special" due to the fact it had served as the General's command train during the war. On this Malone commented that those "folks knew how to fight a war comfortable."

84. Deaver to Vandenberg, March 17, 1948, Malone MSS, 1948 correspondence file.

85. Gregory Bern, *Behind the Red Mask* (Bern Publications, 1948), 323; William B. Ziff, "Mr. Marshall Suffers Lapse of Memory," *Flying*, November 1947, 17–18, Taft MSS, Box 602, ERP 1947 file; Edna Lonigan, "If Freedom Fails," *Human Events*, May 28, 1947, Taft MSS, Box 714, Marshall Plan 1947 file 2 of 2.

86. Taft address to the Lincoln Club, St. Paul, Minnesota, February 12, 1948, Taft MSS, Box 603, ERP 1948 file 2 of 4.

87. Taft address to the Economic Club of Detroit, February 23, 1948, Taft MSS, Box 616, foreign policy 1948 file 2 of 3.

88. Norman Thomas, Postwar World Council News Bulletin, March 1948, Taft MSS, Box 896, foreign policy file. The Postwar World Council, a progressive organization committed to anti-communism without the draft or any emphasis on militarism, counted among its members John Dos Passos, Frank Zeidler and A. Philip Randolph, as well as Thomas.

89. Nelson Lichtenstein, *Walter Reuther*, 329–330.

90. Taft address at Middletown, March 20, 1948, Taft MSS, Box 616, foreign policy file 1 of 3.

91. Taft notes on Marshall Plan, Taft MSS, Box 602, ERP 1947–8 file 1 of 2.

92. See John Malsberger, *From Obstruction to Moderation*, chapter 5. Taft and Malone shared an instinctive fear of federal government power and a desire to avoid social conflict by not prioritizing one section of society over another, preferring to think of America as a unified social whole rather than as a collection of interest groups. They would claim that New Deal liberalism privileged both particular social groups and foreign policy measures, and was therefore "un-American."

93. *Congressional Record*, vol. 94, 80th Congress, 2nd Session, March 12, 1948, 2618.

94. Ibid., 2642.

95. Michael Hogan, *The Marshall Plan, passim*; Robert Collins, *The Business Response to Keynes* (New York: Columbia University Press, 1981).

96. *Congressional Record*, June 3, 1948, 7000.

97. Ibid., June 7, 1948, 7244.

98. See Aaron Friedberg, *In the Shadow of the Garrison State*: chapter 5, and especially 158, 162, 166; Eliot Cohen, *Citizens and Soldiers: The Dilemmas of Military Service* (Ithaca: Cornell University Press, 1985).

99. Aaron Friedberg, *In the Shadow of the Garrison State*, 162. Friedberg argues convincingly that Republican power in Congress and a general antipathy toward peacetime compulsory service made a limited draft the most the administration could expect in the 1940s.

100. *Congressional Record*, June 8, 1948, 7341; 7239.

101. Ibid., June 10, 1948, 7659.

102. Debate on the CIA analyzed and quoted in Rhodri Jeffreys-Jones, "Why Was the CIA Established in 1947?" *Intelligence and National Security* 12, no. 1 (January 1997).Taft speech to Denver Lincoln Club, February 14, 1948, Taft MSS, Box 616, foreign policy 1948 file 2 of 3.

103. Hamilton Long to Martha Taft, June 10, 1948, Taft MSS, Box 616, foreign policy 1948 file 1 of 3.

104. Dr. Samuel Guy Inman, "Bogota Failed As Democratic Rally: Drew Red Herring Across Economic Plight of Continent," *Worldover Press Newsletter*, June 4, 1948, Taft MSS, Box 616, foreign policy 1948 file 1 of 3. For an in-depth analysis, see Lars Schoultz, *Beneath the United States: A History of US Policy Toward Latin America* (Cambridge: Harvard University Press, 1998): chapter 17, entitled "Combating Communism with Friendly Dictators." Schoultz also quotes Marshall's comments on Latin American self-sufficiency: Schoultz, 333.

105. Bender to Taft, July 14, 1947, Taft MSS, Box 615, foreign policy 1947 file 3 of 3.

106. Taft notes on foreign policy, Taft MSS, Box 615, ibid.

107. Felix Morley, "A Sample of Secret Diplomacy," *Human Events*, January 28, 1948, Taft MSS, Box 616, foreign policy 1948 file 1 of 3.

108. The anti-communist foreign policy of the late 1940s did not preclude support for domestic liberal programs, but it did make it harder to harness public and political support when the dominant message of the period showed America to be a society free from state control and damaging social discord. Jane De Hart Mathews was one of several historians pointing to the Cold War "not just as a political response to . . . [international] problems but also as a revitalization movement designed to eliminate foreign influences and revive traditional values and beliefs in a period of societal stress." See De Hart Mathews, "Art and Politics in Cold War America," *American Historical Review* (October 1976): 787. While Mathews sees this phenomenon affecting only the right wing, the present study argues that the right gained considerable political legitimacy it would not otherwise have had from the unintentional side-effects of the foreign and domestic anti-communist outlook of mainstream liberalism.

4. Varieties of Liberalism in the 1948 Campaigns

1. This is a particularly American historical view with very wide acceptance. See, for example, Alonzo Hamby, *Beyond the New Deal: Harry S. Truman and American Liberalism* (New York: Columbia University Press, 1973), chapters 9–11; John K. White, *Still Seeing Red: How the Cold War Shapes the New American Politics* (Boulder: Westview Press, 1997), chapter 2; James Patterson, *Grand Expectations: The United States, 1945–1974* (New York: Oxford University Press, 1996), 156–164. Contemporaries did not have to approve of this interpretation to accept its basic tenets; Phyllis Schlafly, for example, a right-wing Republican, would assume the same analysis in her diatribe on the reasons behind Republicanism's decline after the war: Schlafly, *A Choice Not an Echo* (Pere Marquette Press, 1964).

2. See Elizabeth Fones-Wolf, *Selling Free Enterprise: The Business Assault on Labor and Liberalism, 1945–1960* (Urbana: University of Illinois Press, 1994); Nelson Lichtenstein, *Walter Reuther: The Most Dangerous Man in Detroit* (Urbana: University of Illinois Press, 1995); Michael K. Brown, "Bargaining for Social Rights: Unions and the Reemergence of Welfare Capitalism, 1945–1952," *Political Science Quarterly* 112, no. 4 (Winter 1997–1998): 645–674.

3. Ickes to Truman, March 27, 1948, Ickes MSS, Box 90, Truman 1948 file 1 of 3.

4. Michael Straight, "Truman Should Quit," *New Republic* (April 5, 1948): 5. In a fascinating attempt to reshape slightly his position in the years after 1948, Straight in a 1975 article entitled "Days with Henry Wallace" argued that he had instantly regretted allowing Wallace to continue writing in the *New Republic* in 1948; the periodical's editorial position during the first half of that year suggests that such a schism, if it existed, was not ideological. See Dorothy Wickenden, ed., *The New Republic Reader: Eighty Years of Opinion & Debate* (New York: Basic Books, 1994), 11.

5. James Loeb to Paul Douglas, March 10, 1948, Paul Douglas MSS, Chicago Historical Society, Chicago, Illinois, Box 1078, ADA folder 2.

6. See Steven Gillon, *Politics and Vision: The ADA and American Liberalism, 1947–1985* (New York: Oxford University Press, 1987), chapters 1 and 2, for an account of the growing hostility toward Truman in the Democratic Party before the 1948 convention.

7. The classic hatchet job on Wallace remains Dwight Macdonald, *Henry Wallace: The Man and the Myth* (New York: Garland, 1948). See also Alonzo Hamby, *Beyond the New Deal, passim*; Steven Gillon, *Politics and Vision*, chapter 2. A more sympathetic portrait is John Culver and John Hyde, *American Dreamer: A Life of Henry A. Wallace* (New York: Norton, 2000). Even this recent biography provoked a strong anti-Wallace reaction: see Geoffrey Wheatcroft, "The Prince of Wallese: Chickens, Communists and Henry Wallace," *Times Literary Supplement*, November 24, 2000: 28–29.

8. The literature on the essential conservatism of the New Deal agenda is vast, but two important works are Daniel Rodgers, *Atlantic Crossings: Social Politics in a Progressive Age* (Cambridge, MA: Belknap Press, 1998), which argues that in a time of economic emergency states look to existing ideas about social relief rather than inventing new ones, and David Plotke, *Building a Democratic Political Order: Reshaping American Liberalism in the 1930s and 1940s* (Cambridge: Cambridge University Press, 1996), which argues the Roosevelt and Truman administrations had to be ideologically circumspect in order to hold the various components of their political coalition together.

9. See Patrick Reagan, *Designing a New America: The Origins of New Deal Planning, 1890–1943* (Amherst: University of Massachusetts Press, 1999), chapter 8 and epilogue; Alonzo Hamby, "The Vital Center, the Fair Deal, and the Quest for a Liberal Political Economy," *American Historical Review* (June 1972): 653–678.

10. Steven Gillon, *Politics and Vision*, 51.

11. "Will the Third Party bring us peace and prosperity?," Town meeting broadcast, April 27, 1948, Paul Douglas MSS, Box 1082, magazine articles file. Taylor and Martin debated Dorothy Thompson and Dwight Macdonald.

12. "Ten Extra Years": Wallace speech to the national convention of Alpha Phi Alpha fraternity, Tulsa, Oklahoma, December 28, 1947, Douglas MSS, Box 1083, PCA/Third Party file. For an analysis of the southern civil rights movement in the 1940s and its links to Wallace, see Patricia Sullivan, *Days of Hope: Race and Democracy in the New Deal Era* (Chapel Hill: University of North Carolina Press, 1996), chapters 7 and 8. For a discussion of organized labor links to Wallace and the left, see Steven Fraser, *Labor Will Rule: Sidney Hillman and the Rise of American Labor* (New York: The Free Press, 1991), chapters 17 and 18.

13. Albert Fitzgerald speech in Chicago, April 10, 1948, Paul Douglas MSS, Box 1083, PCA file. For a discussion of the argument that organized labor was losing its political power to influence industrial policy, see Nelson Lichtenstein, *Walter Reuther: The Most Dangerous Man in Detroit* (Urbana: University of Illinois Press, 1995), especially chapter 13.

14. Remarks of Rexford Tugwell, Chicago Stadium, April 10, 1948, Paul Douglas MSS, Box 1083, PCA file.

15. Michael Straight, "What Happened in the Bronx," *New Republic* (March 1, 1948): 7. In the same issue, on page 6, an IPO poll was quoted which claimed to show that Henry Wallace's strength was great enough in February 1948 to cause the Democrats to lose New England, the Mid-Atlantic, and middle western states of America in November. The poll suggested that 15% of independent voters supported Wallace. See AIPO poll, February 15, 1948, *Public Opinion Quarterly* (Summer 1948): 361.

16. Curtis MacDougall, *Gideon's Army*, vol. 2 (New York: Marzani & Mansell,

1965): 325. MacDougall's well-researched three-volume history of the Wallace movement is particularly interesting given that he was a member of the Progressive Party and stood as its candidate for the Senate against Paul Douglas in Illinois in 1948.

17. *New Republic* (March 1, 1948): 7.

18. Samuel Lubell, *The Future of American Politics* (2nd edition, New York: Doubleday, 1956): 92. A useful account of the difficult history of the ALP during and after World War Two is provided in Steven Fraser, *Labor Will Rule*: especially 517–522.

19. Henry Wallace, "Conspiracy Against Housing," *New Republic* (March 1, 1948): 10; Wallace, "Whipped-Up Hysteria," ibid. (March 29, 1948): 10; "Wallace Sees Plot to Enslave Workers," *New York Times*, April 9, 1948, 20. Some recent historiography has given some credence to Wallace's views of the effects of Cold War liberalism on the working class. See Nelson Lichtenstein, "From Corporatism to Collective Bargaining: Organized Labor and the Eclipse of Social Democracy in the Postwar Era," in Steve Fraser and Gary Gerstle eds., *The Rise and Fall of the New Deal Order, 1930–1980* (Princeton: Princeton University Press, 1989), 122–152.

20. See, for example, the *New York Herald Tribune*, February 20, 1948, which argued that "the third party has suddenly taken on a new importance." The *New York Times'* labor editor, A. H. Raskin, argued in that newspaper on April 7, 1948, 20 that "millions of Americans are likely to turn to Henry A. Wallace, even though they have little regard for the Russia first group that surrounds him."

21. This point appears in more recent historiography on civil rights. See Manning Marable, *Race, Reform, and Rebellion: The Second Reconstruction in Black America, 1945–1982* (London: Macmillan, 1984), 27, 63; Thomas Sancton, "Slowly Crumbling Levees," *New Republic* (March 8, 1948): 18–21; Philip Singer and Gilbert Cranberg, "Norway's Solution: By Planning for Abundance and Freedom, a Vigorous Labor Government Has Licked the Communist 'Menace'," ibid. (January 12, 1948): 22–23.

22. Quoted in Michael Straight, "Test for the Steelworkers," *New Republic* (May 24, 1948): 10.

23. The Wallace group had asked liberal Democrats to file on the Progressive ticket, but almost all had refused. See *New York Times*, March 27, 1948, 7; C. B. Baldwin to the *New Republic* (October 18, 1948): 30. Baldwin argued that Progressives had only filed against Douglas and Holifield to protect their place on the ballot, and that they had voted for Douglas in the Democratic primary and "thus contributed heavily to her nomination."

24. MacDougall, *Gideon's Army*, chapter 19; *New Republic* (September 20, 1948): 10; Gillon, *Politics and Vision*, 52–53. The Communist tendency led to serious schisms in the Wallace movement in Colorado, New Mexico, and districts like Helen Douglas's in California in 1948. An AIPO poll, July 21, 1948, found that 51% of

respondents felt Wallace's party was "run by Communists," and only 21% did not. This proportion was roughly the same across all income groups. See *Public Opinion Quarterly* (Fall 1948): 565. Dwight Macdonald referred to Wallace's ideology as "Stalinoid liberalism" in his *Henry Wallace: The Man and the Myth* (New York: Vanguard Press, 1948), 65.

25. MacDougall, *Gideon's Army*, 333–336.

26. Wallace, "On Testifying in Washington" (*New Republic*, April 26, 1948): 10.

27. Wallace, "The Tyrant's Doctrine," ibid. (May 24, 1948): 11.

28. MacDougall, *Gideon's Army*, 330.

29. *New Republic* (March 1, 1948):9; (September 27, 1948): 32.

30. McCarran to Peterson, March 16, 1948, Pat McCarran MSS, Nevada Historical Society, Reno, Nevada, Box 46, Politics 1948 file. The reader should be aware that the organization of the McCarran papers was subject to review at the time of writing, due to their somewhat eccentric filing system devised by the late Senator's daughter.

31. Truman acceptance speech, Philadelphia, July 15, 1948, in Gregory Bush, ed., *Campaign Speeches of American Presidential Candidates 1948–1984* (New York: Frederick Ungar, 1985), 4–9. See also *New York Times*, September 15, 1948, 6 for the text of Truman's campaign speech at Indianapolis in which he backs federal health insurance.

32. Alfred Baker Lewis to James Loeb, February 3, 1948, ADA papers, reel 31, section 36.

33. *New York Times*, April 11, 1948, IV, 8; "The Negro in Politics," *New Republic*, (October 18, 1948): 14–15.

34. The *New Republic* argued on May 10, 1948, 13, that the "Red hysteria, the crop of local anti-labor laws and the barrage of 'American way' advertising in press and radio are symptomatic of big business' feeling that the lines are drawn, at home and abroad, and now is the time to put on the heat."

35. *New York Times*, April 7, 1948, 18; April 10, 1948, 8.

36. Speeches by Wallace and Baldwin in New York, September 21, 1948, Ickes MSS, Box 91, Wallace 1946–7 file.

37. Polls showed support for Wallace peaking at 7.5% in very early 1948, before sliding to 4% by November. When *Fortune* asked voters in September 1948 whether they would agree or disagree with "a candidate who said that we are being too tough with Russia," 87% said they would disagree. Interestingly, 56% of avowed Wallace supporters said they would disagree with such a stance, and only 32% said they agreed the United States was "too tough" on the Soviets, while 63% of respondents in an August poll supported the Mundt-Nixon bill. Compare these figures with those showing a popular response to the question of whether government should do more for the poor in November 1948: 43% said it should, but 35% said government did

enough and 14% said the state did too much, a combined figure of 49%. Wallace's domestic progressivism held little attraction for an electorate more concerned with an ever-reinforced antipathy toward communism. See *Public Opinion Quarterly* (Winter 1948): 767, 760–761, 756, 781.

38. "Kennedy Raps Roosevelt Attitude Toward Russia—Tells Danvers Chamber of Foreign Policy," *Salem Evening News*, May 8, 1948, JFK MSS, Box 99, Russian policy file.

39. The issue of the narrowing of the American political spectrum in the 1940s is discussed in John Malsberger, *From Obstruction to Moderation: The Transformation of Senate Conservatism, 1938–1952* (Selinsgrove: Susquehanna University Press, 2000), although Malsberger attributes the rise of liberal Republicanism purely to the growth of the modern industrial state. There was also, I would argue, a growing consensus in the Cold War era on the limits of liberalism.

40. Jason Dorman to Taft, December 2, 1947, Taft MSS, Box 165, Arizona file; Edward and Vivian Agnes to Taft, November 17, 1947, Taft MSS, Box 165, California A file; Elizabeth Scales to Taft, December 12, 1947, Taft MSS, Box 165, Arizona file.

41. "Bob Taft—Workhorse of the Senate," *Chicago Sunday Tribune*, Magazine, June 1, 1947.

42. Taft, "My Political Credo," Taft MSS, Box 238, 1948 Campaign miscellany (publicity) file.

43. Taft speech at Youngstown, April 21, 1948, Taft MSS, Box 1288, Stassen 1945–8 file 2 of 3; Taft campaign leaflet "Do We Want a Man Who . . . , " Taft MSS, Box 1288, Stassen 1945–8 file 1 of 3; Taft, "My Political Credo," Taft MSS, Box 238, 1948 campaign miscellany (publicity) file.

44. Elizabeth Fones-Wolf, *Selling Free Enterprise*: 51.

45. Ickes to William Black, September 25, 1947, Ickes MSS, Box 86, Taft file 1 of 2.

46. Jensen to Roscoe S. Jones, Joseph Martin MSS, BFJ-2 file.

47. Republican organizer speech on radio station WLW Ohio, April 24, 1948,Taft MSS, Box 1288, Stassen file 1 of 3; *Tulsa Tribune*, September 28, 1946, Taft MSS, ibid.; Typed sheet "Wake Up Republicans!" Taft MSS, Stassen file 3 of 3.

48. Ickes column, "Man to Man," April 28, 1948, Taft MSS, Box 1288, Stassen file 1 of 3; *The Machinist*, April 15, 1948, Taft MSS, Box 1288, Stassen file 3 of 3. Taft actually made use of this article by checking up on the Minnesota law and contrasting it unfavorably with the more "liberal" Taft-Hartley federal law, casting Stassen as the conservative. See memo from Labor Committee counsel Tom Shroyer to Taft, April 23, 1948, Taft MSS, ibid.

49. Confidential transcript of a conference between Joseph Stalin and Harold Stassen, April 9, 1947, for broadcast in the U.S. on May 3, 1947, Taft MSS, Box 615, foreign policy 1947 file 1 of 3.

50. Stassen, "Special Appeal to French and French-Canadian Voters'; Clare Hoffman, "We Are Entitled to Know," April 15, 1948, Taft MSS, Box 1289, Stassen speeches file 1 of 2.

51. Report on GOP questionnaire by McIntyre Faries, GOP California National Committeeman, August 25, 1948, Knowland MSS, Box 89, Republican Activities 1948 file.

52. Knowland to Reichel, August 26, 1948, Knowland MSS, Box 89, ibid.

53. Confidential 1948 Election Report by George Smith, GOP Policy Committee Staff Director, Wallace White MSS, Library of Congress, Box 63, 1948 Presidential campaign file.

54. Warren speech in Chicago, October 6, 1948, Knowland MSS, Box 89, Warren campaign file.

55. Dewey interview March 29, 1948, Taft MSS, Box 1285, Dewey 1944–48 file.

56. Dewey speech at Boston, October 28, 1948; Dewey speech at the Hollywood Bowl, Los Angeles, September 24, 1948, Taft MSS, Box 1285, ibid.

57. Dewey speech at Des Moines, September 20, 1948, in Gregory Bush, ed., *Campaign Speeches of American Presidential Candidates 1948–1984*, 16–22.

58. E. M. Biggers to Clarence Brown, October 3, 1947, Taft MSS, Box 205, New York 1948 file.

59. Morley to Taft, March 18, 1948; Taft to Grenville Clark, March 31, 1948, Taft MSS, Box 896, foreign policy 1948 file.

60. McCormick to Taft, June 30, 1948, Taft MSS, Box 899, Senators correspondence 1948 file.

61. Hendley family to Taft, October 29, 1947; Hendley family to George Marshall, September 24, 1947, Taft MSS, Box 197, Nevada file.

62. William Harrison to Dewey and Warren, July 5, 1948, Knowland MSS, Box 88, 1948 Campaign file 2.

63. Confidential election report, White MSS, Box 63, campaign file. For Taft's campaign strategy, see the series of radio spots made for Taft using voices representing manual workers, farmers and so forth as having benefited from Taft's patronage, Taft MSS, Box 239, radio material file.

64. Halleck address over NBC network, July 28, 1948, Taft MSS, Box 1285, Dewey RNC 1948 file. See also Joseph Martin MSS, file 115.4 for Republican speeches on the 80th Congress.

65. Fletcher to Knowland, April 20, 1948, Knowland MSS, Box 88, California GOP Congressmen 1948 file. Knowland worked on the campaigns of a number of struggling Californian colleagues that year.

66. State by state field reports, October 1948, Knowland MSS, Box 88, 1948 campaign file 7.

67. Minnesota state report, October 1948, Knowland MSS, Box 88, 1948 campaign file 7.

68. For a study of the unusual nature of Minnesota state politics, particularly the history of the growth of radical agrarian-labor activism in the early twentieth century, see Richard Valelly, *Radicalism in the States: The Minnesota Farmer-Labor Party and the American Political Economy* (Chicago: University of Chicago Press, 1989).

69. Orville Freeman to Don Davison, administrative assistant to President Truman, July 28, 1949, Anderson MSS, Box 1052, Minnesota file.

70. Ethel Epstein to Herbert Lehman, April 3, 1948 and September 3, 1948, Lehman MSS, ADA special file 17a.

71. GOP state report in West Virginia, October 1948, Knowland MSS, Box 88, 1948 campaign file 7.

72. See "Neely in West Virginia," *New Republic*, October 25, 1948, 15. The article argues specifically that Neely's strength came from a combination of moderate liberalism and support for U.S. Cold War policy.

73. GOP report, Knowland MSS, Box 88, 1948 campaign file 7.

74. GOP leaflet "The Veterans' Case Against the Democrat New Deal," Anderson MSS, Box 1046, Hurley debate file.

75. *Chicago Daily Tribune*, October 5, 1948; *Silver City Daily Press*, New Mexico, undated editorial, Anderson MSS, Box 1046, Libelous arts file.

76. Hurley debate, July 25, 1948, Anderson MSS, Box 1048, Hurley-Anderson debate file.

77. Anderson radio speech, October 30, 1948, Anderson MSS, Box 1047, OPA/radio address file.

78. Anderson speech, undated, Anderson MSS, Box 1046, Hurley debate file.

79. Anderson radio address, November 1, 1948, Anderson MSS, Box 1047, 1948 election file; Anderson address "Toward Peace of Mind" at Jefferson-Jackson Dinner, Des Moines, March 6, 1948, Anderson MSS, Box 1047, CPA talks—1948 election file.

80. Hurley-Anderson debate at Los Alamos, July 25, 1948, Anderson MSS, Box 1048, Hurley-Anderson debate file; Anderson address, March 6, 1948, Anderson MSS, Box 1046, CPA/election file.

81. There are a number of studies of Sandburg, among the most recent being North Callahan, *Carl Sandburg: His Life and Works* (University Park: Pennsylvania State University Press, 1987). Sadly the biography makes almost no reference to his political beliefs and activities. A new biography of Douglas has appeared: Roger Biles, *Crusading Liberal: Paul H. Douglas of Illinois* (De Kalb: Northern Illinois University Press, 2002).

82. Paul Douglas, *The Coming of a New Party* (New York: McGraw-Hill, 1932), 23, 88, 96. See Daniel Rodgers, *Atlantic Crossings: Social Politics in a Progressive Age* for a discussion of the transatlantic intellectual and political conversations over social reform that took place in the first half of the twentieth century.

83. Paul Douglas, "Rooseveltian Liberalism," *The Nation*, June 21, 1933, 702–703, a review of Rexford Tugwell, *The Industrial Discipline* (New York: 1933), reproduced in Howard Zinn, ed., *New Deal Thought* (New York: Bobbs-Merrill, 1966), 53–56.

84. *Official Congressional Directory*, 89th Congress, 2nd Session (Washington DC: GPO, 1966): 43; Paul Douglas, *In the Fullness of Time: The Memoirs of Paul H. Douglas* (New York: Harcourt, Brace, Jovanovich, 1971); Paul Douglas speech at Champaign, IL, September 22, 1948, Douglas MSS, Box 1191, articles on Douglas's Senate work file.

85. Douglas to Ickes, January 14, 1948, Ickes MSS, Box 55, Paul Douglas file. There can be little doubt that Douglas was right about Communist infiltration of the third party: see "Communists Open Member Drive, Will Recruit Wallace Adherents," *New York Times*, April 12, 1948, 1. However, Douglas used the communist issue as a tool to discredit *all* progressive opponents in Illinois.

86. "Paul Douglas: His Policy," *New Republic*, June 28, 1948, 20–21.

87. Paul Douglas, *In the Fullness of Time*, 137.

88. Walter Johnson to Ickes, February 16, 1948, Ickes MSS, Box 55, Douglas file.

89. Wetle to Ickes, February 8, 1948; Barnard to Ickes, February 4, 1948, Ickes MSS, ibid.

90. Paul Douglas, "The American Occupation of Haiti," *Political Science Quarterly* (June and September 1927), reprint page 62, Paul Douglas MSS, University of Chicago, Special Collections, Box 1, folder 4.

91. See correspondence in Ickes 55, Douglas file. The comment on the atomic bomb is made in Douglas, *In the Fullness of Time*, 498.

92. "MacDougall: His Policy," *New Republic*, September 20, 1948, 30–31.

93. Paul Douglas radio speech, May 27, 1948, Paul Douglas MSS, Box 1084, 1948 speeches file.

94. FDR Jr. speech to the ADA convention, Clevelend, February 19, 1948, Douglas MSS, Box 1078, ADA file. See Steven Gillon, *Politics and Vision*, 52.

95. Paul Douglas to Rev. Father E. V. Cardinal of Chicago, January 14, 1948, Douglas MSS, Box 1078, ADA file 2.

96. Douglas to Sidney Hyman, August 16, 1948, Douglas MSS, Box 1081, Hyman file; Douglas, "Antidote to Communism," University of Chicago Magazine, December 1947, Douglas MSS, Box 1079, campaign literature file.

97. Douglas to the Editor, *Chicago Tribune*, September 11, 1948.

98. Douglas speech at Champaign, IL, September 22, 1948, Douglas MSS, box 1191, articles 1949–54 file.

99. Douglas speech at ADA Roosevelt Day dinner, Washington, January 29, 1949; Douglas speech to the NY Liberal Party annual state dinner, May 25, 1949, Douglas MSS, Box 955.

100. Paul Douglas speech at Springfield, IL, January 7, 1948; Press release Janu-

ary 13, 1948 on the resignation of Rabbi Jacob Weinstein from the Illinois PCA Board, Douglas MSS, Box 1086, campaign material file 2.

101. See Bill V. Mullen, *Popular Fronts: Chicago and African American Cultural Politics, 1935–1946* (Urbana: University of Illinois Press, 1999): especially chapters 2 and 7. For an overview of the Chicago machine and its politics, see Paul Green and Melvin Holli, eds., *The Mayors: The Chicago Political Tradition* (Carbondale: Southern Illinois University Press, 1987).

102. Paul Douglas to Sidney Hyman, August 16, 1948, Douglas MSS, Box 1081, Hyman file.

103. "MacDougall: His Policy," *New Republic*, June 28, 1948; "MacDougall for Senator" newspaper advertisement, Douglas MSS, Box 1083, PCA/Third Party file.

104. The Labour Party in Britain, for example, experienced internal wrangling over the nuclear bomb, involvement in the Cold War, and the direction of welfare state policies as the social democratic impulse grew in strength after World War Two. See, for example John Campbell, *Nye Bevan and the Mirage of British Socialism* (London: Weidenfeld & Nicolson, 1987); Kenneth Morgan, *Labour in Power, 1945–1951* (Oxford: Clarendon Press, 1984). See also Tim Tilton, *The Political Theory of Swedish Social Democracy through the Welfare State to Socialism* (Oxford: Oxford University Press, 1990) for a discussion of debates within the Swedish left.

105. Timothy Thurber advances this thesis when discussing the evolution of American liberalism in the 1960s. See Thurber, *The Politics of Equality: Hubert H. Humphrey and the African American Freedom Struggle* (New York: Columbia University Press, 1999).

106. Senator Scott Lucas (D-Illinois) campaign leaflet, 1944, Douglas MSS, Box 1082, Scott Lucas file.

107. Tugwell to Ickes, February 17, 1948; Ickes to Tugwell, February 27, 1948; Barnard to Ickes, March 4, 1948, Ickes MSS, Box 55, Douglas file.

108. Douglas to Ickes, March 29, 1948, Ickes MSS, Ibid.

109. An example is the fact that progressives in Illinois in 1948 were routinely attacked and picketed. See "Progressives are stoned," *New York Times*, September 3, 1948, 14, about the stoning of MacDougall and his caravan at West Frankfurt, Illinois.

110. Harold Ickes, "An Appeal to the Liberals of America"; Ickes to Herbert Lehman, October 14, 1948, Lehman MSS, Ickes file 1934–1952, 410.

111. Curtis MacDougall, *Gideon's Army*, vol. II (New York: Marzani & Mansell, 1965): chapter 16.

112. Charles Merriam to Ickes, February 24, 1948, Ickes MSS, Box 55, Paul Douglas file.

113. Humphrey procured ten times as many votes as the leftist candidate in the DFL primary. "A book could be written," argued the *New Republic* in its October 18,

1948 issue, page 8, "on how the Humphrey forces gained control of the Democratic-Farmer-Labor Party, cleansed it of the communist stigma, and restored it as a power to be reckoned with on election day." By this stage the *New Republic* had abandoned its earlier ambivalence toward the Wallace forces and stood behind the ADA liberals.

114. Michael Heale, for example, notes the fact that anti-communism was more than an elite political phenomenon; it was also a popular phenomenon amongst Catholic and ethnic voters in blue collar constituencies in Boston, New York, and Chicago. See Heale, *McCarthy's Americans: Red Scare Politics in State and Nation, 1935–1965* (London: Macmillan, 1998): *passim*.

115. Ickes to McGrath, September 14, 1948, Ickes MSS, Box 71, McGrath file.

116. See Hamby, *Beyond the New Deal*, 261–263.

117. See Jennifer A Delton, *Making Minnesota Liberal: Civil Rights and the Transformation of the Democratic Party* (Minneapolis: University of Minnesota Press, 2002).

118. Javits to New York *Herald Tribune*, February 18, 1949, Javits MSS, 1/1/1; Javits remarks to Liberal Party Institute, New York, 1949, Javits MSS, 1/1/2; Javits speech to Young Republican Club, Minneapolis, New York *Herald Tribune*, September 28, 1950, Javits MSS, 8/2/18.

119. Javits speech on "civil rights, health, and education," 1948, Javits MSS, 1/1/1.

120. Chicago *Sun-Times*, July 16, 1948, Douglas MSS, Box 1079, civil rights file.

121. Committee to Elect Paul Douglas campaign release, 1948, Douglas MSS, Box 1081, endorsements file. For a full treatment of the politics of southern sectionalism in 1948, see Robert Garson, *The Democratic Party and the Politics of Sectionalism, 1941–1948* (Baton Rouge: Louisiana State University Press, 1974).

122. William Benton to Hubert Humphrey, November 3 and October 2, 1948, William Benton MSS, University of Chicago, Special Collections, Box 273, folder 4, Humphrey file.

123. Humphrey to Benton, June 25, 1952, Benton MSS, Box 273, folder 4.

124. Benton form letter to doctors, September 8, 1950, Benton MSS, Box 318, folder 5; Benton to Truman, February 21, 1950, Benton MSS, Box 280, folder 8.

125. *The Secret Diary of Harold L. Ickes*, Volume II (New York: Simon & Schuster, 1954), 115.

126. Douglas speech to the ADA convention, April 9, 1949, Douglas MSS, Box 955, ADA file.

127. It is possible to date the emergence of identity liberalism of the sort that came to prominence in American political discourse in the 1960s and 1970s to the 1948 election, a liberalism that old left activists like Eric Hobsbawm and Todd Gitlin decried as "a blind alley where universal demands are cast aside in favor of narrow battles around race, ethnicity, gender and sexuality." See Robin Kelley, *Yo' Mama's Disfunktional! Fighting the Culture Wars in Urban America* (Boston: Beacon Press, 1997), 11.

128. Patricia Sullivan, *Days of Hope*, 241.

129. There is a vast literature on this issue. See Ira Katznelson et al, "Limiting Liberalism: The Southern Veto in Congress, 1933–1950," *Political Science Quarterly* (Summer 1993): 283–306; Julian Pleasants and Augustus Burns, *Frank Porter Graham and the 1950 Senate Race in North Carolina* (Chapel Hill: University of North Carolina Press, 1990); Patricia Sullivan, *Days of Hope*: chapter 8; Jonathan Bell, "Conceptualising Southern Liberalism: Ideology and the Pepper v. Smathers 1950 Primary in Florida," *Journal of American Studies* 37, no. 1 (April 2003): 17–45; Michael Klarman, "How *Brown* Changed Race Relations: The Backlash Thesis," *Journal of American History* (June 1994): 81–118. See also David Plotke, *Building a Democratic Political Order*, chapter 10. Plotke argues on page 310 that the "Cold War reinforced core elements of the Democratic order while encouraging a conservative turn within it," and that, on issues like race relations, the "Cold War provided a large supply of ammunition for conservatives to attack domestic reform efforts as Communist-inspired and therefore illegitimate."

130. *Congressional Record* reprint, July 3, 1947, RN yl, PPS 208 (1947): 40.

131. ADA political questionnaire completed by the New Orleans chapter, 1948, ADA papers, reel 106, section 10.

132. Address of F. Edward Hebert on WNOE radio, August 9, 1948, ADA papers, reel 106, section 10.

133. ADA political questionnaire, New Orleans chapter, 1948, ADA papers, reel 106, section 10.

134. For a complete analysis of the presidential results, see the *New York Times*, November 7, 1948.

135. Details of the 1948 elections and districts can be found in several sources, the best being the *Congressional Quarterly*, week ending August 4, 1950, 853–860; *Congressional Directory*, 80th Congress, 2nd Session (Washington DC: GPO, 1948). Overall the GOP lost Senate seats in Wyoming, West Virginia, Kentucky, Illinois, Minnesota, Idaho, Iowa, Oklahoma, and Delaware.

136. De Vuono to Martha Taft, October 26, 1949, Taft MSS, Box 911, political—Republican 1949 file 1 of 2.

137. Henry Cabot Lodge, "Think Anew and Act Anew—The Republican Future," December 1948, Lodge MSS, HCL speeches, microfilm reel 4 (P5/9).

138. George Smith, Confidential 1948 Election report to members of the GOP Policy Committee, White MSS, Box 63, 1948 campaign file.

139. Spangler to Taft, July 14, 1949, Taft MSS, Box 911, political—Republican 1949 file 1 of 2.

140. Spangler speech, January 26, 1949, Taft MSS, Box 911, Ibid., file 2 of 2.

141. Cutler address, February 9, 1950, Saltonstall MSS, carton 128, Republican Party 1950 file 1 of 4.

142. Irving Ives interview on "Meet the Press," January 7, 1949, Taft MSS, Box 911, political Republican file 1949 2 of 2.

143. *New Republic* (November 22, 1948): 5; (November 15, 1948): 1.

144. Walter Reuther to Paul Douglas, March 31, 1948, Douglas MSS, Box 1082, labor file. For a detailed discussion of the retreat from left-of-center social reform in the late 1940s see Nelson Lichtenstein, *Walter Reuther*: chapter 13. On page 300 Lichtenstein argues that Reuther "was trapped, first by the poisoned legacy of obsessive anti-communism, then by an alliance with an unreformed Democratic Party, and finally by the transformation and demobilization of the UAW itself." See also Colin Gordon, "Why No Health Insurance in the United States? The Limits of Social Provision in War and Peace, 1941–1948," *Journal of Policy History*, 9 , no. 3 (1997): 277–310; Alan Derickson, "Health Security for All? Social Unionism and Universal Health Insurance, 1935–1958," *Journal of American History* (March 1994): 1333–1356; Michael K. Brown, "Bargaining for Social Rights: Unions and the Reemergence of Welfare Capitalism, 1945–1952," *Political Science Quarterly*, 112:4 (Winter 1997-1998): 645-674.

145. Nelson Lichtenstein, *Walter Reuther*, 282, 286.

146. Lewis Feuer, "Russia and the Liberals," *New Republic* (November 8, 1948): 14–16. Feuer himself opposed Soviet communism, but argued that liberals must "realize that communism is but one manifestation of a profound socio-economic need." In failing to differentiate adequately between anti-communism and anti-progressivism, Cold War liberals, Feuer argued, were failing to provide an alternative to idealistic communism for people around the world, as well as in the relatively prosperous United States.

5. Transnational Perspectives and Images of the State, 1949–1950

1. Marjorie Shearon, Notes on British trip no. 11, November 4, 1949, Taft MSS, Box 798, Social Security 1949 file 1 of 3.

2. Shearon report no. 12, November 23, 1949, Taft MSS, Ibid.

3. Dr.William Sweet, "Recent Impressions of Medical Practice in Great Britain," *New England Journal of Medicine* vol. 240 (February 3, 1949): 168–172; Dr. Otto Geier in the *Cincinnati Enquirer*, April 3, 1949. Another example is "Britain's Crisis Shows Dangers of Socialism," *Akron Beacon Journal*, July 10, 1949. The American Institute of Public Opinion published two British polls in November 1950 asking respondents their views of the NHS. See *Public Opinion Quarterly* (Spring 1951): 173–174.

4. Most British doctors opposed to the NHS joined the "Fellowship for Freedom in Medicine" led by Lord Horder. Horder attended the AMA convention in Atlantic City in June 1949 to solicit support for his cause from American sources. See Joseph Lawrence of the AMA to Taft, June 2, 1949, Taft MSS, Box 643, Health file 2 of 3.

5. J. L. Macauley to Taft, April 12, 1949; Taft to Macauley, April 30, 1949, Taft MSS, Box 643, National Program for Medical Care 1949 file 1 of 3. Taft statement May 23, 1949 in *JAMA* (June 25, 1949): 716.

6. *Congressional Record* reprint, October 13, 1949, Taft MSS, Box 499, Britain file 1.

7. *American Medicine and the Political Scene*, December 15, 1949, Taft MSS, Box 499, Ibid.

8. Morris Fishbein, "Health and Social Security," *JAMA* (December 25, 1948): 1254–1256. For a more scholarly analysis of the workings of the NHS in Great Britain, see Nicholas Timmins, *The Five Giants: A Biography of the Welfare State* (London: HarperCollins, 1995).

9. "Don Iddon's Diary" column, undated, Taft MSS, Box 1033, political general M-Mc 1951 file.

10. Patrick Gordon Walker, UK Commonwealth Secretary, speech to Woolwich Labour Party, May 9, 1951, Patrick Gordon Walker MSS, Churchill College, Cambridge, UK, section 3, box 3.

11. Taft introduced the speech, delivered on May 11, 1949, into the *Congressional Record*, July 11, 1949, McCarran MSS, Box 47, Communism file. Palmer argued that he was "not intellectually prepared to make any fine distinction between socialism and communism" in his attack on the Labour government.

12. Copies of the various health insurance bills in the 81st Congress can be found in Taft MSS, Box 640, Health hearings 1949 file. Humphrey to Minnesota doctors, May 27, 1949, Taft MSS, Box 643, national program of medical care 1949 file 2 of 3.

13. The existing literature on this topic focuses on this theme. See Colin Gordon, "Why No National Health Insurance in the US?" *Journal of Policy History* 9, no. 3 (1997): 277–310; Jacob Hacker, *The Divided Welfare State* (Cambridge: Cambridge University Press, 2002): chapter 5; Monte Poen, *Harry S Truman Versus the Medical Lobby: The Genesis of Medicare* (Columbia: University of Missouri Press, 1979).

14. "The President's Message and the Compulsory Health Insurance Bill," *JAMA* (May 7, 1949): 111; J. Donald Kingsley testimony before the Senate subcommittee on health, May 23, 1949, *JAMA*, June 25, 1949, 705.

15. Ibid., 719.

16. "A Voluntary Federal Aid Health Program—Senator Robert A. Taft's Constructive Answer to Socialized Medicine," from Taft's 1950 Senate campaign, Taft MSS, Box 639, Health, 1951 file.

17. Morse to Taft, May 18, 1949, Taft MSS, Box 912, Senate correspondence file.

18. Shearon to Taft, April 25 and May 19, 1949, Taft MSS, Box 643, Health, 1949 file 1 of 3.

19. "Our National Health—A 4 Way Debate," *NEA Daily News Page*, May 4, 1949, Taft MSS, Box 643, national program 1949 file 2 of 3.

20. *JAMA* (September 2, 1950): 46–47, Ickes MSS, Box 52, Committee for the Nation's Health file. The inauguration in July 1950 of new AMA chairman Elmer Henderson was broadcast nationwide for the first time, including his speech attacking federal insurance as part of a "fundamental struggle" against "a socialist state." This represented a vital link between the mass media and growing popular suspicion of the state in the Cold War era. See *New Republic*, July 17, 1950, 7.

21. Dulles address before the American Political Science Association, December 28, 1949, entitled "The Blessings of Liberty," Herter MSS, folder 1362.

22. *Congressional Record* reprint, June 30, 1949, "Socialism—American Variety," Herter MSS, folder 1266.

23. Proceedings of the Interim Session of the House of Delegates of the AMA, St Louis, November 30–December 1, 1948, *JAMA* (December 18, 1948): 1171,1172.

24. Proceedings of the AMA House of Delegates Conference, Atlantic City, June 6–10, 1949, *JAMA* (June 25, 1949): 694–696. See Colin Gordon, *Dead On Arrival: The Politics of Health Care in Twentieth Century America* (Princeton: Princeton University Press, 2003), 141–147.

25. Dr P. Huss of the Allied Medical Arts Committee to Mr Dowdell, a patient, October 25, 1950; William Benton form letter, October 30, 1950; Benton to Thomas Feeney, September 8, 1950, William Benton MSS, Box 318, folder 5. See also Colin Gordon, *Dead On Arrival*, 221–222.

26. Dr H M Maroni to Benton, October 10, 1950; Phil Levy to Benton, September 6, 1950, Benton MSS, Box 318, folder 5.

27. Feeney to Benton, September 20, 1950, Benton MSS, Box 352, folder 10.

28. Benton to J. Howe, December 28, 1950, Benton MSS, Box 318, folder 7.

29. Bulletin no. 12, Compulsory Health Insurance Committee, Herbert Lehman MSS, C235–16; *Niagara Falls Gazette*, November 3, 1949, Lehman MSS, C235–25.

30. Anonymous doctor to Maguire, October 30, 1949, Lehman MSS, C235–34.

31. Lucas to Lehman, November 1, 1949, Lehman MSS, C235–25. See also Lehman MSS C235–26 and C235–27 for files of correspondence between Lehman and doctors, most of it hostile.

32. *New York Medicine*, October 20, 1949; Lehman form letter, October 26, 1949, Lehman MSS, C235–25.

33. Frederick Lehmann to Lehman, October 28, 1949, Lehman MSS, C235–25.

34. Hollander and Froise to Lehman, Lehman MSS, C235–29. See also Senate campaign pamphlets file C235–33 and speeches file C236–8. For material on the ALP issue, see publicity file C235–34.

35. Lehman address over WCBS, November 7, 1949; Lehman speech at ADA meeting, New York, November 6, 1949, Lehman MSS, C236–8.

36. Lehman to Frances Perkins, November 17, 1949, Lehman MSS, Perkins file 704.

37. *JAMA* (May 27, 1950): 377.

38. *JAMA* (July 1, 1950): 783–785; (July 15, 1950); (June 24, 1950): 744.

39. *JAMA* (November 11, 1950): 930–931; (November 18, 1950): 1008.

40. AIPO poll, March 23, 1949, *Public Opinion Quarterly*, Summer 1949, 356–358.

41. "Senator Humphrey's Position on Health Program Clarified," *JAMA* (November 12, 1949): 785.

42. Nixon speech transcript, undated, "Record of the 81st Congress," RN yl, PPS 208 (1950):72. See also Nixon speech to a GOP meeting at Modesto, California, March 24, 1950, RN yl, PPS 208 (1950): 6.

43. Nixon speech notes for a Bakersfield station stop, April 1950, RN yl, PPS 208 (1950):7.

44. Nixon statement to candidates' meetings, April-June 1950, RN yl, PPS 208 (1950): 8.

45. Macy open letter, October 3, 1949; Gwinn remarks in House, June 30, 1949, Herter MSS, folder 1266.

46. Taft speech to the Mortgage Bankers Association of America, January 25, 1949, Taft MSS, Box 655, Housing 1949 file 2 of 4.

47. Gwinn speech, "Public Housing—Disastrous Here and Abroad," June 4, 1948, Taft MSS, Box 655, Housing 1949 file 1 of 4.

48. "OASI: A Report to the Senate Committee on Finance from the Advisory Council on Social Security," (Washington DC: GPO, 1948); see also "The Income of the Aged in 1948–1949: A Summary with Particular Reference to OASI Beneficiaries and OAA recipients," Taft MSS, Box 798, Social Security 1945–8 file. Out of 2.2 million Americans over 65 living alone in 1949, 1.1million received Social Security, but only 300,000 of those received OASI benefits. The other 800,000 had not worked in the same job for long enough or consistently enough to qualify for federal benefits, or found that their employment was not covered, so relied entirely on federal-state assistance programs, which were not dependent upon individual contributions to the federal insurance system.

49. Reuther to Taft, May 11, 1950, Taft MSS, Box 799, Social Security file 3 of 4.

50. See, for example, Charles Hook, Chairman of Armco Steel Corp., to Taft, January 17, 1950, Taft MSS, Box 799, Social Security file 2 of 4.

51. Taft notes on HR6000, Taft MSS, Box 798, Soc. Sec. File 1 of 3; Taft to W. Randolph Burgess, April 13, 1950, Taft MSS, Box 799, Soc. Sec. File 1 of 4.

52. R.C. Townsend to Taft, November 25, 1949, Taft MSS, Box 798, Soc. Sec. File 2 of 3; Mrs. C. E. Gerard to Taft, January 19, 1950, Taft MSS, Box 799, Soc. Sec. File 2 of 4. W. Rulon Williamson, former actuary of the Social Security Administration, also pushed Taft to oppose the reserve aspect of Social Security and levy a standing tax to finance those already retired: Williamson to Taft, December 20, 1949, Taft

MSS, Box 798, Soc. Sec. File 1 of 3. For a contemporary defense of the state control of social relations in the workplace relating to issues of gender and the elderly, see Professor J. Douglas Brown, "Incentive and Mobility Under Social Insurance," lecture given at the University of Michigan lecture series on public affairs, August 8, 1950, Taft MSS, Box 800, Soc. Sec. 1950 file 3 of 4. A stimulating critique of Social Security as being a tool of social control is provided by Frances Piven and Richard Cloward, *Regulating the Poor: The Functions of Public Welfare* (New York: Pantheon, 1971).

53. Curtis speech, October 4, 1949; Noah Mason, October 10, 1949, Taft MSS, Box 798, Soc. Sec. 1949 file 2 of 3; Hugh Butler to Taft, June 13, 1950, Taft MSS, Box 799, file 3 of 4.

54. Shearon to Taft, December 18, 1949, Taft MSS, Box 798, Soc. Sec. 1949 file 1 of 3.

55. Shearon, *American Medicine and the Political Scene*, December 29, 1949, Taft MSS, Box 798, file 2 of 3. In March 1950 the title of this weekly publication with wide circulation in medical circles was changed to *Challenge to Socialism*.

56. Shearon testimony, April 13, 1949, *American Medicine and the Political Scene*, April 21, 1949, Taft MSS, Box 643, National Health file 1 of 3.

57. Shearon to Brewster, January 8, 1950; *Challenge to Socialism*, May 25, 1950; Shearon article "Fraudulent HR6000 Forced Through Senate by Lucas, George, Taft, and Millikin Coalition," *Challenge to Socialism*, June 22, 1950, Taft MSS, Box 800, Soc. Sec. File 3 of 4.

58. Mills quoted in Julian Zelizer, *Taxing America: Wilbur D Mills, Congress, and the State, 1945–1975* (Cambridge: Cambridge University Press, 1998): 75. Zelizer provides a clear account of the ways in which congressional Democrats like Mills steered federal tax and social security policy to achieve a modicum of social welfare within the limits of the American political structure.

59. Walter Reuther to Taft, May 11, 1950, Taft MSS, Box 799, social security file 3 of 4.

60. Herbert Lehman speech to the National Convention of the American Federation of Musicians, New York, June 6, 1951, Benton MSS, Box 275, folder 1.

61. Walter Reuther to Paul Douglas, March 31, 1948, Douglas MSS, Box 1082, labor file. A masterly discussion of the growth of corporate welfare in the late 1940s, symbolized by the "Treaty of Detroit" and the deradicalization of organized labor as it moved increasingly into the Cold War liberal network, is provided in Nelson Lichtenstein, *Walter Reuther: The Most Powerful Man in Detroit* (Urbana: University of Illinois Press, 1995).

62. "Full Employment Conference of Americans for Democratic Action," July 28, 1949, Lehman MSS, C236–35. The conference also heard speeches from representatives of the AFL, the CIO, independent businessmen, the Secretary of Labor, and

Connecticut Governor Chester Bowles. For useful discussions of the evolution of fiscal liberalism see Alan Wolfe, *America's Impasse: The Rise and Fall of the Politics of Growth* (New York: Pantheon, 1981) and Alonzo Hamby, "The Vital Center, the Fair Deal, and the Quest for a Liberal Political Economy," *American Historical Review* (June 1972): 653–678.

63. "Full Employment Conference of Americans for Democratic Action," July 28, 1949, Lehman MSS, C236–35.

64. An excellent overview of the Truman administration's agricultural policy remains Allen Matusow, *Farm Policies and Politics in the Truman Years* (Cambridge: Harvard University Press, 1967).

65. George Aiken remarks in *Congressional Record*, 81st Congress, 1st session, April 7, 1949, 4113ff. Whitney Gillilland, GOP state chairman for Iowa, release, June 14, 1949, Taft MSS, Box 485, agriculture file 2; *Human Events*, February 23, 1949, Taft MSS, Box 485, agriculture file 1.

66. See Matusow, *Farm Policies and Politics in the Truman Years*, chapter 9.

67. Carl Rice to Clinton Anderson, September 13, 1950, Anderson MSS, Box 1052, Kansas file; *Des Moines Sunday Register*, March 19, 1950, section IV, 1, plus material in Anderson MSS, Box 1052, Iowa file.

68. Benton radio commercial no. 3, Benton MSS, Box 319, folder 1; Philip Levy to Benton, October 12, 1950, Benton MSS, Box 318, folder 1.

69. RNC report, "Setback for Socialism," Herter MSS, folder 1265.

70. Nixon, Washington Report, February 26, 1948, RN yl, PPS208 (1948): 10.

71. The development of a right-wing strategic anti-communist agenda with respect to Asia is examined in Bruce Cumings's superlative introduction to his edited volume *Child of Conflict: The Korean-American Relationship, 1943–1953* (Seattle: University of Washington Press, 1983), 3–55, and especially 9–11.

72. Martin speech on China, February 13, 1951; Lincoln Day speech, Brooklyn, NY, February 12, 1951, Martin MSS, folder 118.1, 1951 speech files.

73. Knowland to Lawrence Fouchs, February 15, 1950, Knowland MSS, Box 66, China file.

74. Smith to Pat McCarran, February 18, 1949, McCarran MSS, Box 48, China aid 1949 file.

75. McCarran speech, August 3, 1950, McDonald MSS, Box 3, file I/1/66.

76. McCarran speech, October 4, 1948, McCarran MSS, Box 46, speeches 1948 file.

77. Taft speech in Senate, January 11, 1950; Luce article in "American China Problems," pamphlet published by the Institute of Chinese Culture, Washington, D.C., Taft MSS, Box 506, 1950 Formosa/China file.

78. Bolton, "The Strategy and Tactics of World Communism," supplement III, 1948, Taft MSS, Box 617, foreign policy 1949 file 3 of 4.

79. Kohlberg to Jessup, December 8, 1949, Luce MSS, Box 182, Kl-Kohlberg file; Kohlberg press release, September 17, 1951, Luce MSS, Box 187, 1951 Kohlberg file.

80. Nixon statement at California GOP candidates' meetings, April-June 1950, RN yl, PPS 208 (1950): 8.

81. McCarran release, April 17, 1949, McCarran MSS, Box 48, China aid 1949 file.

82. Kohlberg, "The Road to Peace," February 21, 1950, Luce MSS, Box 182, Kl-Kohlberg file.

83. The main proponent of the decline of bipartisanship view is David Kepley, *Collapse of the Middle Way: Senate Republicans and the Bipartisan Foreign Policy, 1948–1952* (New York: Greenwood Press, 1988). A good discussion of the ways in which a Cold War consensus smothered left political discourse after 1945 is provided in Christopher Lasch, *The Agony of the American Left* (Harmondsworth: Penguin, 1973): chapter 3.

84. JFK speech, Salem, MA, January 30, 1949, JFK MSS, Box 95, China file; JFK speech to the Miami Chamber of Commerce, October 18, 1949.

85. Douglas on radio broadcast "Meet Your Congress," December 31, 1950, Knowland MSS, Box 247, Paul Douglas file.

86. Douglas, *In the Fullness of Time: The Memoirs of Paul H. Douglas* (Boston: Harcourt, Brace, Jovanovich, 1971), 493.

87. "American Forum of the Air" broadcast with Taylor and Knowland, August 15, 1949, Knowland MSS, Box 299, August, 1949 speeches file.

88. Israel Epstein, "Return to New China," *People's China*, October 16, 1951, reproduced by the American China Policy Association, December 5, 1951, Luce MSS, Box 187, Kohlberg file.

89. Malone press release, August 30, 1950, Knowland MSS, Box 260, correspondence M file.

90. Lemke speech in House, April 27, 1950, Anderson MSS, Box 1044, Brannan plan publicity file. Lemke interestingly linked in his critique to the administration's agricultural policy, arguing that the American federal state was deliberately tailoring one to the other.

91. *Congressional Record*, vol. 96, 81st Congress, 2nd Session, April 25, 1950, 6129, 6478. The eight dissenters, seven Republicans and one Democrat, were Henry Dworshak (R-Idaho), William Jenner (R-Indiana), Olin Johnston (D-South Carolina), James Kem (R-Missouri), George Malone (R-Nevada), Kenneth Wherry (R-Nebraska), John Williams (R-Delaware), and Milton Young (R-North Dakota). Harry Byrd (D-Virginia), William Langer (R-North Dakota), and Homer Capehart (R-Indiana) indicated their opposition in absentia.

92. Hazlitt, "The Illusions of Point IV," June 1950, Taft MSS, Box 750, Point IV file.

93. *Amarillo Daily News* editorial, June 4, 1949, Connally MSS, Box 229, NATO file 1 of 2.

94. Acheson broadcast on CBS, March 18, 1949, Connally MSS, ibid. Spain was excluded from NATO in an attempt to shield the organization from charges of double standards in its defense of democracy, although the Truman administration did permit an unofficial Spanish plenipotentiary, Jose Lequerica, to reside in Washington, prompting regular attacks from liberals like Wallace and Ickes. See, for example, Ickes to Truman, January 4 and January 22, 1951, Ickes MSS, Box 90, Truman file 3 of 3. In 1951 the United States recognized the Franco regime formally and accepted Lequerica as its ambassador, a man Ickes referred to as "that poisonous little reptile" and "a passionate enemy of democracy."

95. Department of State, "Collective Security in the North Atlantic Area," *Foreign Affairs Outlines: Building the Peace*, Spring 1949, no. 19, Connally MSS, Box 229, NATO file 1 of 2.

96. Taft notes on NATO, undated, Taft MSS, Box 617, foreign policy 1949 file 4 of 4. Donnell's contribution to the debate is neatly summarized and documented by Bernard Lemelin, "From Internationalism to Neo-Isolationism: Senator Forrest Donnell of Missouri and American Foreign Policy," *The Society for Historians of American Foreign Relations Newsletter*, vol. 29, no. 4, December 1998.

97. Transcript of Watkins's Senate speech, June 1, 1949, Taft MSS, Box 617, foreign policy 1949 file 4 of 4.

98. For a useful discussion of the 1919–20 debate, see Lloyd Ambrosius, *Woodrow Wilson and the American Diplomatic Tradition: The Treaty Fight in Perspective* (Cambridge: Cambridge University Press, 1987).

99. *Congressional Record*, vol. 95, 81st Congress, 1st Session, July 20, 1949, 9786.

100. RNC Report, "Notes on the North Atlantic Treaty," April 1949, Taft MSS, Box 617, foreign policy 1949 file 1 of 4; *Congressional Record*, July 21, 1949, 9880.

101. *New York Times*, July 13, 1949, "Mr. Taft and the Pact."

102. Taft notes on NATO, Taft MSS, Box 617, file 4 of 4; Wallace to Taft, July 5, 1949, Taft MSS, Box 617, file 3 of 4.

103. RNC Report, "Notes on North Atlantic Treaty," April 1949, Taft MSS, Box 617, file 1 of 4.

104. Cox to Tom Connally, July 6, 1949, Connally MSS, Box 229, North Atlantic Pact file 1 of2.

105. The eleven were Guy Cordon (Oregon), Forrest Donnell (Missouri), Ralph Flanders (Vermont), William Jenner (Indiana), James Kem (Missouri), William Langer (North Dakota), George Malone (Nevada), Robert Taft (Ohio), Arthur Watkins (Utah), Kenneth Wherry (Nebraska), and Milton Young (North Dakota). The development of Cold War strategy toward a more wide-ranging commitment to repulse Soviet expansion is significant, and is attested to by the fact that Flanders and Watkins had never voted against foreign policy measures before, and Taft, Cordon and Young rarely did so.

106. Aaron Friedberg, *In the Shadow of the Garrison State: America's Anti-Statism and Its Cold War Grand Strategy* (Princeton: Princeton University Press, 2000): 107–108.

107. *Congressional Record*, vol. 96, 81st Congress, 2nd Session, June 26, 1950, 9155, 9158.

108. Douglas, *In the Fullness of Time*, chapter 31.

109. Pepper Senate speech, August 31, 1950, Holland MSS, Pepper Library, 812/76.

110. Pepper primary campaign leaflet 1950, Pepper MSS, 204B/2/6A.

111. *Congressional Record*, June 26, 1950, 9186–9188.

112. Taft speeches on Korea, June 28 and July 24, 1950, Taft MSS, Box 670, Korea file 1 of 3.

113. See Bonner Fellers, GOP National Committeeman and ex-Army General, article "We Need a New Strategy—Now," sent to Taft, July 25, 1950, Taft MSS, Box 670, Korea file 2 of 3.

114. Smith interview on ABC, July 1, 1950, Taft MSS, Box 670, Korea file 1 of 3.

115. Taft to Ickes, August 1, 1950, Ickes MSS, Box 86, Taft 1948–51 file.

116. Ickes to Taft, July 28, 1950 and August 9, 1950, Ickes MSS, Box 86, ibid; Acheson speech at the National Press Club, Washington, D.C., January 12, 1950, Taft MSS, Box 670, Korea file 1 of 3.

117. Nixon, Washington Report, January 25, 1950, RN yl, PPS 208 (1950): 1. Nixon stated that the "time when we can approve foreign aid expenditures for humanitarian reasons alone, no matter how laudable, is gone."

118. Truman to Harold Ickes, Ickes MSS, Box 90, Truman 1948–51 file 2 of 3.

119. See Richard Freeland, *The Truman Doctrine and the Origins of McCarthyism: Foreign Policy, Domestic Politics, and Internal Security, 1946-1948* (New York: Knopf, 1972), *passim*; Athan Theoharis, *Seeds of Repression: Harry S Truman and the Origins of McCarthyism* (New York: Quadrangle, 1971); Ellen Schrecker, *Many Are the Crimes: McCarthyism in America* (Princeton: Princeton University Press, 1998).

120. Nixon "Americanism" Rally at Ocean Park, California, November 1, 1950, RN yl, PPS 3/1019.

121. Keefe speech in Congress, April 6, 1939, quoted in unattributed document, "Communists and Russophiles in US Labor Unions and Government, 1933–1949," Taft MSS, Box 618, foreign policy 1949 file 1 of 2.

122. McCarthy address to the Republican State Convention, Milwaukee, June 9, 1950, Tydings MSS, series V, Box 7, file 5, McCarthy speeches 1950.

123. Malone press release, October 17, 1951; ibid., April 10, 1951, Knowland MSS, Box 260, Correspondence M file. See also Malone's speech to the Western States GOP Conference in Seattle, October 15, 1951, in ibid., where he associates anti-Americanism with New Deal economic and trade policies.

124. *Congressional Record* reprint, February 21, 1950, 2151, Knowland MSS, Box 90, file 6.

125. Hoover interview "How Communists Operate," *US News and World Report* (August 11, 1950), Celler MSS, Box 20, Internal Security printed material file.

126. McGrath speech to the Advertising Club of New York, April 19, 1950, Celler MSS, Box 20, HUAC printed material file.

127. Liberal bloc memo, October 1, 1950; Philip Levy to Bill Benton, October 4, 1950; John Howe to Bill Morgenstern, September 29, 1950, Benton MSS, Box 318, folder 3.

128. Internal Security Act 1950, McCarran MSS, Box 50, ISA file 2.

129. Benton to Truman, September 27, 1950, Benton MSS, Box 280, folder 8; Truman veto of the Internal Security Act, *New York Times*, September 23, 1950.

130. James Farmer to McCarran, May 7, 1949; R.F. Schilling to McCarran, May 22, 1949, McCarran MSS, Box 49, Communism file; James Farmer to McCarran, June 21, 1950, McCarran MSS, Box 51, ISA 1950 file.

131. Henry Allen to McCarran, November 29, 1950, McCarran MSS, Box 51, ibid.

132. Truman message to Congress, September 22, 1950, McCarran MSS, Box 50, ISA file 1 of 2.

6. The American State on Trial

1. Richard Nixon speech for candidates' meetings before the California Senate primaries, Spring 1950, RN yl, PPS 208 (1950): 8.

2. Douglas broadcast over ABC California, September 6, 1950, RN yl, PPS 3/41.

3. Douglas repeatedly attacked Downey in a series of letters and telegrams to him on subjects ranging from the California Central Valley irrigation project to Social Security. See Douglas to Downey, December 16, 1949 and January 31, 1950, Downey MSS, Bancroft Library, UC Berkeley, Box 2, Helen Douglas file. In the January letter she accused Downey of wanting to restrict old age benefits to the very poor. Downey stood down because of ill health before the June primary and threw his support behind Douglas's main Democratic rival, Manchester Boddy.

4. See Helen Gahagan Douglas, *A Full Life* (Garden City, NY: Doubleday, 1982), 160–61, 224.

5. An excellent overview of postwar California politics, including political sketches of Malone, Unruh and the like, can be found in John Jacobs, *A Rage for Justice: The Passion and Politics of Phillip Burton* (Berkeley: University of California Press, 1995): chapter 2.

6. Helen Douglas, *A Full Life*, 296.

7. Fulton Lewis broadcast, October 3, 1949, RN yl, PPS 3/122. For the text of Raymond Darby's speech for the GOP nomination, see his Inglewood speech, June 8, 1949, RN yl PPS 3/97 and his platform, PPS 3/113a. He followed much more closely

the policy-based line common in 1946 than Nixon, but lost all the primaries in 1950, failing to carry a single county. Nixon carried all counties except Sacramento, Contra Costa, and Fresno, which, interestingly, were pro-Douglas areas. Until 1959 all candidates in California could file in all party primaries, and occasionally won both main party candidacies. Governor Warren achieved this in 1946; Senator Knowland did so in 1952.

8. Nixon to Bill Brennan, LA GOP organizer, October 7, 1949, RN yl PPS 3/130; Nixon circular to California local GOP organizations, October 21, 1949, RN yl, PPS 3/153.1.

9. Nixon announcement of his candidacy for the U.S. Senate at Pomona, California, November 3, 1949, RN yl, PPS 3/66.

10. Chotiner to Hillings, November 8, 1949, RN yl, PPS 3/184.

11. Nixon statewide broadcast from San Diego, October 30, 1950, RN yl, PPS 208(1950).37.

12. RN yl, PPS 3/74. The votes on which Douglas and Marcantonio had agreed included aid to Greece and Turkey, a free press amendment to UNRRA in 1945, and an amendment to UNRRA refusing relief to Communist countries unless supervised by the United States.

13. See Nixon speeches "Response to Douglas' Charges," October-November 1950, RN yl, PPS 208 (1950): 40 and 41; Douglas campaign leaflet "Nixon's Big Lie in California," PPS 3/3.

14. Helen Douglas, *A Full Life*, 313; Douglas speech to International Oil Workers National Convention, Long Beach, August 18, 1950, RN yl, PPS 3/38.

15. 1950 GOP Campaign manual, RN yl, PPS 3/86 (copy 1).

16. GOP release, "Voters Should Study Voting Record of Helen Gahagan Douglas," RN yl, PPS 3/58.

17. Nixon radio speech script, RN yl, PPS 208(1950).44.

18. *Alhambra Post Advocate*, September 8, 1950; RN yl, PPS 3/70.

19. See all material in RN yl, PPS 3/14—20.

20. Lonigan, domestic policy record, RN yl, PPS 3/24–25.

21. Lonigan to Nixon, July 25, 1950, RN yl, PPS 3/30; Nixon to Brennan, September 2, 1950, PPS 3/31. The references included possible praise of Douglas at a Communist Political Association Meeting in San Francisco or Oakland in 1944, and her associations with the Civil Rights Congress.

22. Nixon speech at Ventura, April 21, 1950, RN yl, PPS 3/944.

23. See James Reston in the *New York Times*, November 2, 1950, in an article entitled "Intellectual Left Silent in Campaign," 23. Reston noted that most leftists were "strangely quiet in this election," and that the "trend is more noticeable in California than anywhere else, partly because [Douglas and Roosevelt] are under severe attack as left-wingers." He gave an example of a Hollywood dinner for Douglas, to

which barely twenty of the seventy-odd invited turned up; "the excuses given by the others were . . . somewhat feeble."

24. Helen Douglas, *A Full Life*, 301.

25. Douglas speech over KMPC radio, October 9, 1950, RN yl, PPS 3/44.

26. See Douglas-Ickes correspondence throughout 1950, Ickes MSS, Box 55, Helen Douglas file, *passim*. See also Clinton Anderson's article for *Democratic Digest*, August, 1950, "Let's Look At the 1950 Senate Elections," Anderson MSS, Box 1050, Article 1950 file. Ickes made good on his promise to help Douglas, openly supporting her in his *New Republic* column and indirectly appealing to his readers for donations to her campaign. See *New Republic*, October 16, 1950, 18.

27. Manchester Boddy, "The Struggle for Security Dominates All Forms of Life," *Los Angeles Daily News*, April 7, 1950, Anderson MSS, Box 1052, California file.

28. Creel speech, unattributed, Rn yl, PPS 3/1015.2. The alleged Communist organizations included the Civil Rights Congress, the Win the Peace Conference, and the Joint Anti-Fascist Refugee Committee. The list was exactly the same as that used against Claude Pepper in Florida the same year. Indeed, Karl Mundt, campaigning in South Dakota for his colleague Francis Case in 1950, used the Pepper pamphlet, and sent it to Nixon for use in California. The association of proponents of state solutions to social problems with totalitarianism was extremely popular in 1950, and represented a marked intensification of this type of campaign. See Mundt to Nixon, May 8, 1950, RN yl, PPS 3/471.

29. *Los Angeles Sentinel*, October 5, 1950, RN yl, PPS 3/535A. The Nixon campaign used this editorial as campaign material in African American communities across the State.

30. *Los Angeles Sentinel*, August 31, 1950; October 5, 1950; October 12, 1950.

31. 1950 Senatorial Election in California results tally and analysis, RN yl, PPS 3/1069–1071. Clearly Douglas's lack of funds or wider party support had also taken their toll, but most analyses inevitably focus on popular antipathy toward liberalism in the context of rising anti-communist sentiment. Few analyses attempt to probe the nature or causes of anti-liberal feeling. Irwin Gellman sees anti-New Deal opinion as existing independently of images presented to the electorate in the campaign and political policy pronouncements, and thus links, as Nixon did, anti-communism to anti-liberalism. See Gellman, *The Contender: Richard Nixon—The Congress Years, 1946–1952* (New York: The Free Press, 1999): chapters 14–16. See Greg Mitchell, *Tricky Dick and the Pink Lady: Richard Nixon versus Helen Gahagan Douglas—Sexual Politics and the Red Scare, 1950* (New York: Random House, 1998) for an alternative view that stresses the campaign strategy as a cause of the large Nixon victory.

32. Helen Douglas, *A Full Life*, 334; Moley analysis, *Newsweek*, August 28, 1950; Knowland MSS, Box 90, file 6. So unpopular was Douglas by 1951 thanks to the ide-

ological nature of the Republicans campaign that the possibility of her being appointed to the United Nations caused a huge popular outpouring of vitriol against her. An enormous selection can be found in Knowland MSS, Box 247, Helen Douglas file. One correspondent told Knowland that Douglas had "been on the side of the forces which are trying to destroy what has given us the life we cherish." The writer adds in the same letter that he opposes "all the so-called 'social welfare' schemes of Mr. Truman." Anti-statism and the association of communism with liberalism were closely related: The Bennett family to Knowland, January 17, 1951, in ibid.

33. See James Patterson, *Congressional Conservatism and the New Deal: The Growth of the Conservative Coalition in Congress, 1933–1939* (Lexington: University of Kentucky Press, 1967), esp. 280–281; Caroline Keith, *For Hell and a Brown Mule: The Biography of Millard E. Tydings* (Lanham, MD: Madison Books, 1991).

34. Tydings speech to Congress, April 2, 1935, Tydings MSS, Series II, subseries 1, box 2, speeches on economic recovery 1933–40 file.

35. Tydings radio broadcast, WBAL Baltimore, April 20, 1947, Tydings MSS, Box 7, April file.

36. Tydings Subcommittee of the Armed Services Committee Report on McCarthy's Charges and Lodge and Hickenlooper's minority report in Lodge MSS, Speeches, microfilm reel 5.

37. Fulton Lewis broadcasts May 24 and April 25, 1950, Tydings MSS, Series V, Box 7, file 2.

38. "Be For Butler" leaflet, Tydings MSS, Series III, Subseries 2, Box 5, John Marshall Butler file.

39. Butler GOP primary platform, Tydings MSS, ibid.; Butler speech at Savage Community Hall, Maryland, October 17, 1950, *Baltimore News-Post*, October 17, 1950, John Marshall Butler Scrapbooks, Maryland Historical Society, Baltimore, Maryland, vol. 1, 1950.

40. Tydings and Fallon material in Tydings MSS, Series III, subseries 2, Box 9, 1950 primary material file.

41. Davey Lewis leaflet, "The Life and Times of 'Milord' Tydings," Tydings MSS, III, 1, Box 3, campaign material file.

42. Butler campaign leaflet, Tydings MSS, III, 2, Box 5, John Marshall Butler file.

43. See Robert Griffith, *The Politics of Fear: Joseph R. McCarthy and the Senate* (Lexington: University Press of Kentucky, 1970), 127–128.

44. Tydings campaign questionnaire sent out to all county Democratic organizations, Tydings MSS, III, 2, Box 5, campaign questionnaire file.

45. Much of the correspondence is anonymous, all follows similar lines. See Tydings MSS, V, Box 3, file 10—Lewis broadcasts correspondence October 12–20, 1950.

46. *The Reporter*, June 6, 1950, Tydings MSS, V, Box 5, file 6.

47. Republican National Committee, Research Division, Report, "The 1950 Elections—A Statistical Analysis," Knowland MSS, Box 90, file 6.

48. Results listed in full in Tydings MSS, III, 2, Box 12.

49. Report of the Senate Subcommittee of Privileges and Elections on the Maryland Senatorial Election of 1950, August 3, 1951, Knowland MSS, Box 242, Hugh Butler file.

50. Vic Johnson memo, "The Political Situation in Utah," April 1, 1950, Taft MSS, Box 539, 81st Congress 1950 file.

51. The *New Republic*, October 2, 1950, 15–16, referred to the AMA campaign as "the largest and loudest campaign ever prepared by a professional organization," and alleged that its cost, combined with various tie-in ads from corporations and business groups, totaled over $20 million. These funds could provide one year's medical costs for over 160,000 families earning less than $3000.

52. *Editor and Publisher*, August 26, 1950; Dingell speech to the House, September 14, 1950, *Congressional Record* reprint, JFK MSS, Box 95, Democratic Party speeches file.

53. *Washington Post*, November 4, 1950, 9.

54. Philip Levy to Bill Benton, September 6, 1950, Benton MSS, Box 318, folder 5; Benton to Joe Kusaila and John Howe, September 5, 1950; Levy to Benton, October 12, 1950, Benton MSS, Box 318, folder 1.

55. *New York Times*, October 15, 1950, section IV, 6.

56. Dirksen speech, undated, Knowland MSS, Box 247, Dirksen file.

57. Prescott Bush radio interview for the 1950 campaign, October 13, 1950, Benton MSS, Box 318, folder 7.

58. It is vital to recognize that anti-radicalism pervaded national discourse in 1950 in ways that it had not five years before. For example, media coverage of an anti-Korean War demonstration in New York in August, 1950 actively sought to discredit the demonstrators as "left-wingers" who staged "a noisy riot" in order to secure "peace strictly on Russia's terms." When discussing the aims of the demonstrators, who were in any case numerically insignificant, even a British newsreader's voice dripped with sarcasm. See Gaumont-British News, library number 1732, August 10, 1950, on *The Origins of the Cold War, 1945–1950* (CD Rom, 1999), by the Inter-University History Film Consortium and the British Universities Film and Video Council, newsreel 8: War in Korea.

59. Illinois Democratic State Central Committee release, "Dirksen vs. Dirksen on National Defense and Foreign Affairs," Anderson MSS, Box 1052, Illinois file.

60. Dirksen Champaign speech, Knowland MSS, Box 247, Dirksen file.

61. Benton draft speech, nd; Benton to Joe Kusaila, October 10, 1950, Benton MSS, Box 318, folder 9.

62. J. J. Perling to Anderson, August 21, 1950, Anderson MSS, Box 1050, Senate

Campaign Committee material 1950 file; Perling memo "Who Heartened the Kremlin?," August 21, 1950, ibid., Isolationist bloc file; Democratic Pamphlet "Debunking the Republican Manifesto," in ibid., "Debunking the Republican Manifesto" file; "An isolationist Congress . . . " in "On the Record With Frank Carlson," in ibid., "On the Record With Frank Carlson" file. All underlining is in the original text.

63. See Anderson MSS, Box 1050, "Who Voted to Strengthen the Free World" file.

64. Anderson, "Let's Look At the 1950 Senate Elections," in *Democratic Digest*, August, 1950, 13–16, Anderson MSS, Box 1050, *Democratic Digest* file.

65. *Washington Post*, October 29, 1950, 13. The journalist used the term "pure political poison" in referring to the Senate campaign in Indiana, where Democrat Alexander Campbell disowned his prior commitment to health insurance and against the Internal Security Act in his attempt to unseat Republican Senator Homer Capehart. See also *New York Times*, October 21, 1950, 7: "Doctors Alerted for Nebraska Poll," which details AMA and Republican attempts to unseat Democrat Eugene O'Sullivan in Omaha using "appeals in patients' bills" and "appeals on food trays." See also ibid., November 4, 1950, 9, for a discussion of similar tactics in Colorado. In all cases the GOP was successful, and suggests that the anti-statist campaign in 1950 was carefully targeted in key constituencies where liberals were vulnerable.

66. McCormack to Anderson, September 15, 1950, Anderson MSS, Box 1052, New Hampshire file. McCormack referred to Tobey as "Lahey," a mistake he corrected in another letter dated September 18, 1950.

67. *New Hampshire Morning Union*, August, 19, 1950, Anderson MSS, Box 1052, ibid.

68. *Newport Guardian*, "As We See the N.H. Senate Race," Anderson MSS, ibid.

69. See *New York Times*, September 13, 1950 and October 14, 1950, 9.

70. Jacob Javits, *Javits: The Autobiography of a Public Man* (Boston: Houghton Mifflin, 1981), 153.

71. Moley, "Republican Advance and the ADA," *Newsweek*, July 31, 1950, Knowland MSS, Box 90, file1.

72. *New York Times*, March 5, 1950, 10. See also Lodge's article "Modernize the GOP: Specifications for a Republican Program," in *Atlantic Monthly*, March 1950, Lodge MSS, speeches microfilm reel 5. Lodge specifically rules out a radical program, arguing that "in the field of social legislation we must not try to outbid the Democrats" and that the GOP "should inaugurate a form of tax reduction which will encourage the growth of new economic activity."

73. Benton radio talk number 3, Benton MSS, Box 319, folder 1.

74. Javits statement to the New York Young Republican Club, January 12, 1950; statement of Javits and Clifford Case (R-New Jersey) on a GOP health plan, May 31,

1949, Javits MSS, 1/1/2; Javits testimony to the House Committee on Education and Labor on FEPC, May 12, 1949, Javits MSS, 1/1/1. FEPC formed an important component of federal and state-level political activity in the late 1940s. See Timothy Thurber, *The Politics of Equality: Hubert H Humphrey and the African American Freedom Struggle* (New York: Columbia University Press, 1999).

75. See Margaret Chase Smith with William Lewis Jr., *Declaration of Conscience* (Garden City, NY: Doubleday, 1972).

76. Jacob Javits to Richard Landau, editor of the *Young Liberal Digest*, August 12, 1950, Javits MSS, 8/2/3.

77. UAW-CIO leaflet, "Taft Wants Taxes on YOU Not Big Business," Taft MSS, Box 280, CIO-PAC 1949–1950 file; *Ohio Monthly Review* (April-May 1950): 2, Taft MSS, Box 318, elections file 4.

78. "The Taft Record," Taft MSS, Box 303, Ferguson literature file.

79. Cartoon "Doughboys!," in ibid.

80. H. R. Leonard to the President's Secretary, December 7, 1949; Clinton Anderson to Leonard, February 7, 1950, Anderson MSS, Box 1052, Ohio file.

81. UAW-CIO leaflet "Taft Plays Commie Game," Taft MSS, Box 280, CIO-PAC file; "The Taft Record," Taft MSS, Box 303, Ferguson file.

82. Citizens' Committee for Ferguson, "Independent Comment," 3, Taft MSS, Box 303, ibid.

83. See Mike Davis, *Prisoners of the American Dream: Politics and Economy in the History of the US Working Class* (London: Verso, 1986): 88–93. Davis argues that the CIO became "an integral component of the administration's escalating anticommunist crusade," with a detrimental impact on labor radicalism. See also Taylor Dark, *The Unions and the Democrats: An Enduring Alliance* (Ithaca: Cornell University Press, 1999).

84. "Light, Not Heat, on the British Health Plan," *CIO News*, March 13, 1950, 10, Taft MSS, Box 303, *CIO News* file 2 of 2.

85. Speech "The Party of American Principles," undated, Taft MSS, Box 310, file 7; campaign material draft 1950, Taft MSS, Box 310, file 12.

86. "Answer to Another PAC Lie—Who Raised the Minimum Wage to 75¢ Per Hour?," Taft MSS, Box 303, 1950 campaign investigation materials file; Taft radio broadcast, Station WLW Cincinnati, November 4, 1950, Taft MSS, Box 278, WLW broadcast file.

87. See *New York Times*, August 13, 1950 and *News and Views of Today's World*, May 28, 1950. *The Buckeye Labor News*, published by the Labor League for Taft, carried headlines like "Record Proves Taft is Labor's Best Friend," Taft MSS, Box 278, *Buckeye Labor News* 1949 file.

88. Taft MSS, Box 275, files 3 and 2. James Maxwell, observing the Taft campaign, noted that the "various sections of the body politic are as carefully compartmentalized

as . . . in a well-run consumer survey." Taft was able to use the media to portray himself as the people's friend, whereas Ferguson set out "pre-adolescent ideas delivered in the style of someone who has only recently mastered the rudiments of the language." See *New Republic* (October 23, 1950): 10–12. Historians tend to agree that Taft's campaign was more effective than Ferguson's: see James Patterson, *Mr. Republican: A Biography of Robert A. Taft* (Boston: Houghton Mifflin, 1972): chapter 30.

89. *Labor World,* September 1950; *Labor Digest,* September 1950, Taft MSS, Box 275, file 1. Former New Dealer Donald Richberg was one of many others to express this view in the torrid anti-leftist environment of 1950. See *New York Times,* October 29, 1950, 63: "Socialism trend seen by Richberg."

90. "Taft-Hartley Act Wins Union Membership Okay—Rank and File Like It!" Taft release, Taft MSS, Box 307, labor 1950 file.

91. Winifred Cody to Taft, September 5, 1949, Taft MSS, Box 304, ibid.

92. Taft broadcast, November 4, 1950, Taft MSS, Box 278, WLW broadcast file.

93. Taft to Rebecca Shriver, December 24, 1949, Taft MSS, Box 912, social legislation 1949 file.

94. *Labor Digest* special edition, "Truman and His Fair Deal Administration," Taft MSS, Box 275, file 5.

95. Taft to Ernest Ach, April 8, 1950, Taft MSS, Box 917, foreign policy file.

96. Taft speech at Dayton, September 13, 1950, Taft MSS, Box 309, file 5—National Defense.

97. Article for the International Relations Club, Bryn Mawr College, April 29, 1950, Taft MSS, Box 292, campaign miscellaneous file 6.

98. Taft to Herbert Hoover, November 21, 1950, Taft MSS, Box 920, political Republican file 2 of 4.

99. See vote tallies and statistics in Taft MSS, Box 318, file 1.

100. Taft campaign circular, "The Job We're Trying to Do," Taft MSS, Box 318, ibid.; Memorandum from the Opinion Poll Research Corp. of NY, November 9, 1950, Taft MSS, Box 920, political file 2 of 4.

101. Taft to Arthur Vandenberg, November 11, 1950, Taft MSS, Box 921, Senators 1950 file.

102. Taft to John Bricker, November 24, 1950, Taft MSS, Box 921, ibid.

103. This was certainly the view of the national press at the time. See the *New York Times,* (October 23, 1950): 19; (October 29, 1950), IV, 7. The *Times* argued that "dyed-in-the-wool Democrats" opposed Ferguson because "if Ferguson were victorious, labor leaders might try to take over the party" in a socialist coup. The *New Republic* shared this view. See *New Republic* (November 20, 1950): 8. Despite this, journalists were still astounded at the size of the Taft victory.

104. Claude Pepper diary, January 12, 1950, Pepper MSS, S439/2/6; George

Smathers speech at the Orange Bowl, Orlando, January 12, 1950, Smathers MSS, box 110, general political file.

105. Smathers speech, ibid.; Pepper speech in *Miami Herald*, March 31, 1950, Pepper MSS, 204B/1/15. An example of a Republican anti-statist definition of liberalism is Robert Taft's radio broadcast in Cincinnati on November 4, 1950, shortly before the general election, in which he attacked big government, calling it "the fundamental issue of liberty against socialism." See Taft MSS, , Box 278, radio broadcast Nov. 4, 1950 file.

106. Truman to Sheridan Downey, May 23, 1946, Downey MSS, Box 4, Townsend file.

107. George Smathers Oral History, interview with Donald Ritchie, Senate Historical Office, Washington, D.C., 1989, 25. The hostility seems to have been mutual, at least before Truman's left-turn in the 1948 election and thereafter. See Pepper diary, May 27, 1946, Pepper MSS, S439/2/3, in which he wrote that Truman "is so utterly off track and has a certain regrettable vindictiveness about him."

108. See Pepper diary, January 5, 1949, Pepper MSS, S439/2/5A, in which he wrote that Truman's State of the Union address in the wake of his 1948 victory was a "magnificent message. More for more people than any previous message. . . . I applauded constantly."

109. Smathers Oral History, 27. See Tracy Danese, *Claude Pepper and Ed Ball: Politics, Purpose, and Power* (Gainesville: University Press of Florida, 2000), chapter 9, for the standard argument that Pepper's foreign policy positions defeated him in 1950.

110. Text of Elmer Davis broadcast, April 29, 1950, Pepper MSS, 201/123/21.

111. *Jacksonville Journal*, editorial, nd, Pepper MSS, 204A/45/1.

112. *Tampa Sunday Tribune*, April 7, 1950, Pepper MSS, 204G/1/14A.

113. Memo to Smathers "Welfare and Statism," nd, Smathers MSS, Box 110, untitled folder.

114. Figures supplied in the Committee for the Nation's Health bulletin, May 21, 1951, Pepper MSS, 201/93/1. Some of this anti-health insurance propaganda, according to this bulletin, "showed up regularly in bills sent to patients by their private doctors." See also *New York Times*, October 21, 1950, 7: "Doctors Alerted for Nebraska Poll," which details AMA and Republican attempts to unseat Democrat Eugene O'Sullivan in Omaha using "appeals in patients' bills" and "appeals on food trays." See also ibid., November 4, 1950, 9, for a discussion of similar tactics in Colorado. In all cases the GOP was successful, and suggests that the anti-statist campaign in 1950 was carefully targeted in key constituencies where liberals were vulnerable.

115. Louis Orr to Dr Arthur Schwartz of Beverly Hills, CA, April 10, 1950, Pepper MSS, 201/93/1. This letter is one of a number in this file sent to Pepper by physicians

sympathetic to his cause and appalled by the AMA tactics. There would be many more whom Pepper would not be aware of.

116. American Forum of the Air, January 29, 1950, "Do We Want National Health Insurance in the United States?," Pepper MSS, 203B/1/21.

117. Cartoon "Cleaning Out the Underbrush," for publication in the *Jacksonville Times*, Anderson MSS, Box 1052, Florida file. The use of foreign caricatures to undermine leftists was extremely common in the 1950 elections. In North Carolina, for example, the "Know the Truth Committee" for Willis Smith's campaign used a cartoon depicting Frank Graham as a supporter of British socialism, driving down a highway on the wrong side of the road (the left), and explaining to a patrolman that he had learned the habit "in Socialist England, where I studied." See Pleasants and Burns, *Frank Porter Graham and the 1950 Senate Race in North Carolina* (Chapel Hill: University of North Carolina Press, 1990), 134.

118. Smathers advertisement in the Florida press, 1950, Anderson MSS, Box 1052, Florida file. Smathers is portrayed in photographs as displaying particularly "American" traits, named as "Outstanding Young Man of Miami" in 1940 and a successful lawyer and U.S. attorney. The assertion was that he was self-made, while Pepper was a creature of the state.

119. CIO memo in Anderson MSS, Box 1051, general material file. The *New Republic* took a similar line, arguing after the primary that Pepper was "done in by a ganging-up of the conservative, anti-Pepper Democrats of his state with big money Republicans from the north." See "The Lesson of the Primaries," *New Republic*, May 15, 1950, 5–6.

120. Statement of the Florida Medical Committee for Better Government, May 1950, Taft MSS, Box 294, file 6.

121. *Challenge to Socialism*, March 30, 1950, Taft MSS, Box 800, social security file 3 of 4.

122. Felix Morley, "The Lesson of the Primaries," *Barron*'s magazine, June 19, 1950; R. C. Way to Taft, March 8, 1950, Taft MSS, Box 920, Political Republican file 1 of 4.

123. Reece speech on his decision to stand for Congress in Tennessee, May 20, 1950, Taft MSS, Box 920, ibid.

124. Wesley E. Garrison to Taft, March 3, 1950, Taft MSS, Box 920, Political Republican file 3 of 4.

125. Tracy Danese dates the emergence of a significant role for the GOP in Florida politics to 1958. See Danese, *Claude Pepper and Ed Ball*, 227.

126. Joseph S. Bair Jr. to Young GOP members, nd, Pepper MSS, 204A/48/2.

127. *Dayton Journal-Herald*, March 15, 1950, Pepper MSS, 204G/1/12. The writer, Dwight Young, was the publisher of the newspaper.

128. Lloyd C. Loomis, "The Red Record of Senator Claude Pepper," RN yl, PPS 3/21.

129. Karl Mundt to Nixon, May 8, 1950, RN yl, PPS 3/471.

130. "Is Senator Pepper a Communist?," Pepper MSS, 204G/2/7.

131. *Haines City Herald*, February 2, 1950, Pepper MSS, 204E/8/6.

132. Ickes to J. Parnell Thomas, June 27, 1947, Ickes MSS, Box 90, HUAC file.

133. Smathers Oral History, 27; 36–37. Infamous stories abound of Smathers having appealed to social conservative biases in Florida by stating that Pepper's sister was a "thespian" and that Pepper "practiced celibacy." Smathers denies these stories, and argues that both he and Pepper were equally committed to civil rights.

134. Interestingly, the Soviet newspaper *Izvestia* used the Florida case as well as several others in 1950 with which to launch an attack on American democracy as "a wild orgy" masterminded by racists and big business. See *New York Times*, October 30, 1950, 9.

135. *American Legion Magazine*, November 1950, Pepper MSS, 204E/4/5.

136. Flyer in Pepper MSS, 204A/48/4.

137. Sloan McRea, Dade county manager for Smathers, to Jim Clements, Pepper campaign organizer, nd, Pepper MSS, 204A/48/4, stating the ad was "a deliberate attempt [by Pepper] to influence the race through the placing of misleading advertising copy." Clements denied the allegation.

138. *St Petersburg Times*, January 26, 1950, Pepper MSS, 204A/48/1.

139. Claude Burnett to Pepper, June 20, 1949, Pepper MSS, 204A/37/11.

140. A. Campbell to Pepper, April 29, 1950, ibid.

141. See Alan Brinkley, *The End of Reform: New Deal Liberalism in Recession and War* (New York: Knopf, 1995); Numan Bartley, *The New South, 1945–1980* (Baton Rouge: Louisiana State University Press, 1995), 69–73. On page 69 Bartley argues that liberals' "concern for economic reform and for the redistribution of wealth abated as liberals identified national and international corporate expansion with the growth of democratic values."

142. Smathers speech to the New York Southern Society, December 1, 1950, Smathers MSS, Box 96, 1950 general file.

143. Smathers radio script #32, Smathers MSS, Box 110, speeches file.

144. Quotes taken from Smathers press releases and radio spots, Smathers MSS, Box 110, unmarked file.

145. McLellan Smith, of Washington DC, to Pepper, August 31, 1950, together with a whole file of vitriolic letters, in Pepper MSS, 201/133/9.

146. See Holland MSS, Box 362, socialized medicine files (January–February file, March file, April–December file).

147. Ross Beiler, "General Aspects of Campaign in Greater Miami as Revealed by Poll," March 7, 1950, Pepper MSS, 204A/50A/1.

148. Dade county primary results tabulation and precinct map, Spessard Holland MSS, Claude Pepper Library, Florida State University, Tallahassee, Florida, Box 806, folder 11.

149. Laurence Lee to Anderson, May 9, 1950, enclosing unattributed clipping on the results, Anderson MSS, Box 1052, Florida file.

150. *Florida Federationist*, February 9, 1950, Pepper MSS, 204E/8/6.

151. *Union Record*, March 1950; W. C. Belch to Pepper, March 29, 1950, Pepper MSS, 204A/32/25. There are a number of other pro-Pepper letters from union members in this file.

152. George Weaver to Jack Kroll, "Survey of Potential Negro Vote in Florida," June 24, 1949, Pepper MSS, 204A/11/37. See Tracy Danese, *Claude Pepper and Ed Ball*, chapter 8 for full details of divisions in labor support for Pepper, particularly in the railroad industry.

153. Jean Begeman, "Million Dollar Senators," *New Republic*, April 9, 1951, clipping in Paul Douglas MSS, Box 1233, election laws file.

154. Taft to G. Worth Agee, February 27, 1950, Taft MSS, Box 920, political file; B. Carroll Reece congressional nomination speech, May 20, 1950, Taft MSS, Box 920, political Republican file 1 of 4.

155. *Congressional Quarterly Weekly Report*, March 23, 1951, Paul Douglas MSS, Box 1233, 1950 Campaign file.

156. Helen Douglas, *A Full Life*, 328.

157. Jean Begeman, "Million Dollar Senators," *New Republic*, April 9, 1951, Douglas MSS, Box 1233, election laws file.

158. *Congressional Quarterly Weekly Report*, March 23, 1951, Douglas MSS, box 1233, 1950 campaign file.

159. Taylor radio address, 1950 campaign, undated, Anderson MSS, Box 1052, Idaho file.

160. Burtenshaw pre-primary advertisements, Anderson MSS, ibid.

161. Glen Taylor, *The Way It Was With Me* (Secaucus, NJ: Lyle Stuart Inc., 1979), 151.

162. Ibid., 197–198, 267.

163. Taylor radio address, 1950 general campaign, undated, Anderson MSS, Box 1052, Idaho file.

164. Burtenshaw speech at rally sponsored by Blaine county Democrats, published in the *Idaho Daily State Journal*, September 14, 1950, Anderson MSS, ibid.

165. Johnson, "The Political Situation in Idaho," Taft MSS, Box 539, 81st Congress 1950 file.

166. See correspondence and material in Celler MSS, Box 41, Havenner and Shelley file. The Celler papers also demonstrate how untenable Marcantonio's position had become in 1950; upon his death in 1954, Celler gave a eulogy, which resulted in a flood of condemnatory, often anti-Semitic, letters to Celler. See Celler MSS, Box 44, Marcantonio file.

167. Gus Tyler in the *New Republic* was not unusual in arguing that the odd

thing about the 1950 elections was "NOT the loss of seats by the Democratic Party but that the Democrats lost so *few* seats" in 1950. See Tyler, "The Mid-term Paradox," *New Republic*, November 27, 1950, 14–15. This analysis fails to note that the 1950 Republican campaign was carefully targeted in collaboration with private interest groups against key liberal Democrats such as health insurance sponsors Andrew Biemiller (D-Wisconsin), Elbert Thomas (D-Utah), John Carroll (D-Colorado), Helen Douglas (D-California), Scott Lucas (D-Illinois). Almost all those targeted were defeated, and Democrats who held their ground, such as in Massachusetts and New Jersey, were often lukewarm toward social reform. Only in New York did liberalism appear triumphant, with Herbert Lehman's reelection to the Senate.

168. Celler speech "The Strength of the Democratic Party," at a dinner honoring Senator Herbert Lehman (D-New York), New York, February 6, 1951, Celler MSS, Box 536, 82nd Congress file.

169. The editorial column in the *New York Times*, November 9, 1950, 32, endorses this view, arguing that the elections showed that the "Democratic 'Fair Deal' has met with a resounding check" and that there must be "a substitution of other methods of reform and progress for some of the particular methods which the President has chosen." The *New Republic* took a slightly different tone, arguing that a "lack of a central positive theme" meant that "individual Democrats fell before a unified Republican assault." See *New Republic* (November 20, 1950): 6–7.

170. See *Los Angeles Times* (March 30, 1950): 10. Francis Townsend sent the article to Sheridan Downey, expressing alarm at the rightward turn in the Democratic Party in 1950. See Townsend to Downey, March 30, 1950, Downey MSS, Box 4, Townsend file.

7. All Internationalists Now

1. See voting record for the 82nd Congress in Lodge MSS, Box 69, file 5, and Box 70. A full roll-call of all Congresses from the 80th to the 83rd is provided in Martin MSS, Box 88.

2. Taft to E. W. Jamieson, December 3, 1952, Taft MSS, Box 1185, social legislation file. Taft argued that he was "certainly not in favor of repealing the old age and survivors insurance, or the unemployment insurance laws. I do feel, however, that there are quite a number of bureaus which can be eliminated."

3. See Bruce Cumings, "Introduction: The Course of Korean-American Relations, 1943–1953" in Cumings, ed., *Child of Conflict: The Korean-American Relationship, 1943–1953* (Seattle: University of Washington Press, 1983), especially 32–38; Melvyn Leffler, *A Preponderance of Power: National Security, the Truman Administration, and the Cold War* (Stanford: Stanford University Press, 1992).

4. Aaron Friedberg, *In the Shadow of the Garrison State: America's Ant-Statism*

and Its Cold War Grand Strategy (Princeton: Princeton University Press, 2000), 115–118.

5. Paul Douglas Senate speech, January 15, 1951, Taft MSS, Box 490, 1950–51 file.

6. Paul Douglas, *Economy in the National Government* (Chicago: University of Chicago Press, 1952), 232.

7. JFK testimony before the Senate Foreign Relations Committee on the question of sending troops to Europe, February 22, 1951, JFK MSS, Box 95, Troops to Europe file.

8. Aaron Friedberg, *In the Shadow of the Garrison State,* 110.

9. Henry Cabot Lodge speech "We Are Not Divided," January 11, 1951, Taft MSS, Box 490, foreign policy 1950–51 file.

10. Taft in ibid.

11. Rogers speech, "The New American Foreign Policy," March 15, 1951, Rogers MSS, Box 9, folder 142.

12. See Lodge speech in Taft MSS, Box 490, foreign policy 1950–51 file.

13. Rogers speech, Rogers MSS, Box 9, folder 142.

14. See David Kepley, *Collapse of the Middle Way: Senate Republicans and the Bipartisan Policy, 1948–1952* (New York: Greenwood Press, 1988), 104–105.

15. Robert Taft, *A Foreign Policy for Americans* (Garden City, NY: Doubleday, 1951); Review by Lewis Galantiere in the *Saturday Review of Literature* (November 17, 1951): 13, Taft MSS, Box 945, Book reviews file.

16. Douglas speech, January 15, 1951, Taft MSS, Box 490, foreign policy 1950–51 file.

17. AIPO Poll, August 4, 1950, *Public Opinion Quarterly* (Winter 1950–51): 819. The remaining 7% of respondents had no opinion. In every poll reported in the *POQ* taken after 1948 asking Americans about the Soviet threat, over 60% of respondents argued that it was serious. In one startling example of public terror, 49% responded positively, and only 42% negatively, to the following question in March 1951: "Would you . . . be willing to risk your life, or have some member of your family risk his life, to keep the Russians from taking over western Europe?" See AIPO poll, March 18, 1951, *ibid.*, Summer 1951, 382.

18. Taft address to the Founders' Day Republican Banquet, Detroit, October 15, 1951, Taft MSS, Box 490, armed forces 1952 file 8.

19. Bruce Cumings, for example, makes the plausible contention that North Korea had its own reasons for wanting the unification of the peninsula unrelated to Soviet or Chinese policy. See Cumings, ed., *Child of Conflict,* 40; Melvyn Leffler, *A Preponderance of Power,* 506–511. Leffler argues on page 508 that policymakers "exaggerated the salience of ideological ties and subordinated the importance of nationalist aspirations among Communist leaders."

20. Dorothy Thompson to Taft, February 17, 1951, Taft MSS, Box 490, file 7.

21. *Congressional Record,* vol. 96, 81st Congress, 2nd Session, June 28, 1950, 9338.

22. See George Malone, *Mainline* (New Haven, CT: The Long House, 1958), *passim.*

23. *Congressional Record,* vol. 97, 82nd Congress, 1st Session, August 1, 1951, 9305, 9310.

24. Albert C. Wedemeyer, *Wedemeyer Reports!* (New York: Henry Holt & Co., 1958), 438.

25. Paul Douglas address to the annual dinner of the American Municipal Congress, December 5, 1950, ADA papers, reel 32, section 55.

26. Werdel quoted in the *Economic Council Letter,* no. 261, April 15, 1951, Taft MSS, Box 969, foreign policy B file 1 of 2.

27. Merwin Hart, "Conspiracy?," in ibid.

28. See Bruce Cumings's useful definition of "rollback" anti-statism in his *Child of Conflict,* 9. See also Rick Perlstein, *Before the Storm: Barry Goldwater and the Unmaking of the American Consensus* (New York: Hill & Wang, 2001); Robert Alan Goldberg, *Barry Goldwater* (New Haven: Yale University Press, 1995).

29. *Congressional Record: Major Speeches and Debates of Senator Joe McCarthy Delivered in the US Senate, 1950–1951* (New York: Gordon Press, 1975), 159–160.

30. Bricker press release, March 13, 1953, Taft MSS, Box 498, Bricker amendment file 5.

31. See Duane Tananbaum, *The Bricker Amendment Controversy: A Test of Eisenhower's Political Leadership* (Ithaca: Cornell University Press, 1988); Richard Davies, *Defender of the Old Guard: John Bricker and American Politics* (Columbus: Ohio State University Press, 1993), chapter 10; Youngnok Koo, *Politics of Dissent in U.S. Foreign Policy: A Political Analysis of the Movement for the Bricker Amendment* (American Studies Institute, Seoul National University, 1978); Arthur Schlesinger, Jr., *The Imperial Presidency* (Boston: Houghton Mifflin, 1973).

32. "How Stalin Hopes We Will Destroy America," unattributed, Taft MSS, Box 953, Communism file 3 of 3.

33. "America! Return to Constitutional Government!," published by "Leaflet Revivalism," Los Angeles, Taft MSS, Box 1168, political Republican W 1952 file.

34. George Raymond to Taft, August 21, 1951, Taft MSS, Box 953, Communism file 3 of 3.

35. Helen Kelly to Taft, February 28, 1952, Taft MSS, Box 1101, Communists 1952 file.

36. Myrtle Amis to Knowland, February 1950, Knowland MSS, Box 66, China file. The number of such letters grows exponentially after the twin events of the fall of China and the McCarthy allegations, and examples can be found in any of the congressional manuscript sources cited.

37. *San Francisco News*, January 15, 1952, Knowland MSS, Box 160, 1952 scrapbook.

38. John Lechner to Taft, June 26, 1951; Jack Tenney to Ray Bogue, March 20, 1951, Taft MSS, Box 953, Communism file 2 of 3.

39. AEL pamphlets in ibid.

40. Robert P. Newman, "The Lingering Poison of McCarranism," deposited at the Nevada Historical Society, Reno, Nevada. See also Newman, *Owen Lattimore and the "Loss" of China* (Berkeley: University of California Press, 1992).

41. McCarran, "Eliminating Subversives from Government," Speech to the 1952 Metal and Non metallic Mineral Mining Convention and Exposition, Denver, September 22, 1952, McCarran MSS, Box 56, Communism 1952 file.

42. Analysis of S.716 (McCarran-Walter) by the American Enterprise Association, undated, McCarran MSS, Box 55, 1951 anti-communism file.

43. The votes to override the veto were 278–113 in the House (107 Democrats and 170 Republicans for, 90 Democrats and 23 Republicans against), and 57–26 in the Senate (25D and 32R for, 18D and 8R against).

44. Lehman press release concerning a speech in Detroit, October 25, 1952, JFK MSS, Box 100, McCarran Act file.

45. See, for example, Arthur Wiley of New Jersey to McCarran, June 28, 1952, McCarran MSS, Box 54, McCarran-Walter file. The contents of the letter do not bear repeating, but it is one of several hundred similar examples.

46. David Ford to McCarran, June 30, 1952; F. W. Barnes to McCarran, June 30, 1952; J. M. Tyne to McCarran, June 28, 1952; Frank E. Holman to McCarran, June 28, 1952, McCarran MSS, ibid.

47. See, for example, David W. Reinhard, *The Republican Right Since 1945* (Lexington: University of Kentucky Press, 1983); Jerome Himmelstein, *To the Right: The Transformation of American Conservatism* (Berkeley: University of California Press, 1990), 40. Both argue that Taft's Old Right philosophy was marginalized in favor of an anti-communist, internationalist alternative. To accept this is to take the idea of anti-communism in an international context at face value, rather than as an ideological tool for attacking political opponents.

48. Taft speech draft, May 14, 1952, Taft MSS, Box 431, Chicago convention file 4.

49. Taft broadcast, June 19, 1952, Taft MSS, Box 460, press releases file.

50. Akers to David Ingalls, Taft campaign leader, June 7, 1952, Taft MSS, Box 442, doctors general 1952 file.

51. C.A. Maino to Taft, April 11, 1952; reply by Taft's secretary Jack Martin, April 19, 1952, Taft MSS, Box 1185, social legislation 1952 file.

52. Taft to Dr. J. M. Cox, June 11, 1952, Taft MSS, Box 1185, social legislation 1952 file.

53. Doctors for Taft Committee release, February 17, 1952, Taft MSS, Box 460, press releases file.

54. John E. Bangs to Taft, January 28, 1952, Taft MSS, Box 1185, social security A-B file.

55. William Ayres letter to his constituents, April 17, 1952, Taft MSS, Box 1184, Senators correspondence file.

56. Winrod Wichita Prayer Circle newsletter, 1952, Taft MSS, Box 435, miscellaneous 1952 file. See Leo Ribuffo, *The Old Christian Right: The Protestant Far Right from the Depression to the Cold War* (Philadelphia: Temple University Press, 1983); David Bennett, *The Party of Fear: From Nativist Movements to the New Right in American History* (Chapel Hill: University of North Carolina Press, 1988).

57. Christian Nationalist Crusade poster, undated, Taft MSS, Box 435, ibid.

58. *Headlines and What's Behind Them*, March 15, 1952, Taft MSS, Box 1106, Eisenhower file 2 of 2. Taft received this paper from a number of worried supporters who argued that such attacks might hurt his candidacy. See Taft MSS, Box 435, file 6.

59. "Eisenhower's Record is Pro-Communist," Taft MSS, Box 1286, Eisenhower 1952 file 1 of 2.

60. Wedemeyer's release on agreeing to chair Taft's campaign committee, May 5, 1952, Taft MSS, Box 460, press releases file.

61. Taft radio broadcast, June 1, 1952, Taft MSS, Box 1285, Eisenhower 1952 file.

62. "Win with Taft" telecast, June 19, 1952, Taft MSS, Box 1285, ibid.

63. See Taft to Senator H. Alexander Smith, November 13, 1952, and Smith to Taft, November 17, 1952, Taft MSS, Box 1184, Senators correspondence file. See also Francis Wilcox Oral History, Senate Historical Office (1984), 137–138. Wilcox was the Chief of Staff of the Senate Foreign Relations Committee in this period, and said that by 1953, "he took a more reasonable approach toward things," meaning Taft joined the "bipartisan" anti-communist group on foreign policy.

64. "The Eisenhower Campaign—A Copy Policy," Lodge MSS, Box 23, file 3.

65. Eisenhower-Nixon letter, October 24, 1952, Taft MSS, Box 1107, Eisenhower 1952 file 2 of 2.

66. Eisenhower leaflet, "I Like Ike," 1952, Taft MSS, Box 1286, Eisenhower 1952 file 1 of 2.

67. Taft statement, April 24, 1952, Taft MSS, Box 1286, Eisenhower 1947–52 file.

68. GOP report on the ADA, Taft MSS, Box 1289, Stevenson 1949–52 file.

69. Powell, "What the American Negro Wants," *US News & World Report*, September 5, 1952, JFK MSS, Box 110, Negroes file.

70. Republican National Committee File, "Creeping Socialism," July 1952, Taft MSS, Box 461, GOP candidates file 3 of 3. The comparison to a drug addict suffering through withdrawal is a reference to the return to power of a Conservative government, led once again by Winston Churchill.

71. *Common Sense: The Nation's Anti-Communist Paper,* September 15, 1952, Anderson MSS, Box 1056, political material 1952 file.

72. See ADA notes; Governor Val Peterson (R-Nebraska) broadcast, September 22, 1952, Taft MSS, Box 1289, Stevenson 1949–52 file.

73. Truman speech at Tacoma, October 2, 1952, Taft MSS, Box 1289, Truman file 1948–52 1 of 2.

74. Stevenson speech at the Veterans' Memorial Auditorium, San Francisco, September 9, 1952, quoted in the *New York Times,* September 10, 1952, Taft MSS, Box 1289, Stevenson 1949–52 file; GOP notes on the ADA, 19, in ibid.

75. Chester Bowles to Stevenson, September 10, 1952, Benton MSS, Box 279, folder 11. The term 'Bevanism' is a reference to the emerging schism in the British Labour Party in the 1950s between left-wing followers of former Health minister Aneurin Bevan and the party leadership over nuclear disarmament and the possibility of ending defense links with the United States. India was a nonaligned nation in the Cold War in the 1950s, which Bowles saw as a major problem in the developing world as well as on the Labour left.

76. "Vote for Governor Adlai E. Stevenson and the Democratic Party," Benton MSS, Box 279, folder 11.

77. Benton to Stevenson, April 15, 1952 and August 7, 1952, Benton MSS, Box 279, folder 11.

78. Hubert Humphrey to Bill Benton, September 30, 1952, Benton MSS, Box 273, folder 4; Chase Going Woodhouse to Benton, September 30, 1957, Benton MSS, Box 282, folder 5.

79. See materials in Benton MSS, Box 322, folder 4 and also Box 324, folder 3.

80. Phil Levy to Bill Benton, August 21, 1950, Benton MSS, Box 347, folder 1.

81. *The Nation,* October 18, 1952; Mitchell memo, undated; Stevenson speech at Columbus, Ohio, October 3, 1952, Anderson MSS, Box 1056, political material 1952 file; Stevenson quoted in Phil Levy to Bill Benton, August 21, 1952, Benton MSS, Box 347, folder 1. Stevenson did not oppose federal support for medical care in its entirety, but did not make such a proposal a cornerstone of his campaign, allowing Republicans to dominate political debate.

82. Stevenson speech, Academy of Music, Brooklyn, October 31, 1952, in Gregory Bush, ed., *Campaign Speeches of American Presidential Candidates 1948–1984* (NY: Ungar, 1985), 56, 55.

83. Benton to Dr. Creighton Barker, September 5, 1952, Benton MSS, Box 347, folder 1; Bob Clafferty to Benton, Benton MSS, Box 352, folder 10.

84. Benton to James Doyle, Democratic organizing committee of Wisconsin, September 18, 1952, Benton MSS, Box 322, folder 4. See Michael Paul Rogin, *The Intellectuals and McCarthy: The Radical Specter* (Cambridge: MIT Press, 1967) for an analysis of the social context of McCarthyism in Wisconsin.

85. See Mary L. Dudziak, *Cold War Civil Rights: Race and the Image of American Democracy* (Princeton: Princeton University Press, 2000) for the argument that the Cold War helped encourage moves toward civil rights legislation at the same time as it marginalized more ambitious movements for social change. An excellent treatment of the limits of World War Two liberalism in its definition of the "Four Freedoms" is Robert B. Westbrook, "Fighting for the American Family: Private Interests and Political Obligations in World War II," in Richard Wrightman Fox and Jackson Lears, eds., *The Power of Culture: Critical Essays in American History* (Chicago: University of Chicago Press, 1993), 195–221.

86. Herter speeches at Worcester and at Lowell, August 12 and 29, 1952, Herter MSS, folder 892; Herter biography, Herter MSS, folder 892(a); "A Truly Progressive Record," Herter MSS, folder 893.

87. Herter speech at a Boston Garden Republican Dinner, June 6, 1952, Herter MSS, folder 894(a).

88. Speech material, undated, Herter MSS, folder 894.

89. Herter speech, Democrats for Herter meeting at the Boston Sheraton Plaza, undated, Herter MSS, folder 893.

90. Herter release, undated 1952, Herter MSS, folder 893(a); Herter speech to the GOP State Convention at Montpelier, Vermont, undated 1952, Herter MSS, folder 1280.

91. Herter TV speech, September 5, 1952, Herter MSS, folder 891(a); Herter speech "On Communism," undated, Herter MSS, folder 1175.

92. Memorandum of Herter's meeting with Dean Acheson, March 21, 1950, Herter MSS, folder 890.

93. Lodge speeches on WBZ TV, October 17 and October 27, 1952, Lodge MSS, Box 9, file 6.

94. Lodge civil rights speech for general campaign use, Lodge MSS, Box 9, file 2.

95. Lodge speech to the Retail, Wholesale, and Department Store Union (CIO) Convention, Boston, January 28, 1952, JFK MSS, Box 112, Lodge campaign speeches analysis file.

96. Lodge campaign poll, September 5, 1952, Lodge MSS, microfilm collection Ms-N166, reel 18.

97. Lodge speech over WBZ TV, October 17, 1952, Lodge MSS, Box 9, file 6.

98. William M. Higgins to Taft, February 13, 1951, Taft MSS, Box 1031, political general 1951 file.

99. John McCarthy to Lodge, November 6, 1952, Lodge MSS, Box 16, file 1.

100. Kelly to JFK with complete precinct election returns, JFK MSS, Box 103, Barnstaple file. Kelly was particularly excited by the fact that Kennedy nearly took Hyannis ward, an area Lodge should have taken for granted, receiving 617 votes to Lodge's 703.

101. Kennedy received a breakdown of the vote in this district from David Powers of the Congressional Research & Statistics Service, testimony to his interest and surprise at the result. See JFK MSS, Box 103, Correspondence—campaign help file.

102. Kennedy speech on WNAC TV, October 5, 1952, Lodge MSS, Box 10, file 26.

103. JFK speech to an AFL audience, undated 1952, JFK MSS, Box 99, labor file.

104. Waltham debate background book II, JFK MSS, Box 102, Book II file.

105. Foreign policy speech draft, JFK MSS, Box 102, foreign policy speeches file; Kennedy-Lodge voting record comparison, JFK MSS, Box 98, economy 1952 file.

106. Report on Lodge's voting record, JFK MSS, Box 112, report on Lodge file.

107. "List of Issues which Affect Nationality Groups," JFK MSS, Box 108, nationality issues file.

108. Albanian American Committee form letter, 1952, JFK MSS, Box 103, special groups file.

109. Radio script, undated 1952, JFK MSS, Box 108, Irish file.

110. Sieniewicz to Kennedy, August 20, 1952, JFK MSS, Box 110, Scandinavian file.

111. JFK to Douglas, August 22, 1952, JFK MSS, Box 99, Economy file.

112. For a breakdown of the primary results, see the State of California Statement of Vote, Consolidated Direct and Presidential Primary Election, June 3, 1952, compiled by Frank M. Jordan, Secretary of State, Knowland MSS, Box 92, campaign endorsements 1952 file.

113. Memorandum on the GOP strategy discussion, Los Angeles, June 7, 1951, Knowland MSS, Box 91, file 3.

114. Knowland campaign speech for general use, 1952, Knowland MSS, Box 91, file 2.

115. Knowland 1952 campaign manual, Knowland MSS, Box 92, 1952 campaign file.

116. Frank Mackey to Knowland, May 24, 1951 with accompanying pamphlet, Knowland MSS, Box 91, Republican national party file.

117. GOP campaign strategy report by the Eugene Castle Publicity Machine, New York, 1952, Knowland MSS, Box 91, file 1. Emphasis original.

118. Borough campaign leaflets "An Open Letter to the Democrats of California" and "Vote Against the Anti-Labor Senator," Knowland MSS, Box 93, Borough campaign file.

119. Borough statement in the *San Francisco People's World*, June 17, 1952, Knowland MSS, Box 93, scrapbook.

120. For a full list of House and Senate results in California see Knowland MSS, Box 66, elections file 1. One interesting result was the defeat of Republican right-wing Presidential hopeful, and bitter foe of Earl Warren, Thomas Werdel, who lost his seat in the 14th district to Democrat Harlen Hagen. Redistricting in 1952 had not helped Werdel, but it was also clear that to appeal to a broad base in California one had to appear to be the moderate in contrast to one's extremist opponent. Knowland

carried this off effectively state wide, but Hagen, a Cold War liberal, was able to do so against a far right opponent in the 14th district (Kern, Kings, and Tulare counties). Because of the nature of anti-totalitarian ideology, however, this "vital center" was becoming increasingly unable to defend the expansion of government.

121. Joseph Alsop column, "Republican Death Wish," August 30, 1952; Wilson to Knowland, August 22, 1952, Knowland MSS, Box 92, 1952 campaign urgent file.

122. Taft to Dirksen, August 6, 1952, Taft MSS, Box 1184, Senators correspondence file.

123. Alsop, "Republican Death Wish," Knowland MSS, Box 92, 1952 campaign urgent file.

124. Eisenhower speech at Everett, WA, October 6, 1952, Knowland MSS, Box 91, file 2.

125. The *Elkhart Truth*, October 11, 1952, 1, Taft MSS, Box 453, 1952 engagements file 8—Indiana.

126. See the *New York Journal*, June 20, 1952, Taft MSS, Box 431, Chicago convention file 5.

127. Frank Robinett to Clarence Baldwin, GOP Connecticut State Chairman, September 16, 1951, Lodge MSS, Box 19, "Dirt" file.

128. J. M. Martinez to Luce, September 15, 1952, Luce MSS, Box 195, correspondence folder 11—Mar-Maz.

129. Stevenson to Anderson, November 18, 1952, Anderson MSS, Box 1056, correspondence re 1952 campaign file. The Democrats did well to hold the Republicans to tiny majorities in the House and Senate, but a clear pattern can be established in that almost all those who won stressed their anti-communist credentials. Thus Knowland trounced the Socialist Borough in California while in Missouri Stuart Symington defeated Republican James Kem for being an isolationist and therefore not committed enough to anti-Sovietism. All defeated Senate Republicans were either portrayed as isolationists (in Washington, Missouri, and Montana) or tied to the "appeasement" policies of the administration (Lodge in Massachusetts). Overall, there was little turnover of seats in either the House or Senate. In the upper chamber the GOP gained seats in Wyoming, Arizona, Connecticut, and Kentucky on strongly anti-left platforms, and regained the Michigan seat lost after Vandenberg's death. The Democrats almost recouped those losses in the four states listed above in brackets. Liberal Republican Wayne Morse of Oregon abandoned the GOP in protest at what he perceived as the party's abandonment of its liberal past, and sat as an independent in the 83rd Congress.

Conclusion

1. Pepper's musings on becoming involved in New York or California politics in the wake of his defeat in 1950 are mentioned briefly in his diary that year. See entries for June 12, 1950, July 24, 1950, July 25, 1950, July 27, 1950, Pepper MSS, S439/2/6.

2. Pepper to Herbert Lehman, October 16, 1958, Lehman MSS, Claude Pepper special file 703. Lehman had by this time retired from the Senate, but had contributed $250 to Pepper's 1958 campaign as he and other northern liberals struggled to extend their political network to a South riven by racial and sectional animosities in the wake of the *Brown* decision.

3. Bryan Jennings, chairman of the Citizens Committee for Holland, form letter, August 11, 1958, ibid.

4. See Michael Klarman, "How *Brown* Changed Race Relations: The Backlash Thesis, *Journal of American History* (June 1994): 81–118; Anthony Badger, "Whatever Happened to Roosevelt's New Generation of Southerners?" in Robert Garson and Stuart Kidd, eds., *The Roosevelt Years: New Perspectives on American History, 1933–1945* (Edinburgh: Edinburgh University Press, 1999), 122–138.

5. My awareness of abstract theories of equality that inform American liberalism draws heavily on Michael Walzer, *Spheres of Justice: A Defence of Pluralism and Equality* (Oxford: Martin Robertson, 1983); John Rawls, *Political Liberalism* (New York: Columbia University Press, 1993). See also Duncan Kennedy, "Radical Intellectuals in American Culture and Politics, or My Talk at the Gramsci Institute" in his *Sexy Dressing Etc: Essays on the Power and Politics of Cultural Identity* (Cambridge: Harvard University Press, 1993), 1–33.

6. As in Aaron Friedberg, *In the Shadow of the Garrison State: America's Anti-Statism and Its Cold War Grand Strategy* (Princeton: Princeton University Press, 2000). See also Alonzo Hamby, "The Vital Center, the Fair Deal, and the Quest for a Liberal Political Economy," *American Historical Review*, 77, no. 3 (June 1972): 653–678; Alan Brinkley, *The End of Reform: New Deal Liberalism in Recession and War* (New York: Knopf, 1995).

7. This argument applies most obviously to health care, but also to other forms of social insurance. See Jacob Hacker, *The Divided Welfare State: The Battle over Public and Private Benefits in the United States* (Cambridge: Cambridge University Press, 2002); Colin Gordon, *Dead on Arrival: The Politics of Health Care in Twentieth Century America* (Princeton: Princeton University Press, 2003).

8. David Plotke, *Building a Democratic Political Order: Reshaping American Liberalism in the 1930s and 1940s* (Cambridge: Cambridge University Press, 1996).

9. See Meg Jacobs, "'How About Some Meat?': The Office of Price Administration, Consumption Politics, and State Building from the Bottom Up," *Journal of American History*, 84, no. 3 (December 1997): 910–941; Nelson Lichtenstein, *Walter Reuther: The Most Dangerous Man in Detroit* (Urbana: University of Illinois Press, 1995).

10. This idea forms part of Christopher Lasch's critique of Cold War liberalism. See his *The Agony of the American Left* (Harmondsworth: Penguin, 1973).

11. In any case, other observers have demonstrated the existence of a transatlantic

community of ideas that sometimes bypassed or overcame American institutional obstacles to state building. See Daniel Rodgers, *Atlantic Crossings: Social Politics in a Progressive Age* (Cambridge, MA: Belknap Press, 1998).

12. *New Republic* (August 23, 1948): 25. Here Lynd reviews a book about New Zealand's experiment in social democracy in the 1940s, arguing that unlike American liberalism the Labour government in Wellington believed in "the synthesis of democratic politics with a socialized economy, the combination of liberty and equality." To Lynd, the Cold War was partly to blame for the difference between America and New Zealand in this respect. The book he reviewed is Leslie Lipson, *The Politics of Equality: New Zealand's Adventures in Democracy* (Chicago: University of Chicago Press, 1948).

BIBLIOGRAPHY

Primary Sources

Papers and Manuscripts

Eva Adams Papers, Special Collections, University of Nevada, Reno, Library.

Americans for Democratic Action Papers (Microfilm), Cambridge University Library, Cambridge, UK.

Clinton P. Anderson Papers, Library of Congress, Washington, D.C.

William Benton Papers, Special Collections, Regenstein Library, University of Chicago, Chicago, Illinois.

John Marshall Butler Scrapbooks, Library of Maryland History, Maryland Historical Society, Baltimore, Maryland.

Tom Connally Papers, Library of Congress, Washington, D.C.

Paul Douglas Papers, Chicago Historical Society, Chicago, Illinois.

Sheridan Downey Papers, Bancroft Library, University of California, Berkeley, California.

Patrick Gordon Walker Papers, Churchill College, Cambridge, UK.

Christian Herter Papers, Houghton Library, Harvard University, Cambridge, Massachusetts.

Spessard Holland Papers, Claude Pepper Library, Florida State University, Tallahassee, Florida.

Spessard Holland Papers, Special Collections, University of Florida, Gainesville, Florida.

Harold Ickes Papers, Library of Congress, Washington, D.C.

Jacob Javits Papers, Special Collections, State University of New York at Stony Brook, Stony Brook, New York.

William F. Knowland Papers, Bancroft Library, University of California, Berkeley, California.

Robert La Follette Jr. Papers, La Follette Family Papers, Library of Congress, Washington, D.C.

John F. Kennedy Papers, John F. Kennedy Presidential Library, Boston, Massachusetts.

Herbert Lehman Papers, Lehman Suite, Columbia University, New York, NY.

Henry Cabot Lodge Papers, Massachusetts Historical Society, Boston, Massachusetts.

Clare Boothe Luce Papers, Library of Congress, Washington, D.C.

George Malone Papers, Nevada Historical Society, Reno, Nevada.

Joseph Martin Papers, The Joseph Martin Institute of Law and Society, Stonehill College, North Easton, Massachusetts.

Pat McCarran Papers, Nevada Historical Society, Reno, Nevada.

Joseph McDonald Papers, Special Collections, University of Nevada, Reno, Library.

Richard M. Nixon Pre-Presidential Papers, Archive, The Richard Nixon Library and Birthplace, Yorba Linda, California.

Claude Pepper Papers, Claude Pepper Library, Florida State University, Tallahassee, Florida.

Edith Nourse Rogers Papers, Radcliffe College, Cambridge, Massachusetts.

Leverett Saltonstall Papers, Massachusetts Historical Society, Boston, Massachusetts.

George Smathers Papers, Special Collections, University of Florida, Gainesville, Florida.

Robert A. Taft Papers, Library of Congress, Washington, D.C.

Millard E. Tydings Papers, Archives, McKeldin Library, University of Maryland, College Park, Maryland.

Wallace White Papers, Library of Congress, Washington, D.C.

George Wingfield Papers, Nevada Historical Society, Reno, Nevada.

US Government Documents and Publications

US Bureau of the Census, *Statistical Abstract of the United States, 1957,* 78th Edition. Washington, D.C. 1957.

US Congress, *Congressional Directory, 79th Congress, June 1946*

US Congress, *Congressional Record,* vols. 91, 92, 93, 94, 95, 96, 97, 98, 99, 100,. 1945–1954.

US Congress, *Senate Committee Hearings,* vols. 816, 844, 850, 870, 981.

Galambos, Louis, ed. *The Papers of Dwight D. Eisenhower,* vols. XIII, XIV. Baltimore: Johns Hopkins University Press, 1989.

Ritchie, Donald, ed. *Minutes of the Senate Democratic Conference, 1903–1964.* Washington, D.C.: US Government Printing Office, 1998.

———. *Minutes of the Senate Republican Conference, 1903–1964.* Washington, D.C.: US Government Printing Office, 1999.

Memoirs and Published Sources

Blum, John Morton. *Roosevelt and Morgenthau: A Revision and Condensation of "From the Morgenthau Diaries."* Boston: Houghton Mifflin, 1970.

Bush, Gregory, ed. *Campaign Speeches of American Presidential Candidates 1948–1984.* New York: Frederick Ungar, 1985.

Davies, Joseph E. *Mission to Moscow: A Record of Confidential Dispatches to the State Department, Official and Personal Correspondence, Current Diary and Journal Entries, Including Notes and Comment up to October 1941.* New York: Simon & Schuster, 1941.

Douglas, Helen. *A Full Life.* Garden City: Doubleday, 1982.

Douglas, Paul. *The Coming of a New Party.* New York: McGraw Hill, 1932.

———. *Economy in the National Government.* Chicago: University of Chicago Press, 1952.

———. *In the Fullness of Time: The Memoirs of Paul H. Douglas.* Harcourt, Brace, Jovanovich, 1971.

Flanders, Ralph. *The American Century.* Cambridge: Harvard University Press, 1950.

Gunther, John. *Inside USA.* Curtis Publishing, 1947.

Pat Holt Oral History Interview, Senate Historical Office, Hart Senate Office Building, Washington, D.C. 1985.
Ickes, Harold. *The Secret Diary of Harold L. Ickes.* New York: Simon & Schuster, 1953.
Javits, Jacob K. with Rafael Steinberg. *Javits: The Autobiography of a Public Man.* Boston: Houghton Mifflin, 1981.
"Remembering William F. Knowland." Regional Oral History Office, University of California, Berkeley, 1981.
Lodge, Henry Cabot. *As It Was*. New York: W.W. Norton, 1976.
———. *The Storm Has Many Eyes*. New York: W.W. Norton, 1973.
Macdonald, Dwight. *Henry Wallace: The Man and the Myth.* New York: Vanguard, 1948.
MacDougall, Curtis D. *Gideon's Army*, 3 volumes. New York: Marzani & Munsell, 1965.
Malone, George. *Mainline*. New Canaan, CT: The Long House, Inc. 1958.
Pepper, Claude and Hays Gorey. *Eyewitness to a Century.* San Diego: Harcourt, Brace, Jovanovich, 1987.
Smith, Margaret Chase, with William C. Lewis, Jr. *Declaration of Conscience.* Garden City, New York: Doubleday, 1972.
George Smathers Oral History Interview, Senate Historical Office, Hart Senate Office Building, Washington, D.C. 1989.
Taft, Robert A. *A Foreign Policy for Americans*. New York, 1951.
Taylor, Glen. *The Way It Was With Me.* Secaucus, NJ, Lyle Stuart Inc. 1979.
Earl Warren Oral History Project, Regional Oral History Office, University of California, Berkeley.
Welles, Sumner. *The Time for Decision.* Cleveland: World Publishing, 1944.
Francis O. Wilcox Oral History Interview, Senate Historical Office, Hart Senate Office Building, Washington, D.C. 1984.

Newspapers and Journals
Baltimore Sun 1950, 1962
Journal of the American Medical Association, 1946–1950
Los Angeles Times 1946, 1948, 1950, 1952
Los Angeles Sentinel 1946, 1950
New Republic 1947, 1948, 1950
Newsweek 1950
New York Times 1946, 1947, 1948, 1949, 1950, 1951, 1952
Public Opinion Quarterly 1946, 1947, 1948, 1949, 1950, 1951, 1952
Wall Street Journal 1994
Washington Post 1946, 1950

Secondary Sources

Books

Barnard, William. *Dixiecrats and Democrats: Alabama Politics 1942–1950.* Tuscaloosa: University of Alabama Press, 1974.
Bartley, Numan, *The New South, 1945-1980.* Baton Rouge: Louisiana State University Press, 1995.

Biles, Roger. *Crusading Liberal: Paul H. Douglas of Illinois.* De Kalb: Northern Illinois University Press, 2002.

Borstelman, Thomas. *The Cold War and the Colorline: American Race Relations in the Global Arena.* Cambridge: Harvard University Press, 2001.

Boyle, Kevin. *The UAW and the Heyday of American Liberalism, 1945–1968.* Ithaca: Cornell University Press, 1995.

Brinkley, Alan. *The End of Reform: New Deal Liberalism in Recession and War.* New York: Alfred A. Knopf, 1995.

———. *Liberalism and Its Discontents.* Cambridge: Harvard University Press, 1998.

Chafe, William H. *Never Stop Running: Allard Lowenstein and the Struggle to Save American Liberalism.* New York: Basic Books, 1993.

Chafe, William H. and Hardvard Sitkoff, eds. *A History of Our Time: Readings on Postwar America.* Oxford: Oxford University Press, 1995.

Culver, John. and John Hyde. *American Dreamer: A Life of Henry A. Wallace.* New York: Norton, 2000.

Cumings, Bruce, ed. *Child of Conflict: The Korean-American Relationship, 1943–1953.* Seattle: University of Washington Press, 1983.

Crawford, Alan. *Thunder on the Right: The New Right and the Politics of Resentment.* Pantheon, 1980.

Dallek, Robert. *Franklin D. Roosevelt and American Foreign Policy, 1932–1945.* New York: Oxford University Press, 1979, revised 1995.

Danese, Tracy. *Claude Pepper and Ed Ball: Politics, Purpose, and Power.* Gainesville: University Press of Florida, 2000.

Dark, Taylor. *The Unions and the Democrats: An Enduring Alliance.* Ithaca: Cornell University Press, 1999.

Davis, Mike. *Prisoners of the American Dream: Politics and Economy in the History of the US Working Class.* New York: Verso, 2nd ed. 2000.

Davies, Richard O. *Defender of the Old Guard: John Bricker and American Politics.* Columbus: Ohio State University Press, 1993.

Delton, Jennifer A. *Making Minnesota Liberal: Civil Rights and the Transformation of the Democratic Party.* Minneapolis: University of Minnesota Press, 2002.

Dionne, E.J. *They Only Look Dead: Why Progressives Will Dominate the Next Political Era.* New York: Touchstone Press, 1996

———. *Why Americans Hate Politics.* New York: Simon and Schuster, 1991.

Doenecke, Justus P. *The Literature of Isolationism: A Guide to Non-Interventionist Scholarship, 1930–1972.* Colorado Springs: Ralph and Myles, 1972.

———. *Not to the Swift: The Old Isolationists in the Cold War Era.* Lewisburg: Bucknell University Press, 1979.

Dubofsky, Melvyn. *The State and Labor in Modern America.* Chapel Hill: University of North Carolina Press, 1994.

Dudziak, Mary L. *Cold War Civil Rights: Race and the Image of American Democracy.* Princeton: Princeton University Press, 2000.

Edmonds, Robin. *The Big Three: Churchill, Roosevelt and Stalin in Peace and War.* London: Penguin, 1992.

Evans, M. Stanton. *The Future of Conservatism.* Garden City: Doubleday, 1969.

Evans, P., Dietrich Rueschemeyer, and Theda Skocpol, eds. *Bringing the State Back In.* Cambridge: Cambridge University Press, 1985.

Feinman, Ronald M. *Twilight of Progressivism: The Western Republican Senators and the New Deal.* Baltimore: Johns Hopkins University Press, 1981.
Fones-Wolf, Elizabeth. *Selling Free Enterprise: The Business Assault on Labor and Liberalism, 1945–1960.* Urbana: University of Illinois Press, 1994.
Fraser, Steve. *Labor Will Rule: Sidney Hillman and the Rise of American Labor.* New York: The Free Press, 1991.
Fraser, Steve, and Gary Gerstle, eds. *The Rise and Fall of the New Deal Order, 1930–1980.* Princeton: Princeton University Press, 1989.
Freeland, Richard M. *The Truman Doctrine and the Origins of McCarthyism: Foreign Policy, Domestic Politics, and Internal Security, 1946–1948.* New York: Knopf, 1972.
Friedberg, Aaron. *In the Shadow of the Garrison State: America's Anti-Statism and Its Cold War Grand Strategy.* Princeton: Princeton University Press, 2000.
Fromkin, David. *In the Time of the Americans.* Vintage, 1995.
Gaddis, John L. *The United States and the Origins of the Cold War, 1941–1947.* New York: Columbia University Press, 1972.
Garceau, Oliver. *The Political Life of the American Medical Association.* Cambridge: Harvard University Press, 1941.
Garson, Robert. *The Democratic Party and the Politics of Sectionalism, 1941–1948.* Baton Rouge: Louisiana State University Press, 1974.
Gellman, Irwin. *The Contender: Richard Nixon: The Congress Years, 1946–1952.* New York: The Free Press, 1999.
Gillon, Steven. *Politics and Vision: The ADA and American Liberalism, 1947–1985.* New York: Oxford University Press, 1985.
Goldberg, Robert Alan. *Barry Goldwater.* New Haven: Yale University Press, 1995.
Gordon, Colin. *Dead on Arrival: The Politics of Health Care in Twentieth Century America.* Princeton: Princeton University Press, 2003.
———. *New Deals: Business, Labor, and Politics in America, 1920–1935.* Cambridge: Cambridge University Press, 1994.
Graham, Otis L. *Toward a Planned Society: From Roosevelt to Nixon.* New York: Oxford University Press, 1976.
Green, Paul, and Melvyn Holli. *The Mayors: The Chicago Political Tradition.* Carbondale: Southern Illinois University Press, 1987.
Griffith, Robert. *The Politics of Fear: Joseph R. McCarthy and the Senate.* Lexington: University Press of Kentucky, 1970.
Griffith, Robert, and Alan Theoharis, eds. *The Specter: Original Essays on the Cold War and the Origins of McCarthyism.* New York: New Viewpoints, 1974.
Hacker, Jacob. *The Divided Welfare State: The Battle Over Public and Private Social Benefits in the United States.* Cambridge: Cambridge University Press, 2002.
Hamby, Alonzo L. *Beyond the New Deal: Harry S. Truman and American Liberalism.* New York: Columbia University Press, 1973.
———. *Liberalism and Its Challengers: FDR to Reagan.* New York: Oxford University Press, 1985.
Hartmann, Susan M. *Truman and the 80th Congress.* Columbia: University of Missouri Press, 1971.
Heale, Michael J. *McCarthy's Americans: Red Scare Politics in State and Nation, 1935–1965.* London: Macmillan, 1998.

Herring, George C. *Aid to Russia, 1941–1946: Strategy, Diplomacy, the Origins of the Cold War.* New York: Columbia University Press, 1973.

Himmelstein, Jerome L. *To the Right: The Transformation of American Conservatism.* Berkeley: University of California Press, 1990.

Hirshfield, Daniel. *The Lost Reform: The Campaign for Compulsory Health Insurance in the United States from 1932–1943.* Cambridge, MA: Harvard University Press, 1970.

Hodgson, Godfrey. *The World Turned Right Side Up: A History of the Conservative Ascendancy in America.* Boston: Houghton Mifflin, 1996.

Hogan, Michael. *A Cross of Iron: Harry S Truman and the Origins of the National Security State, 1945–1954.* Cambridge: Cambridge University Press, 1998.

———. *The Marshall Plan: America, Britain, and the Reconstruction of Western Europe, 1947–1952.* New York: Cambridge University Press, 1987.

Hofstadter, Richard. *The Paranoid Style in American Politics and Other Essays.* Cape, 1966.

Horowitz, David, ed. *Containment and Revolution.* Boston: Beacon Press, 1967.

Horowitz, Irving Louis, ed. *Power, Politics and People: The Collected Essays of C. Wright Mills.* New York: Oxford University Press, 1963.

Howe, Irving, and Lewis Coser. *The American Communist Party: A Critical History.* Praeger, 1962.

Hunt, Michael. *Ideology and U.S. Foreign Policy.* New Haven: Yale University Press, 1987.

Jewell, Malcolm E. *Senatorial Politics and Foreign Policy.* New York: Greenwood Press, 1962.

Kaplan, Amy, and Donald E. Pease, eds. *Cultures of United States Imperialism.* Durham: Duke University Press, 1993.

Katznelson, Ira, and Mark Kasselman. *The Politics of Power: A Critical Introduction to American Government.* 3rd ed. New York: Harcourt, Brace, Jovanovitch, 1987.

Kazin, Michael. *The Populist Persuasion—An American History.* Basic Books, 1995.

Kepley, David. *Collapse of the Middle Way: Senate Republicans and the Bipartisan Foreign Policy, 1948–1952.* New York: Greenwood Press, 1988.

Kirwin, Harry W. *The Inevitable Success: Herbert R. O'Conor.* Westminster, MD: The Newman Press, 1962.

Kleppner, Paul, ed. *The Evolution of American Electoral Systems.* New York: Greenwood Press, 1981.

Kolko, Gabriel. *Main Currents in Modern American History.* New York: Harper & Row, 1976.

Kolko, Joyce, and Gabriel Kolko. *The Limits of Power: The World and United States Foreign Policy, 1945–1954.* New York: Harper & Row, 1972.

Koo, Youngnok. *Politics of Dissent in US Foreign Policy: A Political Analysis of the Movement for the Bricker Amendment.* American Studies Institute, Seoul National University, 1978.

Lacey, Michael, ed. *The Truman Presidency.* Cambridge: Cambridge University Press, 1989.

Lasch, Christopher, *The Agony of the American Left.* Harmondsworth, Penguin, 1973.

Ladd, E.C. and C. Hadley. *Transformations of the American Party System.* New York: W.W. Norton, 1975.

Leff, Mark. *The Limits of Symbolic Reform.* Cambridge: Cambridge University Press, 1984.
Leffler, Melvyn. *A Preponderance of Power: National Security, The Truman Administration, and the Cold War.* Stanford: Stanford University Press, 1992.
Lichtenstein, Nelson. *Walter Reuther: The Most Dangerous Man in Detroit.* Urbana: University of Illinois Press, 1995.
Lipset, Seymour Martin. *American Exceptionalism: A Double-Edged Sword.* New York: W.W. Norton, 1996.
Lora, Ronald. *Conservative Minds in America.* Rand McNally, 1971.
Lowitt, Richard, ed. *Politics in the Postwar American West.* Norman: University of Oklahoma Press, 1995.
Malsberger, John. *From Obstruction to Moderation: The Transformation of Senate Conservatism, 1938–1952.* Selinsgrove, PA: Susquehanna University Press, 2000.
Maney, Patrick. *"Young Bob" La Follette: A Biography of Robert M. La Follette, Jr. 1895–1953.* Columbia: University of Missouri Press, 1978.
Matthews, Donald R. *U.S. Senators and Their World.* Chapel Hill: University of North Carolina Press, 1960.
Matusow, Alan. *Farm Policy and Politics in the Truman Years.* Cambridge, MA: Harvard University Press, 1967.
May, Lary ed. *Recasting America.* Chicago: University of Chicago Press, 1989.
Mayhew, David. *Placing Parties in American Politics: Organization, Electoral Settings, and Government Activity in the Twentieth Century.* Princeton: Princeton University Press, 1986.
McAuliffe, Mary Sperling. *Crisis on the Left: Cold War Politics and American Liberals, 1947–1954.* Amherst: University of Massachusetts Press, 1978.
Melanson, Richard A. and Kenneth W. Thompson, eds. *Foreign Policy and Domestic Consensus.* The University Press of America, 1985.
Miles, Michael W. *The Odyssey of the American Right.* New York: Oxford University Press, 1980.
Milkis, Sidney. *The President and the Parties: The Transformation of the American Party System Since the New Deal.* New York: Oxford University Press, 1993.
Milward, Alan. *The European Rescue of the Nation State.* London: Routledge, 1992.
Minogue, Kenneth, ed. *Conservative Realism: New Essays in Conservatism.* London: HarperCollins, 1996.
Mitchell, Greg. *Tricky Dick and the Pink Lady: Richard Nixon vs. Helen Gahagan Douglas—Sexual Politics and the Red Scare, 1950.* New York: Random House, 1998.
Montgomery, Gayle B. and Johnson, James W. *One Step From the White House: The Rise and Fall of Senator William F. Knowland.* Berkeley: University of California Press, 1998.
Mullen, Bill. *Popular Fronts: Chicago and African American Cultural Politics, 1935–1946.* Urbana: University of Illinois Press, 1999.
Nash, George H. *The Conservative Intellectual Movement in America Since 1945.* Basic Books Inc. 1976.
Neustadt, Richard E. *Presidential Power and the Modern Presidents: The Politics of Leadership from Roosevelt to Reagan.* The Free Press, 1990.
Newman, Robert. *Owen Lattimore and the "Loss" of China.* Berkeley: University of California Press, 1992.

Oshinsky, David. *Senator Joseph McCarthy and the American Labor Movement.* Columbia: University of Missouri Press, 1976.

Ornstein, Norman J. Thomas E. Mann, and Michael J. Malbin. *Vital Statistics on Congress 1989–1990.* Washington, D.C: Congressional Quarterly, Inc. 1990.

Ostrander, Gilman M. *Nevada: The Great Rotten Borough, 1859–1964.* New York: Knopf, 1966.

Parmet, Herbert S. *Richard Nixon and His America.* Smithmark, 1990.

Paterson, Thomas G., ed. *Cold War Critics: Alternatives to American Foreign Policy in the Truman Years.* Chicago: Quadrangle Books, 1971.

———. *Meeting the Communist Threat: Truman to Reagan.* New York: Oxford University Press, 1988.

Patterson, James. *America's Struggle Against Poverty, 1900–1994.* 4th Ed. Cambridge: Harvard University Press, 1994.

———. *Congressional Conservatism and the New Deal.* Lexington: University of Kentucky Press, 1967.

———. *Grand Expectations: The United States, 1945–1974.* New York: Oxford University Press, 1996.

———. *Mr. Republican: A Biography of Robert A. Taft.* Boston: Houghton Mifflin, 1972.

Pells, Richard. *The Liberal Mind in a Conservative Age: American Intellectuals in the 1940s and 1950s.* New York: Harper & Row, 1985.

Pickett, William B. *Homer E. Capehart: A Senator's Life, 1897–1979.* Indianapolis: Indiana Historical Society, 1990.

Pleasants, Julian M. and Augustus M. Burns III. *Frank Porter Graham and the 1950 Senate Race in North Carolina.* Chapel Hill: University of North Carolina Press, 1990.

Plotke, David. *Building a Democratic Political Order: Reshaping American Liberalism in the 1930s and 1940s.* Cambridge: Cambridge University Press, 1996.

Poen, Monte. *Harry S. Truman versus the Medical Lobby: The Genesis of Medicare.* Columbia, MO: University of Missouri Press, 1979.

Radosh, Ronald. *Prophets of the Right: Profiles of Conservative Critics of American Globalism.* New York: Simon and Schuster, 1975.

Rawls, John. *Political Liberalism.* New York: Columbia University Press, 1993.

Reagan, Patrick. *Designing a New America: The Origins of New Deal Planning.* Amherst: University of Massachusetts Press, 2000.

Reichard, Gary. *The Reaffirmation of Republicanism: Eisenhower and the 83rd Congress.* Nashville: University of Tennessee Press, 1975.

Reinhard, David W. *The Republican Right Since 1945.* Lexington: University of Kentucky Press, 1983.

Ritchie, Donald. *A History of the United States Senate Policy Committee, 1947–1997.* Washington, D.C.: GPO, 1997.

Rodgers, Daniel. *Atlantic Crossings: Social Politics in a Progressive Age.* Cambridge, MA: The Belknap Press, 1998.

Rogin, Michael P. *The Intellectuals and McCarthy: The Radical Specter.* Cambridge: M.I.T. Press, 1967.

Schlafly, Phyllis. *A Choice Not an Echo.* Pere Marquette Press, 1964.

Schoultz, Lars. *Beneath the United States: A History of U.S. Policy Toward Latin America.* Cambridge: Harvard University Press, 1998.

Schrecker, Ellen. *Many Are the Crimes: McCarthyism in America.* Princeton: Princeton University Press, 1998.

Schuparra, Kurt. *Triumph of the Right: The Rise of the California Conservative Movement, 1945–1966.* Armonk, New York: M.E. Sharpe, 1998.

Scobie, Ingrid Winther. *Center Stage: Helen Gahagan Douglas.* New York: Oxford University Press, 1992.

Shafer, Byron. *Present Discontents.* Chatham House, 1997.

Shaffer, William R. *Party and Ideology in the United States Congress.* University Press of America, 1980.

Sinclair, Barbara. *Congressional Realignment, 1925–1978.* Austin: The University of Texas Press, 1982.

Spritzer, Donald E. *Senator James E. Murray and the Limits of Postwar Liberalism.* New York: Garland Publishing Inc. 1985.

Starr, Paul. *The Social Transformation of American Medicine.* New York: Basic Books, 1982.

Stromer, Marvin E. *The Making of a Political Leader: Kenneth S. Wherry and the United States Senate.* Lincoln: University of Nebraska Press, 1969.

Sullivan, Patricia. *Days of Hope: Race and Democracy in the New Deal Era.* Chapel Hill: University of North Carolina Press, 1996.

Sundquist, James L. *Dynamics of the Party System.* Washington, D.C: The Brookings Institute, 1973, revised 1983.

Theoharis, Athan. *Seeds of Repression: Harry S. Truman and the Origins of McCarthyism.* New York: Quadrangle, 1971.

Thompson, Francis. *The Frustration of Politics: Truman, Congress, and the Loyalty Issue, 1945–1953.* Rutherford: Farleigh Dickinson University Press, 1979.

Thurber, Timothy. *The Politics of Equality: Hubert H Humphrey and the African American Freedom Struggle.* New York: Columbia University Press, 1999.

Tilton, Tim. *The Political Theory of Swedish Social Democracy Through the Welfare State to Socialism.* Oxford: Oxford University Press, 1990.

Trattner, Walter I., ed. *Social Welfare or Social Control? Some Historical Reflections on Regulating the Poor.* Knoxville: University of Tennessee Press, 1983.

Trubowitz, Peter. *Defining the National Interest: Conflict and Change in American Foreign Policy.* Chicago: University of Chicago Press, 1998.

Ulam, Adam B. *The Rivals: America and Russia since World War II.* New York: Viking Press, 1971.

Valelly, Richard. *Radicalism in the States: The Minnesota Farmer-Labor Party and the American Political Economy.* Chicago: University of Chicago Press, 1989.

Walzer, Michael. *Spheres of Justice: A Defence of Pluralism and Equality.* Oxford: Martin Robertson, 1983.

Weed, Clyde. *The Nemesis of Reform: The Republican Party During the New Deal.* New York: Columbia University Press, 1994.

Weir, Margaret, Orloff, Ann Shula Orloff, and Theda Skocpol, eds. *The Politics of Social Policy in the United States.* Princeton: Princeton University Press, 1988.

Westerfield, H. Bradford. *Foreign Policy and Party Politics, Pearl Harbor to Korea.* New Haven: Yale University Press, 1955.

White, John K. *Still Seeing Red: How the Cold War Shapes the New American Politics.* Boulder: Westview Press, 1997.

Wickenden, Dorothy, ed. *The New Republic Reader: Eighty Years of Opinion & Debate.* New York: Harper-Collins, 1994.

Wolfe, Alan. *America's Impasse: The Rise and Fall of the Politics of Growth.* New York: Pantheon Books, 1981.

Zelizer, Julian. *Taxing America: Wilbur D Mills, Congress, and the State, 1945–1975.* Cambridge: Cambridge University Press, 1998.

Articles

Badger, Tony. "State Capacity in Britain and America in the 1930s." in David Englander, ed. *Britain and America: Studies in Comparative History, 1760–1970.* Open University Press, 1993.

Brinkley, Alan. "The Problem of American Conservatism." *American Historical Review* 99, (April 1994).

Brown, Charles C. "Robert A. Taft, Champion of Public Housing and National Aid to Schools." *Cincinnati Historical Society Bulletin* 26 (July 1968): 224–253.

Brown, Michael K. "Bargaining for Social Rights: Unions and the Reemergence of Welfare Capitalism, 1945–1952." *Political Science Quarterly* 112, no. 4 (Winter 1997–1998): 645–674.

Cook, Rhodes. "Theme of a 'Do-Nothing' Congress Does the Trick For Truman." *Congressional Quarterly* 53 (February 18, 1995): 503–505.

De Hart Mathews, Jane. "Art and Politics in Cold War America." *American Historical Review* 81 (October 1976): 762–787.

Derickson, Alan. "Health Security for All? Social Unionism and Universal Health Insurance, 1935–1958." *Journal of American History* (March 1994): 1333–1356.

Derickson, Alan. "The House of Falk: The Paranoid Style in American Health Politics." *American Journal of Public Health* 87, no. 11 (November 1997): 1836–1843.

Gordon, Colin. "Why No Health Insurance in the United States? The Limits of Social Provision in War and Peace, 1941–1948." *Journal of Policy History* 9, no. 3 (1997): 277–310.

Jacobs, Meg. " 'Democracy's Third Estate': New Deal Politics and the Construction of a 'Consuming Public'." *International Labor and Working Class History*, no. 55 (Spring 1999): 27–51.

———. " 'How About Some Meat?': The Office of Price Administration, Consumption Politics, and State Building from the Bottom Up, 1941–1946." *Journal of American History* 84, no. 3 (December 1997): 910–941.

Jeffreys-Jones, Rhodri. "Why Was the CIA Established in 1947?" *Intelligence and National Security* 12, no. 1 (January 1997).

Kaplan, Lawrence A. "The United States and the Origins of NATO, 1946–1949." *Review of Politics* 31, April 1969.

Katznelson, Ira. "Considerations on Social Democracy in the United States." *Comparative Politics* (October 1978): 77–99.

Katznelson, Ira, Kim Geiger, and Daniel Kryder. "Limiting Liberalism: The Southern Veto in Congress, 1933–1950." *Political Science Quarterly* (Summer 1993): 283–306.

Kazin, Michael. "A People Not a Class: Rethinking the Political Language of the Modern U.S. Labor Movement." *The Year Left* III, 1988.

———. "The Grass-Roots Right: New Histories of U.S. Conservatism in the Twentieth Century." *American Historical Review* 97 (February 1992).

Klarman, Michael. "How *Brown* Changed Race Relations: The Backlash Thesis." *Journal of American History* (June 1994): 81–118.

Leff, Mark H. "Revisioning U.S. Political History." *American Historical Review* 100 (June 1995): 829–853.

Lemelin, Bernard. "From Internationalism to Neo-Isolationism: Senator Forrest C. Donnell of Missouri and American Foreign Policy." *The Society for Historians of American Foreign Relations* Newsletter 29, no. 4, December 1998.

Riddick, Floyd M. "American Government and Politics: The First Session of the 80th Congress." *American Political Science Review* 42, no. 2(August 1948): 677–693.

———. "American Government and Politics: The Second Session of the 80th Congress." *American Political Science Review* 43, no. 3 (June 1949): 483–491.

Schappsmeier, Edward L. and Frederick H. "Scott W. Lucas of Havana: His Rise and Fall as Majority Leader in the United States Senate." *Journal of the Illinois State Historical Society* 70, no. 4 (November 1977): 302–320.

Schlesinger, Jr. Arthur. "The Two Joes—and Korea: Five Ways of Explaining the Rise of McCarthyism." *Times Literary Supplement*, September 22, 2000, 14–15.

Sugrue, Thomas J. "Crabgrass-Roots Politics: Race, Rights, and the Reaction Against Liberalism in the Urban North, 1940–1964." *Journal of American History*, (September 1995): 551–578.

Westbrook, Robert B. "Fighting for the American Family: Private Interests and Political Obligations in World War II." In Richard Wrightman Fox and Jackson Lears, eds. *The Power of Culture: Critical Essays in American History.* Chicago: University of Chicago Press, 1993, 195–221.

INDEX

COLUMBIA STUDIES IN
CONTEMPORARY AMERICAN HISTORY

Alan Brinkley, General Editor

Lawrence S. Wittner, *Rebels Against War: The American Peace Movement, 1941–196*	1969
Davis R. B. Ross, *Preparing for Ulysses: Politics and Veterans During World War II*	1969
John Lewis Gaddis, *The United States and the Origins of the Cold War, 1941–1947*	1972
George C. Herring, Jr., *Aid to Russia, 1941–1946: Strategy, Diplomacy, the Origins of the Cold War*	1973
Alonzo L. Hamby, *Beyond the New Deal: Harry S. Truman and American Liberalism*	1973
Richard M. Fried, *Men Against McCarthy*	1976
Steven F. Lawson, *Black Ballots: Voting Rights in the South, 1944–1969*	1976
Carl M. Brauer, *John F. Kennedy and the Second Reconstruction*	1977
Maeva Marcus, *Truman and the Steel Seizure Case: The Limits of Presidential Power*	1977
Morton Sosna, *In Search of the Silent South: Southern Liberals and the Race Issue*	1977
Robert M. Collins, *The Business Response to Keynes, 1929–1964*	1981
Robert M. Hathaway, *Ambiguous Partnership: Britain and America, 1944–1947*	1981
Leonard Dinnerstein, *America and the Survivors of the Holocaust*	1982
Lawrence S. Wittner, *American Intervention in Greece, 1943–1949*	1982
Nancy Bernkopf Tucker, *Patterns in the Dust: Chinese-American Relations and the Recognition Controversy, 1949–1950*	1983
Catherine A. Barnes, *Journey from Jim Crow: The Desegregation of Southern Transit*	1983
Steven F. Lawson, *In Pursuit of Power: Southern Blacks and Electoral Politics, 1965–1982*	1985
David R. Colburn, *Racial Change and Community Crisis: St. Augustine, Florida, 1877–1980*	1985
Henry William Brands, *Cold Warriors: Eisenhower's Generation and the Making of American Foreign Policy*	1988

Marc S. Gallicchio, *The Cold War Begins in Asia: American East Asian Policy and the Fall of the Japanese Empire.* 1988

Melanie Billings-Yun, *Decision Against War: Eisenhower and Dien Bien Phu* 1988

Walter L. Hixson, *George F. Kennan: Cold War Iconoclast* 1989

Robert D. Schulzinger, *Henry Kissinger: Doctor of Diplomacy* 1989

Henry William Brands, *The Specter of Neutralism: The United States and the Emergence of the Third World, 1947–1960* 1989

Mitchell K. Hall, *Because of Their Faith: CALCAV and Religious Opposition to the Vietnam War* 1990

David L. Anderson, *Trapped By Success: The Eisenhower Administration and Vietnam, 1953–1961* 1991

Steven M. Gillon, *The Democrats' Dilemma: Walter F. Mondale and the Liberal Legacy* 1992

Wyatt C. Wells, *Economist in an Uncertain World: Arthur F. Burns and the Federal Reserve, 1970–1978* 1994

Stuart Svonkin, *Jews Against Prejudice: American Jews and the Fight for Civil Liberties* 1997

Doug Rossinow, *The Politics of Authenticity: Liberalism, Christianity, and the New Left in America* 1998

Campbell Craig, *Destroying the Village: Eisenhower and Thermonuclear War* 1998

Brett Gary, *The Nervous Liberals: Propaganda Anxieties from World War I to the Cold War* 1999

Andrea Friedman, *Prurient Interests: Gender, Democracy, and Obscenity in New York City: 1909–1945* 2000

Eric Rauchway, *The Refuge of Affections: Family and American Reform Politics, 1900–1920* 2000

Robert C. Cottrell, *Roger Nash Baldwin and the American Civil Liberties Union* 2000

Wyatt Wells, *Antitrust and the Formation of the Postwar World* 2002

Cyrus Veeser, *A World Safe for Capitalism: Dollar Diplomacy and America's Rise to Global Power.* 2002

Michael Janeway, *The Fall of the House of Roosevelt: Brokers of Ideas and Power from FDR to LBJ* 2004